St

Br

Star Trek and the British Age of Sail

The Maritime Influence Throughout the Series and Films

Stefan Rabitsch

McFarland & Company, Inc., Publishers
Jefferson, North Carolina

ISBN (print) 978-1-4766-6463-7
ISBN (ebook) 978-1-4766-3419-7

LIBRARY OF CONGRESS CATALOGUING DATA ARE AVAILABLE

BRITISH LIBRARY CATALOGUING DATA ARE AVAILABLE

Manufactured in the United States of America

McFarland & Company, Inc., Publishers
Box 611, Jefferson, North Carolina 28640
www.mcfarlandpub.com

For the ones who still shine their light upon us long after they are gone; this one is for you, grandma (1934–2013)

The threads that bind ...*

... for my uncle and my aunt whose door (and swimming pool) is always open for me.

... for my grandpa who was the first and truest friend I have ever had, and who has been a trusted sounding board when no one else would listen.

... for my dad who instilled in me an acute appreciation for the outdoors and all things wild, showing me that nature is the only place where I can find solace and serenity.

... for my brother who is the best wingman I could ever hope for, who has always got my back, and who shares a "bond of brothers" with me to the end of the line.

... for my sister who was right there beside me on the quarterdeck of the imagination, always punctilious and ready to set sail for the far side of the world regardless of our preferences for turnips.

... for my mum who simply had to put up with a lot.

... for Bianca who probably had to put up with the most.

*No matter what charge you bring against the values and convictions you presume to be inherent in this dedication, I simply *know* beyond the shadow of a doubt that while water is sweet, blood is thicker.

Table of Contents

Abbreviations Used

ST:TOS	*Star Trek: The Original Series*
ST:TAS	*Star Trek: The Annimated Series*
ST:TNG	*Star Trek: The Next Generation*
ST:DS9	*Star Trek: Deep Space Nine*
ST:VOY	*Star Trek: Voyager*
ST:ENT	*Star Trek: Enterprise*

Clear all moorings...

So we beat on, boats against the current, borne back ceaselessly into the past.

—F. Scott Fitzgerald, *The Great Gatsby,* 1925

Give me the wheel of a sailing ship
And the surge of the briny main,
Bring on the wind till the hawsers sing
And the spars and the lanyards strain.

—Capt. Eugene W. Roddenberry, "Sailor's Prayer," 1945

"All I ask is a tall ship, and a star to steer her by." You could feel the wind at your back in those days. The sounds of the sea beneath you. And even if you take away the wind and the water, it's still the same. The ship is yours. You can feel her. And the stars are still there, Bones.

—Captain James T. Kirk, *ST:TOS,* "The Ultimate Computer," 1968

Well, ... it seems as though we're truly sailing into the unknown.

—Captain Jean-Luc Picard, *Star Trek Nemesis,* 2003

Preface

In defense of popular culture and science fiction—this book project has been informed and sustained by vigorous efforts of making science fiction (sf) television and film into viable and potent vehicles for teaching cultural studies at the tertiary level. Since such a project does not easily conform to the contemporary discourse of academic knowledge *production*, which seems to place more value on the immediate applicability, economic viability and/or quantifiable measurability of research, it stands in need of a simple albeit powerful defense. The often mistakenly presumed triviality of engaging with sf artifacts, which still prevails in certain quarters of academia, demands to be dispelled by emphasizing the scientific value and the academic relevance of sf. Notwithstanding the implicit polemic, there is a need to engage with popular culture artifacts and mass media products simply because they matter. The key lies in the fact that these forms are *popular*. They are consumed by and thus speak to large segments of cultural bodies. Hence, they contain meaning(s) in that they are both reflections and refractions of the culture(s) in which they are conceived. In simple terms, such artifacts are prime conduits for understanding not only what one or more cultural bodies are concerned with at the moment, but also where these concerns come from. For example, to contemporaries of Shakespeare, his plays were very much a part of Elizabethan popular culture. The works of Edgar Allan Poe intimated romantic, gothic, and macabre refractions of Antebellum America and Jacksonian democracy. As tools for doing cultural studies, contemporary forms of popular culture, their potency and their relevance, are particularly pertinent.

We find a democratizing spirit at the heart of sf's wide range of allegorical intentions. The genre is informed by the very basics of the scientific method—from the posing of a question, the subsequent construction and testing of a hypothesis in observations and/or experiments, to the drawing of conclusions and the dissemination of the knowledge thus gained. Sf challenges its audience with a seemingly simplistic yet intellectually provocative question: *What if?* This is especially true for mass media phenomena such as *Star Trek*, which has enjoyed a global resonance for more than fifty years. The research conducted and the knowledge produced as part of this book project has directly fed into their innovative application in the cultural studies classroom on both the undergraduate and graduate level. As a genre, sf—and sf television, film, and video games in particular—consistently dares to ask questions. Sf narratives are not mere escapist fantasies. They are infused with the moral imperative to critically question and re-question the very world—natural and cultural—we live in. The broad allegorical intentions of sf, which speak to its intellectually empowering and thus democratizing spirit, can be circumscribed by posing the following questions:

What if we engage critically with sf?
What if the characters that unnerve us teach us to value cultural diversity?
What if the science that intrigues us leads to a future career?
What if the physical anomalies that baffle us help us to think outside the box?
What if the technology that disturbs us strengthens our sense of ethical responsibility?
What if today's sf audiences are tomorrow's problem solvers by being culturally aware and responsible citizens?

Not only do sf stories offer us nodes for thinking differently about the world we live in, but more specifically, they allow us to grasp to what extent our worldviews are culturally constructed and mediated. Consequently, their inherent mutability affects the stories that we tell each other, (re)informing how we look at the world in the first place. In *Teaching Science Fiction* (2011), Andy Sawyer opines that sf's "speculative nature ... invites a speculative response; it requires engagement with thought-experiments that confront and often overturn passive acceptance of contemporary conditions" (1). Sf stories do that by openly declaring their opposition to a status quo in marrying their allegorical intent with the discourses of feminism, postcolonialism, postmodernism, queer theory, ecocriticism, post- and/or trans-humanism. Alternatively, they may exaggerate a historicized status quo as immutable and unchanging. This dialectic not only informs *Star Trek*'s transatlantic double consciousness, as explored in this book, but it also shapes the approaches I take in my sf seminars.

While the immediate outcome and impact of my endeavors cannot readily be cast into benchmarks, the resolute responses to working with sf by students provide clear indicators. Involving a myriad of contexts/texts, they do not shy away from the hard work that engaging with sf entails. Instead, they meet the challenge with a mix of enthusiasm and critical zeal. It is the students' accomplishments which inevitably confirm and, dare I say it, secure the importance and relevance of sf in the cultural studies curriculum. At this point I would also like to acknowledge a debt of gratitude I owe to my PhD advisor, mentor, and *friend,* Heinz Tschachler. He has been a trusted advocate of my scholarly endeavors over many years. Without him, I would not be where I am today. In the spirit of scholarly pursuit and sf alike: "Let's see what's out there. Engage!" (*ST:TNG,* "Encounter at Farpoint," 28 Sep 1987).

Introduction: These Are the Voyages...

This book begins with a simple query: What is *Star Trek* really? Answers to this question are by no means in short supply. Inarguably one of the most iconic and widely known science fiction (sf) universes in popular culture, it is often described as the "vision" of its principal creator—Gene Roddenberry. While not an *auteur,* he and his team of writers and producers developed a new sf television show in the 1960s which presented a hopeful and positivistic outlook on a future of human space exploration. It was a "prescriptive vision," according to Jeffrey Lamp, "for how a constructive future may and perhaps should look" (194). Spanning more than forty years of entertainment history, it has spawned a number of spin-off series and feature films. In the process, the *Star Trek* continuum (U.S. 1966–) also attracted a globally dispersed viewership of "invested audiences" who are commonly known as Trekkies or Trekkers. Using *Star Trek* as a node of shared interests, they formed a participatory fan culture. By appropriating the diverse contents of *Star Trek* as a media artifact, they redefined it for themselves as a "philosophy" and/or "a way of life" which celebrates diversity as the cornerstone of the community's inclusiveness. *Star Trek* fandom then became the initial proving ground for what has since emerged as the field of fan studies. It serves not to forget that *Star Trek* is also a multi-million-dollar entertainment and merchandise "franchise" which encompasses but is not limited to home videos, DVDs, apparel, action figures, innumerable novels, technical manuals for fictional future technology, and board/video games. Chris Gregory has listed *Star Trek* as "one of the most valuable 'cultural properties' in the world" (2).

The popularity, range, and longevity of *Star Trek* have not escaped scholarly attention either. Daniel Bernardi has defined *Star Trek* as "a *mega-text*" (7) that replicates and perpetuates the racialized discourses of dominant U.S. culture, while Lincoln Geraghty has described it as "a historical narrative discourse" (18) retelling the American Puritan Jeremiad in outer space. Matthew Kapell has framed the archetypes and icons found in *Star Trek* as "a kind of contemporary *Gesamtkunstwerk*," i.e., an American "mythos" (2) at large. Certainly, as Jeff Greenwald has proclaimed, emphatically albeit cryptically, *Star Trek* "means something" (6). However, Darcee McLaren has pointed out that "[t]here is no single meaning in *Star Trek* ... it will have multiple meanings, it will be interpreted differently by the same people at different times and by different people at the same time" (233).

Yet, whatever *Star Trek* is, it is *also* a story-world that is modeled on the British Golden Age of Sail, a fact that has largely escaped scholarly attention and eluded systematic delineation.[1] On March 11, 1964, Roddenberry outlined his idea for a new sf television series in a document he simply titled "STAR TREK IS...." It contains two basic intertextual building blocks that would become the shorthand definitions for *Star Trek* which he and the production team then used for years afterwards: "Wagon Train to the stars" *and* "Hornblower in space." A popular television Western with a distinctive semi-anthological format and proto-ensemble cast who found themselves in a new location each week, *Wagon Train* (U.S. 1957–65) presented semi-allegorical stories about a broad range of contemporary issues. The series essentially told a wide range of morality plays which were regularly infused with social criticism, ranging from Cold War consensus culture and race relations to changing gender roles and substance abuse. "HornblowSter" refers to a series of eleven novels, an unfinished novel, and a few short stories by British author Cecil Scott Forester. They chronicle the rise of the eponymous hero, a fictional Royal Navy officer during the heyday of the Age of Sail at the end of the 18th and the beginning of the 19th century. Published between 1937 and 1962, the Hornblower saga enjoyed great popularity in the U.S. during and after World War II. Forester's sea novels were particularly successful with a segment of a young, white, predominantly male Anglo-American readership. Next to Roddenberry, it was a generation which included a young John F. Kennedy. Spanning diverse locales (from European to Caribbean and Pacific waters), the Hornblower novels offered the coming-of-age story of a meritocratic albeit complex character who navigated a world that was morally and ideologically clear-cut. In the face of a deeply polarized world order—the West against the Rest—Forester delivered a reassuring fable of continuing Anglo-American righteousness and superiority, packaged in stories of heroism, adventure, and escapism.

As is commonly known (and reiterated by actors, producers, writers, and fans alike), *Star Trek* was originally pitched as being little more than a Space Western at a time when the Western reigned supreme on the American media landscape. Using the genre's language, President Kennedy declared the 1960s as the "New Frontier." Yet, *Star Trek*'s world of future space exploration was never intended as a Space Western, but was in fact modeled on the British Golden Age of Sail found in the romance of Napoleonic sea fiction.

Star Trek, then, posits a science-fictional world, i.e., an imaginary framework, which builds on and sustains a continuum of histories/stories that partakes of the myth of the American West *and* the myth of the British Golden Age of Sail. In other words, *Star Trek* is given meaning through a double *vraisemblance*. Jonathan Culler has explained *vraisemblance* as a process "in which a text may be brought into contact with and defined in relation to another which helps make it intelligible" (140). Consequently, the *Star Trek* continuum is governed by two distinct yet interrelated and compatible themes—the *frontier* and *Rule Britannia*. Together, they form a transatlantic double consciousness at the heart of *Star Trek*. In short, *Star Trek* simply is "Wagon Train to the stars" and "Hornblower in space." Such a holistic definition demands preliminary framing and decoding.

By default, the *Star Trek* continuum[2] is still viewed, investigated, and problematized from a predominantly American point of view not least because a significant number of *Star Trek* scholars hail from American shores. Even if they are not American, they often deconstruct the very Americanness of *Star Trek*. Critics easily looked past Roddenberry's intertextual ruse of selling a Space Western when in fact he staged modern morality plays about American society in a science-fictional format in order to sneak controversial topics past the television censors. Even so, it has done little to change the default repertoire of critical lenses through which *Star Trek* is usually viewed. After all, *Star Trek* indeed has multifaceted roots in American culture. Yet, whenever space adventures are defined in frontier terms, critics, fans, and casual viewers alike tend to quickly equate them with Kennedy's space race with the Soviets. While of course not necessarily incorrect, the comparison often draws on presumed knowledge and shared cultural assumptions rather than an accurate juxtaposition of the Western, the president's New Frontier ideology, and sf stories. Paying uncritical attention to *Star Trek* as a *faux* Space Western is also problematic insofar as it is in part driven by the national exceptionalism inherent in the myth of the American West, and the American monomyth at large; this is another reason why the significance of *Star Trek* as being *also* "Hornblower in space" has yet to be fully explored and appreciated. While we may often think of the frontier as a quintessentially American phenomenon, we must not forget that it sustains many links of similarity and compatibility with European colonial and imperial experiences. David Mogen has argued that "it is not always meaningful to separate the American frontier experience from European colonial experience when discussing the *operative analogy* in a given science fiction text" (19, emphasis added). Consequently, analogical complexity, transatlantic continuity, and Anglocentric co-presence are crucial trajectories in understanding *Star Trek* as "Wagon Train to the stars" and "Hornblower in space." This book will therefore reassess *Star Trek* as an artifact of American popular culture which not only tells American stories for predominately American audiences, but also looks back across the Atlantic for a British maritime legacy to tell its continuum of Anglocentric histories/stories.

Star Trek's transatlantic double consciousness can be made visible, and indeed audible by way of a condensed yet paradigmatic example: the opening narration and theme music for *Star Trek: The Original Series* (U.S. 1966–9). The "final frontier" obviously echoes President Kennedy's New Frontier rhetoric; the frontier was a political metaphor of change and progress which quickly became a free-floating ideological signifier that *also* pertained but was not limited to the American space program. Less frequently commented upon is the fact that the mission shared by *Star Trek*'s principal starship captains—"to boldly go where no man [or no one] has gone before"—is a thinly veiled echo of Captain James Cook's journals. Upon having travelled further south than anyone before him, he recorded the following in his journal entry of January 30, 1774: "I whose ambition leads me not only farther than any other man has been before me, but as far as I think it possible for man to go" (331). What is more, the opening narration is accompanied by Alexander Courage's iconic theme music. The three opening notes of the *ST:TOS* fanfare, underscoring the first three words of narration, are exactly the same as the ones used in Robert Farnon's suite composed for *Captain Horatio Hornblower R.N.* (Raoul Walsh, U.S. 1951)—the film adaptation of the first three *Hornblower* novels. Robert Wise, who directed *Star Trek: The Motion Picture* (U.S. 1971), recalls in a 2006 DVD extra, "A Bold New Enterprise," that the film's soundtrack and Jerry Goldsmith's adaptation of Courage's theme was to evoke "visions of sailing ships." This example shows how deeply the transatlantic double consciousness permeates the fabric of the *Star Trek* continuum.

Celebrating a shared transatlantic cultural continuum between Britain and the U.S., the mythologized British Golden Age of Sail serves as the primary model for *Star Trek*'s worldbuilding. A maritime endowment, *Rule Britannia* is embedded in five maritime dimensions which shape the ontology of *Star Trek*'s future world in space. They encompass operational discourses, nomenclature, visual and conceptual aesthetics, and character archetypes as well as rituals, traditions, and an entire maritime milieu.

The first maritime dimension speaks to *Star Trek*'s rich naval corpus of descriptive and performative language. The corpus contains, for example, a clear hierarchy of naval ranks and designations for individuals who perform specific shipboard functions. They mix and mesh structures which are rooted in the age of wind and sail with contemporary naval jargon. The bodies governed by these hierarchies operate on recognizable patterns of order(s), fostering a tone of naval nostalgia characteristic of the discourse of civility, graciousness, and deference displayed by the gentleman/officer protagonists in naval fiction. Rather than being "demeaning" (Rayner 163), such naval forms of order and power bear distorted connotations of respect, morality, and courtesy which ties them to how they are used in sea romances. The corpus also encompasses descriptive terms for the interior, the exterior, and the movement of starships as well as naval phraseology reminiscent of sailing orders. *Star Trek*'s naval corpus is neither solely British nor purely American, but rather attests to a shared transatlantic, Anglophone discursive construct. As exemplified especially in starship nomenclature, its historio-mythical *core*, which draws from a British maritime legacy, is often draped with a symbolic *veneer* that is deceivingly indicative of the U.S. Navy's post–World War II legacy.

By way of visual aesthetics and a conceptual maritime similitude, the second maritime dimension circumscribes a complete oceanic paradigm. Operating in this oceanic paradigm, starships are re-imagined and disguised sailing vessels transposed into outer space. Even though Starfleet ships do not look like sailing ships—their greyish color being reminiscent of modern navy ships—they behave and function like sailing ships. This becomes obvious when they come alongside each other or when they engage in battle. Key aesthetic markers are the correlative motions of starships; they are characterized by a relatively close distance between vessels, their proportionally steady speeds, and the approximated two-dimensionality of their movements in the zero gravity environment of space. This pronounced "horizontal attitude" is best observed when two or more vessels engage in battle. They are reminiscent of the romanticized conventions and glamour of frigate duels. The *frigate*-trope is also used to transpose into space the premise of long-distance, independent cruises, which were the signature assignments for frigates during the Golden Age of Sail. The broad mission parameters and the discretionary powers usually carried by frigate captains prompted Roddenberry to compare the role of Starfleet vessels to such British warships of the past. Even when more resources, especially CGI technology, became available in the newer series, aesthetics did not radically change but were maintained as part of *Star Trek*'s established naval worldbuilding rules. With Captain Cook's three voyages in the Pacific serving as pertinent reference points, *Star Trek* extrapolates a world of future space exploration similar to the age of discovery. As such, *Star Trek*'s disguised sailing vessels stand in stark contrast to the trope of the aircraft carrier and dogfights in space. The latter represent the *aero*nautical paradigm which dominates all other major American sf universes in film and television. Not only is it rooted in a mid-20th century historical framework, but also within a decidedly American frame of reference.[3] A similar difference applies to space itself which is presented as a reconfigured seascape. Space may be the "final frontier," but it is encoded in oceanic terms. By literalizing the metaphor, *Star Trek*'s "ocean of space" takes on physical and physiognomic qualities of a maritime environment. In *Star Trek*'s oceanic paradigm, star systems appear like island groups and foreign lands on the horizons of the star-bound explorers. Starships go into standard orbit like a sailing ship would stand into a bay to find an anchorage. This is the place to survey, chart, and observe. The planet's surface, i.e., the landing-zone of the shore party/away team, is analogous to a beach as a zone of contact, conflict, and negotiation.

The third maritime dimension addresses the archetypal *Star Trek* captain in naval terms. Starfleet captains are *not* space cowboys regardless of the family ancestry that some of them lay claim to and despite a number of critics who have read *Star Trek*'s central character as a cowboy-type, Cooperesque/Wisterian frontier hero[4]; this even goes for James T. Kirk. The historical and fictional models that served as reference points for the captain's character archetype bespeak a different genealogy. Horatio Hornblower, who himself is a fictional permutation of romanticized British naval heroes such as Horatio Nelson, Edward Pellew, and Thomas Cochrane, provided the paradigmatic blueprint which holds true for all principal starship captains. Hornblower was used to craft a composite archetype of the Enlightenment mariner as a "fighting naturalist in space" out of the mythologized persona of the quintessential maritime warrior—Horatio Nelson—and the epitome of maritime exploration—James Cook. After all, Starfleet captains are interstellar masters and commanders as well as spaceborne naturalists and scientists. According to Roddenberry, the archetypal starship captain further shares a genealogy with Sir Francis Drake, Admiral Louis Antoine de Bougainville, and Captain Robert F. Scott. In Hornblower, we find a distinct character formula which represents a particular permutation of the attributes and circumstances that hold true for any sea captain in fiction: their solitary existence, which is determined by their hierarchical distance from their crew, their geographic isolation from their homeland, and their seemingly divine powers which govern every aspect of the lives placed under their command. He is someone who ultimately bears the sole responsibility for his decisions despite being revered instead of feared by his men. He allows for open communication and complete trust among his "band of brothers." Driven by innate zeal, he is prone to take the initiative and to use his common sense not only to go beyond his orders, but also to question, and sometimes even defy them if he deems it necessary to achieve the successful outcome of his mission. His advancement by merit rests on a paradox which is coupled to a lack of political ambition. All he wants is to be in command of a ship while his successes usually lead to promotion which in turn takes him further away from the profession he prefers. This sketch of the Hornblower archetype, which holds true for all principal Starfleet captains regardless of ethnicity or gender, would not be complete without a general lack of domestic happiness. It is accentuated by an incessant psychological struggle shaped by self-doubt and the generic loneliness of command. In short, *Star Trek*'s "Hornblowers in space" perennially re-enact the much romanticized Nelson Touch.

The first three maritime dimensions coalesce in a fourth which emerges as a pastiche-like repertoire of naval customs, artifacts, performative texts, and the nautical performers who stage them. Together, they draw a validating parallel of similitude between life at sea and life in space. The Captain's Log is a key component because it facilitates the historicized telling of *Star Trek*'s narratives. It is both a naval tradition and a historiographic archive used to record events, chart spaces, and add explanatory commentaries. It is akin to the narrative journals written by naval officers in the past. Their privileged position as chroniclers allowed them to produce historical knowledge. Members of Starfleet re-enact the past by going through the motions of celebrating seemingly archaic naval rituals. Most of these rituals are accompanied by a key auditory marker—the bosun's pipe—and overt references to a bygone age of wind, sail, and wooden vessels. Poetically reproaching the sophisticated technology of the future, intertextual references and borrowings are sometimes used to add a romantic lament for said past. For example, John Masefield's poem "Sea-Fever" (1902) occupies a distinct place in *Star Trek*, as does Herman Melville's *Moby Dick* (1851); and cadets at Starfleet Academy still sing the Royal Navy March *Heart of Oak* (1759/60). All of this is enhanced by the visual presence of naval paraphernalia such as navigational instruments, model ships, and pictures of sailing vessels. They conspicuously appear in the *mis-en-scène* whenever a direction is sought, questioned, tested, or in the need of a course correction.

The fifth and last maritime dimension encases the other four in a maritime milieu. *Star Trek*'s future world in space poses as a Neo-Enlightenment which is informed by romanticized voyages of discovery and their supposedly benign and disinterested forms of exploration. It, however, also espouses an Anglocentric teleology of reason, progress, and civilization which stands in a dialectic relationship with the exotic, colonized Other, and the processes of their subsequent Othering. Governed by the laws, politics, and exigencies of distance, the future is reconstituted along the lines of an uncompressed maritime fabric of space and time. It is purposefully out of step with our compressed postmodern, postindustrial, and virtualized perceptions of space-time. *Star Trek*'s Neo-Enlightenment celebrates a normative, Anglocentric view of modernity that transcends American claims to national exceptionalism. Rather, it (re)tells a continuous telos of modernity shared and carried by two consecutive, Anglophone, cultural, political, and economic hegemonies. Following the *translatio studii et imperii* topos, we can trace the continuity of Anglocentric modernity from the "formal" British Empire to the "informal" empire of the U.S. The benevolent albeit disguised "empire of good intentions" found in the United Federation of Planets is their obvious heir.

The cancellation of *Star Trek: Enterprise* (U.S. 2001–5), the launch of the *Star Trek* reboot, and *Star Trek*'s return to television with *Star Trek: Discovery* (U.S. 2017–) afford us an opportunity to develop a fresh and synoptic (i.e., compendious and thematic rather than episodic and chronological) look at the *Star Trek* continuum. When *ST:ENT* was cancelled in 2005, it became the final incarnation of the original *Star Trek* world as it had been conceived in the 1960s. Shortly thereafter Paramount tasked a new creative team, spearheaded by director J.J. Abrams who had not worked on any previous incarnations of *Star Trek*, to reboot the franchise. While recasting the characters of *ST:TOS* with new actors, *Star Trek* (U.S. 2009), *Star Trek into Darkness* (U.S. 2013), and *Star Trek Beyond* (Justin Lin, U.S. 2016) created a parallel universe positing a new imaginary framework. By employing a staple sf plot device, they no longer had to adhere to the rules and the established fictional history that governed the Prime Universe. While the *Star Trek* reboot certainly offers a new avenue for critical inquiry in the future, it will not be considered in this book since it is *markedly* different from the original.[5] It remains to be seen how *ST: DSC* and the two new animated *Star Trek* shows (announced in 2018) will continue the continuum's legacy on television. Judging by the first season of *ST: DSC*, the series seems to attempt a delicate balancing act; it aims at presenting a departure from what came before (though less radical than the reboot), while offering the first "genuine" 21st century permutation of the *Star Trek* idea in aesthetical, narratological, and, possibly, ontological as well as ideological terms. It is safe to say, however, that after its inaugural season, *ST:DSC* has exposed *Star Trek*'s worldbuilding to considerable strain. What is more, the bulk of *Star Trek* scholarship, regardless of whether it focused on individual characters/episodes/series, one or more specific themes and/or the entire universe, was published between the late 1990s and mid–2000s. Hence, most of it was constrained by *Star Trek*'s on-going production. *Star Trek*'s 50th anniversary in 2016 was then an ideal moment not only to go back to *Star Trek*'s conception, but also to explore the *continuities* that have shaped its science-fictional world since then. Gary Westfahl has reminded us that "despite the efforts of later series to establish their own distinctive identities," they were "obliged to work within the parameters of concepts established in the 1960s" (2002: 273). Ina Rae Hark has confirmed that the "parameters of what would become the Trek universe developed out of a number of choices made about the premise for the original series" (8).

These parameters translate into a set of rules which senior production and writing staff established and occasionally amended in order to ensure coherence and familiarity on the part of the audience. These patterns of coherence manifest onscreen, but the processes that regulate them largely take place across the multiple levels of television production. They can be accessed through production-related material, i.e., the written and codified "archive" of *Star Trek*'s production history. Apart from Roddenberry's series pitch, it comprises series bibles and guidelines for writers and directors, which delineate the ground rules for the various contributors to *Star Trek*'s different incarnations, as well as technical manuals, providing condensed FAQ-type introductions to the world of *Star Trek*, its language, symbols, and cosmology. Also included are memos that were exchanged between senior production and writing staff in which they negotiate and regulate the mechanics of *Star Trek*'s world. While the bulk of the *Star Trek* continuum was written and produced after Roddenberry's death in 1991, the establishing of "ground rules" was largely his doing. He also nurtured his successors, such as Rick Berman and Michael Piller, who in turn mentored subsequent writers and producers, including Brannon Braga, Jeri Taylor, Ronald D. Moore, Ira Steven Behr, and Bryan Fuller. While not an *auteur*, Roddenberry nonetheless regulated his creation to a point where the premise and especially the worldbuilding rules of *Star Trek* could no longer be *radically* changed lest his successors endanger the degree of familiarity, narrative comfort, and recognition of the audience. Writers and producers repeatedly refer to pre-existing and/or already established rules and formats, i.e., the *Star Trek* canon, in the production archive. The main premise of *Star Trek*'s world is treated as an *a priori* fact.

Trawling through these materials allowed me to chart a *mare incognitum* that bears an inescapably British signature. Straddling the dialectic of maritime military might and maritime exploration, this sea of contextual flotsam points to the intentional and systematic nature of the maritime narrative embedded in *Star Trek*'s world. It points out five maritime dimensions, as outlined earlier, and lies on a bearing that demands a transatlantic remapping of the *Star Trek* continuum.

Despite significant changes in production, distribution and, more generally, American cultural contexts, when viewed synoptically, the *Star Trek* continuum emerged as a procedural presence on the American and the global media landscape. It saw perpetual updates of the "original" idea conceived by

Roddenberry and his creative team. The continuous attempts and efforts of their successors to integrate both sequels and prequels, as well as more disparate elements and stories, resulted in an arguably coherent science-fictional world and the history/story of a future that spans roughly the late 21st to the late 24th century. These same production-related materials provide the code that effectively allows us to understand the cultural significance and relevance of *Star Trek*'s two key intertexts. They indicate the extent to which its sf world partakes of the myth of the British Golden Age of Sail; Roddenberry's act of *vraisemblance* goes far beyond merely modeling Captain James T. Kirk (William Shatner) on Horatio Hornblower (see Illustration 1).

Consequently, this book takes the shape of a contextual manual for *Star Trek*'s transatlantic double consciousness which consists of two main parts: (1) a primer, and (2) a voyage. By "theorizing from the site of practice" (Hutcheon 226), this manual is a product of using *Star Trek*'s own codes and relating them back to their multiple constituent contexts/texts. Re-historicizing the well-known origins of *Star Trek*, along with its fifty years of output, entails a systematic juxtaposition of *Star Trek*'s corpus of episodes and films with the *Hornblower* novels and other relevant naval histories/stories. By synoptically investigating both of Roddenberry's intertextual reference points within the same critical framework, it is possible to read, understand, and reconcile *Star Trek*'s science-fictional world as "Hornblower in space" *and* "Wagon Train to the stars" in equal measure. After all, these two intertextual reference points are compatible inasmuch as they share the telos of the grand narrative of western modernity. It is not a question of dismissing the frontier in favor of *Rule Britannia*, but particular emphasis is placed on the detailed delineation of the latter.

The first contact between veteran producer/director, and initially consulting producer of *Star Trek: Discovery* (U.S. 2017–), Nicholas Meyer, and the world of *Star Trek*, provides an anecdotal albeit illuminating example. When asked to write and subsequently direct *Star Trek II: The Wrath of Khan* (U.S. 1982), he encountered the world of *Star Trek* with a peculiar mix of confusion and recognition. Initially, he had very little knowledge of *Star Trek*. When Meyer went back and watched episodes of *ST:TOS* and the first motion picture, he "didn't understand the world, the people, or the language," while at the same time it "vaguely reminded [him] of something, something for which [he] had great affection" (77–9). When the epiphany—"What was *Star Trek* but Hornblower in space?"—hit him, "a great many things fell readily into place" (79–80). It was with some satisfaction when he learned about Roddenberry's affinity for the Hornblower novels, the world of wind and sail, and the "parameters of the universe Roddenberry set up" (81).[6] Once he had recognized Hornblower's

naval corpus	"a flavor of Naval usage and terminology" "naval parlance" "semimilitary" "It was set up as a Navy command structure and Gene always mentioned Horatio Hornblower" "seminavigational" "include the names of famous fighting ships" "rank, when properly used, can be a pleasant way of acknowledging seniority—of showing respect.... I think man will always want this type of thing ... we enjoy the use of these courtesies"
naval aesthetic and the literalization of metaphor	"The mission of the U.S.S. *Enterprise*? Isn't it something like that of, say, English warships?" "Very close" "performing a well-defined and long-range Exploration–Science–Security mission" "naval flavor" "it is usually like a naval battle, with broadsides being fired off" "infinite space promises just as much life and adventure as our own oceans"
maritime archetype(s)	"[a] space-age Captain Horation [sic] Hornblower" "his continuing struggle with himself" "resembles the captain of an 18th century ship of the line" "similar men in the past.... Drake, Cook, Bougainville and Scott" "in those days ... broad discretionary powers" "a show about Captain Hornblower in outer space!" "'Number One' ... since the Earth's seventeenth century when the second-in-command of sailing ships became generally known as 'First Lieutenants'"
veneer of nautical heritage, rituals and intertexts	"retains remnants of tradition known to Nelson and Drake" "the narrative device of the ship's log" "the same 'band of brothers' feeling" "the naval lineage as an important component of Star Trek" "many of the traditions, titles, and much of the terminology of the past have been maintained" "an acknowledgement of the naval heritage of Starfleet"
maritime milieu and *translatio imperii/translatio studii*	"The situation of this interstellar society is almost exactly analogous to the Earth of the eighteenth century" "and yet, everything we do is usually based on the English" "the *Enterprise* operates far away and virtually out of touch with higher authority" "Just as bold men once discovered and subdued new continents here on Earth" "a period of exploration and discovery" "Out of contact with the Admiralty"

ILLUSTRATION 1. A mosaic of (con)textual flotsam. Sources: Roddenberry, "STAR TREK Is..." 3–5 and 8–12, "STAR TREK GUIDE" 2, 14 and 17, and "WRITER/DIRECTOR'S GUIDE STAR TREK: The Next Generation" 4, 13, 24 and 40; Alexander 518; Whitfield and Roddenberry 173, 178 and 185; Duncan 79; Gerrold 11–12 and 218; Moore "Exclusive.")

intertextual presence in *Star Trek,* he "suddenly knew what *Star Trek* wanted to be and how [he] could relate to it" (80).

Paraphrasing the words of Captain Picard in *Star Trek Nemesis* (Stuart Baird, U.S. 2002), *Star Trek* presents us with a science-fictional world in which we sail into the unknown of the future by actually sailing into the known of the past. Engage!

Part I: Elementary, Dear Trekker (A Primer)

The transatlantic remapping of *Star Trek*'s world is rooted in an understanding of sf in general, and sf film and television in particular, as a genre which is inherently intertextual and historiographic. Sf uses and abuses histories and icons in order to tell stories that create and maintain stable yet estranged worlds which are still analogous to and thus sufficiently recognizable in relation to the ontological pasts and presents of our collective cultural memories. The same process of selecting and arranging discourses, icons, agents, settings, attitudes, spaces, and times into meaningful sequences governs both histories and stories. They are differentiated only by ideological and political claims to power, legitimacy, and truth. Despite its often-cited future-oriented and utopian outlook, sf is essentially nostalgic and even reactionary in its "analogical historicity" (Suvin 83). In sf television, in particular, analogy, similitude, and plausibility are routinely achieved by intertextually tapping into culturally significant myths which are then transposed into a science-fictional framework. They are then told and retold in a formulaic process of repetition and modulation which is key to maintaining coherence and familiarity on the part of the viewers.

The estrangement and subsequent worldbuilding in *Star Trek*'s "imaginary framework" (8), can be summarized by asking the science-fictional question of *what if* humanity began to travel to the stars; and *what if* the resulting utopian future was like "Wagon Train to the stars" and "Hornblower in space"? Through its intertextually anchored *vraisemblances, Star Trek* receives analogical historicity while also partaking in two culturally significant, nationally specific but ideologically compatible myths. The frontier and *Rule Britannia* are the discursive, symbolic, and ideological essences of these myths as much as they are the governing principles and central themes of *Star Trek*. They ensure the continuing plausibility, verisimilitude, and consistency of its sf world with regards to: (1) its ever-changing contexts of production and reception, and (2) the internal logic of a historicized maritime future in outer space. As themes, the frontier and *Rule Britannia* shape the *Star Trek* continuum in the form of two recognizable, structuring sets of discourses and sign systems. They perform two central, logical yet different functions. Drawing on *Wagon Train*'s format, *Star Trek* installed the frontier as a *topical/allegorical theme*, which enabled commentary on the "big issues" of the day (e.g., race, gender, religion, politics, technology, ethics). These broad allegorical intentions have been the source of many critical appraisals of *Star Trek*. As a metaphor, the frontier provides discursive and symbolic flexibility perpetually reshaped in relation to changing contexts. Channeled through a transatlantically informed perception, reactionary thought, and nostalgic conviction, which actually preceded the New Frontier context of the 1960s, *Rule Britannia* became *Star Trek*'s *operational/functional theme*. Delineating the mechanics of *Star Trek*'s worldbuilding, it provides permanence and coherence through repetition and permutation.

1. Logical, or at Least Plausible

Genre and Science Fiction

Any approach to sf storytelling must lay bare its formal understanding of genre and briefly delineate what might be called a problematics of definition.[1] Genre can generally be understood as a cultural practice of conventions which results from the perpetual renegotiation of meaning between creators of cultural artifacts (writers, producers, directors, etc.), the artifacts themselves (novels, television episodes, graphic novels, etc.), and their audience (readers, viewers, gamers, etc.). This process takes place in overlapping zones of contact and conflict within the confines of a capitalist market economy. Sf builds on an organic, procedural, and thus historically mutable understanding of intra-, inter- and extra-membranous workings of genre. Reasons for adopting an organic approach to genre are manifold. Labeling any artifact as sf is framed by the implied question of how we arrive at such a description. For a long time, the efforts of genre theorists were geared towards delineating the most paradigmatic model for a particular type of story (e.g., the typical crime or western story). However, the process of grouping texts together based solely on shared characteristics found in a representative range of artifacts proved to be impractical and inadequate. Even in the early years of sf criticism, scholars argued for abandoning a strict demarcation of genre boundaries in favor of more adaptable and reader-oriented models. Darko Suvin, who is credited with having had the most significant impact on sf criticism, has offered that genres are "ecological units, interacting and intermixing, imitating and cannibalizing each other" (21). Such an understanding espouses a high degree of intertextuality in the form of intergeneric and intermedial migrations of entire myths, characters, settings, themes, icons, and discourses.

The metaphor of a *membrane* circumscribes genre boundaries and interaction between genres most clearly. Unlike an impregnable stockade, a membrane has the qualities of a permeable node of contact and exchange. It transfers molecules, and grows and adapts along with the osmotic pressure that the demands of a larger textual organism put on the membrane. Interlocking layers of membranes operate not only between genres that are traditionally thought of being closely related, but also between more distant genre cell clusters. What is more, the metaphor is also viable when we look at the contours of adaptation processes across media. Interlocking membranes not only apply to different texts and groups of texts by way of their creators' practices, but they also envelop the audience as it takes a crucial place in the ecology of texts. By now, some variation of reader/audience-response criticism has become the norm in sf studies. The genre membrane that outlines the contours of sf is particularly porous when observed in its immediate neighborhood of genre clusters—fantasy proper and horror—which are frequently grouped together as the Fantastic. While there are not many characteristics that are "unique" for sf, there are a few formal processes and elements, along with their narratological and aesthetic constraints, which allow us to point to the membrane's selective permeability. They help us to cordon off a large albeit historically mutable range of sf artifacts across media from its immediate neighbors. When engaging with sf one has to be "a Darwinist and not a medicine-man" (36), or, I hasten to add, at least *pretend* to be a Darwinist.

Any examination of sf artifacts not only has to acknowledge the problematics of definition of what sf is and how it works, but also has to steer a clear course through it. The forces of our market-driven capitalist economy cannot be entirely ignored either. The labeling of any artifact as sf is economically motivated and ultimately also shapes the audience's perception and understanding of the artifact. After all, the term "science fiction" was first coined by pulp magazine editor Hugo Gernsback in order to carve out a niche for *Amazing Stories* on the American market in 1926. He defined sf as a "charming romance intermingled with scientific fact and prophetic vision" (qtd. Wolfe 43). The impact of pulp magazines is significant not only because it was literally a genre-defining period for American sf, but also because the pulps, together with radio dramas and B-movie serials, were the precursors for early American sf television both in terms of content and form. The main root of the problematics of definition then lies in the fact that three overlapping albeit partially incongruent traditions of discourse evolved concurrently with the genre itself. Each is engaged in the discussion of what is/is not sf, what was/was not sf, and how sf works/does not work. Right from the beginning of the pulp era, sf readers, i.e., fans, contributed to the critical discussion of stories in letters to magazine editors and in fanzines. Fans also engaged actively with creators of sf, i.e., writers, editors, and producers, who in turn developed their own vernacular. Lastly, scholars also contributed to the discussion by importing theories and methodologies primarily from literary studies. As a result, the challenge of the problematics usually revolves around five key issues: definition, classification, theme, context, and technique. By pointing out the selective permeability of the sf genre membrane vis-à-vis its fantastic neighbors, we begin to see and understand the few elements and processes that are distinctive of sf.

What Suvin defined as the "presence and interaction of estrangement and cognition" in an "imaginary framework alternative to the author's empirical environment" (7–8) is perhaps best understood as an *imagined world*. Sf stories create worlds which are made to appear otherworldly, altered and/or estranged from our everyday lives and cultural memories in discourse, form, and symbolism. Ontologically complete and following *plausible* laws, they manifest in the performance of cultural practices which are framed by physical environments, ecologies, and cosmologies. The process of building an sf world is triggered, facilitated, and maintained by the introduction, presence, and validation of the (e)strange(d), i.e., those elements which set the sf world apart from our primary reality. Termed the "novum" (63), it pushes the audience to acknowledge and make sense of the subsequent split with their historical and naturalistic existence. At this point of divergence, an sf world posits the simple yet thought-provoking question "what if." It aims at engaging the audience in a thought-experiment of hypotheticals. They willingly suspend their disbelief by extrapolating from what they are familiar with and by building analogies. In a Hegelian effort to achieve cognition, they essentially oscillate between that which is known and the knowable unknown. The process follows a parabolic trajectory from the known to the unknown "not by avoiding the formulaic and the familiar but by sending old vehicles off on new trajectories and furnishing them with the texture of experience" (Attebery 15). In the past, a formalist definition like Suvin's was put to normative uses, establishing a canon of sf and separating the proverbial wheat from the chaff. To steer through the problematics of definition, it is more practical to renegotiate the flexibility and intentional openness inherent in his definition.

Unlike the worlds created by other fantastic genres, sf lays an empirical claim to realism, historicity, and a closer ontological similitude with humanity's past and present. Sf worlds are grounded in the cognitive/scientific episteme. When we engage with an sf world, we validate our suspension of disbelief by adhering to an approximation, or semblance of the logic and rationale commonly attributed to the scientific method. In short, sf imitates the scientific method; it usually does not practice it. Governed by (pseudo-)scientific laws and explanations, an sf world simply has to appear plausible. Explaining its own sense of wonder, making it plausible, and thus making it appear "more" real speak to sf's genre-distinctive need. This plausibility clause sets sf apart from other fantastic genres on the story and narration levels as well as in terms of the cognitive demands placed on the audience. Fantasy proper and horror posit largely unexamined answers, taking the implausible, the inexplicable, and the impossible at face value. By comparison, sf initially poses questions and arrives at answers by way of scientifically plausible—not necessarily accurate—explanations which are consistent with the imaginary world thus created. Magic, and horror, too, work precisely because they are not explained, nor explainable. These genres are neither obliged to be subjected to a cognitively validating view of the world they help to create, nor do they have to adhere to any constraints of (pseudo-)scientific plausibility. People simply cast a spell and something happens; in sf, however, people more often than not deliver some sort of explanation, or speculation that sounds sufficiently scientific, reasonable, and thus plausible.

Consequently, I treat the *Star Trek* continuum as a formal manifestation of sf. Whether it can or should be considered canonical or not, or whether it makes for "quality" sf or not, bears little to no relevance for producing a contextual manual for its transatlantic double consciousness. *Star Trek* simply is sf. It follows the basic formal criteria which place it within the sf genre membrane. The systematic delineation of its maritime endowment, i.e., its "secret" British history, has no intentions of making any value judgment about the paradigmatic qualities that *Star Trek* might have as an sf artifact. Following historical and contextual trajectories proves more fruitful and meaningful in this respect.

The protozoan impulses, which coalesced into shaping significant parts of the sf genre membrane, point to sf's most potent premises, intentions, and presuppositions. They are also paradigmatic for the two themes that govern the *Star Trek* continuum and their different functions, respectively. There are as many sf genre histories as there are definitions. Even so, from a synoptic point of view, sf storytelling shares a generic genealogy with many other types of stories. They range from the fabulous/epic voyage, the Robinsonade, the utopias of the Baroque and the Renaissance to the political writings of the Enlightenment and, of course, the gothic and scientific romance. Whether we turn to the works of Iambulus, Euhermerus, Lucian of Samosata, Thomas More, Jonathan Swift, Mary Shelley or Jules Verne, they all share—to varying degrees—the estranging effects inherent in sf worlds. While these historical examples are hardly exhaustive, they circumscribe two impulses that bear importance for conceptualizing *Star Trek*'s transatlantic double consciousness. First, there is a political and democratizing timbre resounding throughout sf. Building on critical, allegorical, and didactic intentions, sf places the objects and/or subjects of its commentary within estranged and thus isolated locales

Historically, the second impulse espoused a predominantly maritime worldview—best exemplified by classic epic odysseys, Thomas More's *Utopia* (1516), or Jonathan Swift's satires—which often included colonial/imperial tendencies.[2] By way of underscoring the portentous qualities of these impulses, Gene Roddenberry once stated the following in an interview: "I was creating the show *Star Trek* and thinking maybe I could do what Jonathan Swift did" (qtd. Alexander 570).

Transposing these impulses wholesale into outer space and strapping them over the *Star Trek* continuum, it becomes clear that they are mirrored in its intertextually installed themes. The frontier is a purely metaphorical yet culturally correlative canvas, i.e., a topical theme, which acts as an adaptive and pedagogical allegory for the changing socio-cultural contexts that shaped *Star Trek*'s long history. *Rule Britannia*, on the other hand, provides an operational theme in the form of stable and consistent worldbuilding mechanics which are seaborne, naval, and British in origin. Both shape, inform, and maintain *Star Trek*'s formal categorization as sf.

The Best of Both Worlds: Conceptualizing Star Trek's *Transatlantic Double Consciousness*

The particulars of worldbuilding are governed by (1) the specific use of language in sf which is coupled to (2) the historiographic nature of the genre, especially its historicized futures. Moreover, worldbuilding also makes use of (3) a pronounced intertextual practice of presuppositions, mythomorphism, and *vraisemblance*. Even so, we are prone to neglect the workings of building an sf world since once learned, understood, and internalized, they are taken for granted. Sf criticism tends to "derive from what happens in the fiction, from its story," according to Carl Malmgren, while "the generic distinctiveness of SF lies not in its story but in its world" (7). In short, an sf world, and the meanings embedded within it, is not subservient to the plot it accommodates but rather constitutive of it. Operating within the selective permeability of the genre's membrane, an imaginative world amounts to rules of continuity and consistence which, in turn, ensure the world's meaningfulness. Analogies play an essential part in achieving meaning in sf as a genre of "cognitive estrangement."

Initiated by one or more nova, an sf world comes into being with the help of the audience. They engage in an extrapolative and cognitive exploration of plausible differences between the sf world and the audience's empirical environment. Since our everyday reality is informed by the past(s) and present(s)—both historical and fictional—of our collective memory, the process does not happen in a conceptual vacuum. Cognition of an imaginary framework is successful only when there is *re*cognition of similitude between the ontology of the fictional/estranged world and that of the real/empirical world. Cognitive estrangement then occurs by oscillating between reasonable extrapolation under the plausibility clause of sf, and analogies to the historical existence of the audience. After all, we cannot imagine and/or make sense of that which we do not know yet without using known referents. Building analogies is essentially "an extrapolation backwards ... to the past of the Earth, from geological through biological to ethnological and historical" (Suvin 29). Despite sf's often-cited future-oriented and utopian outlook, many sf worlds display built-in reactionary and nostalgic tendencies. The analogical building of sf worlds together with their recognition on the part of the audience tend to rely more on the application and negotiation of metaphor than metonymy. For example, this is the reason why we might not readily recognize Starfleet ships as sailing vessels of the Royal Navy transposed into outer space—neither in terms of their aesthetics, nor in the nature of their missions. Similarly, it might be challenging to fathom how and why *Star Trek*'s hyper-technological and utopian future was described as being similar to the late 18th and early 19th century Age of Sail. Analogical recognition is even more difficult in visual sf because visual tangibility serves as relief for the audience in that it requires them to do less "cognitive work" when compared to reading an sf novel. In short, estrangement makes difficult analogical recognition, which demands particular attention to the use of discourse.

We can stay with the principal ships of *Star Trek* in order to exemplify sf's discourse of estrangement. As a *species*, a starship, which can travel faster than the speed of light, may seem not only unfamiliar and estranged, but also fantastical yet not necessarily implausible. A starship belongs to the *genus* "ship" which increases the degree of familiarity and cognition. It then becomes even more meaningful and thus recognizable once we know which type of ship—"English warships" ("THE STAR TREK GUIDE" 27)—fulfilling which type of mission—"assisting colonists, aiding in scientific exploration, putting down conflicts, helping those in distress, regulating trade, engaging in diplomatic missions" (4)—it was modeled on. The same analogical process applies to specific characteristics of a starship. For example, Starfleet ships are equipped with a tractor beam, which Roddenberry explained as "the 'grappling hook' and 'towing line' of our future century" (21). However, analogical recognition of *Star Trek*'s disguised sailing ships is made more complicated again by a general lack of contextual knowledge of the ocean, sailing ships, and seafaring in our 20th and 21st century everyday reality. After all, our modes of transportation and communication are no longer chiefly determined by maritime agents, their agendas, and the uncompressed maritime space and time that constituted their world. Even so, despite its current unavailability and the unlikeliness of FTL-travel, a starship becomes a recognizable species by way of a historical analogy.

The importance of language in speaking and writing sf's estranged worlds into cognitive existence is, of course, much broader, encompassing metalinguistics, neology, and exolinguistics. Together, they contribute to the historiographic practices and thus the historicized character of the genre and its worlds. In audio-visual sf in particular, language often becomes either a subject in its own right, or a means for transforming familiar language in order to corroborate the strangeness of what the audience sees and hears. As a subject, it leads to speculation about how communication with extraterrestrials could be established. Sf creators often introduce a technologically plausible solution, like *Star Trek*'s universal translator, which renders alien languages into English in real time. At the same time, they also provide neologisms which supposedly "explain" the workings of such a fantastic piece of technology. The *Star Trek* continuum is a particularly good case in point. Often mocked as Treknobabble, its excessive blending of (pseudo-)scientific and (pseudo-)technical language is a neological means for cognitively validating the strangeness of its hyper-technological future. In such a case, language is then used transformatively, and, in the strictest sense, also nonsensically since we can only speculate about its meanings. Even so, the bulk of language we find in any type of fiction has to be clear lest communication between the creator(s), the text, and the audience breaks down and meaning is lost. Analogical recognition and validation of that which is estranged in sf is achieved not only by transforming language itself, but also by shifting the context in which a specific set of discourse is usually used. It essentially amounts to "placing untransformed language into transformed context" (Csicery-Ronay 20). Jonathan Culler has argued that "[t]o understand the language of a text is to recognize the world to which it refers" (135). For example, in the world of *Star Trek*, people speak a naval language, which originates in the operational discourses of British Napoleonic sea fiction, vis-à-vis Treknobabble. *Star Trek*'s naval corpus helps to transplant the gentlemanly tone of civility, courtesy, and deference characteristic of texts like the Hornblower novels into outer space.

The use of language in sf is closely interwoven with the historicizing practices of the genre. Sf worlds are historiographic archives of stories set and recorded in the future. While of course not all sf texts are set in fictional futures, the genre's membrane is especially permeable to future-oriented tendencies. The future is a potent territory since it allows sf creators to deal with "the present and the past as special cases of a possible historical sequence seen from an estranged point of view" (Suvin 81). While the future has not happened yet, it can be told from a historicized perspective as if it has already taken place. Hence, science-fictional futures are always historicized because "[a] past that is not yet known is a form of the future" (Csicery-Ronay 4). The rise of modern science and its intersection with capitalism created an aggregate of epistemological and teleological forces that inform sf's predisposition to creating historical futures. The scientific method, which gained broader traction roughly in the first third of the 19th century, redefined time along an exclusively linear trajectory. Later aided by the concept of evolution, most scientific thought "acquired a time direction ... of gradual, irreversible, inevitable change" (Malmgren 3–4). The anticipatory outlook of "western civilization" was also fueled by the rise of a capitalist market economy and the industrial revolution. Capitalist means of production and consumption helped to spatialize time—time became a new space—in the transition from farm time to factory time. Production outputs, wages, and shareholders' dividends represent the anticipated outcomes that will happen in the future as measured by the factory clock. The aggregate effect these forces have had on acts of discourse, especially in English-language sf,[3] is particularly telling. The memories of western modernity's "moment" and its telos of linear progress continue to reverberate in certain sf artifacts; and *Star Trek* is a paradigmatic example.

Sf worlds are inherently historiographic and thus historicized because they construct "micromyths of the historical process" (Csicery-Ronay 6). Throughout the *Star Trek* continuum, the *Captain's Log* explicitly announces the historicized nature of the future not least because it provides a star*date*. On the one hand, the log is a romanticized naval tradition reminiscent of the narrative journals of explorers such as Captain James Cook. On the other hand, it is also an archive of historiographically recorded events, geographically charted spaces, culturally defined bodies, and explanatory commentaries. Like their genealogical predecessors, starship captains then become the privileged chroniclers of historical knowledge. Recorded and archived futures like *Star Trek*'s maritime Neo-Enlightenment of the 22nd, 23rd and 24th century replicate and continue the way western histories are written, i.e., their historiography. "History cannot be imagined without a conception of the past having a future" (79). When historians write histories, they do so in narrative form by inserting themselves in a historical sequence right before the events, circumstances, and personages they are looking at. They then narrate the sequence as it unfolds from that point in time. Consequently, a certain past then becomes the virtualized future of an earlier past. The same virtual character of writing history also applies to the analogical historicity of science-fictional futures.

While all these discursive processes highlight the historicizing power of sf's genre membrane, they also point to how quickly the analogical historicity of sf futures can become dated in relation to the empirical world. Whether sf stories are set in near or distant futures, spanning mere minutes or many centuries, they inevitably bear the imprint of the historical moment that marked their creative conception. Historically anchored and archived sf worlds "retain a stylistic encoding of their point of origin," which is important for "a thorough understanding of how the extrapolated future works" (Stockwell 12). The "datedness" of sf futures and the relation to their point of origin provides an entry point to piece together *Star Trek*'s transatlantic double consciousness from a more holistic vector of sf criticism. We can construct a meaningful conduit between an sf world and the cultural influences and ideological forces that shaped the context(s) of its conception. In any sf story, one or more nova are used to initiate a world that diverges from the audience's empirical reality which essentially translates into a simple "what if" question. In other words, any sf world puts forth a proposition which demands to be cognitively validated. Every proposition a text makes, includes both the explicit and implicit presuppositions of its creators and the audience. Consequently, any proposition offered by an sf world is always intertextual. Such a complex interrelation of texts and contexts makes a contextual manual for *Star Trek*'s transatlantic double consciousness not only plausible but, indeed, necessary.

Vraisemblance is a useful concept especially for understanding the workings of sf television. Jonathan Culler has defined *vraisemblance* as an act "in which a text may be brought into contact with and defined in relation to another text which helps make it intelligible" (140). It allows us to decode the analogical recognition needed to validate an estranged sf world as much as it exposes its presuppositions. *Vraisemblance* points out the systematic interrelation between sf worlds, texts, creators, audiences, and contexts. Both the "attraction" and the "challenge" of sf's intellectually stimulating premise arguably lies "in the working out of its vraisemblance" (Malmgren 11). Relying on *vraisemblance* is a common practice when creators conceive a new fictional world; and it is deeply ingrained in television production where it is clearly observed when a new TV series is pitched to studios. A TV sales pitch usually draws on its addressees' (studio executives, board members, senior managers, etc.) knowledge of commonly shared cultural and especially medial reference points in order to make meaningful "that which is new." Usually following an "it's like ..."–formula, the most concise format of a pitch is essentially a straightforward act of *vraisemblance.*

There are a number of examples which corroborate the significance of this intertextual practice and its inherent meaning for arriving at analogical recognition and historicity. For example, J. Michael Straczynski, creator and showrunner of *Babylon 5* (U.S. 1993–8), more than once stressed that his show "would attempt to do for scifi television what *Hill Street Blues* did for cop shows" (1991, JMSNews.com). The reference was to highlight a move from episodic storytelling to a more sequential form which would allow for more complex, long-term, and preplanned story arcs and character development. More recently, James D. Parriott pitched the series *Defying Gravity* (U.S. 2009) as "*Grey's Anatomy* in space." What is more, its near-future setting was also based on the BBC documentary mini-series *Space Odyssey: Voyage to the Planets* (UK 2004). *Vraisemblance* can also be established when a new show seeks to renegotiate the formulas of the genre labels it would usually attract. Ronald D. Moore's re-imagined *Battlestar Galactica* (U.S. 2003–9) is a case in point; aiming for "Naturalistic Science Fiction," he essentially pitched the show as "Taking the Opera out of Space Opera" (1).

It serves to pause and take stock of the overarching science-fictional proposition of *Star Trek*. The title alone ties together the outcome of all the nova, or "novum effects" (Csicery-Ronay 75) of *Star Trek* in the form of a premise. Its sf world imagines a future where humanity is on *a trek to the stars*—an adventurous voyage in outer space. Hence, *Star Trek* poses the question of what if humanity develops the means to traverse interstellar space and thus makes contact with alien life. The proposition builds on three presuppositions: (1) Faster-than-light travel is possible, (2) extraterrestrial life exists, and (3) meaningful communication with alien life can be established. Moreover, the sf world thus imagined can be cognitively validated as plausible so that the audience willingly suspends their disbelief. Gene Roddenberry used two intertextual building blocks as a means to make all of *Star Trek*'s presuppositions and its premise enticing, meaningful, and marketable. Condensing the science-fictional proposition into the "language of television," he stated that "STAR TREK is a 'Wagon Train' concept—built around characters who travel to worlds 'similar' to our own, and meet the action-adventure-drama which becomes our stories" ("STAR TREK Is ..." 3). This act of establishing *vraisemblance* between *Star Trek* and the TV series *Wagon Train* (U.S. 1957–65) quickly morphed into the often-cited pitch: "Wagon Train to the stars." Roddenberry then went on to delineate the "principle [sic] character," who was in charge of this trek to the stars, as "[a] space-age Captain Horation [sic] Hornblower" (5). Commanding a "cruiser," he is on a "well-defined and long-range Exploration-Science-Security mission which helps create our format" (3).[4] His second act of *vraisemblance* further defined *Star Trek*'s world in relation to the main protagonist and his naval world found in C.S. Forester's novels. Consequently, *Star Trek*'s imaginary framework—its sf world of cognitive estrangement—puts forth the proposition of a historicized future of human space exploration which is analogous to "Wagon Train to the stars" and "Hornblower in space."

Through this intertextually anchored double *vraisemblance*, *Star Trek*'s "what if"-proposition not only receives analogical historicity, but also partakes in two nationally specific albeit ideologically compatible myths. Sf stories may take the form of myths, take part in and/or become a part of myths.[5] While more responsive to mythomorphism, sf's genre membrane is less permeable to mythopoeia.[6] The need to define myth only adds to the list of terms which notoriously suffer from an inflation of meaning. In general, myth is best understood as a totality of narratives and the meaningful arrangement of discourses, symbols, and artifacts in order to tell these narratives. Groups of people use myths as a means to establish and maintain their shared identity as a cultural community. Through them, a group structures and thus makes sense of its cultural memories, i.e., the past, in order to tackle everyday life in the present while promulgating and negotiating its hopes and fears about the future. The potency of myths has been used to great albeit detrimental effects in the creation and continuation of national mythologies. After all, myths are "ideology in narrative form" (qtd. Kapell 3). Myths are thus the main means to structure, access, and negotiate cultural memories; and *Star Trek* is rich in cultural memories and meanings.

The TV show *Wagon Train* ties into the myth of the American West and its presupposition of Manifest Destiny. This myth turned the violent subjugation of subsequently mythologized spaces found in the North American West into an identity-defining national project for the United States over the course of the 19th century. "[E]ssentially a tale of progress," the myth translates into "a justification of violent conquest and untrammeled development" (Hine et al. 192). C.S. Forester's Hornblower novels, in contrast, belong to a quintessentially British sub-genre of historical fiction. They are a part of the myth of the British Golden Age of Sail. Mythologized on a national level, this era reached its apex during the Napoleonic Wars at the end of the 18th and the beginning of the 19th century. The outcome of the conflicts reverberated well into the 19th century and shaped the advent of the 20th century. As the victorious naval superpower, Britain saw it as their imperial mission to bestow and "benevolently" enforce *Pax Britannica* on a global scale through hegemonic power and progress.

While *Wagon Train* and Hornblower point us to the mythological "what" *Star Trek* participates in, the two intertextual shorthand definitions do not yet reveal "how" these myths inform *Star Trek*'s world. By virtue of the double *vraisemblance*, the discursive, symbolic, and especially the ideological essences of the two respective myths were distilled into the two governing principles of *Star Trek*'s "imaginary framework." Together, they result in thematic coherence. We do not have to go far in order to find the singularly defining essence of the myth of the American West—the frontier. A structuring image, it permeates the myth. It is a rather illusive, indeed ironic space where wilderness is arguably transformed into civilization enabling the American national project of democracy and progress. The frontier enjoys a trifold spatialized existence: geographical, historical, and psychological; the latter points to its most potent manifestation as a space of the imagination. After all, the frontier, as David Mogen has argued, "has always functioned as a symbolic territory expressing our aspirations and our deepest fears, as well as our ironic sense of the tragedy brought by progress" (17). James Thomson's ode *Rule Britannia* (1740) helps us to ascertain the essence of the myth of the British Golden Age of Sail. We hardly have to look beyond the ideologically charged imperative in the chorus as it is usually sung: "Rule Britannia! Britannia rule the waves" (qtd. Gregg 87). Though written and first performed slightly before the British Golden Age of Sail proper, the ode comprises the dominant building blocks and imagery that shape the myth. Britain's national identity and sense of mission are defined in relation to oceanic spaces. Naval figures carry Britain's sense of "benevolent" mission to all seven seas. They are the primary agents of empire, straddling a dialectic of maritime military might and maritime exploration. Their work is instrumental in expanding a commercial enterprise of imperial proportions.

The two ideological essences were then realized as the central themes of *Star Trek*. As governing principles, they ensured the continuing plausibility, verisimilitude, and consistency of its sf world with regards to (1) the ever-changing cultural contexts of production and reception, and (2) the internal logic of building and maintaining a historicized maritime future. The frontier provided discursive and symbolic flexibility inherent in its qualities as a largely metaphoric space that could be adapted to changing contexts. *Rule Britannia* furnished permanence and coherence of worldbuilding along nostalgic and, indeed, reactionary lines. It is possible to argue, of course, that there is hardly any common ground between the myth of the American West and the myth of the British Golden Age of Sail. Each plays a significant role in the culturally dominant national identity of two distinct national cultures; and they seem to differ significantly from each other. It helps, however, to take a step back and look at the proverbial "bigger picture" and look past the effects of establishing identity by way of difference—a process central to any national project. Both are, in fact, products of the grand narrative of western modernity.[7]

Consequently, the transatlantic compatibility of the two myths and the two themes are secured via a shared telos, i.e., a shared purpose or goal. *Star Trek*'s transatlantic double consciousness speaks to the wholesale transposition and continuation of this telos in a fictional albeit historicized future. The telos espouses a reactionary utopian nostalgia for two pasts of Anglocentric modernity, and a belief in the inevitable triumph of humanism and progress. The telos permeated the flawed Anglocentric mission of benevolently bestowing the fruits of modern western civilization upon "the rest" of the world. The British Empire and the United States saw themselves as successive standard-bearers of this mission. The telos also encompassed the application of knowledge, which was wrestled from the cosmos thanks to the scientific method, to modes of industrial production and consumption. Not only was western modernity's belief in humanism ethnocentric, but it was distinctively Anglocentric. After all, most of western modernity was dominated by the succession of two socio-economic, cultural, and political Anglophone hegemons passing the torch from a formal to an informal empire.[8] After bringing forth "incomplete" truths—ranging from capitalism and communism to nationalism and fascism—the grand narrative of modernity has since come under the ironic scrutiny of postmodern thought. The *Star Trek* continuum is also haunted by the postmodern specter of doubt, distrust, and deconstruction especially in the three post–Roddenberry series. *ST:DS9*, in particular, was repeatedly hailed as the most postmodern incarnation of *Star Trek*. Even so, while the series sometimes questions the humanist paradigm, it does not abandon and/or radically alter *Star Trek*'s utopian outlook on the future.[9]

Star Trek's unerringly humanist belief in a hopeful future is key to its persistent Anglocentric telos of modernity as well as the compatibility of its themes; the same goes for the nostalgia and reactionism found at the heart of its utopian future. Apart from continuing to dethrone grand narratives of positivistic truth, postmodernism also unhinged their principal agent—the human self as a coherent entity—from the epistemological nodes of identity, meaning-making, and knowledge. Yet, if postmodern thought "renders all narratives of progress, utopianism in essence, meaningless," then *Star Trek*, as Bruce Isaacs has observed, "attempted to recuperate the boldest of them all: a faith in an *essential* human being" (186, original emphasis). *Star Trek*'s future keeps the self centered at the heart of a humanist universe which in turn ties into an essential albeit sometimes misunderstood quality of utopia.

The study of utopias and utopian thought is a scholarly quagmire where disagreements, contradictions, and multiple definitions abound. Any form of positivistic utopia is, however, essentially not only nostalgic, but also reactionary. Using popular period films of the 1980s for illustrative purposes, Linda Hutcheon has argued that nostalgia, even when exposed as problematic, still makes us participate as agents of the colonial project.[10] She has observed that this "is the nostalgia of those who believe in 'progress' and innovation, a nostalgia (again, paradoxically) for more simple, stable worlds—such as those of the putatively static society they destroyed" (1998). Hence, utopian models such as the one offered by *Star Trek* "reflect on what has been lost rather than what can be gained" (Isaacs 189). Therein we find an additional key for unlocking its utopian future as both nostalgic and reactionary by way of its transatlantic double consciousness. *Star Trek*'s stories are told in reactionary form in that they constantly look back along the shared telos of Anglocentric modernity in order to celebrate its unimpeded continuation in a fictional future. A continuum of texts, *Star Trek*'s 'imaginary framework' is governed by the repetition and permutation of its two themes. They serve to maintain familiarity and recognition with regards to *Star Trek*'s allegorical intentions and the workings of a historicized future which is in fact a re-imagined maritime past. Together, they have continuously shaped *Star Trek* stories for more than forty years of television history.

A Brief Note on Television

In the multi-author nature of *Star Trek*'s production,[11] the tension between authorial power and the regulated dispersal thereof has to be weighed against the behavioral patterns of and demands on television audiences. They, in turn, are governed by the conventions, norms, and evolution of the medium. While television has changed considerably since its advent in the 1950s—especially in terms of technological advancements of filming, means of distribution, and changing modes of viewing—it remains a well-structured medium. Key to television drama is the mode of repetition which is juxtaposed with degrees of suspense providing crucial modulation. Between the mid–1980s and the mid–1990s, television went through a paradigmatic shift towards *televisuality*. Triggered by the intersection of technical developments, especially lighting technologies, cinematography, and the use of CGI, the medium became "more" visual. This, in turn, led to a reduction of dialog-centered storytelling. Equally important was the gradual transition from episodic storytelling, i.e., every TV episode is more or less a discrete entity producing a high degree of closure at the end, to more sequential forms which have since become the industry norm. The transition also coincided with significant changes in distribution such as a shift from broadcasting to narrowcasting, cult television, boutique productions, and home video technology, which initiated a culture of the perpetual re-watch. Even so, repetition remains key as it ensures continuity. After all, as John Caldwell has noted, "continuity is one of the chief aspects of a television aesthetic" (qtd. Johnson-Smith 62). Television's mode of repetition and modulation provides a formal conceptual frame for the thematic continuity of *Star Trek*.

The value of repetition, and thus familiarity and comfort on the part of the audience, points to a cultural significance of television storytelling which is rooted deep in the human condition. Television is a means for emulating ancient, pre-print modes of storytelling, most notably oral traditions.[12] Audience comfort and recognition through repetition and familiarity are central aspects of oral storytelling. "Like 'fireside' listeners of traditional storytellers," Chris Gregory has suggested, "television's audiences delight in continual repetition, in fantastic heroics and dream-like imaginary scenarios, and in melodramatic high tragedy and comedy" (8). The repetitive and regulated nature of a television continuum like *Star Trek*, which is codified and archived in primary production material, attests to the fact that showrunners, producers, and writers are, of course, keenly aware of the mythical and well-structured dimensions of television storytelling. The themes that govern *Star Trek*'s world were remarkably resilient. They remained in place despite the paradigmatic changes that occurred on the television landscape, especially with regards to narrative formats, production techniques, and distribution, moving from episodic to more sequential storytelling, and from a dialog-centered mode to more visual foregrounding of the background in a milieu of televisuality. In order to be successful and economically viable, any television series needs to maintain its audience. For example, while we might be overwhelmed by the sheer number and implied diversity of *Star Trek* stories, let us not forget that every episode and film speaks to "the gradual, continuous rediscovery of things that the readers/viewers already know and wish to know again" (Johnson-Smith 52).

It is possible to use one of *Star Trek*'s own discursive formations to theorize and conceptualize its intertextually appropriated themes vis-à-vis the mechanics of television—the IDIC. Short for *Infinite Diversity in Infinite Combinations*, Roddenberry initially conceived the IDIC as a marketing ploy to sell more *Star Trek* merchandise. Subsequently, the IDIC was introduced into the *Star Trek* world as the central philosophical principle of the Vulcans.[13] We can also use it as a critical tool for looking at the workings of *Star Trek* from the inside out. When we apply it to television's mode of repetition and modulation, and the resulting thematic continuity that governs *Star Trek*, we can reconfigure IDIC into: finite diversity in semi-finite combinations. *Star Trek* relies on a few "foundational narratives," as Lincoln Geraghty helps us to remember, i.e., "the same stories, only slightly different each time" (26–27).[14] *Star Trek* was repeatedly defined by way of two "foundational narratives"—*Wagon Train* and *Hornblower*. Hence, every incarnation of *Star Trek* is a repetition and permutation of "Wagon Train to the stars" and "Hornblower in space." Via the theme of the frontier, *Star Trek* always lays claim to the moral imperative inherent in its telling of allegorical stories about American issues, or providing American answers to questions that are of a more universal nature. By the same token, *Star Trek*'s future world of space exploration always builds on a historicized and nostalgic transposition of Hornblower's naval world into outer space.

For a passionate albeit critical aficionado, there is hardly a task more daunting than the attempt to introduce *Star Trek* in its entirety insofar as it is even possible, let alone practical. The *Star Trek* continuum encompasses a history of the future which extends roughly from the late 21st to the late 24th century. As a media phenomenon, it grew out of the exclusively episodic format of its original incarnation (*ST:TOS*) and its animated spin-off (*ST:TAS*), which gave rise to a distinct fan culture.[15] *Star Trek* then moved onto the silver screen in a series of motion pictures before being reincarnated four times in the growing serial and televisual nature of the medium between the late 1980s and the early 2000s. While becoming more serial, *Star Trek* has yet to harness the potential of a fully pre-planned/sequential format. The *Star Trek* continuum emerged as a procedural presence on the American, indeed, the global media landscape which saw regular "updates" and thus modulation of the original idea/vision as conceived by Roddenberry. The perpetual attempts and efforts of his successors to integrate sequels and prequels, along with more disparate elements and stories, resulted in a coherent whole of a science-fictional world.

2. Space. The Final Frontier

What then has *Star Trek* exactly to do with (a) *Wagon Train*? After all, outer space in *Star Trek* is discursively *not* realized as a frontier geography. The crews of Starfleet ships are *not* passengers on a re-imagined wagon train to the stars.[1] The starship captain is *not* a composite character of a wagon master and a dashing young cowboy-scout, and neither are the rituals performed by these interstellar explorers reminiscent of a mid–19th century, land-based milieu of the American West. The added lens of primary production material point to the extent of how *Star Trek* partakes in the myth of the American West, how its conception was entangled with the Western during the 1950s and early 1960s, and, ultimately, how the frontier was installed as one of two themes governing its imaginary framework. The significance of Roddenberry using *Wagon Train* as an intertextual reference point was twofold. First, his act of *vraisemblance* was rooted in selling *Star Trek* convincingly to studio executives who were familiar with producing Westerns. *Wagon Train* was a meaningful point of reference, suggesting the economic viability and practicality of making an sf television series that, in contrast to space opera and rocketmen shows of the 1950s such as *Tom Corbett, Space Cadet* (U.S. 1950–5), was geared towards an adult audience. Second, *Wagon Train* was used as a ruse, disguising what *Star Trek* really was. Recognizing and capitalizing on the allegorical intent encoded in the imagined frontier of *Wagon Train,* he installed the frontier as a metaphoric canvas in *Star Trek.* He drew on the show's semi-anthological structure and its relatively large recurring cast who encountered different dramatic situations every week. They staged morality plays that emphasized basic American values such as individualism, progress, egalitarianism, and a sense of mission. *Wagon Train* essentially provided a television format for *Star Trek* using the metaphoric force of the frontier to tell allegorical stories at a time when the frontier was contextually infused with presidential vigor and the *image* of liberal progressivism.

Roddenberry's act of *vraisemblance* must of course be understood vis-à-vis President Kennedy revitalizing the frontier as a metaphor to describe the opportunities, challenges, and threats that the American people faced in the "revolutionary" decade of the 1960s. Emphasizing its existence as a largely imagined space, David Mogen has asserted that "the significance of the term 'frontier' derives from its application as metaphor, as much as or more than from its uses as an accurate description of historical processes" (26). Evoking powerful national nostalgia in his acceptance speech for the Democratic Party Nomination in 1960, Kennedy used one of the many geographic endpoints of westward expansion—California—as a beachhead for a liberal-progressive leap of the imagination. The mobility, mutability, and polysemy inherent in the president's metaphoric use of the frontier corresponds with it being installed as an allegorical/topical theme in *Star Trek*. Even so, Kennedy's New Frontier ideology, and its science-fictional echoes, were encased and maintained by an awareness for transatlantic cultural continuities. They underscored that many key American values are historically, culturally, and ideologically shared by all English-speaking peoples. Individual enterprise, scientific rationalism, a belief in progress, and a sense of "benevolent" mission are in fact just parts of a larger story arc that conjoins the telos of Anglocentric modernity. Consequently, it is pertinent to also take a look at the president's "private myth," which, according to John Hellmann, was "driven since childhood by fantasies of British adventurers" (122). Not only does it point us to a largely hidden discourse undergirding the New Frontier—its ideological "far side"—but it also provides us with a transatlantic segue for remapping *Star Trek*'s world along British lines.

Wagon Train to the Stars

The TV Western *Wagon Train* offered a readily recognizable segment of the American experience out west. It is easy to imagine a train of covered wagons, wheels creaking relentlessly, as it traverses the vast spaces found in the American West—prairies, rolling hills, valleys, canyons, mountain passes, and high deserts—transporting myriads of different people towards an imagined promise of rebirth, renewal and/or redemption. Every season a new train set out from Missouri to California under the command of a wagon master and his company. While usually rather monotonous, the trains' repeated treks on television were replete with dramatic encounters. They involved the passengers, the literal and metaphorical baggage they brought with them, the wagon master's company, and whoever and whatever they crossed paths with.[2] The qualities of the imagined frontier as a metaphoric canvas onto which almost any type of story could be projected, permeated *Wagon Train* like the proverbial "red thread." Echoing the intentions and subtexts of especially movie Westerns in the 1950s, *Wagon Train* employed the frontier—much like *Star Trek* would do later—as an allegorical theme to provide commentary on and social criticism of contemporary American culture. This was the show's basic format which connected the diverse range of semi-anthological stories it offered on a weekly basis. Its format also set the show slightly apart from other TV-Westerns which were either of the gunfighter/lawman or the homesteading variant—*Rawhide* (U.S. 1959–65) was arguably its closest relative. Contextualizing *Wagon Train* during the golden age of TV and movie Westerns sets us on a trajectory that will lead us to the decline of the genre Western which spawned intertextual links with other genres, most notably, with sf.[3]

As the disappearance of the geographic frontier was bemoaned and academically historicized in Frederick Jackson Turner's far-reaching "Frontier Thesis" (1893),[4] it also gave birth to the Western as a literary genre which would continue to nurture the frontier in countless permutations. While artist Frederic Remington supplied much of the Western's iconography, Owen Wister's novel *The Virginian* (1902) provided the paradigmatic literary model. It included a nameless cowboy protagonist as well as a highly ritualized, chivalric gunfight. *The Virginian* provided a formula which was, according to Robert Hine et al., "entirely masculine, restoring health and re-creating American men as self-reliant individuals" (199). The formula of the Western made it an ideal vehicle for early filmmakers. Hundreds of movie Westerns were produced in the wake of *The Great Train Robbery* (Edwin S. Porter, U.S. 1903), ranging from *The Covered Wagon* (James Cruze, U.S. 1923) and *Stagecoach* (John Ford, U.S. 1939) to *My Darling Clementine* (John Ford, U.S. 1946), *Shane* (George Stevens, U.S. 1953), and *The Searchers* (John Ford, U.S. 1956); the latter heralded the brief rise of Spaghetti Westerns in the mid–1960s. Westerns became a career vehicle for pioneering actors such as Bronco Billy Anderson and Tom Mix. They turned Gary Cooper, John Wayne, and Clint Eastwood into popular culture icons before, during and well after World War II. The prolific output of genre novelists such as Zane Grey and Louis L'Amour, and many more writers of the purple sage, was paralleled by movie Westerns. The dime novel tradition of the 19th century also found its continuation in pulp magazines. Ultimately, all of this together culminated in the golden age of the Western across the American media landscape which lasted roughly until the mid–1960s.

While the Western of course grew and evolved over five decades in the wake of World War I, the Great Depression, and World War II, for millions of Americans the genre remained the premiere popular culture means of escaping from and coping with everyday life. The genre, however, also began to increasingly reflect the growing tensions between social and ideological consensus, conformity, and change in the post-war years. The Western became a narrative vehicle which ambiguously oscillated between reaffirming the myth of the American West—privileging white, middle class, Anglo-Saxon, heterosexual, Protestant men—and pointing out its unfulfilled promises; the myth blatantly failed women, Native Americans, Latinos, African Americans, and other people of color. Consequently, traditional stories of America's heroic conquest of the West existed vis-à-vis diverging narratives which challenged the myth and/or used its images to probe contemporary American life.[5] During the 1950s, television and movie Westerns served as a quintessential prelude to and discursive repository for President Kennedy's rhetorical masterpiece of defining the following decade as the New Frontier. They paved the way for him because "[o]n the screens of both theaters and living rooms, westerns addressed major social issues of the 1950s through coded and displaced maneuvers" (Hellmann 118).

The decade of 1950s witnessed the rapid growth of television as a new mass medium. Early TV Westerns, like *Hopalong Cassidy* (U.S. 1952–4) and *The Lone Ranger* (U.S. 1949–57), were exclusively directed at a juvenile audience. Their resounding success, especially with young American boys, can be attributed to a rather simple moral formula: good always triumphed over evil; and it was easy to tell these two apart since the good guys always wore white hats whereas their adversaries donned black ones.[6] Concisely outlined in Gene Autry's *Cowboy Commandments*, the heroes of these shows adhered to a chivalric code which encompassed fairness, truthfulness, helpfulness, and patriotism as well as a strong work ethic and the absence of any racial or sexual bias. The repetitive and naive nature of this code has to be understood vis-à-vis the politically charged climate of the Second Red Scare. The McCarthyism of the early 1950s pushed television, together with other media, into being HUAC-friendly.[7] The discrediting of Senator McCarthy and his witch hunts for suspected Communist sympathizers harbingered a paradigm shift for the TV Western in the mid–1950s. Accentuating the transition from juvenile to more adult-oriented formats, a shift in allegorical fervor and social critique spilled over from movie Westerns.[8] Television studios recognized the growing economic potential of TV Westerns. What began with *Gunsmoke* (U.S. 1955–75), quickly became an overpowering presence on the American television landscape, boasting popular titles such as *Maverick* (U.S. 1957–62), *Rawhide* (U.S. 1959–65), *Bonanza* (U.S. 1959–73), and *Have Gun—Will Travel* (U.S. 1957–63). The latter had Gene Roddenberry in the writing credits of no less than twenty-five episodes. There is no doubt that the TV Western reigned supreme by the end of the decade[9]; and, of course, there was *Wagon Train*.

The show was inspired by John Ford's classic Western *Wagon Master* (U.S.

1950). Producers Howard Christie, Richard Lewis, and Frederick Shorr used the film's premise of a wagon train crossing the vastness of the American West and extended it to develop the show's distinctive format. In total, *Wagon Train* ran for eight seasons; five of which it could be found among NBC's best-rated shows before it was sold to ABC in 1962 where it received its final three seasons. When compared to its immediate competitors, it stood out in terms of its production dimensions, its television format, and its narrative conventions. At $100,000 per episode, the show had an unusually high production budget for a TV Western. It allowed the series not only to attract quality writers, but also made it possible to engage top-billed guest stars[10] who became central to the show's format. The basic format was such that the main story focused on one and/or more passengers on the train, showcasing their reasons, intentions and/or motivations for heading out West. While the regular cast also received stories of their own, the wagon master and his crew mainly provided commentary and continuity. "[N]ot a conventional Western at all but a dramatic anthology that happened to be set in the nineteenth-century American West," Gary Yoggy has asserted that the show's format "permitted scriptwriters a wide range of plots dealing with character development and kept the program consistently sophisticated and engrossing" (175–6). In other words, the stories were not necessarily locked into the representations of the geographic and historical American West; neither were they dependent on nor constitutive of a world which was built with the discourses, iconography, archetypes, rituals, and *mise-en-scène* associated with the American West. The passengers served as entry points for the exploration of topical themes, issues, and concerns. The series employed imagined frontier spaces as a metaphorical canvas onto which any story could be projected.

Following the lead of newer movie Westerns,[11] *Wagon Train* told a wide range of allegorical stories and morality plays which were regularly infused with social criticism. The show featured many domestic stories which showcased the negotiation of female gender roles found especially in traditional marriages. Episodes oscillated between giving a voice to women who were less conformist—also in the professional world featuring, for example, skilled female doctors—and curbing behavior that was still deemed too controversial for women in the 1950s. Such stories also included didactic morality plays about characters dealing with the detrimental effects of substance abuse, especially alcoholism. Some also commented on the growing concerns about juvenile delinquency. Other episodes produced a broad spectrum of commentaries on religious beliefs and practices; for example, the ethical conundrums of refusing medical treatment based on fundamentalist religious doctrines. There were a series of political stories which usually featured government representatives, the U.S. Army, or shady third-party go-betweens. Such episodes allowed for commentary on secret arms trading with natives, the involvement in proxy wars, general wide-spread corruption, and war crimes in POW camps. They also brought forth more personal stories about presumed enemy collaborators, cowardice, conscientious objectors, and what is now known as PTSD.

By contemporary standards, *Wagon Train* mostly took the moral high ground, advocating the resolution of racial conflicts by negotiating and developing mutual understanding rather than resorting to violence. Writers also attempted to be *tentatively* revisionist when it came to portraying the exploitation of and racial prejudice towards Native Americans. Certain "Indian scenarios" occasionally became a foil for pointing at growing civil rights struggles; for example, educated native lawyers and sympathetic white attorneys variably mustered legal responses to fight the forced removal of a native community from their territory. Not only were racial themes used to comment on deeply held WASP anxieties about racial equality, but also to present more lighthearted views on intercultural misunderstandings and stereotypes. While the good of the train's covenant was portrayed as paramount, a number of stories had members of the crew, usually the wagon master, stand up and speak for individual passengers who happened to be different in one way or another. Hence, the show also promoted moral courage and individualism under the pressure of civic complacency. "This format managed to keep Wagon Train rolling for eight seasons," and provided, according to Gary Yoggy, "a pattern" (176). This pattern informed not only *Rawhide* and *The Virginian* (U.S. 1962–71), but also points at the intertextual node of contact between *Wagon Train* and *Star Trek* as delineated by Roddenberry. Moreover, it also points to the continued use of the frontier as a thematic conduit for commenting on contemporary and/or historical subject matters.

In 1956, Gene Roddenberry resigned from the LAPD to become a full-time television writer. He expanded on his work with Ziv Television Productions who had hired him as a technical advisor for police procedurals. He worked as a writer on a new but short-lived anthology show titled *The West Point Story* (U.S. 1956–8). Roddenberry continued to develop stories for other shows. He drafted concepts for entire TV series while also making his first forays into producing. His prolific contribution to CBS's *Have Gun—Will Travel* went a long way to establish his credits. He moved on to pitch, sell, and produce the series *The Lieutenant* (U.S. 1963–4) for MGM. "The program portrayed human drama in a military setting, examining social questions of the day" (Alexander 186). Even though the show was ultimately not successful, Roddenberry met a number of people, actors, production and writing staff, whom he would assemble for his next project. While producing *The Lieutenant*, he began to work on a new idea. He combined new impulses with elements and concepts he had discarded in the past which together coalesced into the first pitch for *Star Trek*.

Simply titled "STAR TREK Is ...," Roddenberry committed his concept to paper on March 11, 1964. Presented as "[a] one-hour dramatic television series," he is quick "to put it in a language of television," in that "STAR TREK is a 'Wagon Train' concept—built around characters who travel to worlds 'similar' to our own, and meet the action-adventure-drama which becomes our stories" (1–3). In order to sell *Star Trek* convincingly to studio executives, who were familiar with making Westerns, *Wagon Train* was a meaningful point of reference to stress the economic viability of his idea. It served to illustrate the nuts and bolts of making an sf TV show which was geared towards an adult audience. What is more, *Wagon Train* also served as a ruse. Inspired by the allegorical intent of *Wagon Train*, Roddenberry capitalized on the mutability of the frontier as a metaphoric canvas offering what Wallace Stegner called "a geography of hope" (qtd. Aquila 14). Thus, it was bound to resonate well with the progressive, hopeful and utopian outlook offered in President Kennedy's New Frontier, which included but was not limited to the exploration of space. Pitching a *faux* Space Western was Roddenberry's way to sneak what were then considered possibly contentious and provocative topics past television's regulatory boards and censors.[12] *Wagon Train* essentially provided a television format and narrative premise for *Star Trek* which allowed him and his creative team to tell stories about contemporary society; stories that allegorized and thematized topical problems, issues, and questions while offering a positive and progressive outlook for the future.

Roddenberry then took his pitch to television studios with a view to selling his show. First, he approached CBS. Even though their representatives expressed great interest, they ultimately rejected the proposal. After all, they were arguably concerned about receiving potential competition for their new sf show *Lost in Space* (U.S. 1965–8) which they were developing with Irwin Allen at the time. Gene also had little luck at MGM. The prevalent attitude towards doing "serious" sf on television was curtailed by the fact that studios and networks regarded it as too expensive. His next stop was at NBC, where he was more successful. Executives were still on the fence about the practicality, feasibility, and marketability of producing an sf show with what was then considered a rather large recurring main cast who would visit new alien places on a weekly basis. Even so, they asked Roddenberry to develop a few story outlines that could serve as the basis for a pilot episode.

Ultimately, they commissioned "The Cage" (1964/5) as the first pilot which was produced at Desilu Studios. The episode features a recognizable starship *Enterprise*, captained by Christopher Pike (Jeffrey Hunter). While the cast and characters were not, with the exception of Spock (Leonard Nimoy), the same of what would later become *ST:TOS*, the basic *Star Trek* format, its world, its allegorical intent and social criticism, and its maritime worldbuilding were already in place in their embryonic form. While investigating the distress call of a long lost starship on an uncharted planet, the captain is captured by powerful mind-controlling aliens. They are dependent on the emotions and thoughts of other species in order to sustain their civilization whose evolutionary development had ground to a standstill. The story offered a thinly veiled critique of substance abuse and the forced enslavement of "subordinate" peoples for the sole purpose of satisfying the needs of a social elite. In order to break out of situations of dependency and oppression, it showed that human characters must confront and overcome their most primal desires and fears. Unfortunately, the test screenings of the pilot were not successful. Executives and the test audience concluded that the story was too demanding, too complex, and "too cerebral." They were also concerned about a few casting choices, especially the alien and female leads. While the original pilot was rejected, the basic premise and format of the show were given a second chance.

The Western genre in general, and *Wagon Train* in particular, remained reference points for practical issues of production, like writers who were unfamiliar with sf storytelling. Starting with Roddenberry's series pitch, these references served to underscore that the fantastic encounters of the crew could be made economically feasible by harnessing the potential of recycling and reusing props and sets of other shows and films. They also served a more specific purpose with regards to believability of character and story. In his series pitch, these practical considerations and arguments were the prelude to nineteen short "story springboards" (13). Even though most of them were never developed into full episodes later, they all clearly betray a thinly veiled allegorical, satirical and/or socially critical theme which permeates and connects them. For example, in the "The Perfect World," the crew would make landfall on a planet where the local civilization would be roughly at the same stage as Earth in 1964. There, they would encounter "perfect order, no crime, no social problems, no hunger or disease," which ironically would be enforced by "incredible police barbarism," and framed by "despotic communism carried to its extreme" (*ibid.*). Though gradually subsiding in intensity after the Cuban Missile Crisis of 1962, a story like "100 A.B. Or, 'A Century After the Bomb'" would have struck a topical chord with the living memories of contemporary viewers. Such a story would have addressed their collectively shared anxiety over a possible nuclear war which had been festering since the early 1950s. It would have presented "a terrifying parallel as we examine what might be our own world a few decades after an atomic holocaust" (14). A story titled "Kongo" foreshadows how morality tales about race relations and the rights of the individual would ultimately become a staple in *Star Trek*. According to the outline, the crew would visit a planet whose society is reminiscent of the "Old Plantation Days ... with the slight exception of it being white savages who are shipped in and auctioned at the slave mart" (16).

The series bible for *ST:TOS*—"THE STAR TREK GUIDE. THIRD REVISION" (1967)—added more substance to how *Star Trek* can be understood vis-à-vis the Western. Combating misconceptions and a lack of knowledge about sf storytelling, Roddenberry repeatedly drew parallels to the Western as a common frame of reference which many television writers at the time were familiar with. He referred to the Western in order to emphasize how the stories he intended them to tell were not inherently different from other types of stories. The series bible instructed them to check whether their story became tied up in "the wonder of it all" and the glitz of sf, and how to revise accordingly. Serving as a marker to understand *Star Trek*'s relationship with the Western, he used *believability* as a keyword throughout the document, conflating the telling of stories about "today" with recognizable values and behaviors displayed by the characters. For example, Roddenberry stated: "We did *not* recreate the Old West as it actually existed; instead, we created a new Western form, actually a vast colorful backdrop *against which any kind of story could be told*. And who was our character? Essentially, *today's* man, with attitudes, values and morals the audience understood and could accept" (3, original emphasis). Television and movie Westerns of the 1950s/60s are used as an obvious foil for re-encoding the genre's contemporary social commentary and criticism in *Star Trek*. These references reinforce one of the two protozoan impulses that had informed sf since long before the genre was called sf—its satirical undercurrents and social critique. The premise of *Star Trek* as a "Wagon Train concept/format," equating believability of character and story with allegorical intentions, social commentary and topicality, was later reiterated and cemented in the series bible for *ST:TNG*—the "WRITER/DIRECTOR'S GUIDE STAR TREK: THE NEXT GENERATION" (1987). Roddenberry invited "writers to consider premises involving the challenges facing humanity today (the 1980's and 90's)" (4). Once again "believability" served as a keyword to stress the adaptability of the *Star Trek* format to new contexts which, in the case of *ST:TNG*, meant the late 1980s and early 1990s. Governed by the frontier as a theme, this basic format was subsequently treated as an *a priori* fact in the production material of later shows.

Invoking space as the "final frontier," as we hear it in the opening credits of *ST:TOS* and *ST:TNG*, gives us access to a relatively simple act of *vraisemblance*.

However, it also evokes more complex contextual, ideological, and political realities which ultimately point towards nothing less than a transatlantic cultural continuity. As the "final frontier," outer space reverberated with immediate, powerful, and topical contextual resonance in the 1960s. Whenever space and space adventures are defined in frontier terms, critics, fans and casual viewers alike are quick to equate them with the U.S. space race with the Soviets. While of course not incorrect, it is often done somewhat haphazardly, drawing on presumed knowledge and shared assumptions. Such a view eschews the multilayered complexity involved in *Star Trek*'s frontier—a theme installed vis-à-vis the "far side" of President Kennedy's New Frontier.

The British "Far Side" of Kennedy's New Frontier

The multilayered meanings of the New Frontier can be accessed through a few significant presidential speeches. Upon closer inspection and contextualization, they reveal more than the obvious reference points that are usually used to talk about space exploration in frontier terms. Speaking about, promoting, and remembering outer space in a frontier discourse points to a proverbial marriage of convenience and enthusiasm. Kennedy's New Frontier also lays bare the power of symbols in the nation's imagination. Advocates of the Mercury, Gemini, and Apollo programs regularly pointed to and adopted the language from two speeches President Kennedy gave on the nation's space effort. The first was a special message on urgent national needs given in person before a joint session of Congress on May 25, 1961; the second, dubbed "the Moon speech," the president delivered at Rice University on September 12, 1962.[13] They have since served as the textual repertoire for space boosters in their continuous attempts to cast space exploration in frontier terms. Interestingly, however, barring one exception, overt references to the frontier vis-à-vis space exploration are conspicuously absent in both speeches. Speaking at Rice, the president juxtaposed the growth of aeronautical industries in Texas with "what was once the furthest outpost on the old frontier of the West will be the furthest outpost on the new frontier of science and space." Even so, Kennedy's objectives for the nation's space effort still made space exploration *a* New Frontier of the 1960s. Consequently, it is still important for understanding the frontier theme in *Star Trek*. By making outer space the "final frontier," *Star Trek* points at dimensions of the New Frontier that are less literal and less analogical. They greatly add to the symbolic and ideological baggage of the theme.

Firstly, and most obviously, *ST:TOS* posits a hyper-technological, utopian future of the 23rd century which espouses a belief in positivistic progress through scientific and technological development. Roddenberry conceived this future at a time when the public's confidence in the good of technology and science was still rather high before it rapidly declined in the second half of the 1960s and the early 1970s. Space exploration, in particular, "remained a technology of optimism" (McCurdy 100). Unlike the horrid misuses of technology in Vietnam, or the rampant secret wiretapping conducted by various government institutions, space technology did not become a target of countercultural attacks. Subsequently, the optimism about space exploration became "frozen" as a thematic constant in *Star Trek*'s frontier. Secondly, it is also entangled in the space frontier as being essentially a prestige project and ploy to foster trust in the federal government. The space program repeatedly served as an example for the Kennedy and Johnson administrations to show the American people that the government could successfully coordinate and carry out a large and complex project, affecting "real" change and thus progress. Kennedy's speech at Rice showed that the race for the moon was not only a prestige project aimed at energizing Americans, but also to impress upon other countries, especially developing nations in danger of falling for Communism, that the United States laid claim to the leadership of the western world.[14] Internationally, outer space turned into yet another ideological and symbolic battleground of the Cold War. On the domestic front, the space program was used to show and convince a nation, which traditionally distrusts its federal government, that it could tackle and solve other complex challenges besides putting a man on the moon (e.g., the conflict in Vietnam, Civil Rights legislation, the War on Poverty, etc.). Most of them were fraught with just as many problems as the space program. However, people did not learn about the problems that actually plagued the space program until later. While most policy responses to these challenges showed signs of mismanagement and/or disastrous failure as the decade wore on, space exploration remained a paradigmatic beacon of the New Frontier.

Since the frontier theme in *Star Trek* is obviously more expansive than being just a science-fictional echo of the space frontier, it is necessary to look at Kennedy's New Frontier in its entirety. With crucial echoes found in his inaugural address, the key to the New Frontier as a political and rhetorical metaphor lies in his 1960 acceptance speech for the Democratic Party Nomination. The speech provides an additional key to unlock the contemporary resonance of space as the "final frontier" in *ST:TOS* as well as the perpetual existence of the frontier theme in the *Star Trek* continuum. Opening the address with a swift attempt to dispel concerns about his Catholic faith, Kennedy continued with an appraisal of the status quo. He covered international concerns, chiefly the influence of Communism and the threat of a nuclear war, before addressing domestic issues which spoke to population growth, racial discrimination, and technological advances. He then turned them into threats, challenges, and opportunities for the future as represented by the new decade; for the latter he invoked the "New Frontier" as a metaphorical descriptor. In a rhetorical move, he used one of the many geographic endpoints of westward expansion—the venue of the DNC in California—as a point of departure for a leap of the imagination.[15] The New Frontier was essentially *a metaphor of change and progress* which, together with other catchphrases like Kennedy's intentions "to get the nation moving again," and to deal with "unfinished business," became a free-floating ideological signifier. "[B]oth domestic problems and foreign controversies were among the potential real-life settings for this metaphorical landscape" (Hellman 120). First and foremost, the New Frontier circumscribed measures to contain Communism, followed by economic and then civil rights and social policies. Ultimately, it was the promise of positive change by way of setting right the wrongs of the nation's past and present that connected all the different applications of the New Frontier. This also added considerable and lasting momentum to the frontier theme in *Star Trek*.

The New Frontier articulated and reflected Kennedy's *image* of liberal progressivism. He presented the New Frontiers of the 1960s as opportunities to fix not only the broken promises of rebirth/redemption found in the myth of the American West, but also to heal the wounds of America's revolutionary national project on the whole. Prefigured by TV and movie Westerns in the 1950s, which critiqued the dominant discourses that had been used to tell myth of the American West, Kennedy *also* pointed to the proverbial elephants standing in the room of the national psyche. The major wounds and sins incurred by the nation's forbears, such as slavery, racial and gender discrimination, genocide, the exploitation and destruction of the environment, could no longer be ignored—"I tell you the New Frontier is here, whether we seek it or not." Regardless of the President's violent and untimely passing, the nation's psychohistorical wounds have of course remained a source of unfinished business to this very day. Consequently, the frontier as *Star Trek*'s allegorical/topical theme continued to address "unfinished business" in both domestic and international spheres of American influence. It was an attempt to replicate the image of progressivism *ad infinitum*. When *ST:TOS* first aired, it stood as "an extraterrestrial morality play," which addressed "superpower conflict, fascism, civil rights, and interracial sexuality" (McCurdy 103). The later incarnations of *Star Trek* continued to allegorically heal wounds, redress sins and deal with unfinished business via the frontier theme—whether it was the gender politics of the 1990s, or the trauma incurred by 9/11 that informed *ST:ENT* shortly before it was cancelled.

Casting the space race and space exploration into the mold of the New Frontier amounted to making use of an easy metaphor. However, once we place the operative and historical analogies that were actually used to make sense of the magnitude of the American space program under scrutiny, we quickly find that the frontier does not easily apply—neither in language nor in symbolism. Interestingly, but perhaps not surprisingly, overt references to outer space in frontier terms are conspicuously absent in Kennedy's speeches on the nation's space effort. For example, all the operative analogies he used in his "Moon speech"—describing the process of going into outer space and exploring its unknown wonders—were of a maritime nature.[16] What is more, "one of the most popular analogies," McCurdy has observed, drew "on the public's memory of sea captains ... maritime explorers ... European mariners" (140–1). Add to this the following: as much as the projected images of liberal and progressive change shaped *Star Trek*'s frontier theme as the science-fictional echo of Kennedy's New Frontier, so have the socio-cultural, political and ideological realities lying underneath it. Both point back across the Atlantic, following a predominately British trajectory.

The first few years of the 1960s, especially Kennedy's successful campaign against Richard Nixon, are popularly remembered as a radical departure from what preceded them—the paternalist Eisenhower administration and the consumerism-induced complacency of the 1950s. Contextual realities, however, were less dichotomous. Rather than a radical break, the early 1960s were a transitional period which accommodated polyvocal tensions and compatibilities between conservative, reactionary, and progressive ideas.[17] The same transitional qualities also informed the "flipside" of Kennedy's image of liberal progressivism. While his New Frontier rhetoric exploited the difficult task that Republicans had to attractively sell the status quo, Kennedy still had to position his program close to the political center. His youthful and charismatic Hollywood-image helped him greatly in that it made him *appear* to be radically different. The range for "real" progressive change was, of course, severely curtailed by the political realities of the Cold War. The American populace was also caught in the transitional currents and eddies of the early 1960s. "Although America seemed a less satisfied, materialistic, and conformist society by the time of Kennedy's inauguration," James Giglio has asserted that "Americans were unready for the sweeping changes of the 1960s," in that "[m]ost were gradualists, willing to wait" (29).

While perhaps an unusual entry point, there is a secondary, and decidedly transatlantic motif which runs through Kennedy's acceptance speech for the nomination at the DNC convention. Couched in pronounced Anglophilia, it can be used as a symbolic segue to the romantic and heroic "far side" of the

New Frontier. Not only does his speech point to the continuation of an Anglocentric hegemony under the auspices of the U.S., but it also speaks to the extent of how much the New Frontier ideology was influenced by Kennedy's personal myths and heroes. He repeatedly referred to political figures in English and British history to signal and demarcate major segments in his speech.[18] For example, when he criticized the seemingly autocratic self-appointment of Nixon as the Republican heir apparent, he pointed to two examples from English history where one political ruler was followed by an obvious albeit less adept successor—Henry II and Richard I as well as Oliver and Richard Cromwell. Similarly, he invoked Winston Churchill, for whom he had held a particular affinity since adolescence, to realign the audience's gaze towards the future before providing a summary of issues, challenges, revolutions, and uncertainties that would wait for them. After having defined the New Frontier, Kennedy cited Prime Minister David Lloyd George to underscore the metaphor's liberal progressivism. The latter was an icon of 20th century liberalism. He facilitated major changes which formed the basis of the modern British welfare state. A successful prime minister during World War I, he also fostered and expanded the Great Rapprochement between Britain and America. John Hellmann contends that the president's "identification with heroes of British history would be translated into his vision of America as the legitimate successor to the Empire as defender of freedom in the world" (35), a responsibility which he announced and welcomed in his inaugural address.[19]

The *image* of Kennedy's liberal progressivism was rooted in his persona as the romantic/hero president. At the center of a modern political aristocracy, he reigned from the White House as a New Camelot.[20] His persona was built on a "private myth," which points to Kennedy's fascination with British history, adventure and romance, and his strong identification with the mission and values arguably shared by all "English-speaking peoples" (122). The romance of the heroic models Kennedy had identified with since childhood had a lasting impact on the persona he cultivated throughout his political career.[21] He "developed a private image of self-reliance, intelligence, and courage modeled on his British heroes" (16). The tales of Ivanhoe, Robin Hood, King Arthur and, more generally, the works of Sir Walter Scott and Rudyard Kipling, allowed him to assume the self-image of the heroic individual. He also developed a pronounced interest for the works of Winston Churchill, and he studied the life of Lord Melbourne, mentor of the young Queen Victoria. John Buchan's memoir *Pilgrim's Way* (1940) was reportedly among his favorite books. Kennedy's pronounced Anglophilia thus went far beyond his acceptance speech. His persona left an indelible mark on his government and leadership style, and on the political ideology of his administration, especially in foreign affairs. The style of the Kennedy administration was elitist, command-driven, and openly reminiscent of the antiquated concept of *noblesse oblige*.

While it seems paradoxical for a Catholic American with Irish roots to identify with British heroes and Anglo-Saxon values, Kennedy's Anglophilia was facilitated by the broader context of British-American relations since the Great Rapprochement (1895–1915). Both Kennedy and Roddenberry, who was only four years his junior, "grew up in a cultural milieu in which an American was encouraged to imagine himself part of an English-speaking tradition of democratic and individualist values that extended far beyond American history in both geography and time" (Hellmann 19). While the Western may have reigned supreme on the American media landscape, the shared transatlantic/Anglophone heritage was also visibly present on cinema screens. Between the 1930s and the 1950s, a series of popular films portrayed chapters from Britain's romantic, chivalrous, and imperial past.[22] Historically and geo-politically, America's westward expansion must be viewed within the larger geopolitical paradigm of *Pax Britannica*. Consequently, Kennedy's hero image bore the indelible imprint of universal Anglocentrism which ultimately also informed the "far side" of his New Frontier ideology.

The British relied on their imperial agents, romanticized as heroic, benevolent, aristocratic figures, to maintain and defend *Pax Britannica* in the 19th century. Kennedy's emissaries, such as the Astronaut Corps, the Green Berets, in whose formation he was a chief architect, and the Peace Corps, were conceived and portrayed in a similar vein as they promoted *Pax Americana* in the 20th century. Taking up the baton from those romantic heroes who had inspired the president's hero image, they "could reincarnate the warrior-aristocrats that he had so admired on the frontiers of the British Empire" (Hellmann 141). Like Roddenberry, Kennedy was an avid sailor who referred to his closest advisors as his "band of brothers"; a phrase he borrowed from Admiral Horatio Nelson, who himself had appropriated it from *Henry V*'s St. Crispin's Day Speech as a shorthand for referring to a command paradigm which became institutionalized among the naval elite during his time.

Consequently, it is but a small step to see how and perhaps why less than a year after Kennedy's assassination, Roddenberry took a fictional British hero and his naval world, which were conceived in the same romantic tradition as the president's heroes, and used them as a major intertext for a science-fictional world that would carry on the president's legacy of New Frontier space exploration. While seemingly incongruous, Roddenberry's decision to model *Star Trek* on a historical era, which saw the genesis of Britain's geopolitical dominance and assumed ideological superiority, simply mirrored Kennedy's ideology of continuing Anglocentric hegemony under American auspices. Thus,

Star Trek's frontier theme is entangled with a maritime world that becomes visible once we have turned our attention to the transatlantic "far side" of the New Frontier ideology. It is a world, however, which is no longer readily recognizable or accessible in that it is far removed from our everyday reality. "[E]roded direct knowledge of the sea, ships, and sea-faring" (18), according to Robert Foulke, presents the main difficulty in accessing Britain's maritime past, and thus Horatio Hornblower's world. Consequently, there is a need to compensate for the default lack of knowledge about maritime texts and contexts—spanning historical, linguistic, geographic, technical, and experiential dimensions—whether we hail from a landlocked country, or from a "traditional" maritime culture such as Britain. Our post-industrial, postmodern, and virtualized worldview is no longer chiefly determined by seaborne travel, communication, and commerce.

3. Maritime Histories

The maritime endowment of *Star Trek* draws on the power of legacy found in the myth of the British Golden Age of Sail. Not only is it comparable to but also compatible with the myth of the American West. As a historical period, the British Golden Age of Sail can be located roughly between the end of the Seven Years' War (1763), and the immediate aftermath of the Congress of Vienna (1814–5). The period between the Battle of Navarino Bay (1827) in Greece and the 1840s then signaled the gradual transition from wind power to steam power. Even so, the British Golden Age of Sail is marked by a historical fluidity that transcends the periods of conflict, such as the American Revolutionary War (1775–83) and Britain's prolonged confrontation with Revolutionary, and later Napoleonic France (1793–1802, 1803–15), which naval historians traditionally cite as the main navigational beacons of that age. At the same time great strides were made in maritime exploration. They were mostly fueled by the persistent quests for *Terra Australis Incognita* and the elusive Northwest Passage. The Royal Navy of the fighting and exploring Age of Sail thus was the principal, executive agent of the colonial, and later imperial project of the British Empire. The men of the Royal Navy, particularly its corps of officers, were employed as true Renaissance men; they were reputable soldiers, bold tacticians, diplomatic envoys, clever trade negotiators, adept engineers, meticulous mapmakers, enthusiastic naturalists, ambitious astronomers, and, most importantly, they served as vectors of an Anglophone cultural hegemony. The "Service" was the nation's primary line of defense and protector of trade. In cooperation with other entities, such as the East India Company and the Royal Society, it epitomized, as Jeremy Black has argued, "the sense of the British as the purposeful bringers of knowledge and the standard-bearers of a single world order of beneficial purposes and consequences" (186). Britain's sense of purpose, and ultimately its destiny was conflated with the physical and metaphorical qualities of transoceanic seascapes.

The language of James Thomson's ode *Rule Britannia* (1740) inarguably provides the most concise articulation of the myth. Though slightly antecedent to the British Golden Age of Sail proper, the song furnished the main building blocks which shaped the myth at large. Britain's identity and sense of mission are described in their unique relationship with oceanic spaces to which they are carried by naval figures who are the primary and free agents of this benevolent empire.[1] Thomson's lyrics not only reflect the spirit of the Enlightenment, but also point to proto–Romantic sentiments. The language of power, order, discipline, and knowledge—in a Foucauldian sense—together form a broader British imperial discourse. They shape the vast semiotic surfaces of the sea and the shores it connects. Britain's imperial discourse manifests in two distinct yet interrelated fields—*maritime military might* and *maritime exploration*. Their interplay was then transatlantically reconfigured into the thematic makeup of *Star Trek*'s world in that Starfleet performs a function akin to that of the Royal Navy. Hence, it is not surprising that 350 years in the future, Captain Sisko (Avery Brooks), when he faced a fleet of enemy ships, relies on naval daring, heroics, and tactics similar to those used by genealogical predecessors at the Battle of Trafalgar (1805), or at the Battle of Gravelines (1588).[2] Similarly, it only makes sense that the Northwest Passage, which had eluded naval explorers for over three centuries, would symbolically be discovered by Captain Janeway (Kate Mulgrew) during her sojourn on the other side of the galaxy.[3]

Rule Britannia will be employed as an overarching theme to contain the sometimes conflicting interplay between the fields of maritime military might and maritime exploration. They provide the key trajectories for charting the histories and stories of the British Golden Age of Sail. The same trajectories serve to trace how the myth found its continuation primarily the realm of literature, i.e., the sea novel/naval romance, carrying it well into the 20th century. There, they will lead us to the transatlantic node of contact between *Star Trek* and the Hornblower novels. Like with the frontier, localizing *Rule Britannia* as an operational/functional theme demands its tracking both in history and fiction in order to understand its continuous and continuing presence in *Star Trek*.

"Beat to quarters!": Maritime Military Might

The great naval battles of the period, and their celebrated heroes, articulate most clearly the discursive field of maritime military might. While often remembered as a prodigy, or even anomaly of his times, the historical Nelson was actually the product of a new command culture rooted in the Seven Years'

War. This culture "emphasised manoeuvre and seizing the initiative," Black has argued, "in order to close with the opposing fleet and defeat it in detail after it had been divided by intersecting the opposing line" (149). By combining careful planning and clear communication with all of his subordinates—the famed "Nelson Touch"—the admiral, who was also an accomplished self-promoter, took the initiative on a number of occasions and dealt the French a series of devastating blows. He made a name for himself in engagements such as the Battle of the Nile (1798) and the Battle of Copenhagen (1801), where he famously turned a blind eye to a signal of his superior, telling him to discontinue action. Mortally wounded at Trafalgar—a battle where he disregarded virtually all naval conventions of the day—ultimately ensured that Nelson was transformed into the single most powerful personification of Britain's maritime military might. Nelson's death fed into a national obsession of hero worship which in turn historicized and mythologized scores of other British naval leaders.[4] The resulting pantheon of naval heroes extends as far back as Sir Francis Drake, who became a genealogical predecessor for Nelson's "model of maritime daring and initiative" (Lavery 23). In short, the Age of Sail was permeated by a collective belief in Britain's seaborne identity and national superiority. While divinely ordained, the belief was embodied by the naval vanguards of a transoceanic Anglophone world order.

Britain's sense of hegemonic, cultural superiority became known as the doctrine of *Pax Britannica* in the 19th century. Similar to Nelson's precursors, however, the doctrine's systematic roots and ideological development are also found in the aftermath of the Seven Years' War. Settled in the Peace of Paris (1763), the outcome of the conflict led to an imperial turn in Britain's foreign policy, building on maritime reach and the projection of power. Britain entered the latter half of the 18th century with the feeling that it defined and embodied the pinnacle of western civilization. Emerging again victorious from the conflict with Napoleonic France, Britain saw itself destined to "bringing civilisation to a benighted world and was therefore fulfilling a providential purpose" (Black 179). The naval agents of this doctrine began to figure prominently in the literary works of Romantic thought. Battles, such as Trafalgar, and their heroes entered the national imagination via personal accounts, naval history books, and works of fiction.

Britain's national celebration of its maritime military might stands in a reciprocal relationship with the birth of the sea novel and the genre of naval romance. C.S. Forester's Hornblower novels, which were published between 1937 and 1967, are but a few in a long line of imagined naval heroics and swashbuckling adventures. They largely follow formulas that were conceived at the juncture of Enlightenment reason, proto–Romantic thought, and Romanticism at large. The Romantic imagination and its "cult of sensibility" had a significant impact on the mythologization of Britain's maritime military might in the wake of Trafalgar. The production of maritime historical fiction[5] was already prolific while the Age of Sail experienced its heyday. Literary output, however, increased at the dawn of the Age of Steam. Royal Navy captain turned author, Frederick Marryat, is often credited with being the father of the British sea novel. He enjoyed a prolific career, writing twenty-two novels that dealt with the Royal Navy's exploits during the Napoleonic period. Most of his work was targeted at an adolescent readership. Novels like *The King's Own* (1830), *Peter Simple* (1834), *Mr. Midshipman Easy* (1839), and *Percival Keene* (1842), stand out as his most successful and most widely read stories. They are paradigmatic for the genre of Napoleonic sea fiction in that they build on a coming-of-age formula of meritocracy. Most stories chronicle the protagonists' rise from their humble origins to the highest echelons of society. As is the case in Marryat's novels, the action of independent vessels, which found themselves on detached service, became yet another important narrative template for the genre. These genre conventions would then be readily adopted and continued by authors such as C.S. Forester and Patrick O'Brian in the 20th century; and they also strike a chord with the deep-space missions of Starfleet.

Along with Marryat's genre-defining role, literary giants such as Jane Austen, Robert Southey, Samuel Taylor Coleridge, and lesser known Frederick Chamier, also contributed to the romanticization of the age and its quintessential Nelsonian heroes. Capturing the Romantic *Zeitgeist*, they speak to the literary milieu in which Marryat produced most of his work. These voices of Romanticism, Tim Fulford has observed, "promoted the chivalry of the ocean when the chivalry of the land was in doubt" (162), particularly during the Regency (1811–20). The officers of the Royal Navy became the principal embodiment of this type of chivalry, brandishing characteristics like patriotism, moral incorruptibility, and benevolent paternalism. In their prose biographies of prominent naval figures like Nelson, Southey and Coleridge provided the public with naval saviors who were better equipped to lead the nation than the landed classes who were viewed as increasingly decadent, corrupt, and incompetent. Jane Austen, who had more fictional license at her disposal, romanticized naval officers into the epitome of the gentleman. The central position occupied by the naval officer, especially the ship captain, attests to the fact that, as John Peck has argued, "the individual sailor, particularly the officer, became the gentlemanly embodiment of all the best character traits of the British" (qtd. Parrill 11). However, if readers of naval romances expect tales of heroic adventure and suspense, they will be disappointed. Apart from other literary influences, such as the picaresque novel, "suspense comes second to the development of complex characters and to the expression of ideas" (1). Many sea stories speak to the romanticized belief in upward social mobility through merit. Proto-Romantic sentiments and the sensibilities of British Romanticism were not only reserved for the gallant naval warrior, however, but they were also extended to the explorer/adventurer type of the Golden Age of Sail.

"Land ho!": Maritime Exploration

If Trafalgar and Nelson epitomize British maritime military might, then the three voyages of discovery into the Pacific led by James Cook represent the pinnacle of British maritime exploration. His scientific and colonial exploits made him the archetypal naval explorer of the age. Raised in modest circumstances, Cook ultimately received a commission in acknowledgment of his work as a reliable seaman and accurate naval surveyor in North America during the Seven Years' War. His skills as a mapmaker brought him to the attention of the Admiralty and the Royal Society who were planning at joint mission into the Pacific at the time. The orders for his first voyage (1768–71) are a telling example for the close interrelation of British maritime military might and maritime exploration. His primary objective was to carefully observe the transit of Venus from Tahiti. His observations would contribute data to an experiment with the goal of ascertaining the exact distance between the Earth and the Sun. Sealed confidential, Cook carried a second set of orders. He was tasked with finding the southern continent—*Terra Australis Incognita*—which had been theorized as a counterweight to the northern hemisphere since Antiquity, and claim it for the British crown. Failing that, he was instructed to make a complete survey of New Zealand's coastline and take possession of any other undiscovered islands. Cook succeeded in fulfilling his main mission and claimed the east coast of Australia for Britain. The Pacific, however, remained of great interest to colonial powers. Tasked once again with finding the elusive southern continent, Cook's second voyage (1772–5) dispelled once and for all with this popularly held belief. He failed to accomplish the main objective of his third voyage (1776–9) which was to find a navigable waterway around or across North America—the much coveted Northwest Passage. While he did not return alive, his three voyages contributed much to ascertaining the missing outlines of the globe.

In cooperation with a complement of naturalists and artists, Cook produced and recorded new knowledge which furthered academic pursuits and imperial desires. In turn, they fueled the public's curiosity about faraway lands and exotic peoples. Much of the newly created knowledge was centrally collated in a concerted effort and powerful statement of imperial aspirations. Founded in 1795, it was the task of the Royal Navy's Hydrographic Office to disseminate information in the form of atlases, maps, paintings, engravings, and published letters and journals. Under the direct control of the Admiralty, the emphasis was placed on the distinct role played by British explorers as opposed to those of competing powers, especially the French. Heavily edited by John Hawkesworth, the journals of Cook's first voyage were published as part of a collection—*An Account of the Voyages undertaken by the Order of His Present Majesty for Making Discoveries in the Southern Hemisphere* (1773)—which also included the accounts of earlier expeditions like those by Samuel Wallis and Philip Carteret. Cook's journals, which circulated widely in various editions thereafter, had a significant impact on the mythos of the British Golden Age of Sail. Through them, the British took possession of new lands and ordered the knowledge that had been generated by explorers. Accounts like Cook's also offered a narrative which conveyed scientific authenticity and authority as well as a sense of grandeur that was reminiscent of classical epics. They helped the British to understand and legitimize the providential role they had assumed for themselves. Feeding directly into the doctrine of *Pax Britannica*, the Royal Navy's ability to project maritime military might was tempered by its seemingly benign ventures of exploration. Ships of exploration brought back, as Jeremy Black has argued, "sketches and specimens of creation—human, botanical, and zoological—which helped to equip the science of the age of reason and stimulate the sensibilities of the age of Romanticism" (302). Consequently, the accounts of Cook's journeys also provide a double-coded mix which unveils "the tensions between the ideals of discovery and the realities of intercultural contact" (Gregg 148), in that they "othered" the exotic Other along the lines of the noble/ignoble savage dichotomy.

Expeditions into the largely uncharted realm of the Pacific led to its rise as the quintessentially exotic maritime space in the people's imagination. As early as five decades prior to the publication of Cook's journals, Robinsonadic adventures and travelogues already catered to a large market drunk on South Sea Fever. Literary works like Daniel Defoe's *Robinson Crusoe* (1719) and *Captain Singleton* (1720), and Jonathan Swift's *Gulliver's Travels* (1726), capitalized on the public's interest in faraway shores. They directly contributed to a surge in numbers of young men striving for a seafaring career. Driven largely by ennui and escapism, they were, however, often ill-prepared for the harsh realities of the sea. Travel literature of the early 18th century was widely read until the later waves of exploration in the Pacific. The resulting corpus of maritime tales about exotic lands, peoples and creatures would continue to resonate long after the Golden Age of Sail had ended. Robinsonadic adventures had also set the stage for the widespread dissemination and acclaim of Cook's journals. Not only did his voyages yield new knowledge which would allow for the perpetuation of the Pacific's inherent exoticism, but they would also serve to mythologize the British maritime adventurer/explorer who followed the same gentlemanly virtues as the British maritime warrior.

Coated in heroic sentimentalism, which was bestowed upon the intrepid explorer by editors like Hawkesworth and Canon John Douglas, James Cook and his exploits have occupied the people's imagination for over two hundred years. The general reading public eagerly consumed the accounts of his journeys throughout much of the 19th century. "Cheap abridged accounts of his voyages were available in Sunday schools, and were," according to Glyndwr Williams, "popular reading among Victorian families" (2008: 133). Escapism, adventure, and scientific endeavor, as embodied by Cook, resonated in novels written by Robert Louis Stevenson and R. M. Ballantyne. They shaped the seaborne fantasies and aspirations of entire generations of young men. They even entered some of the domestic settings in Charles Dickens' works. More broadly perhaps, *Rule Britannia* and its multiple intersections with the belief in the "White Man's Burden," which the British Empire took upon itself, reverberated in the oeuvres of Rudyard Kipling and Joseph Conrad in the latter half of the century. Ultimately, this meant that the archetype of the "benign" maritime explorer/adventurer would be carried not only well beyond the 19th century, but also to many shores; as a mythologized and romanticized character, James Cook transcends any single national discourse. Gene Roddenberry also referred to the explorer when he delineated the archetypal make-up of a Starfleet captain being an interstellar master and commander as well as a spaceborne naturalist and scientist. As was the case with Nelson and the fictional descendants of the maritime warrior he spawned, Captain James Cook dominates those complementing spaces of the imagination that are reserved for maritime exploration during the Golden Age of Sail.

The genre of naval romance along with other maritime adventure tales contributed much to the longevity of the mythos of the British Golden Age of Sail. Even though they celebrated—explicitly and implicitly—Britain's seaborne empire and the doctrine of *Pax Britannica,* they also became popular beyond British shores. The mythos of past victories and achievements was responsible for a power of legacy that fed, according to P.J. Marshall, into the "assumption," that the British Empire of the seas "survived until the mid-twentieth century" (42). Britons relished the thought that they would continue to rule the waves while historical realities were increasingly out of step with the myth of British naval supremacy. Prolonged peace led to complacency in the Royal Navy of the 19th century which was followed by a naval arms race—

first with France, and later with Germany. Britain proved and maintained its naval supremacy once more during World War I. When the clouds of war gathered over Europe a second time, however, it became clear that Britain no longer ruled the waves.

This period of conflict, transition, and decline was the immediate historical and cultural context for Forester's Hornblower novels. When Britain faced yet another European tyrant during World War II, Forester nurtured a hero who was born out of a long-standing mythos. He provided meaning to English-speaking peoples on both sides of the Atlantic. Hornblower becoming a transatlantic hero was facilitated by the fact that Britain and the U.S. had gone through a rapprochement which began as early as the 1890s. The historical rift between the mother country and its revolutionary cousins was then healed symbolically with the United States entering World War I as a British ally. The shared Anglocentric *Weltbild* that grew out of the rapprochement attested to the fact that these two nations were "basically similar in their ideals and aspirations" (Perkins 82). "Individualism, political liberties, perhaps peace and Protestantism—these characteristics gave Anglo-Saxons their uniqueness, their superiority—and their bond" (86). While repeatedly tried and tested, the transatlantic rapport between Britain and the U.S. remained strong. Winston Churchill defined it as the "special relationship" at the end of World War II. Nurtured by the restoration of harmony between Anglophone peoples, Forester's hero and his world became a meaningful intertextual reference point for one particular American man.

Introducing Forester and Hornblower

The life of Cecil Scott Forester and the historio-fictional existence of his naval protagonist are intimately and inextricably linked not least because the latter became Forester's alter ego. Even though marginalized and even belittled by literary scholars, the impact that Forester had with his entire oeuvre on 20th century popular literature and generations of readers is beyond reproach. As Stephanie Jones has asserted, he "effectively created the most renowned sailor in contemporary fiction" (37), and thus established the dominant paradigm of Napoleonic sea fiction in the 20th century. Writing in Forester's wake, we find acclaimed authors of the genre such as Patrick O'Brian, Dudley Pope, and Alexander Kent. "Not until Ian Fleming's James Bond crashed into the literary collective consciousness of the Anglo-American reading public in the 1950s," Sanford Sternlicht has argued, "was Hornblower's primacy in escapist fiction challenged" (9). Forester succeeded in drawing millions of readers into a milieu which often seems to be at odds with the immediate experiences of 20th century readers; a disregarded reading community of invested Hornblower fans represents the proverbial exception to the rule. While perhaps challenging to the postmodern reader, the missing historical, technical, linguistic and especially experiential contexts of the Age of Sail continue to be alive and well in naval romance stories. The dissonance between the historical milieu found in the stories and the immediate contexts of Forester's life and Hornblower's publication history was less pronounced than it is now in the 21st century.

Forester was born Cecil Louis Troughton Smith in Cairo in 1899 as the youngest of five children to George Smith, who worked as a teacher for the Egyptian Ministry of Education, and Sarah Troughton Smith. His father decided that all their children should return to England with their mother in order to receive a proper education. They left behind an upper-middle-class life which was comparatively luxurious and comfortable. Later in his life, Forester recalled that "his earliest memory was of being on a fog bound ship at sea" (qtd. Sternlicht 16). Living in suburban London, he and his siblings were placed in council schools to increase their chances of winning scholarships to more prestigious secondary schools and colleges. Attending council schools meant that Cecil's class background isolated him from most of his peers. His mother also insisted on him not mingling with his working-class friends. Consequently, he experienced intense isolation which became the most pertinent theme in his writing career. Restricted to lonely child activities, such as staging mock naval battles of the Napoleonic Wars with paper ships, he also became a voracious reader at an early age. Initially drawn to fiction for young boys written by G.A. Henty and Robert Michael Ballantyne, he also singled out a few of Robert Leighton's adventure stories as early influences. Forester then progressed to reading canonical writers. While he particularly enjoyed Jane Austen, Henry James, and H.G. Wells, he expressly disliked the works of Charles Dickens. Forester advanced to prestigious high schools where he was exposed to harsh forms of punishment. There, he developed an abhorrence of corporeal punishment which later left a distinct imprint on Hornblower's conduct as a commanding officer. Due to a heart condition, young Forester was rejected from serving in the Armed Forces during World War I. For the rest of his life he struggled with finding an answer to the question of how we would behave on the battlefield. He compensated for that by writing about warfare and military leaders. During a brief but unrewarding stint at medical school, he began to write for the campus magazine. Adopting C.S. Forester as his pen name, he decided to become a full-time writer. Even though his approach to writing and his methodology were essentially painful and unrewarding, he kept producing.[6]

At first, Forester was marginally successful as long as he wrote hack biographies about historical figures; but he soon developed a transatlantic reputation. His chronicle of Napoleon's Russian campaign, *A Pawn Among Kings* (1924), was followed by biographies of Josephiné de Beauharnais, Victor Emanuel II, Louis XIV, and Horatio Nelson. His break as a writer of fiction came with the murder mystery/thriller *Payment Deferred* (1926). Well-received by critics, the novel was adapted for the stage and, a little later, also for film, foreshadowing his nascent relationship with the American movie industry. From there, his career continued more auspiciously with the two non–Hornblower novels for which he is most remembered: *Brown on Resolution* (1929) and *The African Queen* (1935). Both were successfully adapted for the screen with the latter starring Humphrey Bogart and Katharine Hepburn. *Brown on Resolution* was even turned into two movies. Forester garnered a valuable reputation during a time when Hollywood exhibited a pronounced affinity for British subject materials.[7] His success in the U.S. led to a transatlantic life. Relocating his family of three to California, he continued to travel back and forth, staying several months in England each year. At the onset of World War II, he worked as a correspondent for the *New York Times* in Spain and Czechoslovakia. Forester was also in the employ of the British Ministry of Information, producing propaganda material in England and in Hollywood. His work for the ministry gave him the opportunity to travel on Royal Navy and U.S. Navy vessels throughout the war.

Hornblower took a gestation period of approximately ten years. Taking his family on extended boating trips in France and Germany to work on travel books, and simultaneously seeking respite from the strictures of Hollywood, Forester brought with him three volumes of the *Naval Chronicle*. Written by Royal Navy officers for their peers between 1790 and 1820, it gave Forester deep insights into the realities of life at sea, the discourse they used to report successes as well as failures, and the strong identification of the nation with its navy. Having grown dissatisfied with working for director Irving Thalberg, he temporarily quit his job in 1937, and booked passage on a freight ship back to England. While making his way to the Panama Canal, the idea of a British frigate captain who was on an independent cruise[8] along the Pacific Coast of South America came to him. The idea was also fueled by his preoccupation with another war looming over Europe. As the freighter neared the end of its six-week journey, Forster disembarked together with Hornblower.

The publication history of the Hornblower novels is "complex" since Forster had not intended for them to become a series (Parrill 65). Hence, they are marked by a chronological fragmentation, a few inconsistencies, and redconning on part of the author. The Hornblower saga was also overshadowed by Forester being diagnosed with arteriosclerosis, which crippled him for the rest of his life, and two severe strokes in 1947 and 1962, respectively. The author died on April 2, 1966, only five months before *Star Trek* aired for the first time.

The Hornblower saga consists of eleven novels, an unfinished novel, and a handful of short stories which, together, put forth an incredibly detailed and immersive world of wind and sail. The career of the novel's eponymous protagonist follows the coming-of-age formula which is found in many if not most sea romances. With Hornblower, Forester provided a paradigmatic model for most Napoleonic naval heroes in 20th century historical fiction. The novels' internal chronology covers a period between 1794 and 1848. What is more, the saga, and thus Hornblower's life, can be divided into three stages: (1) the adventures and maturation of young Hornblower,[9] (2) the prolonged stretch of his golden years as a captain and commodore on independent commands,[10] and (3) his career as a senior flag officer commanding the West Indies station.[11] Two novels in the saga, *Hornblower and the Atropos* (1953) and *Lord Hornblower* (1946), serve as transitions between the respective stages of his life.

Forester succeeded at (re)creating an immersive world of wind and sail in fiction. Hornblower's life is richly adorned with nautical and non-maritime minutiae while also driven by psychological character depth. According to Sternlicht, Forester effectively evokes "a milieu, the life of a British naval officer of the epoch; and a place, the British world of the Romantic period" (112). Forester himself saw his works primarily as "psychological novels" that began with his "interest in the problems of independent command" (qtd. Sternlicht 89). Much of the drama is rooted in Hornblower's world of isolation; he finds himself in a time and space where these two dimensions had not yet been conflated by modern technologies. The protagonist is constantly exposed to four tiers of isolation, ranging from geography, and the hierarchy onboard his vessel, to the social stratification in 18th century society, and his very own idiosyncratic character. "Forester deliberately creates a desperately insecure protagonist," Stephanie Jones has argued, "whose self-confessed weakness can be seen as contributing to his success" (37). The Hornblower saga, however, also offers a failed critique of, or rather a reactionary re-affirmation of military and class hierarchies. The novels were tremendously successful with a segment of a young, predominantly male Anglo-American readership. Nevil Newman has contended that Forester created "a hero whose qualities, while stereotypically British, could flourish in the American literary market" (106).

Locating Cecil, Horatio and Gene in Pax Transatlantica

Once again, the question has to be raised as to why such a quintessentially British set of narratives like the *Hornblower* novels were compatible with the worldview of an aspiring American television writer, let alone why his naval world would serve as the model for *Star Trek*'s worldbuilding. After all, Roddenberry served as a bomber pilot with the Army, *not* the Navy Air Corps, and pursued a career in commercial aviation before joining the LAPD. However, if we re-historicize the *Star Trek* idea not only as a product of the mid- and late-1960s, but rather as a complex distillate of contextual impulses originating during its gestation period in the 1950s and even the 1940s, matters become clearer.

C.S. Forester and his oeuvre were shaped by transatlantic spaces, events, and circumstances. The socio-cultural and geopolitical contexts that nurtured the transatlantic basis for the novels—and Roddenberry's exposure to them—were determined by the prologue to and the outbreak of World War II as much as by the subsequent large-scale shifts of power and influence within the Anglosphere in the opening years of the Cold War. It was a time that saw the rapid decline of the last vestiges of the British Empire. At the same time, the western world witnessed the initially reluctant stirrings of the empire's self-declared ideological successor—the United States. Americans soon ushered in the dawn of *Pax Americana*, a period of "relative peace," vis-à-vis the competing model offered by *Pax Sovietica*. Much like the British Empire, the U.S. also saw itself as "the product of both Classical and Christian civilization," and thus felt ordained to perpetuate an Anglophone cultural hegemony (Black 183). Framed by the 1940s, 1950s, and early 1960s, it was at this node of cultural convergence and transition that C.S. Forester's hero gained popularity.

The Hornblower novels, especially the first four, met with favorable environments on both sides of the Atlantic, turning Hornblower into a common transatlantic symbol. Sanford Sternlicht has stressed that "only *Gone with the Wind* appealed to the Anglo-American collective consciousness as did the Hornblower Saga" (162). In the U.S., the stories were first published in serialized form in the *Saturday Evening Post* and other periodicals, such as *Argosy* and *Collier's Magazine*. These outlets ensured that millions of American readers were introduced to an archetypal British character: the romanticized Nelsonian gentleman hero and his seaborne world of adventure and wonder. The meanings Forester offered had an impact that was twofold; by purposefully spanning transatlantic realms, he tapped into a myth that was met by a receptive sense of Anglocentric continuity and sense of mission in the U.S. Living a transatlantic life himself, Forester created a hero who was able to resonate with both the British and the American self-image as the benign and righteous benefactors of the world. Hornblower was Forester's attempt to do "everything he possibly could to bring Britain and America closer toward a cultural harmony and a closely related identity" (16). As such, he was much sought after for the propaganda campaigns of the armed forces on both sides of the Atlantic. At the core of what resonated well in both national discourses stood the idea of "The Man Alone," a theme reminiscent of Ernest Hemingway's "grace under pressure."[12] Hornblower reached a generation of Americans, including Kennedy, Roddenberry, and conservative political theorist Russell Kirk, that was sensitized to the image of "the collective Englishman" (Hellmann 24). They grew up at a time when American self-perception was permeated by Anglophilia. Forester's novels then offered a triumphant outlook on the trials ahead. More importantly, they also provided a reassuring, reaffirming, and continued, or rather continuing, Anglophone legacy to a segment of a young, predominately male Anglo-American readership.

Roddenberry was first exposed to the myth of the British Golden Age of Sail by way of the Hornblower novels in 1939. David Alexander has noted that Hornblower was "without question, Gene's favorite literary character, he read Hornblower when it was first published in the United States in 1939 and continued to reread the novels until a few weeks before his death" (188). Between his biographer's comments, a telling yet largely unknown poem titled "Sailor's Prayer" that became Roddenberry's first publication in 1945,[13] and his first application of Hornblower as an intertextual shorthand for describing the *Star Trek* idea, there is precious little known about how the novels became his favorite set of narratives, why they continued to resonate with him for the rest of his life,[14] or how and why they became the embedded narrative that structured *Star Trek*'s world. Yet, it is possible to comprehensively infer these seemingly missing links by tying together key character attributes of Hornblower and his maritime world with Roddenberry's personal beliefs and his worldview along with his professional background prior to becoming a scriptwriter/producer. Equally pertinent are the socio-cultural and geopolitical contexts of the 1940s and 1950s during which the idea for *Star Trek* as "Hornblower in space" fermented. This process was also facilitated by Hollywood's affinity for British subject materials, history, and actors, especially in adventure films.

Roddenberry was a self-proclaimed humanist and iconoclast. Similarly, Hornblower, as a 20th century permutation of the Nelsonian hero, can easily be described as an iconoclastic officer who exhibits clear humanistic tendencies.[15] He is a benign commander who cares deeply for his crew while being unable to completely break with the strictures placed upon him by a harsh military service. He always seeks equitable solutions in situations where the strict codes of the Royal Navy would not allow for any exceptions. Following the Nelsonian paradigm, he is also prone to critically reflect on his orders—more often than not turning a blind eye to them. He takes local circumstances into account and seizes the initiative while sometimes appearing to stand in open defiance of his superiors. The captain is also critical of religion; and he would have dispensed with the mandatory Sunday service on his ships if he could,[16] much like Roddenberry had to fight studio executives over the issue of putting a chaplain aboard the *Enterprise*. While always striving to achieve a better social station through merit, Hornblower regularly expresses anti-entitlement sentiments. He is critical of the landed classes and the higher echelons of political power. However, he clearly falls short of being openly revolutionary which would have been antithetical to all the values he defends in the face of Napoleon's tyranny. Even so, the meritocratic rise of the Nelsonian hero, who works himself up the ladder of fame and recognition thereby achieving a higher social status, closely corresponds with a shared belief which is often exclusively attributed to the U.S.—the American Dream. Not only did Roddenberry try to live Horatio Alger's rags-to-riches myth, but he also witnessed how it became the *Zeitgeist* of an entire generation who enjoyed unprecedented upward social mobility after World War II.

Roddenberry's stance on authority, especially military hierarchies, exposes a telling ambiguity and compatibility. He developed a "distrust of authority" (Alexander 69), based on a number of experiences he made during the war. However, he still believed as he wrote later that "man will always want this type of thing" (qtd. Whitfield 185). Roddenberry was anti-conformist in that he believed in using one's common sense rather than blindly following orders without taking the immediate context into consideration. Yet, he neither espoused anti-authority views, nor objected to a well-ordered society. In short, he was rather reactionary, inclined to question established orders without radically subverting them. He definitely did not share the counter-cultural sentiments that erupted in the mid– and late–1960s.[17] Consequently, *Star Trek*'s maritime world celebrates a nostalgic, gentlemanly form of military hierarchy, envisioned by him as "courtesies" (184).

The resonance of character traits and worldview have to be understood vis-à-vis the ideology espoused by the Hornblower novels and the growing polarization of international politics at the onset of the Cold War and its impact on the domestic *Zeitgeist*. The romanticized Napoleonic Wars found in the novels present a clear-cut, polarized *Weltbild*. Representing the epitome of western civilization, the British Empire acts as the bringer and defender of liberty, besieged by the threat of French tyranny. Otherwise simply a benign and seemingly disinterested "meddler," the Royal Navy enforces peace for all by containing, deterring, and openly interfering with Napoleon's plans. The first few Hornblower novels initially served as allegorical vehicles for the fight against fascism in the propaganda machineries of the UK and the U.S. The adversaries Hornblower does battle with, above all Napoleon, are thinly disguised stand-ins for Hitler and other fascist figureheads. At the end of World War II,

Napoleon had not yet been defeated in Hornblower's world. Even so, the milieu of "the west against the rest" offered by Forester continued to resonate well in the American national consciousness, and Roddenberry's, as the conflict between Allies vs. Axis powers was replaced by that between capitalist west vs. communist east.[18] Hornblower's world was compatible with a nation spearheaded by a benign military patriarch, i.e., President Eisenhower, who launched NASA as a "peaceful space program" (Halliwell 7). At the same time, there was a growing albeit largely muted concern about "the loss of the heroic individual" (Hellmann 65–6), soon answered by the dashing, vigorous warrior/hero persona that Eisenhower's successor had crafted for himself. Thus, Hornblower was arguably also compatible with the new, chivalrous image that Kennedy bestowed upon the presidency. This gallant albeit cautious fictional naval officer subsequently transformed, in Roddenberry's eyes, into "a man for all seasons" when the invigorating vision of the future Kennedy promised seemed to have been killed with him in 1963.

The Hornblower novels also served as a reactionary antidote to the domestic fallout of the growing Cold War conflict. In the 1950s, Roddenberry found himself in a milieu of anti-iconoclasm and anti-common sense. Prosperity and upward mobility fed into a growing consumer culture of consensus and the conformity of Levittown. It was a time where the masses were suspicious of intellectuals and where they mistrusted ideas—especially their own. There was widespread "reluctance to speak out on controversial issues," for fear of opposing the "consensus," which was an often-used euphemism for conformity (Halliwell 19–24). This *Zeitgeist* facilitated the wildfire of the Second Red Scare, including McCarthyite witch hunts and HUAC inquiries. Concurrently, the early 1950s also saw a religious revival in the U.S. with a sharp increase of churchgoers; and the line "one nation under god" was added to the Pledge of Allegiance in 1954. Shaping the milieu of conformity, the Korean War tends to be overlooked as a key to the cultural angst of the 1950s. While the reasons for entering World War II along with the resulting worldview were clear for Americans, the impetus for going to war in Korea were more ambiguous.[19] There was an attitude of "unthinking" that spread beyond military hierarchies. Even so, instead of countercultural subversion and revolution, Roddenberry turned to the nostalgic, reactionary stance of the Hornblower novels. They are both a reactionary antidote to conformity and a reaffirmation of Anglocentric preeminence in the western world.

Additionally, Hollywood's affinity for British history, subjects, and actors at the time, makes it seem all but inevitable that Roddenberry and his colleagues would look across the Atlantic for the narrative that would so strongly inform *Star Trek*'s spacefaring. This affinity amounted to a complex arrangement of commercial and ideological factors, which led Hollywood to engage with British imperial and military history especially between the 1930s and the 1950s.[20] There were many British actors under contract in Hollywood and the British film market was second only to the domestic market. Apart from obvious propaganda reasons and the need to support Britain in the face of an increasingly hostile Europe, "Hollywood's interest in movies depicting empire was inspired," according to Brian Taves, "by contemporary imperialism, together with the United States' own growing role on the world scene" (176). Sea adventure and empire films regularly "portrayed Englishmen as personifying the very type of Anglo-American morality and virtues" (72). Military explorer/adventurer types often served as *beau ideal*. Most of these films depicted a blatantly uncritical idealization of the "White Man's Burden," celebrating a benign and paternalistic colonialism. Interestingly, the soundtracks of these films bore a distinct British imprint in that *Rule Britannia* "sometimes became the central structuring motif of an entire score" (71). In view of this prolific transatlantic tradition, Roddenberry's second act of *vraisemblance* was hardly idiosyncratic, then, since appropriating historical and cultural material from Britain for American screen entertainment was a longstanding practice at the time.

Part II: Rule, Britannia! Britannia Rules Outer Space in *Star Trek*! (A Voyage)

The historio-mythical analogies which are used as models for worldbuilding in sf are often greatly obscured by the genre's conventions. After all, sf's *what if* scenarios build on a strong degree of estrangement from the empirical reality found in our ontological pasts and presents. Any fictional world, however, cannot run the risk of losing its "analogical historicity" lest it jeopardizes its discoverable relationship to the real world. Consequently, the way how *Rule Britannia* governs the ontology of *Star Trek*'s future world might at first not be easily recognized and decoded.

Celebrating a shared transatlantic cultural continuum between Britain and the U.S., the mythologized British Golden Age of Sail serves as the primary model for *Star Trek*'s worldbuilding. While occasionally coated with a veneer of American nautical references (i.e., readily recognizable but also misleading symbolic surfaces), the British naval model—*Star Trek*'s historio-mythical core—was maintained and expanded by Roddenberry's successors. It manifests along five interrelated maritime dimensions: a naval linguistic corpus; the starship as a re-imagined sailing ship traversing the partially literalized "ocean of space"; the starship captain as a transposed sentimental Royal Navy Enlightenment mariner, i.e., a "fighting naturalist in space"; the practice of archaic nautical traditions vis-à-vis the presence of naval intertexts and nautical paraphernalia; a future backdrop of benign, imperial, interstellar discovery and colonization.

4. "Off the starboard bow"
Star Trek's *Naval Corpus*

Upon learning that he is to lead a mission on a planet which consists entirely of water, *Voyager*'s helmsman, Lt. Tom Paris (Robert Duncan McNeill), is seized by his life-long fascination with naval stories. Embarking on one of the ship's smaller craft, he enthusiastically proclaims to his fellow crew member: "And, so I thought to myself, who better than Harry to be my first mate?"[1] Since Ens. Harry Kim (Garrett Wang) is seemingly confused by this form of address, Paris patronizingly adds: "Oh, sailor talk. You'll get the hang of it." In *Star Trek*'s hyper-technological future, nautical jargon might seem like a linguistic relic with which only a few would be conversant, but the opposite is actually true.

Star Trek's spacefaring sailors are noticeably proficient in the use of naval language. There are three main units of *Star Trek*'s naval corpus that allow its stories to be told as privileged English-language, transatlantic, nautical artifacts. Naval ranks create clear echelons of power and order which govern the relationships of the spacefaring sailors. They mix and mesh structures that are rooted in the age of wind and sail with contemporary naval jargon. Hence, *Star Trek*'s naval corpus is neither solely British, nor purely American but rather attests to a shared transatlantic, Anglophone discursive construct. Naval ranks also foster and maintain a distinct naval tone of operational discourses used to steer ships between stars. The militaristic origin of such discourses is de-emphasized by infusing the naval tone with forms of romanticized courtesies and civility which are popularly attributed to navy officers in sea romances. Rather than being "demeaning" (Rayner 163), such naval forms of order and power bear distorted connotations of respect, morality, and courtesy which ties them to how they are used in sea romances. The corpus is accentuated by Starfleet officers being well-versed in the use of nautical terms and phrases to name their surroundings, and thus speak them into existence as nautical realities.

Even two of *Star Trek*'s most iconic catchphrases very likely originated in the Hornblower novels. While Hornblower was serving as a midshipman, and later as a lieutenant, the phrase "number one" was repeatedly used to refer to the respective ship's second-in-command.[2] According to *Star Trek* writer and producer Robert Justman, Captain Picard's signature "Make it so!"[3] is a "tribute" to Hornblower (qtd. Okuda 172), who used it at least once to order junior officers to carry out ideas which they had brought to his attention.[4]

The English language in general is permeated by lexical items and idiomatic expressions which have distinct maritime roots.[5] They mostly originated in the age of wind and sail; a fact that many, if not most speakers of English are no longer aware of since our shared experiences of travelling—the stories that we tell about them, and thus the discourses we use—have rapidly shifted from maritime realms and equestrian locomotion to aeronautical spaces and automotive mobility/power. Such a sweeping generalization notwithstanding, it serves to keep the pervasiveness of naval language in mind. *Star Trek* adopts a broad range of naval discourses from its original contexts of wind and sail, occasionally merges them with more contemporary naval terminology, and then re-inscribes the resulting transatlantic naval corpus onto the realities of space travel.

Consequently, it is not surprising that when the crew of the *Enterprise-D* is about to establish first contact with an alien race of hyper-capitalist, spacefaring merchants, they are compared to "the ocean-going Yankee traders of eighteenth and nineteenth century America."[6] The reference serves as a meaningful analogy. Within the crew's frame of reference, these aliens "sail the galaxy in search of mercantile and territorial opportunity." Similarly, when the crew of DS9 discusses the vagaries of serving on a Klingon ship, they conclude that it "is like being with a gang of ancient sea pirates."[7] Once again, the reference to a romanticized image of an ocean-going people in the past of wind and sail is well-taken and understood. On another occasion, when Captain Kirk is about to commandeer to his own ship, he invokes the blessing, "may the wind be at our backs," before ordering his co-conspirators to take the ship out of space dock: "Steady as she goes."[8] Such references may seem oddly out of place and without immediate conceptual resonance since Starfleet operates in the vacuum of space. Even though they might easily be dismissed as mere "metaphor" (Barrett 10), they point out a process where nautical metaphors are either literalized and/or bear strong literal qualities. The repeated appropriation of wind, sail, and oceanic spaces (e.g., the sea, the bay, the beach, etc.) are used to metaphorically, indeed, in some cases, physically overwrite the realities of outer space. In short, *Star Trek*'s historicized future presents itself as an oceanic paradigm that exceeds simple intertextual references. Thus, it also stands in stark contrast to other, more *aero*nautical worldbuilding models in sf television and film.[9]

"Sailor talk" in Space: Rank and File

Most orders given on Starfleet vessels are acknowledged by subordinates with the quintessential naval phrase "aye, aye." Such a simple phrase belies a rich naval corpus of descriptive and performative language. They are used to write and speak *Star Trek* stories as privileged English-language artifacts. Its future celebrates the global dissemination of the English language which began during the Age of Sail, and which, according to *Star Trek*, shall continue to spread in naval fashion throughout the galaxy; or, at least throughout the Alpha Quadrant. In comparison to other sf universes, *Star Trek* is different not only because its ships are not modeled on aircraft carriers or submarines, but also because the link in jargon between the Royal Navy of wind and sail and the contemporary U.S. Navy was acknowledged as a reference point right from the beginning.[10] For example, the Royal Navy's infamous *Articles of War*, which delineated ranks, the duties of sailors and officers, and especially various forms of punishment, were used as a basis for the U.S. Navy's *Articles for the Government of the United States Navy*, which remained in effect until 1951. Similarly, Starfleet is governed by a strict, expansive, and often-quoted set of rules—*Starfleet General Orders and Regulations*. They are, however, much more benign in terms of punishment than their naval predecessors.

Naval ranks and hierarchies are among the most obvious building blocks of the naval corpus. The very first word spoken in *Star Trek* when it first aired was a marker of rank—"Captain's Log"[11]—which inevitably set the naval tone of the show. Strict vertical hierarchies have always been a quintessential element for shipborne communities. They are given a prominent position in *Star Trek* especially since Starfleet ships, like sailing vessels in the past, often operate independently and out of touch with the higher echelons of the fleet's command structure. Starfleet vessels are commanded by an elite caste of senior officers (*captain, commander, lieutenant commander, lieutenant, ensign*). Other members of a starship's crew are often simply addressed as *crewmen*, or summarily referred to as *hands*. Occasionally, characters refer to *warrant* and/or *petty officers*. The higher tiers of Starfleet are populated by flag officers of various ranks (*commodore, rear admiral, vice admiral, admiral* and *fleet admiral*). They are either located at Starfleet Command on Earth, scattered across starbases, or they are in command of flagships. It is, however, important to stress that Starfleet ranks are not used consistently. Some designations slightly change depending on the century in which the respective shows and movies are set. Nonetheless, they are all distinctively naval.

It is difficult to trace Starfleet ranks to one single naval tradition. While some argue that the scheme for Starfleet ranks was originally adopted from the

U.S. Navy, there are a number of aberrations, inconsistencies, overlaps with, and, in some cases, explicit references to Hornblower-esque traditions of wind and sail. The ranks of *captain* and *lieutenant* have been universal constants in naval life for centuries. The duties of modern-day navy captains, however, differ greatly from those performed by captains during the Age of Sail. In many ways, they are much more restricted than their predecessors in their range of command powers and independence. The rank of a sailing ship captain is imbued with the appeal of an independent command. Traditionally, a captain achieved "this 'post rank' by being appointed to command a 'post-ship' [sic], one of the first- to sixth-rate square-rigged ships. The term 'post' was used to differentiate from officers who commanded unrated vessels" (King 14). The symbolism of the number "four," which is used to indicate the rank of a captain, also dates back to an earlier period. For example, when a captain, like Hornblower, approached a larger vessel in a boat, either to take command or report to a superior officer, the sailor at the bow "held up four fingers which indicated the presence in the boat of a captain as a warning for them to prepare the correct ceremonial" (1937: 383). This historic symbolism translated into the four stripes, or rings that are commonly found on epaulettes and uniform sleeves. The symbolism is also maintained by Starfleet. Depending on the uniform design, the rank is indicated either by four stripes on the uniform's sleeves, or by four round rank pips which are worn on the right shirt collar.

The ranks of *commander*, which is usually worn by the first officer of a starship, and *lieutenant* are particularly interesting because they directly draw on traditions of wind and sail. Any officer ranked as lieutenant was "originally the Captain's deputy, literally a 'place holder'" (King 15). The rank of commander was first introduced in the Royal Navy in 1794 to stave off the swelling ranks of captains. Yet, this did not mean that commanders served only as first officers. On the contrary, they could be placed in charge of smaller, unrated vessels; a fact that is still true for commanders in both the Royal Navy and the U.S. Navy today. During the Age of Sail, the *first lieutenant* was the "executive officer of a ship, usually the second in command" (196). It was those officers that Roddenberry had in mind when he described the role of the first officer on a starship. He stated that "'Number One' is a term whose meaning has not changed appreciably since Earth's seventeenth century when the second-in-command of sailing ships became generally known as 'First Lieutenants' (hence Number One being used as the equivalent of First)" ("WRITERS/DIRECTOR'S GUIDE TNG" 24). Likely having originated in the Hornblower novels, this *Star Trek* catchphrase was first used in the failed pilot episode for *ST:TOS* ("The Cage"). There, "Number One" was the designation for a woman who occupied the position of first officer. Later, it became Captain Picard's preferred form of address for Commander Riker throughout the entire run of *ST:TNG*. By contrast, the more contemporary designation of "executive officer," or short "XO," which is a mainstay in other sf universes, is generally not used in *Star Trek*.

Other Starfleet ranks speak to inconsistencies and distinct transatlantic overlaps. Some, like *lieutenant commander*, did not exist during the Age of Sail. It was introduced in both the Royal Navy and the U.S. Navy in the late 19th and early 20th century, respectively; it has been maintained ever since. The most junior rank on Starfleet vessels—*ensign*—which in some navies is "the lowest rank of commissioned officer," clearly draws on U.S. naval tradition since is not a part of Royal Navy structures (King 189). Even so, on a number of occasions, the designation *midshipman* is used.[12] Not only do these "prospective commissioned sea officers" (15), form the lowest tier in the Royal Navy officer cadre, but they are also literary archetypes; most naval heroes in Napoleonic sea fiction enter the Royal Navy as midshipmen and then begin to climb the ladder, following the coming-of-age formula. Interestingly, students who train at the United States Naval Academy (USNA) are enrolled as midshipmen. Prospective Starfleet officers attending Starfleet Academy, however, are called *cadets*. Initially, the latter term was used for "a very small group of prospective commissioned sea officers who held this title while attending the Royal Naval Academy" (15–6); and it is still in use today. Such aberrations, whether intended or not, also include higher ranks such as *commodore*. It has repeatedly fallen in disuse in the navies on both sides of the Atlantic at various points throughout history. Commodores primarily appear in *ST:TOS* and *ST:ENT*.[13] Their function is largely the same as in Napoleonic sea fiction where the rank denotes someone who was "appointed Commander-in-chief of a station or a detached squadron" (14). Other singularities in the same vein include terms such as *port master, dockmaster, ables'man* (able seaman), and the *ship's master*. Even so, they are clearly not given the same significance as the group of senior officers who form the core of *Star Trek*'s naval protagonists. While any viewer might draw a parallel between Starfleet and the contemporary U.S. Navy at first glance, it ultimately remains difficult to classify Starfleet's naval hierarchies along any one naval tradition.

A similar transatlantic mix of antiquated and contemporary naval usage applies to a handful of designations for individuals who perform specific duties on a starship. The same goes for residual symbolism that was encoded in some Starfleet uniforms. For example, *navigators*, like Ens. Pavel Chekov (Walter Koenig), are "responsible for projecting the desired course or trajectory of the vehicle and for determining the ship's actual position" (Okuda 317). In later *Star Trek* series, *helmsmen*, such as Lt. Paris or Ens. Mayweather (Anthony

Montgomery), merged the function of the navigator with their duty of steering the ship.

Medical practitioners on starships, along with the varied functions they perform, also have to be acknowledged as yet another direct point of transatlantic naval convergence. In early *Star Trek* series and films, they are often referred to as *ship's surgeon*—a term that was intermittently used in later spin-offs. Even so, the more contemporary *chief medical officer* (CMO), or simply the *ship's doctor,* became the preferred designations. Both terms allow for a direct comparison with their predecessors during the Golden Age of Sail. Like midshipmen, they are archetypal characters in most Napoleonic sea fiction (much like the Nelsonian captain or the Jonah). Even though a ship's surgeon often did not have a medical degree—the practice of a surgeon was considered a craft—they were still in charge of the crew's general welfare. Considered "equivalent to commissioned officers," however, a "handful of Navy doctors served as official naturalists on both warships and those sent on missions of exploration" (King 17–37).[14] Even though Starfleet medicine has advanced considerably since these "Dark Ages," it is not surprising that starship doctors are modeled after those ocean-bound surgeons. In the writers' guidelines for *ST:TOS,* the duties of the ship's surgeon are delineated as having "medical responsibilities for the health and physical welfare of the crew of the Enterprise and broad medical science responsibilities in areas of space exploration" (12), the latter of which they often perform in conjunction with the science officer. Moreover, the character of the doctor is traditionally "the least military" of the starship crew and "a bleeding humanist" (*ibid.*). The ship's surgeon, who first came to life in Dr. Leonard "Bones" McCoy (DeForest Kelley), was turned into an archetype in the *Star Trek* continuum; much like the starship captain. All of McCoy's successors perform the same duties, tending to anyone's medical needs. They also join landing parties in the search for and the study of new lifeforms, re-enacting the role of naturalists on the alien beaches of the galaxy.

Even though Gene Roddenberry called for clothing to be "naval in general appearance," Starfleet uniforms resemble neither present nor past navy uniform codes ("Star Trek Is..." 11). Starfleet ranks are also devoid of any complex special forces/special branch groupings which are the bedrock of contemporary naval operations. Instead, *Star Trek* offers a simple distinction between three divisions, indicated by three different uniform colors. In *ST:TOS, ST:TAS,* and *ST:ENT,* gold is worn by the command division, red by the security and engineering divisions, and blue by medical and science staff. The color code changed in *ST:TNG, ST:DS9,* and *ST:VOY,* where command officers swapped their colors with those traditionally worn by security and engineering. The case can be made that the color-coding for the security division in *ST:TOS* was very likely inspired by the scarlet tunics of the Royal Marines and their duties onboard Royal Navy ships.[15] In many ways, the marines represent an aberration within the confines of a sailing ship because they were not sailors. They were mostly unskilled landsmen who worked menial/support tasks. However, it is their primary duties and their depreciative portrayal in Napoleonic sea fiction that allow for a comparison with the iconic portrayal the so-called *redshirts*. Historically, Royal Marines were used as the first line of defense, particularly during landings and boarding actions; they were considered expendable.[16] This is also how they are commonly portrayed in Napoleonic sea fiction—the Hornblower novels are no exception.[17] Similar to Royal Marines, Starfleet security and tactical officers are in charge of ship-to-ship engagements, ship-board security, and the guarding and defending of landing parties. The way they are portrayed in *ST:TOS* offers a peculiarly striking parallel to the depiction of the marines in sea novels since the color of their uniforms carries the same connotation of expendability. Over the course of three seasons, hardly a week went by where not one or more security officers fell in the line of duty. They were usually killed in encounters with exotic aliens on shore, or while repelling intruders on the ship. This pattern became so recognizable and indeed iconic that writers, producers, and fans coined the term *redshirt* to refer to those unfortunate souls. The term has since gained wide-spread popular culture status which is largely due to its popularization in *Star Trek* parodies.

"Course heading, Captain?": The Romance of Gentlemanly Discourse

The structural language used to delineate *Star Trek*'s naval hierarchies also begets a particular naval tone that resonates in the operational language. The tone of how *Star Trek*'s naval corpus is actively performed, recalls popular conceptions of naval exchanges between sailors. Projecting a timbre of courtesy, it explicitly draws on the Hornblower novels and the presumed discourse of gentlemanly civility—a mainstay in sea romances. The language officers use to issue, acknowledge, and carry out orders translates into a set of clearly recognizable *schemata* which govern everyday life onboard Starfleet ships. Found throughout the *Star Trek* continuum, these schemata are at the core of its maritime nostalgia. These language patterns are best observed when we juxtapose sailing orders given on the quarterdeck of Hornblower's ship with the ritualized setting and/or changing of a course on the bridge of a starship; both involve giving "sailing orders" to the helmsman and/or the navigator. We find a paradigmatic example in *Hornblower and the Hotspur*:

"Mr Bush! Set all plain sail. Mr Prowse! A course to weather Finisterre as quickly as possible, if you please. Mr Foreman, signal to the Commodore." ...

"Thank you, Mr Foreman. Up helm, Mr Bush. Course sou'west by south."

"Sou'west by south. Aye aye sir" [600].

While starships still display a distinct horizontal attitude in terms of movement, some of the navigational terms are modified to account for imagined bearings in outer space. Even so, as the following example dialog shows, the underlying naval schemata are largely maintained, thus adding considerably to *Star Trek*'s naval tone.

KIRK: Mister Chekov, lay in a course for Troyius. Mister Sulu, impulse drive, speed factor point zero three seven.

SULU: Impulse drive, Captain?

KIRK: Yes, that's correct, Mister Sulu. Sublight factor point zero three seven.[18]

Battle orders also maintain a similarity of schemata. The default battle script usually encompasses the sighting of an enemy vessel, constant reports on its movements, directions for offensive or evasive maneuvers, and commands for targeting and firing.[19] While certainly condensed, Starfleet officers echo the naval nostalgia that is carried by the language used to evocatively describe sailing ship duels in sea novels. They then maintain a similarity in form when engaging in ship-to-ship action in outer space.

KIRA: We've lost the number three starboard shield.

WORF: Come about. The cruiser is taking us too far away from the convoy. Try to keep our portside to the Klingons.

O'BRIEN: Aye, sir....

KIRA: I have phaser lock.

WORF: Fire![20]

The similitude in operational language is closely approximated in and reinforced by visual aesthetics of starship movements (see next chapter).

Not only is *Star Trek*'s naval tone circumscribed by the operational discourses for steering the ship and commanding the crew in battle, but it is also rooted in the romantic misconceptions about the gentleman/officer-heroes of wind and sail. Projected through language, they are shrouded in an apparent air of charming courtesy and deference. Starfleet's naval corpus embraces the same romanticized discourse of civility and politeness. Roddenberry's intentions of making Starfleet not too militaristic, while maintaining naval hierarchies and forms of address point to an anachronism that demands further explanation.[21] Even though Starfleet does not impress highly sought-after "space sailors" anymore, as it was common practice during the Age of Sail, Jeff Greenwald has noted that it is "not a democracy ... it's a very good tyranny. A good, working tyranny" (100). Particular inflections in *Star Trek*'s naval tone belie a constituent element found in sea romances. A specific form of address, which was discontinued in contemporary Anglophone navies, provides us with a key. Whether addressing an officer or a crewman, the term "mister" was prefixed to their names. This tradition is occasionally even applied to female characters in *Star Trek*; the Vulcan officer trainee "Mister Saavik" (Kirstie Alley) serves as a case in point. "It functions to keep alive ... the conventions of sailing," as Michèle and Duncan Barrett have argued, "rather than polite manners" (46). However, this is not how Starfleet's naval hierarchies and the naval tone they foster, are connoted. It serves to understand how and why Roddenberry weaved military ranks and the trappings of war into his future of benign space exploration. For him, "rank, when properly used, can be a pleasant way of acknowledging seniority—of showing respect" (qtd. Whitfield 185). In the directors' guidelines for *ST:TNG*, he emphasized that "the word 'sir'" is "an acknowledgement of the naval heritage of Starfleet" (40). This heritage is then rooted in the romanticized discourse spoken by Royal Navy gentlemen/officers found in sea novels.

Even though the common sailor entered the history books as the most foulmouthed representative of Georgian society—and, they are also depicted as such in sea fiction—the privileged cadre of naval officers are usually portrayed as gentlemen. They were expected to conduct, and especially articulate themselves as such. The idealized image of the naval officer is largely a product of British Romanticism and the impact it had on the national pantheon of naval heroes. Their gentlemanly conduct and graciousness then became a mainstay in Napoleonic sea fiction. In texts like the Hornblower stories, "we escape into a world where etiquette and order seem to rule," as King has argued, "and where even war had its civilities" (xiii).[22] Various expressions, such as the ubiquitous "if you please" (added to almost every order even in the heat of battle), indicate the gentlemanly romance in naval fiction. Officer training instills an elaborate discursive protocol and etiquette which forms the base tone required and expected of gentlemen; expressions like "Mister Bush's compliments, sir," "Mister Bowles's respects, sir," or "I'd be obliged" are cases in point. The gentlemanly qualities of the romanticized and archetypal discourse of politeness and courtesy constitute a crucial inflection in *Star Trek*'s naval tone. Roddenberry reactionarily inscribed the naval corpus with the same accentuation of civility and deference he found in the Hornblower stories. Rather than being degrading, such naval forms of order and power bear distorted connotations of respect, ethics, and graciousness.

Of Bows and Sterns

Star Trek's naval corpus would be incomplete without a compact set of descriptive terms and nautical phraseology. Casting the discursive net wide in nautical dictionaries as well as the Hornblower texts, reveals an appreciable number of terms and expressions. Not only do they call to mind Starfleet's wind and sail heritage, but they also merge it with a more contemporary naval register.

Many terms can be grouped together into spatial descriptors, denoting directions and specific places in and around starships. Extending from a vessel's centerline, a ship has *starboard* and *port* sides. *Fore* and *aft* point to spaces in the front and in the rear of a ship, respectively. Since they are also shown from above and below, the terms *dorsal* and *ventral* designate the top and bottom parts of the ship. However, a starship also has a *bow* and a *stern*. Reminiscing about the construction of his ship, Captain Archer (Scott Bakula) recalls the time when they "laid the *keel* for Enterprise" (emphasis added).[23] Once completed, they went on a *shakedown cruise*. If something is lost in the *bowels* of the ship, or an intruder is on the loose, the *vessel* will be searched from *stem* to *stern*. In battle, one ship might *bear down* on another one. The *hull* might subsequently be hit *amidships*, even though cannon balls and musket fire have been replaced by *torpedoes* and phasers. Ships as well as peace treaties can be *scuttled*. When their intentions are peaceful, ships simply lay *alongside* each other. They often also take position off the starboard or port bow. Yet, they may also come up the *beam* of a ship. The particular *rig* of a vessel indicates its configuration; and Starfleet engineers are as adept at *jury-rigging* the ship's systems to solve a problem as the carpenter and his mates are at rigging a substitute mast after a heavy engagement. In the guidelines for writers of *ST:TOS,* the tractor beam was conceived as the 24th century equivalent of a "grappling hook and towing line" (21). And when a Starfleet vessel does not sail between the stars, it might be *moored* in a *berth* in space*dock*.

The richness of nautical terms also applies to starship interiors. A ship has multiple *decks* whose walls are called *bulkheads*, and they also feature *hatchways*. The most prominent place on a starship is the *bridge*, which is located at the very top of the vessel. "The concentration of controls ... on the bridge," Jonathan Rayner has opined, "follows the installation of centralised 'combat information centers' on board Navy vessels in the post-war period" (163). The bridge on a Starfleet ship, however, conveys a different atmosphere. After all, a CIC is usually located in the bowels of a ship; sf shows and movies which extrapolate this command-center paradigm—and the distinct aeronautical discourse that comes with it (e.g., *Battlestar Galactica, Space 2063*)—show it as a cavernous, barely-lit room. It is densely packed with duty stations, monitors, a tactical plot, and radar equipment surrounding a central command and control station. While most officers no longer stand at their stations in *Star Trek*—there is even a much coveted *captain's chair*—a Starfleet bridge retains a residual similitude with the quarterdecks of old. They are brightly lit, open spaces. Some of them also feature wooden elements; the bridges on the *Enterprise-D* and *Enterprise-E* are particularly good cases in point. The layout of the bridge echoes this similitude. They all face *for'rad* and tend to feature a section in the back of the room which is slightly raised and separated from the central command and steering section by a *railing*. The layout recalls the separation between quarterdeck, which was the station of the captain, senior officers, and helmsman, and the poop deck which extended to the rear of a sailing vessel. Not only is the quarterdeck "considered virtually sacred," it is also used "as a promenade by the officers," as evidenced by Starfleet captains getting out of their chairs in order to pace back and forth (King 361). The *helm* also goes by the name of *con*. When someone is ordered to *take the con*, they are either placed in charge of steering, or in temporary command of the bridge and thus the ship on the whole.[24] A few starships even have a *skylight* installed in the ceiling of their bridge. On sailing ships, a skylight cut into the quarterdeck to provide light in the captain's cabin. While bridge designs clearly feature a separate room labeled *head*, it is part of *Star Trek* lore that toilets were never actually shown on screen.

When not on the bridge or at their duty stations, senior officers and crewmen can be found in their *quarters*, which are occasionally also referred to as *cabins*. When they go on holiday, they take *shore leave*. The ship's doctor takes care of medical matters in *sickbay*, while prisoners are thrown in the *brig*. The massive amount of provisions and spare parts are *stowed* in *cargo holds/cargo bays*. Some missions may require the *hauling* of specific goods from one star system to another. Even in the 24th century, they have not yet solved the problem of *stowaways*.[25] If people do not order food via replicators, it is prepared in a *galley* that serves the *mess hall*. In *ST:ENT*, they even revived the tradition of *stewards* waiting on senior officers. There is also a *wardroom* which is often used for formal dinners and diplomatic meetings. Even though most of *Star Trek*'s stories center on the senior officers, occasionally the audience is given the view from the *lower deck*, which used to be the place "where seamen lived and the ship's heaviest guns were located," and which came to denote "all the men who were not officers" (King 284).[26]

This broad range of nautical terms is complemented by a compact set of nautical phraseology. Most nautical phrases used throughout the *Star Trek* continuum pertain to orders usually given to the helm. When a starship leaves spacedock the captain orders to *clear all moorings*. Occasionally, captains meta-phorically *weigh anchor*[27] before continuing their journey. Once a course is laid in, they may choose to remind the helmsman to steer *steady as she goes*, or to keep the ship *straight and steady*. Commands to *go about, come about*, or to *bring the ship about* prefigure course changes. They all derive from the maneuvers of either *wearing around*, or *putting about*. When officers change their mind about something, or when they interject, they often exclaim: *Belay that order!* In the direst situations, *Star Trek*'s naval heroes have no other choice than to sound the general call to *abandon ship*.

The naval corpus, however, also encompasses nomenclature. The importance of names should not come as a surprise in an sf world which embeds distinct nautical meanings even in the names of secondary characters in order to etymologically foreshadow their role in the story. For example, over the course of five episodes of *ST:VOY*'s second season, Lt. Michael Jonas (Raphael Sbarge) lives up to the portentous significance of his nautical name. The *Jonah* is an archetypal character in maritime lore who derives from the eponymous biblical prophet. After defying god's orders, he was swallowed by a large fish/whale as punishment and incentive to repent his sins. To superstitious sailors, the Jonah is synonymous with bad luck. In sea novels, he functions as a scapegoat, traitor and/or jinx. Once a ship's crew elected the collective source of their bad luck, the vessel can only be saved by casting the Jonah overboard both literally and metaphorically. In the same vein, Lt. Jonas brings increasingly more bad luck to *Voyager* in the form of enemy attacks. He decided to defy the orders of his captain and began conspiring with alien enemies who want to steal Starfleet technology. He provides them with inside knowledge. Needless to say, once his traitorous activities are exposed, the crew disposes of him. This only goes to show how deep the nautical theme permeates the world of *Star Trek*. Its transatlantic maritime endowment was written even more powerfully into ship names.

"Let's make sure history never forgets the name [HMS Enterprize*]"*

Everything is in a name. The old adage also holds true for what is arguably the most renowned ship, or rather series of ships in fiction—the *Enterprise*. The iconic status of the starships bearing the name can hardly be overestimated. Jeff Greenwald has asserted that "aside from Noah's Ark, the starship *Enterprise* is the most famous such vehicle ever created" (35). While perhaps presumptuous, a case can be made that the *Enterprise* shares the illustrious company with a small pantheon of vessels, both historical and fictional, that enjoy instant public recognition.[28] The ship's name is, of course, also integrally linked to the stories it helps to facilitate. *Star Trek* stories are as much about the individual vessels, and the one space station, as they are about their crews. Doing a "grand fleet review" of Starfleet ships reveals that the most prominent vessels reflect a transatlantic, Anglophone core of naval nomenclature in both ship names and designations for ship classes. They reflect naval legacies not exclusively confined to the Age of Sail. The fleet's historio-mythical core, which draws from a British maritime legacy, is often draped with a symbolic veneer that is deceivingly indicative of the U.S. Navy's post-war legacy. The resulting dense transatlantic mesh in nomenclature is easily obscured by the obvious prefix USS,[29] the symbolic prominence of which might lead to premature conclusions about whose legacy Starfleet ships carry into space. Even though the names for the multitude of starships are drawn from different sources (e.g., geographic place names, important historical figures, various mythologies), a grand fleet review shows that *Star Trek*'s vision of a post-national and unified Earth is based on a culturally dominant albeit seemingly benign Anglocentric western mind-set. It is a world where the English language is ubiquitous and where American and British names form the inner circle of privileged descriptors.

The starships named *Enterprise* form the apogee of all vessels sharing this name in a purposefully delineated genealogy that resists easy categorization along the lines of a single national naval heritage. In fact, the name is a unique node of converging transatlantic legacies that link the Age of Sail, the large global conflicts of the early 20th century, and contemporary space exploration. Initially, the *Enterprise* was to be named *Yorktown* which would have placed it solely within an American frame of reference, recalling the Siege of Yorktown (1781), and the aircraft carrier of the same name (CV-5) that served in the Pacific during World War II.[30] While *Enterprise* might recall the legacy of two other aircraft carriers (CV-6 and CV-65), it is in fact much more elusive in its cultural distinctiveness. According to *Star Trek*'s fictional history, it does not have American roots. While the initial impetus for choosing this name is very likely linked to the carriers, which enjoyed popular recognition in the 1960s,[31] Starfleet ships are not aircraft carriers transposed into space. What makes this become evident is the way how the historical genealogy of the starship *Enterprise* is celebrated and expanded throughout the *Star Trek* continuum.

The complete, and ultimately transatlantic genealogy of the *Enterprise* was gradually revealed in commemorative displays and the symbolically potent opening credits for *ST:ENT*. Even though the aircraft carrier is featured in these displays, the legacy of the starships *Enterprise* goes back to a sailing vessel. Its design is reminiscent of a frigate. First shown in the officer's lounge in *Star*

Trek: The Motion Picture (Robert Wise, U.S. 1971), it is most clearly displayed in Captain Archer's ready room, which features prominently throughout *ST:ENT*. Talking about the legacy of his ship's name, the captain once remarks to an alien visitor: "This one [pointing at the display] sailed Earth's oceans almost four hundred years ago."[32] This particular episode is set in 2154 which thus locates the sailing vessel at some point during the second half of the 18th century—the heyday of the Golden Age of Sail. Even so, there are no markers in any of the displays that would indicate which naval service the sailing vessel belonged to. A holographically recreated sailing ship named *Enterprise* features as a highly symbolic setting in the opening sequence of *Star Trek Generations* (David Carson, U.S. 1994). The crew dresses up in what were described as British naval uniforms.[33] As was the case with the commemorative displays, we do not see a prefix or anything else that would designate whether it was a Royal Navy or U.S. Navy ship. After all, there were a number of commissioned sailing ships serving in both the Royal Navy and the fledgling Continental, later U.S. Navy in the late 18th and early 19th century.[34]

According to *Star Trek* canon, however, the legacy of the *Enterprise* does not have American roots; a fact that is unequivocally established in the opening credits of *ST:ENT*. The credits blend historical achievements in human exploration with the fictional exploration of space as envisioned in *Star Trek*'s future. In the beginning, they feature oceanic scenes which then give way to early landmarks in aviation before progressing to fictional milestones in space exploration that conclude with the launch of the show's eponymous ship. The images range from a Kon-Tiki raft traversing the vast expanses of the Pacific and the Wright Brothers' first flight at Kitty Hawk, to various members of the Apollo program, the International Space Station (ISS), and the fictional landmark of humanity's first faster-than-light ship—the *Phoenix*. Even though the number of overt markers of American national identity may outweigh the few remaining non–American references, observations by fans and scholars generally remain rather ignorant of the telling arrangement of visuals and powerful semiotics evident in two key title cards.[35] Not only is the aircraft carrier *Enterprise* conspicuously absent, but one title card also shows a square-rigged sailing vessel and its name plate which reads HMS *Enterprize*. This clearly establishes the starship's transatlantic heritage. Disregarding the procession of American-ness that follows, the image of the sailing ship occupies a privileged and specifically marked position in the symbolic narrative of the credits. It sails into the following title card which presents Roddenberry's credits as the creator of *Star Trek*. At the same time, the rolling ocean waves, which carried the ship in the previous frame, gradually morph into a starry horizon as the HMS *Enterprize* is shown sailing towards a cosmic ocean. Since there were approximately six commissioned ships of the Royal Navy bearing this name during the Golden Age of Sail, it remains difficult to ascertain which historical *Enterprise* the credits refer to.[36] Nevertheless, the opening titles of *ST:ENT* give a historicizing nod to the maritime worldbuilding paradigm Roddenberry extracted from the Hornblower novels.

Our understanding of Starfleet's naval nomenclature will improve even further if we acknowledge how the ship's transatlantic genealogy is reinforced by the designations for ship classes. Even though ship classifications are often believed to have been a by-product of the era of steel battleships and dreadnoughts, the practice of separating ships into classes is rooted in the Age of Sail.[37] The original *Enterprise* and its successor, the *Enterprise-A,* both belong to the *Constitution*-class. The namesake for this class is a famous ship in U.S. naval history. The frigate USS *Constitution,* nicknamed "Old Ironsides," is the oldest fully commissioned ship still in service. It won a number of engagements with the Royal Navy during the War of 1812. This conflict is often singled out as a defining moment for the U.S. Navy because it briefly managed to hold its ground against the maritime superpower of the time. The three successors of the *Enterprise-A* all belong to ship classes which do not have any recognizable namesakes in naval history; the *Enterprise-B* belongs to the *Excelsior*-class, the *Enterprise-C* to the *Ambassador*-class, and the *Enterprise-D* is a *Galaxy*-class ship. The latest incarnation of the *Enterprise* so far belongs to the impressive *Sovereign*-class. Since there are no ships or classes that bear this name in the U.S. Navy, it stands to reason that it could have been named after one of the many capital ships designated HMS *Royal Sovereign.* The most likely candidate is a ship-of-the-line which served as the flagship for Admiral Collingwood, who was Nelson's second-in-command at Trafalgar. The qualifier "Royal" was likely dropped because there is no royalty left on Earth in the future. The fact that the *Enterprise-E* is not only the flagship of Starfleet, but also a mighty ship-of-the-line supports the genealogical link. There is a residual echo of merged transatlantic naval legacies which, while primarily encoded in the name *Enterprise,* also extends to designations for starship classes.

Given the starship's iconic status in popular culture, it is not surprising that its historio-fictional legacy is written back onto the real world. The transatlantic linkage bleeds back from the *Star Trek* continuum into contemporary culture and re-inscribes the fictional legacy of the starships onto naval vessels and space vehicles. It is a well-known fact that the prototype for the NASA Space Shuttle (OV-101), which was going to be named *Constitution,* was rechristened *Enterprise* after a coordinated fan-letter campaign prior to its launch in 1976. Roddenberry and the cast of *ST:TOS* were guests of honor at the dedication ceremony.[38] One of the starship's predecessors—the nuclear-powered aircraft carrier—made a guest appearance in *Star Trek IV: The Voyage Home* (Leonard Nimoy, U.S. 1986) when the crew travels back in time to save the future. Since the real *Enterprise* was out at sea, the film was shot on USS *Ranger* acting as a stand-in. Recent developments in space tourism also tapped into the starship's popular culture legacy. Virgin Galactic named its first commercial suborbital spacecraft, VSS *Enterprise* and VSS *Voyager*, after the title ships in *ST:TOS* and *ST:VOY*, respectively. However, there is also a transatlantic residue of the starship's iconic status which has gone unnoticed, or at least uncommented. The high-tech hydrographic survey vessel HMS *Enterprise* is on active duty in the Royal Navy. Launched in 2002, it was nicknamed the "Royal Navy's star ship" (navynews.co.uk, 2011). This goes to show that the transatlantic meanings, which were extracted from Anglophone naval histories and inscribed into the name of the starship, are reciprocally acknowledged and re-appropriated in the naming of contemporary vessels.

An even broader look at the multitude of Starfleet ships, which are either shown and/or referred to throughout the *Star Trek* continuum, reveals that their nomenclature gravitates towards a distinct British/American legacy. In some cases, they form genealogies similar to that of the *Enterprise*, or openly refer to renowned sailing ships. A fair share of these names have been used by both the Royal Navy and the U.S. Navy. In other cases, references are clear; the number of renowned naval warships and/or maritime warriors prevails over any references made to ships of exploration and their commanders. This is somewhat at odds with *Star Trek*'s overall premise for a future world of benign and enlightened exploration of outer space.

American aircraft carriers, which served with distinction during World War II and continued to be important icons in later conflicts, represent one group of vessels whose legacy Starfleet taps into. Ships such as the *Lexington*, the *Yorktown*, the *Saratoga* and the *Hornet*, the *Constitution*, the *Constellation* and the *Intrepid*, stand out. Some carriers, like the *Constitution*, the *Constellation* and the *Intrepid*, all draw on the legacies of sailing ships which served during the War of 1812 and the Barbary Wars (1801–05, 1815). There are certain cases, like the starship *Essex*, whose namesakes are slightly more ambiguous and may allow for a shared transatlantic heritage. The USS *Essex* was a frigate that was captured by the British during the War of 1812 and continued to serve as HMS *Essex*. It then also lent its name to an aircraft carrier. There was, however, also a renowned Royal Navy ship-of-the-line of the same name which served at the famous Battle of Quiberon Bay (1759).

There is an equally large squadron of British vessels which found their way into the ranks of Starfleet by way of providing namesakes. Most of them can be traced back to renowned sailing vessels. The HMS *Victory* takes the lead as the famed flagship of Admiral Nelson which he commanded at Trafalgar. The *Agamemnon* was a ship-of-the-line on which he achieved much of his pre–Trafalgar exploits. Fighting in major fleet actions, the *Majestic,* the *Ajax* and the *Bellerophon* were also iconic vessels during the long conflict with France. The latter bears particular note because Napoleon formally surrendered aboard her after his defeat at Waterloo. The starship *Centaur* likely alludes to the flagship of famous British Admiral Sir Samuel Hood. One of Starfleet's ships, the *Sutherland,* was even named after the first ship-of-the-line commanded by Hornblower. Interestingly, there is also a USS *Horatio*; however, it is difficult to ascertain whether it was named after Hornblower, Nelson, or Hamlet's loyal friend. Royal Navy battleships such as the *Hood,* named after the above mentioned admiral, the *Valiant,* the *Repulse* and the *Exeter,* all of which garnered distinction either during World War I and II, also serve as legacy markers. Lastly, some starships are named after well-known naval warriors such as American Civil War Admiral David *Farragut,* or one of England's earliest swashbuckling heroes, Sir Francis *Drake.*

Confronted with the large number of warships that lent their names to Starfleet vessels, the few references to ships of exploration seem negligible at first. Their namesakes are, however, all the more telling from a transatlantic point of view in that they specifically emphasize the *Rule Britannia* theme. Continuing the voyages of James Cook in outer space, there are at least three starships by the name of *Endeavour* that serve in Starfleet. Similarly, the HMS *Beagle,* which carried Charles Darwin to the Galapagos Islands, also represents a significant reference point for Starfleet's mission to seek new life and new civilizations. The *Challenger* is arguably named after the last ship of the Age of Exploration in the Pacific. HMS *Challenger* "spent the years from 1873–76 systematically studying 68,890 nautical miles of ocean," Martha Veil has noted, and "its discoveries still guide oceanographic research in the Pacific" (137). Both starships, the *Endeavour* and the *Challenger,* have transatlantic legacies encoded into their names. After all, the names of the original sailing/steam-assisted vessels were bestowed upon two of NASA's space shuttles. The eponymous title ship of *Star Trek: Discovery* (U.S. 2017–) bears a similar multifaceted legacy. Also lending its name to a space shuttle, HMS *Discovery* was the vessel that Robert F. Scott, who also served as a reference point for Roddenberry, took to the Antarctic in 1901. Earlier, George Vancouver commanded another HMS *Discovery* on his voyage of exploration. And yet another HMS *Discovery* served as consort ship on Captain Cook's third voyage. The starship USS *Discovery* is to recapture the very spirit inherent in its name. Ultimately, the extended legacy of these ships underscores the dominant position of the Royal Navy in the realm of maritime exploration and discovery.

There are a few more nautical apocrypha which lead to a deeper appreciation of the etymological symbolism encoded in two of Starfleet's better-known ships—*Stargazer* and *Voyager*. Not only is stargazer a colloquial term for referring to amateur astronomers, but it also has a nautical meaning; "in a square-rigged ship, a small sail set above the skyscraper to maximize the power gained from a light wind," is called stargazer (King 416). While the starship *Voyager* shares its name with the eponymous unmanned spacecraft launched in 1977, its etymological root is equally relevant for a starship which is stranded on the other side of the galaxy. While "originally quite precise in its reference to travel by sea," the word "gradually broadened to include other means of conveyance on land" (Foulke xiii).

Previous studies of *Star Trek*'s nomenclature were largely oblivious to the impressive transatlantic borrowing of naval names. As *Star Trek* grew, the producers and writers occasionally looked to non–Anglophone naval histories. Once again, renowned warships received preference, allowing for an appreciative nod towards former enemies of the U.S. Navy and the Royal Navy. A number of ships are named after Japanese aircraft carriers and/or battleships such as the *Yamato*, the *Akagi*, the *Musashi* and the *Kongō*. Russian names are also included in Starfleet with ships like the *Potemkin* and the *Zhukov*. Even so, a grand fleet review reveals the unacknowledged and/or under-appreciated transatlantic naval legacies which are purposefully merged and encoded in Starfleet's nomenclature; especially in one of fiction's most famous vessels—the *Enterprise*. By deconstructing and re-contextualizing the deceivingly simplistic American surface markings/meanings, and the preliminary associations they might carry, we uncovered a privileged, English-language, transatlantic naval core which is rooted in a merged Anglo-American heritage of wind and sail.

5. "All I ask is a tall ship"
Sailing the Ocean of Space

If the title of the officially licensed *Star Trek* wall calendar and the eponymous companion book, *Ships of the Line*, are any indication, then they make it clear that Starfleet ships claim an aesthetic and conceptual kinship of naval similitude with tall ships of the past. The dense transatlantic mesh in naval jargon and nomenclature also envelopes *Star Trek*'s starship paradigm. Due to its distinct transatlantic nature of re-imagined and disguised sailing vessels, which are supported by an oceanic paradigm in outer space, it differs significantly from the predominant trope of the spaceship found in most other American space-based sf TV shows and movies. By partially literalizing the metaphor of the "ocean of space," space takes on physical qualities of a maritime environment in *Star Trek*. Extrapolating a maritime similitude, the trope of *Star Trek*'s starship is conceptually and aesthetically modeled on the romanticized glamour of sailing frigates and ships of exploration—henceforth referred to as the *frigate-trope*. On the one hand, the trope is paradigmatic for the world of wind and sail found in the Hornblower novels. On the other hand, it is reciprocally tied to a number of initial production-related restrictions, such as a low special effects budget, which resulted in the use of model ships and compositing techniques that simply did not allow for more elaborate ship movements. Even when more resources, especially CGI technology, became available, the frigate-trope was not radically changed since it had become an integral part of *Star Trek*'s naval worldbuilding rules.

The trope transposes into outer space the premise of long-distance, independent cruises, which were the signature assignments for frigates during the Golden Age of Sail. The broad mission parameters and the discretionary powers usually held by frigate captains, prompted Roddenberry to compare the role of Starfleet vessels to such British warships of the past. While ships of exploration were sometimes smaller than frigates (e.g., sloops, colliers), the basic premise for their assignments was largely the same. Not only were most voyages of discovery commanded by naval officers, but they also operated independently and largely out of touch with the Admiralty for many months, even years at a time. Since *Star Trek* postulates a world of future space exploration that is similar to the Age of Exploration, it only makes sense that independently operating sailing vessels, which were still powerful enough to hold their own and act as representatives of their respective countries, were morphed into the paradigmatic model for Starfleet ships. As such, *Star Trek*'s disguised sailing vessels stand in stark contrast to the trope of the aircraft carrier and dogfights in space which is wedded to a more aeronautical corpus; that trope is rooted in a mid–20th century American historical framework.

Disguised Sailing Ships in Space

Anyone who examines the principal ships of Starfleet, which all share distinct design conventions, will inevitably agree that they do not look like sailing ships; they do not even have solar sails or solar panels which already find experimental deployment in contemporary space projects. The ship design attests once again to the transatlantic interplay between a highly symbolic American surface, and a historio-mythical British core. A preliminary reading of the literal surfaces of Starfleet ships echoes the deceiving simplicity of its seemingly All-American nomenclature and naval prefixation.[1] Surface markings alone are hardly sufficient to equate Starfleet vessels either with Theodore Roosevelt's "Great White Fleet," or the entirety of the contemporary U.S. Navy[2] since both color coding and the display of pendent numbers are common in most naval forces. While they nominally belong to a fleet, Starfleet ships are rarely shown to travel in squadrons or in larger battle fleets. Compared to the regular rendezvous of two or more Starfleet ships, where they transfer personnel, receive orders or cargo, there are only a few major fleet actions. For the most part, however, the principal vessels of the *Star Trek* series pursue their independent cruises, following a broad set of orders.

It is essential to understand both the iconic status of frigates, especially in sea fiction, and sailing ship aesthetics in general, before their residual influence on *Star Trek*'s ship paradigm can be visualized. During the Age of Sail, "frigates were the most glamorous ships," as King has contended, because they were "the fleet's fast fighters, involved in all sorts of duties and high drama" (11). They were also nick-named "the eyes of the fleet." Unlike the behemoths of ships-of-the-line, which mostly operated in squadrons that stayed closer to shore, a frigate's purpose was to operate independently on long-distance assignments. Thanks to advancements in technology, navigation, and medicine, these ships were "expected to remain at sea literally for years without coming to port" (Davies 24). Frigate commands were much coveted by young officers. They offered the most lucrative opportunities for career advancement, both in terms of prize money and distinction, and thus were a fast-track towards promotion. Frigates usually came with a broad set of assignments.[3] The potential of multifaceted adventures, which frigates offered, made them the preferred paradigm in Napoleonic sea fiction. For example, even though Hornblower commanded different types of vessels throughout his career, C.S. Forester initially located his hero on a frigate.

Frigates were not only limited to military assignments. Their versatility made them one of a few ship types that were also dispatched on circumnavigations and voyages of discovery. The Wallis and Carteret Expedition (1766–8), Admiral Bougainville's *La Boudouse,* and the Challenger Expedition (1873–6) are just a few cases in point. What is more, the terminology used for ships like frigates and smaller types of vessels, which often performed similar duties, was not entirely consistent. Hence, most of these vessels were often generically called *cruisers.* Rather than a label for a specific class of ship, the term circumscribed the broad assignments and missions of such vessels. Sailing cruisers provided one of the conceptual cornerstones of *Star Trek*'s frigate-trope as it comes to life in its disguised sailing ships. Roddenberry already used the model of the independent "cruiser" in the first pitch for *Star Trek,* delineating the starship's mission as "a well-defined and long-range Exploration-Science-Security mission" (3). The opening narration of *ST:TOS* tells the audience that the *Enterprise* was on a five-year mission. The conceptual premise was expanded on and reinforced in that Starfleet ships were compared to English warships and their multi-faceted missions.[4] The conceptual premise also found articulation in ship aesthetic.

On the surface, Starfleet vessels may be reminiscent of modern-day navy ships. However, not only do they perform similar duties like those of sailing frigates "as maids of all work" (Davies 23), but they also *behave* very much like sailing ships. An approximated two-dimensionality places peculiar and thus signature constraints on the spatial alignment, orientation, and movement of starships in outer space. Even though starships traverse astronomical distances, whenever vessels meet, whether in peace or in war, their relative positions and movements are marked by a distinct proximity. This is yet another marker for the residual naval aesthetics of wind and sail. While starships travel at fantastic velocities, a similar naval echo can be observed—though to a lesser degree—in the relative speeds of ships.

Star Trek's maritime two-dimensionality is partially grounded in camera angles and movements that deliver shots of the whole vessel. While the camera can move rather freely, showing a ship from low and/or high angles respectively, the vessels themselves are hardly, if ever, shown upside down. From the audience's point of view, a ship's keel is always at the bottom and its dorsal section always points up. While starships are shown to heel when coming about—and they also pitch and yaw within a limited range of degrees—they rarely spin more excessively along the Z-axis. Generally, they do not perform wild space loopings, barrel rolls, or other aerial maneuvers. This translates into rather conservative spatial alignments which become even more obvious when we take the relative position between ships into consideration.

When vessels come alongside each other, they take up position roughly along the same level. Measured from an imaginary horizontal plane, there is either no, or very little difference between the ships along the Z-axis. While the three-dimensionality of direction and movement was acknowledged in production notes,[5] we see a distinct horizontal attitude dominating most of *Star Trek*'s space shots. Resulting in rather conservative, approximated nautical movements, the horizontal attitude sets the paradigmatic tone for starships. In short, a starship rendezvous is reminiscent of an encounter between two ocean-going vessels.[6] Very similar in aesthetics and conceptualization, they then maintain a naval model in outer space. In peaceful encounters, ships approach each other with their bows facing forward. Alternatively, they may also come alongside each other on a parallel course. In either scenario, they are usually aligned roughly along the same horizontal plane before closing the distance between each other. While a cable's length is approximately 185 meters in nautical terms, the distances maintained between starships also move within the same range; sometimes even less. Keeping similar nautical distances in the vastness of outer space is striking. The ships then proceed to exchange hails and, if required, people beam from one vessel to the other. Logically there is no need to keep a close distance even when transferring people since transporters operate at a range of more than 10,000 kilometers. In some cases, shuttles are used to ferry people and/or cargo between vessels. It is even the standard mode of exchange in *ST:ENT* since transporters are a largely untried technology in that era. This goes to show that *Star Trek*'s ship aesthetics, movements and ritualized encounters were to maintain a distinct naval similitude with the nautical realities found in the past of wind and sail.

Even though Starfleet is supposedly only a semi-military organization, there are many conflicts and ship battles in *Star Trek*. With the exception of a few big fleet actions—most of which take place in *ST:DS9*—the large majority of ship-to-ship engagements involve either one Starfleet ship and a single enemy vessel of varying sizes, or a small group of opponents. The approximated naval aesthetics that govern these ship engagements point to the residual romance of so-called *ship duels*. It is also what sets *Star Trek* unmistakably apart from the dominant trope of the aircraft carrier and dogfights in space found in other sf universes. A crucial mainstay in Napoleonic sea fiction, the presumed heroic glamour and gentlemanly romance of ship duels continue to hold sway over readers. Such encounters are portrayed as an elaborately ritualized form of warfare which is infused with a gentlemanly etiquette. It helps to bear in mind that these single ship-to-ship actions took place at a time when duels were seen as a legitimate and honorable means of resolving conflicts between men of sentiment, i.e., gentlemen. Dueling, as an act of honorable heroism both on land and at sea, was emphatically portrayed in romantic literature and thus entered the popular imagination. Anthony Price has contended that "in some sense all frigate fights were to a greater or lesser degree: the meeting of two captains, with luck and merit mediating the outcome" (255). The basic model of the sailing ship duel, visually echoing the discourse of gentlemanly civility, was then transposed into outer space.[7] Accounting for the vast differences in technology, it was maintained largely by way of similitude and approximation.

For obvious reasons (e.g., discourse time), the movements of individual vessels were speeded up, especially in the later incarnations of *Star Trek*. Even so, correlative speeds between belligerents remained relatively steady, particularly when compared to the fast movements of fighter-jet-type dogfights in other sf universes. More importantly, the distance between opponents in starship duels, and even in big fleet actions, is yet again a crucial marker of maritime similitude.[8] Ever since the interwar years, modern naval warfare has concentrated on putting more and more distance between the ship and the target, relying on long-distance strike capabilities (e.g., cruise missiles, long-range torpedoes, etc.). Consequently, one might assume that in transposing a maritime setting into the future, the awesome weaponry of starships would allow for attacks being launched from even more remote distances. However, this is not the case in *Star Trek* where belligerents essentially stay within sight of each other. Once warning shots have been fired, ships exchange opening barrages which are then followed by a quick succession of maneuvers. They involve not only particularly close passes between ships, but also the same *approximated horizontal attitude* in carrying out these maneuvers as outlined earlier. A starship's main offensive capability is no longer limited to a crushing broadside since weapons such as phasers and torpedoes can be fired in more than just one direction. They are, however, not mounted on turrets which might recall contemporary navy vessels. Instead, they are integrated into the hull. The way in which these weapons are brought to bear during maneuvers are decidedly reminiscent of wind and sail tactics since ships move into positions that allow them to hit the side of an opponent. Also, they cross the bow and/or the stern of their enemies, respectively, to hit what are presumably more vulnerable sections. Such ship duels and battle scenes are then intercut with naval-style battle orders that govern the actions of the bridge officers.

For example, *Star Trek II: The Wrath of Khan* and the first Hornblower novel, *The Happy Return,* bear more than a few casual similarities. The battle sequences between the *Enterprise* and the *Reliant,* which was commandeered by a group of genetically enhanced humans led by Kirk's archenemy Khan Noonien Singh, are in fact closely modeled on the ship duel (*Lydia* vs. *Natividad*) found in the novel. Director Nicholas Meyer recalled that he wrote "a Hornblower script, simply relocating [sic] in outer space" (80). Both *Reliant* and *Natividad* are taken and commandeered by surprise. The *Lydia* and the *Enterprise* are sent to pursue and stop the ships' commanders from carrying out their respective nefarious plans. In both cases, the opponents meet in battle twice. The first leaves them greatly damaged and in need of speedy repairs. Whoever succeeds in jury-rigging their vessels faster will likely have the upper hand in the inevitable second encounter. The ships temporarily retreat and drift apart only to finally track each other down to engage once more. Like the battle between the sailing ships, which takes place during a storm, the starships also fight in a hostile environment—the Mutara Nebula. The ships encounter thunderstorm-like lightening and bad visibility. Thanks to the superior seaman-/spacemanship of Hornblower and Kirk, the *Natividad* and the *Reliant* are left beyond repair. Both captains call on their respective opponents to surrender and thus save their lives, to which both Crespo and Khan respond with a vengeful show of defiance before perishing along with their ships. What is more, Meyer had the film's composer, James Horner, intermediately quote Claude Debussy's *La mer* (1905) to provide "a lovely 'nautical score,'" which aimed to put the audience "in the mind of Captain Horatio Hornblower" (101).

Not only was the maritime similitude with sailing ship duels maintained throughout *Star Trek,* but it was also confirmed by production staff. Even though designers and animators occasionally experimented with new patterns of ship movement, Still Animation Supervisor James Strauss commented on the distinct naval nature found in the concept art and storyboard stills they used when working on special effects: "There is a kind of look and feel in the way ships move and conduct themselves in these pictures, and it is usually like a naval battle, with broadsides being fired off" (qtd. Duncan 79). While the speed of ships and the number of explosions increased thanks to CGI, their maneuvers were still a far cry from aerial dogfights. With a few occasional exceptions, e.g., the daring maneuvers of the *Defiant,* Starfleet vessels continued to adhere to the same paradigm of approximated two-dimensionality and their horizontal attitude. This even applies to the big fleet actions featured in *ST:DS9*, with larger ship-of-the-line-type vessels engaging in close combat. Even though fleets no longer line up from bow to stern to exchange broadsides, they still take up position like on a battlefield before they begin to outflank, cross or break through enemy lines. Being reminiscent of big sailing ship battles, obviously following Nelsonian battle tactics, these capital ships move in close and engage their enemies in a melee. Ships-of-the-line-type vessels steadily maneuver into position to deliver barrages of phaser broadsides, while smaller frigate-type vessels dart between bigger ships to exploit tactical weaknesses.[9] Though ordered infrequently, Starfleet officers show a distinct readiness to ram their large ships into an enemy vessel as a last resort.[10] Also, the mode of how a starship reacts to their immediate surroundings in battle is based on a fallacious postulation. We see the starships rocking and rolling in reaction to direct hits as well as near misses which foreshadows the way how space is reconfigured into an oceanic seascape.

Merging American surfaces with a British historio-mythical core, the frigate-trope can only be fully appreciated when compared to the dominant starship paradigm in other sf series and movies. Most, if not all, other major American space operas and space-based military sf universes transpose into space the legacy of U.S. aircraft carriers during World War II and later conflicts. The carrier-in-space-trope is irrevocably tied to dogfights and other aeronautical characteristics, which lionize the daring feats, romanticized nonchalance, and skills of dauntless flying aces. They claim a predominately American kinship, marrying the jargon of Air Force and Navy operations in the Gulf Wars and Vietnam with the celebrated legacies of American pilots who fought Japanese Zeros in the Pacific. Their legacy goes all the way back to American volunteers who served in the Lafayette Escadrille during World War I. The re-imagined version of *Battlestar Galactica*, the *Star Wars* universe, *Babylon 5*, both *Stargate SG-1* as well as *Stargate Atlantis*, and the short-lived series *Space: Above and Beyond* serve as the most obvious reference points.

The conceptual basis of all these universes is much more militaristic and they are mostly devoid of any claims to space exploration. The discourse used in these series and films is closely modeled on contemporary military jargon, especially fighter pilot slang. The conceptual paradigm of the spaceship and its interaction with other vessels and outer space closely mirrors contemporary aeronautical realities. The principal spaceships are all capital vessels. They maintain iconic features of aircraft carriers, such as the command tower, launching platforms, and flight decks for squadrons of fighters and auxiliary craft. Unlike the frigates of old, most of these spaceships do not operate in isolation.

Like contemporary aircraft carriers, they are a part of a carrier group/fleet. When in battle, the first stage of any engagement does not involve the main vessels in direct combat. While they are also equipped with powerful weaponry, mounted on turrets, they usually provide only cover fire for their main offensive capability—their fighter jets.

Whether they are called *Viper, TIE fighter, X-wing, Starfury, F-302, Death Glider* or *Hammerhead,* they not only look like fighter jets, maintaining either a two- or four-wing configuration, but they also behave as such in combat. Transposing the fighter jet paradigm into a zero–G environment removes all constraints on the aesthetics of movement which are displayed by these craft as they engage in "real" dogfights in space. Pilots also paint victory tallies on the hulls of their fighters along with elaborate squadron insignia. They also provide a different view of space for the audience—the view from the cockpit. It includes contraptions like radar screens, a control column, and a head-up display (HUD). These space pilots wear helmets, flight suits, and they all have call signs. They are either somewhat generic such as *Red Five, Alpha 7,* and *Blue Leader,* or highly individualistic, and thus iconic such as *Starbuck, Apollo,* or *King of Hearts.* Ultimately, the dominant starship paradigm in most space-based sf series and films reflects an exclusively American, aeronautical legacy, and thus underscores the distinct nautical model maintained by *Star Trek.*

The bulk of *Star Trek* stories are set on independently cruising Starfleet ships and revolve around their fantastic encounters on the ocean of space. Though largely anchored at the eponymous space station, *ST:DS9* does not contradict the transatlantic wind and sail paradigm, but rather supports it by way of a carefully crafted maritime complement to the frigate-trope. *Deep Space Nine* is analogous to an exotic/colonial port whose commander has a small squadron of vessels at his disposal. Generally, space stations tend to be viewed as aberrations in that they inhibit dynamic, outward going space adventures. "[A]n awkward subject," Gary Westfahl has asserted, the space station "holds elements of both land and sea, of openness and closure … while the space station is necessarily a strange place in a strange location" (2009: 12–30).

A stationary locale could easily be regarded as a major departure from *Star Trek*'s transatlantic world of disguised sailing ships, especially since the show was described as "The Rifleman in space" (Dillard 152), and "Fort Laramie on the edge of the frontier" (Berman et al. 19). Producers purposefully mythologized Roddenberry's sales pitch for *ST:TOS* by recouping on its analogy in the 1990s. Since the frontier theme has little *literal* substance throughout *Star Trek,* a closer look at the narrative mechanics of *ST:DS9* becomes necessary. As delineated in the series bible, the station is made to fit into *Star Trek*'s *Rule Britannia* theme via more maritime analogies. Not only does the series offer a complement to the frigate-trope, but it is also conspicuously reminiscent of and compatible with the geographic setting and circumstances that Hornblower was confronted with later in his career. Even though critics labeled *ST:DS9* the most postmodern and most postcolonial of the *Star Trek* series,[11] it undoubtedly offers the most colonial setting. Located on the exotic, imperial fringes of the Federation, the station is an essential interstellar crossroads. Its immediate surroundings are much coveted and contested by the big powers in that the region. Since it has enormous economic and strategic value, Starfleet's commanding presence is to provide not only political and military stability, but also to facilitate the gradual assimilation of a local alien people, the Bajorans, into the Federation. The station is described as "the leading center of commerce and scientific exploration ... somewhere between a free port and a flea market" ("Star Trek DS9 Bible" 2–5). The port analogy stayed consistent throughout the series. It is particularly obvious when we look at the central space on the station—the Promenade. The seaside analog is aesthetically validated in that it extends to an upper level where the comings and goings of ships can be observed. Walking along the Promenade is reminiscent of walking along a dock or a pier.

As a port, *Deep Space Nine* is "bustling with aliens of all sorts when a ship's in," and there is "gambling and smuggling ... alien grifters at work here ... bars with sexual holosuites upstairs ... right next to traditional ship's stores, a Bajoran temple," and more (*ibid.*). Commander, later Captain Sisko is placed in charge of this station environment, holding equally broad political, diplomatic, and judicial powers as his fellow ship-bound captains. The port analogy bears considerable resemblance with Admiral Hornblower's posting in Kingston as Commander-in-Chief of the West Indies Station.[12] Located on the imperial fringes, the Indies were the most economically profitable region for the major powers of the Age of Sail. They were also a perpetual powder-keg throughout the 18th and early 19th century. Issues of naval *Realpolitik* shape the mission of both Hornblower and Sisko. Apart from trying to pursue Starfleet's mission of space exploration, *Deep Space Nine* is drawn into a series of volatile affairs that range from trade disputes and coup d'états of local alien governments to the hunt for Federation renegades. They culminate in the eruption of a full-scale interstellar war between established powers in that part of the galaxy and new invading forces from outside. Hornblower, much like Sisko, does not accomplish all of his exploits while staying in port. Being bound to a stationary locale is anathema to the central appeal of every sea story along with its narratological driving force. As admiral, we see Hornblower cruise the Caribbean on one of his squadron's vessels with HMS *Clorinda* serving as his flagship. Since Britain is at peace while Hornblower serves in the West Indies, he repeatedly laments the somewhat downscaled range of his command.[13] Journeys onboard ships facilitate adventures, encounters, and conflicts. Similar to the admiral, Sisko is initially assigned a complement of smaller mid-range vessels.[14] Later in the series, with local tensions rising, the captain takes command of a powerful vessel—the *Defiant*—as his flagship. Ultimately, *ST:DS9* consistently maintained *Star Trek*'s oceanic paradigm by oscillating between an exotic port setting on the colonial fringes of the imperial horizon, and semi-autonomous cruises on ships operating from the station within that particular region of space.

Following the rules of *Star Trek*'s worldbuilding, the entirety of outer space is discursively and, in part, also aesthetically constructed as an oceanic seascape. The starships' mode of propulsion offers a preliminary pointer not only because it harks back to the naval corpus, but also because it partially literalizes the metaphor of transposing the presumed romance of travel by wind and sail into space. Even though the fantastic faster-than-light (FTL) velocity achieved by a starship's *warp* drive has, at first glance, little in common with the infinitesimally slow speed of sailing ships, we can still establish a maritime analogy. Despite the fact that the term "warp" primarily refers to the deliberate distortion of normal space-time, it also bears the etymological residue of an old nautical term. The method of "warping out" a ship from port by means of ropes and cables is a mainstay in Napoleonic sea fiction; and the Hornblower novels are no exception.[15] Casting our discursive net wide yet again, reveals another nautical meaning which allows for the partial literalization of the "sailing ship in space" metaphor within *Star Trek*'s world of high-tech propulsion, theoretical physics and pseudo-scientific explanations. The nautical dictionary of wind and sail also relates the term "warp" to the natural force of wind; "Of wind, to toss or drive a ship violently around" (King 464). Even on the surface, we can juxtapose the volatile forces of wind, which can "warp" a ship along, with the tempestuous powers necessary to propel a starship faster than the speed of light.

Technological progress, especially steam technology, is viewed with an archetypal suspicion in sea novels. The engine is portrayed as an infernal intrusion since it destroys the presumed romance of wind propulsion, i.e., being moved by a natural rather than man-made force. Paradoxically, the powerful warp engine of a starship is used to partially literalize the "romance of sail"[16] with the help of theoretical physics. Invented by writers to enable them to tell stories across interstellar distances, the warp drive is a key sf novum and conceit in *Star Trek*. Even so, the way it supposedly works according to in-universe lore also helps to transpose part of the romance of sailing ships. The analogy is sufficiently simple so that a foray into theoretical physics and so-called *Treknobabble* pseudo-science is not necessary. The basic postulation for the warp drive states that once engaged, the starship does not actually move by its own power. Subspace is another essential element in this equation. *Star Trek* physics postulate that there is another natural medium, i.e., another dimension, undergirding normal space-time. The warp engine creates a "bubble" around the ship which not only temporarily lowers the "apparent mass of an object (with the relationship to the outside universe)" (Okuda 557), but also distorts, that is to say warps the boundaries between space and subspace. The "natural" medium of subspace then propels the starship, enveloped by the warp bubble, forward. In other words, it allows the ship "to ride a 'wave' of space and exceed the speed of light" (Leone 160). Once the bubble is furled, like sails, the ship slows down and stops. If they want to change course, they change the configuration, i.e., the subspace field harmonics of the bubble which is oddly reminiscent of tacking and trimming the canvas of a sailing ship. Though a high-tech machine, equipped with a powerful engine, a starship is not moved by an engine per se. Rather, like a sailing ship, its propulsion depends on the application of technology to harness a natural force. The natural force/medium itself remains unchanged, untampered, and thus uncontrollable. There are many subspace and even normal space phenomena which can seriously impede a starship's movements. Then again, a sailing ship was considered the most advanced and most complex piece of machinery during the Golden Age of Sail. It required large crews with technical skills to operate it. The naval analogy inherent in the warp drive also echoes an early condition set by Roddenberry to free starship travel from quaint contemporary contraptions—"I don't want to see any trails of fire. No streaks of smoke, no jet intakes, rocket exhaust, or anything like that" (qtd. Whitfield 69). Since starships are moved by a natural force, and thus partially literalize the romance of sailing ships, then the leap to acknowledge the fact that *Star Trek* rewrites outer space into a maritime environment remains but small.

"We can't be afraid of the wind": Star Trek's *Cosmic Ocean*

Space may be the "final frontier," but it is encoded in oceanic terms. Outer space is discursively likened to the only other space known to the human imagination that allows us to grasp the infinite vastness of starry realms—Earth's oceans. What is more, by literalizing the metaphor, *Star Trek*'s "ocean of space" takes on physical qualities of a maritime environment. As such, it also offers a habitat to a small yet distinctive population of space-dwelling creatures which are reminiscent of ocean-dwellers on Earth. *Star Trek*'s cosmic ocean also posits analogies to recognizable ritualized patterns of how sailors and their ships related to and interacted with other ocean bound spaces they encountered during their voyages.

Any claim that the physical, aesthetic, and conceptual qualities of outer space are of a distinct maritime nature, creates friction and dissonance with the dominant symbol of space as the "final frontier." The culturally charged metaphor of space as yet another frontier born out of President Kennedy's New Frontier politics extended only marginally beyond its rhetorical quality. Not only does the frontier actually not work as a metaphor for space on a conceptual level, but it also did not really inform the official discourse of the Space Race with the Soviets. Maritime metaphors and analogies shaped both the rhetorical and operational battle for America's supremacy in space exploration. President Kennedy himself used the sea and maritime exploration as reference points on a number of occasions.[17] Nautical metaphors were also much more common in the official communication of the administration as well as in NASA circles than any talk about space as a frontier. Howard McCurdy has found that it was especially "sea captains, who in centuries past crossed vast bodies of water to reach distant lands," that "played an important role in the promotion of space" (140). For example, astronaut Buzz Aldrin borrowed extensively from the Age of Sail to promote various of his space ventures. The same goes for one of the most influential NASA administrators, John C. Fletcher, who reminded people towards the end of the Space Race that "like Darwin, we have set sail upon an ocean: the cosmic sea of the Universe" (qtd. McCurdy 148). While these representative examples clearly expose a maritime undercurrent in the "final frontier" rhetoric, they do not necessarily explain why the sea generally serves as a conceptual analogy for space, especially in sf.

The significance of the sea as a metaphor for outer space can be reduced to a simple visual observation. When looked at from the surface of the open ocean, an observer's horizon typically extends to approximately one mile. "Perched in the rigging of a large ship," Dean King has noted, "a lookout might see the sails of a large ship at 20 miles" (1). Without having an object rise from and/or disappear below the horizon, however, which then belies the curvature of Earth's surface, the oceanic horizon looks very much the same regardless of the height one could occupy on an ocean bound vessel. In short, from an observer's point of view, the sea seems to bleed into the sky, offering a conceptual bridge between two spaces that could not be any more different from each other. Robert Foulke has emphasized the relatively unchanging "attitudes toward the unstable ocean that mirrors an equally mutable sky" (7). He points to how humanity has been visually conditioned for millennia. Whenever we behold the oceanic horizon, it presents itself in a dialectic relationship with the sky; the horizon marks a clear boundary which at the same time seems to be connected to the sky—the boundary blurs particularly well at night. Consequently, without any direct access to the sky and the space beyond, philosophers, scholars, and theoreticians tended to project the natural conditions of the environments they knew onto spaces yet unreached and on the conditions that might be found there. The process of associative comparison formed the conceptual basis of various "ether theories" that shaped natural philosophy, especially cosmology and physics, until roughly the late 19th century.

In the course of human history, ether cosmologies produced a wealth of proto-sf stories which center on voyages into ethereal realms. The protagonists travelled on ships that were largely analogous to oceangoing vessels. In their fantastic encounters, they also maintained a distinct similitude with maritime environments known to people on Earth. Such works range from Lucian of Samosata's *True History* (2nd century CE), Johannes Kepler's *Somnium* (1634), and Christiaan Huygens's *Cosmotheoros* (1698), all the way to the scientific romances of the *fin de siècle* and beyond. In short, this is how the Earth's oceans and modes of maritime transportation have entered the popular imagination, and especially sf worldbuilding. They are arguably the most meaningful analogies for the realities found in outer space. Gary Westfahl has asserted that space as a frontier is "unsatisfactory," when "writers have traditionally fallen back on ... the metaphor of space as a vast ocean" (2009: 32).

In a second season episode of *ST:TOS*, Captain Kirk quotes John Masefield's poem "Sea-Fever" (1902) to draw a validating parallel between interstellar travel and sea voyages in the past. He concludes that "even if you take away the wind and the water, it's still the same."[18] The intertextual reference betrays the constant discursive practice of referring to space in maritime terms that complements *Star Trek*'s extensive borrowing from the nautical dictionary. What it also points to is space being more than a mere passive backdrop when, in fact, it is a rather active force which, like in most sea stories, has to be reckoned with. In the same vein, Captain Picard, upon learning that he and his crew are sent on a mission into a potentially hostile part of space without adequate information, states: "It seems as though we're truly sailing into the unknown."[19] Similarly, at the launch ceremony of the *Enterprise NX-01*, Admiral Forrest (Vaughn Armstrong) sends the ship and its crew on their way with the following comment: "For nearly a century, we've waded ankle-deep in the ocean of space. Now it's finally time to swim."[20] Later in the same episode, the literalized qualities of *Star Trek*'s cosmic ocean are highlighted again when the ship's helmsman draws the captain's attention to the fact that they might encounter rough weather along their course.

MAYWEATHER: I'm reading an ion storm on that trajectory, sir. Should I go around it?
ARCHER: We can't be afraid of the wind, Ensign. Take us to warp four.

While trying to figure out a technical problem, *Voyager*'s self-proclaimed morale officer and ship's cook, Neelix (Ethan Phillips), recalls a time when he "lost a warp nacelle going through a dark matter nebula ... it sent out a dark matter bow wave."[21] Such references represent the discursive norm for how characters give meaning to space. While Archer's reference to wind and Neelix's comment about waves in the vacuum of space may easily be dismissed as empty metaphors, most space phenomena encountered by the crews of Starfleet literalize at least part of the metaphoric qualities inherent in the "ocean of space." This happens in the vein of how the ocean usually functions in sea stories both in literature and in film. As Robert Foulke reminds us "the maritime environment itself can be agent, enemy and arbiter" (10).

Maritime space weather phenomena feature throughout the *Star Trek* continuum. They were already encoded in the worldbuilding rules right from the beginning in the form of aesthetic conceits. These range from equipping the vacuum of space with a soundscape of various swooshing sounds to the fallacious assumption that space is largely not empty. They help to foster cognition and familiarity on part of the audience along distinct nautical lines.[22] These conceits draw on quintessential realities found in a seaborne world. "That world reverses many physical ... realities," like Foulke has noted, since "at sea, motion is imposed upon them, with temporary but debilitating effects" (8). Moreover, the way how ships and crews react to weather phenomena in space follows patterns of behavior and rituals found in sea fiction. The visualization of these phenomena also displays a strong maritime similitude.

In *Star Trek*'s oceanic paradigm, maritime weather and the effects it has on ships can be grouped together roughly along two lines. There are phenomena that affect the movement and stability of vessels. Others either impair sensory vision/detection, or facilitate concealment. The bulk of *Star Trek*'s space weather amounts to manifestations of different storms and the various phenomena that accompany them, like maelstroms, currents, wave fronts, waterspouts, and interstellar fog—i.e., nebulae of different extent and composition. If a starship crew finds itself unable to navigate around a storm, they decide to weather the phenomenon. Not only do the visual and physical aesthetics of such encounters recall the vivid descriptions of storms in sea fiction,[23] but the ritualized patterns of how the crew rides out the storms bear a residual maritime imprint. Space storms often take the shape of large, rolling wave fronts as well as obscure and looming cloud-like formations. When entered, they expose a ship to the shearing forces of currents, particle winds, and electromagnetic discharges.

Even though the audience rarely sees a storm in *ST:TOS*, their effects were still felt on the ship; and the crew repeatedly discussed or referred to the aftermath of phenomena they encountered. In one of the first episodes, the crew learns about the fate of the starship *Valiant*, which was swept off course and ultimately destroyed after encountering a magnetic storm. On another occasion, while trying to return to the ship before becoming trapped by an ion storm, Kirk and his landing party are accidentally transported into a parallel universe. After having lost a crewman in yet another ion storm—which seems to be the most common type—the captain is court-martialed, facing charges of negligence. Even though the storm is not shown, the crew's testimonials take the form of flashbacks which show the bridge crew being tossed around.[24] While there are many storms in *ST:TNG*, one particular phenomenon underscores both the maritime qualities of outer space as well as the approximated two-dimensionality that governs starship aesthetics. In a second season episode, the *Enterprise* encounters a disruption in the space-time continuum which is rendered in the form of a maelstrom that literally sucks the ship from its plane of normal space. The image is reminiscent of an ocean-going vessel about to sink.[25] Even though *Deep Space Nine* is a stationary habitat, it still weathers violent space conditions in an explicitly marked nautical fashion. When a violent plasma storm makes it necessary to evacuate the station, Doctor Bashir (Alexander Siddig) secures his duty station stating: "I've struck the sails and battened the hatches."[26] What may seem as a mere idiomatic expression actually has actually deep etymological roots in the Age of Sail. Sailors used to strap tarpaulin over the gratings of hatchways, fixing it with thin pieces of wood—so-called *battens*—to prevent water from filling the lower decks. As *Deep Space Nine* is enveloped by the ever intensifying storm, the station is also shaken and rattled.

The procedure of battening down the hatches also points to a recurring trope in sea stories which is transposed wholesale into space. Prolonged periods of bad weather meant that a sailing ship was steered small and close-reefed in order to ride out the storm. The crew that was not needed on deck retreated deeper into the ship, occupying themselves with various activities. In *Star Trek*, this maritime trope usually takes the form of "bottle shows," i.e., episodes that take place only on the ship or the station, respectively. Usually trapped by space weather phenomena, the crew closes down all unnecessary operations. They then begin to focus inward while they wait until they can proceed with their routine activities. Retreating inward usually intensifies the social dynamics of these isolated and self-contained communities of spacefarers. For example, regions like the Void or the Barrens can be understood as the outer space equivalents of *doldrums*. Upon entering the Void, Commander Chakotay (Robert

Beltran) observes that "it's like being becalmed in the middle of the ocean,"[27] as his captain faces archetypal doubts over her command abilities.

While *Deep Space Nine* may not encounter as many storms as the vessels and crews of the other series, it is located in the vicinity of one of the most volatile and unpredictable regions on the cosmic ocean—the Badlands. They are perpetually harassed by plasma storms which are visualized as funnel-shaped, fiery columns reminiscent of waterspouts in both form and effect. Navigation is very difficult and fraught with danger. The region is also reminiscent of the difficulties involved in rounding Cape Horn, which represents a mainstay in sea novels, in that the Badlands, much like the Horn, are an obstacle to space travel. Additionally, the Badlands are invested with semi-mysterious qualities which recall the singular status of the Bermuda Triangle in maritime lore. Ships are frequently beaten off course, lost and even destroyed with all hands by powerful currents and eddies. It was also in the Badlands where a massive shockwave swept up starship *Voyager* and hurled it 75,000 light years away from home. Spacefaring sailors encounter a few other regions on the ocean of space that present similar maritime challenges and obstacles such as the Delphic Expanse, the Briar Patch, and the Nekrit Expanse.

Starfleet ships encounter a great many nebulae, which form the second group of maritime phenomena in space. Most are akin to "space fog" in terms of both physical and aesthetic qualities as well as narrative function. Before modern navigational technologies, such as GPS, sonar, and RADAR, fog represented an ominous obstacle to sailors. History is replete with examples of ships getting lost and running aground in foggy conditions, or enemy ships, concealed by fog, waiting to strike. An established *topos* in Napoleonic sea fiction, fog is used as a recurring plot device. Since there were no adequate means of maintaining sensory contact with a ship once it had entered a fog bank, it becomes either a hiding place to escape from an enemy, or a staging ground which offered a tactical advantage for an attack.[28] The fact that fog reduces the relatively simple sensory capabilities available to sailors in the past gives us yet another meaningful key for understanding how *Star Trek*'s oceanic paradigm is actually based on the 18th century naval world. If a more contemporary naval model had been used, there would always have to be some sort of infrared, RADAR or sonar device that allows the spacefarers to "see" even in bad space weather; after all, fog does not represent the same kind of danger and obstacle to modern ships as it did to vessels in the past. Even though Starfleet ships are equipped with powerful sensor technology, their sensory capabilities are usually hampered and/or rendered completely useless whenever they enter a nebula. Despite their high-tech gadgets, we see the future spacefarers re-enact naval modes of navigation which are clearly reminiscent of a pre-high-tech age. The

Star Trek continuum is replete with examples where it becomes necessary for starships to hide from overpowering forces, often licking their wounds after a failed engagement.[29] Conversely, both friendly and enemy ships, even entire fleets, sometimes use "space fog" as a staging area.[30]

Hic sunt dracones

Not only is the "ocean of space" metaphor literalized in that it assumes physical and aesthetic qualities of a maritime environment, but said environment is also populated by space-dwelling creatures. Far from a lifeless void, *Star Trek*'s cosmic ocean teems with life forms which explicitly resemble a specific range of creatures both in looks and behavior. Some of these creatures also draw on the sense of wonder and awe attributed to their ocean-bound archetypes found in maritime lore. Cetaceans serve as the most popular model for so-called "space whales." The crew of *ST:TNG* encounters more than one such creature. On one occasion, they accidentally kill a space whale that was about to give birth. They perform a cesarean and are able to save the youngling, which in turn attaches itself to the ship, thinking the *Enterprise* is its mother. As it begins to drain the ship's power, the crew manages to wean it, leaving it to join a pod of its species. In another episode, the crew attempts to establish first contact with a creature called Gomtuu, which turns out to be a large organic spaceship. The sounds heard on the interior of the creature were drawn from whale songs. Ultimately, the special ambassador assigned to the *Enterprise* for this mission decides to join with Gomtuu thereby alleviating the suffering and loneliness felt by both. A man occupying the bowels of a "space whale" clearly plays on the biblical image of Jonah. The crews of the original *Enterprise* and *Voyager* also encounter cetacean creatures in space. They serve as plot devices for retellings of Herman Melville's *Moby Dick* (1851).[31] In its first season, the *Discovery* encounters a Gormagander; labeled a "space whale" by the crew, they follow Starfleet regulations and initiate a rescue and relocation protocol before they learn that it harbors an unwelcome passenger.[32]

There are other ocean-dwelling species that also provide contours for the creatures encountered on the starry seas. Unbeknownst to the crew of *Deep Space Nine*, the hatching process of what ultimately turns out to be a spaceborne species threatens to destroy the station. Once catastrophe is averted, the entity metamorphoses into its final form, resembling a luminescent stingray. On another occasion, two senior officers encounter a squid-shaped creature. It turns out to be a shapeshifter who belongs to the same race as the station's constable. Similarly, *Voyager* encounters a large swarm of squid-like creatures. When the ship accidentally interferes with their mating ritual, one particular creature mistakes *Voyager* for a sexual rival. *Star Trek*'s cosmic ocean teems with even more exotic creatures. On their very first mission, the crew of *ST:TNG* encounters and helps to free a spaceborne entity that looks like a gigantic jellyfish. Perhaps one of the most exotic species ever encountered by Starfleet resembles a bioluminescent creature of the deep. The crew of the original *Enterprise* discovers a single-cell organism which they label "space amoeba."[33] All these creatures command a sense of wonder and awe mixed with apprehension and danger. They capitalize on the rich tradition of sea monsters found in preindustrial seafaring cultures. These fantastic creatures thus serve to recall the inscription *hic sunt dracones* (trans. "here be dragons") found on maps and globes in the past.

"Standard orbit": Cosmic Bays and Beaches

When we explore the partially literalized metaphor of the "ocean of space" to its fullest extent, then we find that there are key spaces other than the sea that serve as maritime correlatives. These spaces represent the various stages that it takes for spacefaring sailors to interface with the shores of the cosmic ocean. They allow us to draw distinct analogies with the exploration of what was considered the "final frontier" in the 18th century—the Pacific. Whether mariners landed on a large landmass or on a group of small islands, there are certain spaces that functioned as nodes of access, interface, and meaning between the sea and the shore—the *bay* and the *beach*. Star systems, planetary orbits, and a planet's surface serve as correlative locales for these quintessential maritime spaces. Though estranged, mediated, and facilitated by sf's technological trappings, the patterns of interfacing with the cosmic shores are reminiscent of voyages of discovery.

While the ocean can function as both a facilitating as well as an obstructive entity in sea fiction, it ultimately serves one purpose—seafarers need to traverse it so that they can arrive at those places they seek. Even though the exploration of space phenomena is also part of Starfleet's mission, it is, however, "the strange new worlds" and the "new civilizations" which lure the spacefaring sailors. "The professionals of the sea take its hazards and its beauties for granted," as Jonathan Raban has observed, but for "them the land is always full of interest ... its affairs merit description" (5). Consequently, *Star Trek*'s cosmic ocean stands in an inseparable dialectic relationship with its cosmic shores. Moreover, the correlative spaces in its oceanic paradigm—the bays and beaches in outer space—are reminiscent of the maritime realities that were distinctive of voyages into the Pacific. The wealth of scholarly work on Captain Cook's three voyages, and his interactions with the different spaces and peoples he encountered, offers meaningful models to further accentuate *Star Trek*'s oceanic paradigm. After all, Cook also served as a key character component in the archetypal make-up of the Starfleet captain.

Interactions with these correlative spaces roughly follow three recurring stages. Since space serves as an analog for the sea, planetary systems can then be understood as island groups or archipelagoes in space that appear on the horizons of the explorers. During the Age of Sail, the sighting of land, whether it was the coastline of a continent or a small group of islands, was a moment invested with great significance and anticipation. This was particularly the case when a ship had spent long weeks at sea without making any landfall. It was a moment of cautious excitement as well as rational observation.[34] Once land had been sighted, mariners proceeded to make preliminary observations with regards to its location and general features, followed by orders to make preparations for landfall. The process of sighting land from a distance, and at the same time establishing one's own position in relation to it, is maintained in the way how planetary systems appear on the starry horizon of the spacefaring sailors. While many star systems are discovered and sighted for the first time, Starfleet also navigates to places which are already on their star charts. There are innumerable examples of the "technological lookout," i.e., the ship's sensors, detecting planetary systems at varying distances. Once detected, the helmsman/navigator reports to the captain and provides a basic description of the system. For example:

> DATA: Long range sensors detect a T-tauri type star within a pocket of the Ngame cloud.
>
> PICARD: Well, there's nothing unusual about that.
>
> DATA: No, sir. However, the star's single planet falls within the M-class range. It is capable of supporting life.[35]

Once the final destination is reached—for sailors this could be a port, a specific island or a particular stretch of coastline whereas for Starfleet's intrepid explorers this usually means a certain planet, or perhaps a starbase—the next stage of interfacing with the land begins.

Finding a safe place to anchor, usually a safe bay, was the main goal for mariners. There, they would, among other things, take soundings and begin to observe the most pertinent geographic and geological features from a closer vantage point. They would attempt to draw preliminary conclusions about the potential resources they might find, and try to ascertain whether or not the island was inhabited.[36] The planetary orbit is the outer space correlative of the bay. The fact that the main vessels in *Star Trek* usually do not land on a planet's surface allows for the direct comparison between a planetary orbit and a bay. Starting with the pitch for *ST:TOS*, Roddenberry repeatedly noted that the "Cruiser will stay in space orbit" (10). A so-called "standard orbit" provides safe anchorage for the starship where the crew performs ritualized forms of observation, relying on their high-tech equivalents of telescopes. They scan for life signs, both sentient and non-sentient, geological formations, mineral deposits, tectonic activity, energy signatures, and more. In the episode "The Chase," once the *Enterprise* is in standard orbit of the planet Ruah Four, Data reports it as being "a class–M planet. Sixty seven percent of its surface is covered with water. Its landmass contains multiple animal species, including a genus of proto-hominids." The captain then asks for a scan to determine if there are "earthworks or monuments that might indicate a previous civilization." Data determines that no evidence points to "even a primitive culture" having lived there.[37] There are a few notable exceptions to the rule that starships are not supposed to land on a planet's surface. By far the most common way for a larger vessel to touch down on a planet takes the form of a signature trope in sea voyage narratives—the shipwreck. A type of "immobilization ... shipwrecks and disasters in coastal regions," provide riveting material for stories, as Robert Foulke has opined, "perhaps because at those dramatic moments the power and danger of the sea impinge upon the imagination of land dwellers" (12).

A handful of episodes and movies tap into the narrative power of the shipwreck, and we see ships run afoul of the cosmic shores. The unfortunate vessels rarely disintegrate when they enter the atmosphere. Once they crash on the planet's surface, they are irreparably damaged in the process and potential survivors are then forced to abandon the hulk of the ship.[38] In the portentously named *ST:DS9* episode "Rocks and Shoals" (6 Oct 1997), the metaphor of the cosmic shipwreck becomes literalized. Captain Sisko and his crew commandeer an enemy vessel for a mission. Their ship is badly damaged in the process and they crash-land on a nearby planet. They actually crash into the sea, their ship sinks and the survivors wash ashore on a rocky beach, temporarily marooned on the planet. Similarly, *Voyager* crashes on an icy planet after having unsuccessfully attempted to navigate a different dimension of space. They become stuck in the ice and freeze up.[39] The scenario and setting invite a comparison with those unfortunate Arctic explorers whose ships were also caught in the ice, like the Franklin-Expedition (1845). Even so, barring any major disaster, planetary orbits—*Star Trek*'s cosmic bays—offer a safe anchorage and a place where spacefarers observe, scan, and survey.

Since not all observations, neither in the past nor in the future, can be conducted from the safety of the ship, sending shore parties to the surface of the planet provides access to the last correlative space in the oceanic paradigm—

the beach. Cultural historians and anthropologists contributed a lot to making this space one of the most closely scrutinized locales.[40] For maritime explorers, the beach was arguably the most important sense-making space. It was "the interface between the voyagers and the shore, islands, rivers, hills and forests," which, for example, "so concerned Cook and Banks" (Lambert 247). In essence, the Pacific beaches of the 18th century were a maritime frontier space. They were the places where highly ritualized encounters of cultural power and hierarchy took place. They facilitated negotiations of meaning and knowledge, triggered conflicts, and invited a general sense of wonder. In the same vein, a planet's surface, i.e., the landing zone of the so-called "away team," fulfills the function of a cosmic beach. Shore parties land either in a small shuttle craft, or, for reasons of narrative expediency, they beam down using the transporter. Setting their encounters into a maritime perspective, Roddenberry believed that "infinite space promises just as much life and adventure as our own oceans ... where you could open the door of a spaceship, step out on the planet surface, and breathe fresh air. Just as bold men once discovered and subdued new continents here on Earth" (qtd. Whitfield 178). The diverse reasons for making landfall on a planet are unmistakably reminiscent of the romanticized and thus culturally distorted activities and interactions of explorer-heroes. It serves to remember that they traversed the oceans to contribute to imperial projects.[41] The landing on and interaction with the cosmic beaches is a major recurring trope that is maintained throughout the entire *Star Trek* continuum without any significant deviation. The cosmic beaches are places of contact, conflict, and negotiation. The interactions between the spacefaring sailors and the natural environment, and particularly with the many permutations of the "alien Other," also point to how *Star Trek*'s world resembles that of the 18th century; they point to the ideologies of colonialism and the *Zeitgeist* of the Enlightenment which were re-imagined in *Star Trek*'s maritime milieu—its fifth maritime dimension.

For now, the correlative spaces of the bay and the beach, along with the schemata of nautical traditions they help sustain, serve to secure the comprehensive charting of *Star Trek*'s oceanic paradigm. It clearly transcends the boundaries of mere metaphor while it also contributes the final segment to *Star Trek*'s operational naval corpus which is espoused by the first two maritime dimensions. They encompass a set of discourses and visual aesthetics which together point to *Star Trek*'s continuous acknowledgment of a transatlantic heritage, merging contemporary U.S. Navy surfaces with a historio-mythical Royal Navy core. In the 1951 film adaptation of the first three Hornblower novels, the captain (Gregory Peck) muses about the dialectic relationship between the ocean, the act of sailing, and the starry sky with Lady Barbara (Virginia Mayo).

LADY BARBARA: How beautiful the stars are tonight. It's as though we were sailing the heavens instead of the sea.

HORNBLOWER: Well, in a way, we are. We steer from star to star rather than from land to land.[42]

The transpositional jump from sailing the Seven Seas on Earth to traversing the cosmic ocean is but small for *Star Trek*'s "Hornblowers in space." Even so, the modes of how space travel is made analogous to sea voyages, and how they are discursively sustained by a rich naval corpus, do not yet reveal the naval genealogy of those who do the sailing, especially those who are in command.

6. "Captain's prerogative"
Star Trek's *Hornblowers in Space*

The principal Starfleet captains are *not* space cowboys regardless of the family ancestry that some of them lay claim to. When Captain Kirk tries to understand why a group of aliens, intent on probing humanity's moral limits, has his away team re-enact the gunfight at the O.K. Corral, he concludes that it must be because his "ancestors pioneered the American frontier."[1] *Star Trek,* however, only sparingly refers to and/or literalizes the myth of the American West this explicitly. Such instances are the exception, indeed an aberration, rather than the rule.[2] Even so, the deceiving significance of the frontier, as a theme, has not prevented a number of critics from reading the central character in *Star Trek* as a cowboy-type, Cooperesque/Wisterian frontier hero.[3] While not entirely incompatible with the archetypal frontier hero, the historical and fictional models that served as reference points for the archetype of the captain bespeak a different, distinctively naval *and* British origin. Already in the first pitch for *ST:TOS,* Roddenberry introduced the starship captain as a "space-age Captain Horation [sic] Hornblower" (5). Making the archetypal Starfleet captain also a descendant of "similar [naval] men in the past (Drake, Cook, Bougainville and Scott)," he made it fairly clear that "the leading man and central character," was anything but a simple space cowboy.

Nowhere is the maritime endowment provided by the myth of the British Golden Age of Sail more visible than in the archetypal make-up of *Star Trek*'s principal Starfleet captains. They slip into the role of the sentimental Royal Navy officer/hero of the Romantic period. Theirs is a Hornblower-type of heroism that shares and conflates a specific set of traits and behaviors with two of the quintessential representatives of maritime military might and maritime exploration—Horatio Nelson and James Cook. Horatio Hornblower is himself but a fictional permutation of romanticized British naval heroes such as Nelson,

Edward Pellew, and Thomas Cochrane. Consequently, Starfleet captains are agents of an imperial enterprise. Benign, enlightened, and disinterested as they might profess it to be, they are still the genealogical descendants of who Joseph Conrad labeled the "fathers of militant geography" (qtd. O'Sullivan 99). Their portrayal, however, is mostly devoid of any postcolonial accusations and/or revisioning. After all, the "Hornblowers in space" are modeled only on the romanticized personae of their naval ancestors and do not necessarily draw on historical realities.

A telling descriptor will help us illustrate both, the vast range of functions that British naval officers fulfilled as Enlightenment mariners, and how they became condensed into the character of the Starfleet captain. In the movie adaptation of Patrick O'Brian's novel *The Far Side of the World* (1984), a young midshipman muses about the compatibility of military duty and scientific inquiry; they are embodied by the protagonists, Captain Jack Aubrey (Russell Crowe) and the ship's surgeon, Stephen Maturin (Paul Bettany), respectively. The officer-trainee resolves that he could pursue both and become "a sort of ... fighting naturalist."[4] Similarly, "Hornblower in space" is television shorthand for describing a process of adaptation and extrapolation which resulted in Starfleet captains acting as "fighting naturalists" on the cosmic oceans and beaches. Roddenberry used Hornblower as a paradigmatic blueprint to craft the archetypal Starfleet captain by conflating in him the mythologized qualities of the two most widely remembered naval officers of that time. The Hornblower archetype holds true for all principal Starfleet captains regardless of ethnicity or gender. After all, they all are interstellar masters and commanders as much as they are spaceborne naturalists and scientists.

Palmam qui meruit ferat

Found on his coat of arms,[5] Horatio Nelson's family motto acts as a leitmotif for understanding a military service, in which—despite all class restrictions—men of modest, even impoverished circumstances could elevate their social status by their own merit. This was definitely true for Nelson and Cook, who both excelled in their profession as versatile maritime agents of an imperial project; the former exhibited considerable zeal and desire for command, and the latter professional ambition and intrepidity. The Georgian Navy is popularly imagined and remembered as one of the few professional institutions where advancement by merit was possible in an otherwise vertically ossified social world. As such, it provided the backdrop for the coming-of-age formula that has informed the large majority of sea novels since the early 19th century.

They speak to the opportunity of moving from before the mast to the quarterdeck, and in rare cases—as happened with Hornblower—even gain a peerage. Enlightened humanists, the Cook(s) and Nelson(s) in history and in fiction oscillate between acknowledging the worth of individuals and imposing discipline on those under their command.

Men like Nelson and Cook were perceived and remembered by their peers as well as the popular imagination as different from many of their contemporaries in that they appeared to be fairer and more humane in an otherwise brutal seaborne world. The trust they inspired among those who were under their command fostered early precursors of modern command culture. They allowed for clear communication, delegation of responsibilities, and suggestions from their subordinates.[6] Nelsonian heroes were subsequently mythologized into the embodiment of British Romantic sentiment and became idolized and idealized British gentlemen. Though acknowledging historical inaccuracies and contradictions that framed the myths of Nelson and Cook, our character study of Starfleet captains is largely informed by the most popular and thus widely remembered representations of the naval heroes and their fictional descendants. Early on, they emerged in elegies, paintings, monuments, songs, and theater productions. Nurtured chiefly by influential biographers and editors, their works served as basis for writers, advertisers, and filmmakers.[7] Most of these texts illustrate a composite character, i.e., the Enlightenment mariner, who embodies a set of characteristics and behavioral patterns. Forester then conceived Horatio Hornblower in the same vein.

In the immediate aftermath of his death at Trafalgar, Nelson was immediately mythologized, leading to his apotheosis which, in turn, made him the "first British 'pop hero'" (White 68). Two hundred years of fictional representations saw many, including C.S. Forster, contribute to the Nelson myth. In his biography of the hero, *Nelson* (1929), Forester asserted that the many inconsistencies and incongruities of the gallant naval warrior were due to an invisible psychological struggle. His internal fight with self-doubt and self-criticism became one of the distinguishing features of Hornblower (and of Starfleet captains). Forester's Nelson, however, was but one articulation of the imagined admiral. His first biographer, Robert Southey, furnished the main model for the Nelson myth which has since been reiterated in umpteenth permutations. Southey depicted Nelson as "checked by piety and humanity," displaying "interest in, and care for, his subordinates," as well as "constancy in his friendships and agreeable personal manners," and "professional ability" (Czisnik 87). What is more, he portrayed Nelson as "lovable as well as admirable," and created the impression that readers "would vicariously enjoy being under his command" (Fulford 173). While bold and courageous, he was neither fearless nor rash.

His focus on professional achievement and success freed Nelson to rely on his own judgment when making decisions. He is famously remembered for "turning a blind eye" to, or rather interpreting his superiors' orders critically, on a number of occasions.[8] It would be too convenient to interpret his actions as acts of mere disobedience. Nelson followed the Kantian maxim *sapere aude* in that he did not follow orders blindly. Instead, he weighed local circumstances, complexities, and exigencies, and then decided on a course of action that would likely lead to a successful outcome. The naval hero's propensity to interpret and even exceed his orders is a trait that he also shares with Captain Cook. Since Hornblower is cast in the same archetypal mold, it is not difficult to imagine that this kind of behavior became a mainstay in *Star Trek*. It is the exception rather than the rule when Starfleet captains do not "interpret" their orders. As Captain Picard tells Data (Brent Spiner), Starfleet officers should not simply "blindly follow orders"; they are expected to be able to evaluate each situation before acting.[9]

Nelson's ambition and professional zeal were driven neither by fear nor by an excessive lust for power beyond his own command. While his knowledge of Shakespeare amounted to little more than "a few half-remembered quotations" (Harris 188), Nelson adopted the language of *Henry V*, especially his St. Crispin's Day speech, to articulate a precursor of modern-day command culture—the famed Nelson Touch. He established a rapport of mutual trust, clear communication, and protective paternalism with his officers—his "band of brothers." It allowed him to successfully execute tactics and plans which were often viewed as unorthodox. Even though Nelson did not openly speak out against, let alone try to change the brutality that governed the Georgian Navy, this particular portrayal added considerably to his perceived difference in being more humane and fairer. Since Nelson is commonly remembered as someone who did not crave excessive power, he is also not invested with any significant political ambitions—another key characteristic of the Enlightenment mariner. Instead of using his military success to enter politics, like many of his contemporaries (Cochrane, Pellew, and Arthur Wellesley, the 1st Duke of Wellington), Nelson is usually cast as someone who presented himself as a dutiful albeit vain servant. In sea novels, once the protagonist achieves a certain level of success—usually the captaincy/an independent command—he becomes weary of further advancement. Hornblower feels similarly about his knighthood, various honorary titles, and even his peerage. Starfleet captains then take it even a step further in that they despise and/or actively resist promotion to any rank higher than that of captain.

The persona of Captain James Cook, as entertained in the popular imagination, is also a product of a mythologizing process more than two hundred years in the making. The archetypal naval explorer bears considerable similarity with the archetypal naval warrior. Cook is commonly remembered as "a legendary figure, a hero of the Enlightenment, who was said to have brought civilization to the Pacific," as well as "a master voyager who journeyed to unknown places, a seeker of knowledge" (O'Sullivan 1). A benign and benevolent commander and discoverer, Cook shows a noticeable degree of introspection that points to the tendency of imbuing Enlightenment mariners with a troubled psyche. The dominant image of him as military explorer and emissary of western civilization can largely be traced to the works of two men. John Hawkesworth, editor of the journals of Cook's first voyage, turned the explorer into a mainstay in Victorian sea fiction aimed at young boys. Even though New Zealand historian John Beaglehole produced the most thoroughly researched biography of Cook to date, he still depicted the captain in the vein of Hawkesworth. He historicized him as "a heroic figure who surmounted every kind of difficulty to achieve remarkable ends," as O'Sullivan has argued, and "who seldom puts a foot wrong" (51). Much like Nelson and his fictional descendants, Cook goes to great lengths when contemplating his decisions. Not only does he justify them to himself, but he also aims at vindicating his actions in the eyes of his superiors.

The Captain Cook of popular culture is essentially a working class hero. Defining himself through his vocation, he achieved his rise from the ranks to a command position largely by his own merit. He excelled at hydrographic surveys, seamanship, and navigation. As an archetype, he is, however, beset by obsessive meticulousness. Cook quickly developed a profound sense of judgment based in part on necessity and the exigencies encountered on long-distance voyages. Given his long service as a mariner before he embarked on his three Pacific voyages, he drew on a wealth of experience. Consequently, he developed a command style and stance on how to "interpret" orders similar to Nelson's. In a letter to a young French explorer, he stated: "I maintain that someone who only obeys orders will never make a name for himself as a discoverer" (qtd. O'Sullivan 11). Cook is portrayed as displaying a distinct propensity to go beyond the purview of his orders. For example, instead of simply ascertaining the existence of *Terra Australis Incognita,* as specified in his orders, he went ahead and claimed the entire east coast of Australia for the British Crown as soon as he had concluded that it must be the mysterious southern continent. In polemic terms, Cook is commonly represented as an over-achiever.

While the parameters of Cook's missions differed vastly from Nelson's, their command culture and command style was fairly similar. The meritocratic James Cook of the popular imagination has a reasonably lucid understanding of how to handle his officers, his crew, and the supernumeraries who accompany him. Preceding Nelson coining the "band of brothers" paradigm, Cook documented a number of instances where he consulted with his officers on how to proceed at various junctures of his voyages; for example, he did so after completing a survey of New Zealand's entire coastline, or after running aground in the Great Barrier Reef.[10] Even though the explorer cultivated a sterner and more taciturn image on his second and third voyage, his command style still allowed for the delegation of responsibility and cooperative decision-making. Cook is also presented as a much respected, even revered figure especially by a group of midshipmen and master's mates. He nurtured future officers such as George Vancouver, James Cornett, George Dixon, and William Bligh. The trials and tribulations of growing into a command position are one of the recurring tropes in the coming-of-age formula found in most sea novels. Once again Hornblower makes a case in point since he also nurtures a number of subordinates over the years by including them into his decision-making process and by delegating responsibility to them. The fact that we see all principal Starfleet captains taking one, sometimes two of their junior officers under their wings points at the continuation of this trope in *Star Trek*. James Cook is also portrayed as an exception in his display of below-average cruelty and above-average benevolence and patience towards his crew and the many indigenous peoples he came in contact with. It goes without saying that his image is grossly distorted since Cook was usually compared to his Spanish predecessors and French contemporaries both of which were made to appear more barbaric and avaricious. Cook, however, was as much a vector of imperial power projection as other explorers; and the British imperial enterprise was anything but benign. Nevertheless, ever since his death at the hands of an indigenous Hawaiian in 1779, the captain has been eulogized as "the mild hero," and "the emissary of 'humanity'" (Williams 67).

It is beyond doubt that Cook as well as Nelson were floating agents of the British Empire. Both were vectors of power projection; one surveyed and took possession of alien places, while the other defended British interests and sentiments against a continental tyranny. While embodying two distinct yet interrelated fields, the way both are commonly remembered and represented in popular culture makes it clear that they share many characteristics as romanticized, sentimental naval heroes. Even though this is taken from Michelangiolo Gianetti's *Elogio del capitano Giacomo Cook* (1785), the following passage serves as an adequate shorthand for the composite naval warrior/explorer character—"'A Hero,' at once sailor warrior and philosopher, who displayed the qualities of magnanimity, enterprise and tranquility" (qtd. Williams 70). In other words, this amalgam of characteristics merges "chivalry, courage, and fraternal solidarity with the sensibility of attachment to home [the ship] and family [the crew]" (Harris 205). Continuous mythologization and fictionalization turned the British Enlightenment mariner into a floating archetype. He achieved a life in his own right and became detachable from historical actualities and yet remain tethered to the myth of British Golden Age of Sail. Even so, he became sufficiently disentangled from any one particular national discourse so that he could be transferred across imagined cultural borders. He was pulled out of the transatlantic imaginarium by C.S. Forester and sent on his way in the form of Hornblower, who, in turn, found himself cast loose again on the ocean of space.

"The man alone": A Transatlantic Hero Heads into Space

Hornblower is undoubtedly one of those fictional characters who have transcended the imagined boundaries of fiction and history. He is "one of the exceedingly great creatures of the imagination who escape," as Sanford Sternlicht has argued, "from the world of art to an independent reality established by and in the mind of the public, like a Hamlet or a Sherlock Holmes or a Kilroy" (15–6). He assumed a blatantly historical existence as the best-known naval captain in 20th century literature. Not only was Hornblower cast in the romanticized Nelsonian mold, but also minted with personal imprints of his creator—a man who lived a transatlantic life. Thus, he also assumed a transatlantic existence in the imagination of the Anglo-American cultural continuum. For example, in a potent symbolic act, Forester decided that July 4, 1776, would be his hero's date of birth. Even the hero's name is a product of transatlantic coalescence. The name Hornblower derived from Forester's producer in Hollywood—Arthur Hornblow, Jr. However, the author never gave any additional details. The narratological complexity and thus significance of the hero's given name is more notable. Forester chose to imbue Hornblower with the onomastically encoded role of the narrator found in Hamlet's unfailing friend—Horatio. The obvious parallel to Horatio Nelson, which many readers still assume to be the main source of the hero's name, was simply an additional bonus for Forester.[11] The significance and implications could not be more obvious. As the keeper and/or teller of time, Horatio embodies and performs the onomastic meaning of his name in the heterodiegetic narrative found in all but one Hornblower novel.[12] However, the way Forester conceived his protagonist made him a believable yet not necessarily a reliable narrator.

In Hornblower, we find a distinct character formula which represents a particular permutation of the attributes and circumstances that hold true for any sea captain in fiction: their solitary existence, which is determined by their hierarchical distance from their crew, their geographic isolation from their homeland, and their seemingly divine powers which govern every aspect of the lives placed under their command. Forester conceived his hero as "[t]he man alone" (1998: 82).[13] He is somebody who ultimately bears the sole responsibility for his decisions despite being revered instead of feared by his men, and despite allowing for open communication and complete trust among his "band of brothers." Driven by innate zeal, he is prone to take the initiative and use his common sense to go beyond his orders. More often than not, he questions his orders and sometimes even defies them if he deems it necessary to achieve the successful outcome of his mission. His advancement by merit rests on a paradox which is coupled to a lack of political ambition. All he wants to do is to be in command of a ship while his successes usually lead to promotion which in turn takes him further away from the profession he prefers. The Hornblower archetype would not be complete without a general lack of domestic happiness. This is accentuated by an incessant psychological struggle shaped by self-doubt, and the generic loneliness of command.

The character of the Starfleet captain was defined and fully articulated in Hornblower-esque terms in the first three installments of *Star Trek* (*ST:TOS, ST:TAS, ST:TNG*), and then historicized as an established archetype, i.e., the character norm, in the later shows (*ST:DS9, ST:VOY, ST:ENT*) by Roddenberry's successors. All captains share the qualities which Forester ascribed to his protagonist regardless of ethnicity or gender. In pursuing their diverse missions assigned by Starfleet Command, the core of their character results from their continued exposure and reaction to spatial, temporal, hierarchical, psychological, and emotional isolation and/or detachment. Such situations would always arise on missions that severed most lines of communication with home. Based on a set of general orders, the multifaceted isolation and detachment has been the central premise for the format of *Star Trek*'s space-borne adventures since the earliest draft for *ST:TOS*. Drafting his starship captain as "Hornblower in space," Roddenberry equipped him with a basic psychological and behavioral profile. He then went on to define his status as a "man alone" in much greater detail in the guidelines for writers/directors of *ST:TOS*.[14] His descriptions applied equally to Captain Pike (Jeffrey Hunter), first seen in the failed pilot episode "The Cage" (1965), and Captain Kirk. Even though there is Starfleet with "a headquarters somewhere, general orders and a whole command hierarchy," Roddenberry made it clear "to keep Kirk and the Enterprise far away and out of touch" (24–7). His argument was that such a setting would allow writers to create moments of dramatic decisions for the captain more easily. Forester used the same approach as a dramatic mainstay in his novels.

Hornblower is left to his own devices trying to ensure the best possible outcome for any situation he might find himself in. His conduct, his decisions, and their outcome would then hopefully exonerate him in the eyes of his superiors.

Even though some of their orders and mission objectives changed, the contours used to define the character of the captain were continued as a normative practice by the writers and producers of the later series. According to the series bible of *ST:TNG,* the mission of Captain Picard remained largely unchanged; he was "to expand the body of human knowledge ... provide assistance as required to Earth/Federation colonies ... provide for Earth/Federation security," and to "seek out new life, new civilizations" (2). Picard was introduced as a mature and versatile deep space explorer. He had gained considerable experience at independent decision-making while conducting the interstellar equivalent of Captain Cook's voyages—the twenty-two-year mission of the *Stargazer*. Like all principal captains, Picard commands broad powers over his crew, mediating conflicts at his own discretion.

It was only the situations of detachment and the captains' degree of isolation that changed in the post–Roddenberry series. They shifted the emphasis on different aspects of the archetype without ever really changing the basic model. Consequently, when Commander Sisko takes charge of *Deep Space Nine,* he finds himself at the periphery of the Federation. The station is an exotic port of call where the transience of alien multitudes and local color are key leitmotifs. Outlined in the series bible, his mission is essentially colonial in that he "spearhead[s] the arduous diplomatic and scientific efforts that accompany the lengthy entry procedure," (3–5) of the Bajorans into the Federation. Though Sisko is in contact with the higher echelons on Earth more regularly—as is Hornblower while stationed in the West Indies—he repeatedly finds himself in situations where his resolve provides the decisive weight. By that time, the "fighting naturalist" in outer space had become the character norm. When Captain Janeway sets sail on *Voyager* to capture a group of renegades, she finds herself hurdled to the other side of the galaxy. She is instantly placed on the most detached and most independent cruise of all captains, and becomes the woman who is the most alone. She has no support structure except for her crew and she is wholly dependent on her own judgment, taking the responsibilities borne by the archetype to a new level. Even so, the captain is adamant about upholding Starfleet principles and, as outlined in the series bible, she intends to "continue to go boldly, to explore, study, and investigate" (2). Despite, or rather because of the fact that *ST:ENT* is a prequel series, Captain Archer also finds himself detached from Earth. After all, not only is he Starfleet's first deep space explorer, but he is also the face of humanity acting as its ambassador on the interstellar stage. By being and going first, his decisions bear significance in that they set a benchmark for later generations of captains. Staying true to the captain archetype, "he has a strong sense of duty, he's a bit of a renegade—he's not afraid to question orders or even disobey them, if he feels in his gut that he's right" ("STAR TREK ENTERPRISE Bible" n.p.). Consequently, the archetypal premise of "the man alone" can be observed in all of his descendants in outer space.

Variants and Variations: Coming of Age in Space

Not only is any character study of the five[15] principal *Star Trek* captains an exercise in tracking and understanding the hybrid character of the naval warrior and the naval explorer, but it is also a study of variants and variations. Over the course of almost fifty years, none of them appear to be alike—at least at first glance. They are best introduced along Hornblower-esque lines by way of a brief taxonomy. These profiles are all but exhaustive since they only outline certain key aspects of how particular attributes of the archetype manifest themselves more in one captain than the other.

Consequently, Captain Kirk can be called a *naval swashbuckler* since he is more of an action-adventure type of hero. He tends to rush into taking the initiative faster than his fellow captains. Kirk is reminiscent of Hornblower once the latter had achieved post-rank, making a name for himself during the first years of his captaincy. Captain Picard is a *naval stargazer* who, despite being on a broad mission of exploration, finds himself proving his diplomatic finesse in countless negotiations and conflicts which involve many different parties. He approximately mirrors Hornblower's growth in maturity when the latter is given his own squadron and dispatched to the Baltic, and later to northern France in order to deal with political, military, and diplomatic situations that affect all of Europe. Upon assuming command of *Deep Space 9*, Commander, later Captain Sisko takes post in the vein of Hornblower when the latter is transferred to the West Indies. Operating from a stationary habitat, he is a *naval commander-in-chief* who is deeply entrenched in the *Realpolitik* of interstellar exploration, commerce, and a conflict whose outcome affects billions of lives. As with Hornblower, Sisko's moral integrity and his conscience are put to the test more than once.

Captain Janeway embarks as a *naval pathfinder* on a journey of Odyssean proportions when she finds herself stranded on the other side of the galaxy. She nurtures a small family of intrepid voyagers pursuing a single goal—to return home. The journey is marked by her making hard choices which, however, do not preclude her from making new discoveries along the way. *ST:VOY* appears as a conflation of Hornblower's independent cruise in the Pacific and his long journey home as he affects an escape from hostile territory with a crew of only two. Captain Archer clears the moorings of spacedock as a *naval naïf*. Like Captain Cook, who was among the first to comprehensively chart the vastness of the Pacific, *ST:ENT*'s Archer is initially struck by the wonder of it all. His reverence for deep space exploration quickly gives way to his need to grow in command maturity when faced with the political realities of his era. It is a process which takes on the qualities of a baptism by fire. To some extent, Archer's growth mirrors Hornblower's as the latter learns his first valuable lessons at command as a young midshipman. He grows increasingly adaptable as he is exposed to the exigencies of command. He then advances to the rank of lieutenant and leaves the naivety and innocence of the midshipman, who infamously had been seasick in port, far behind.

Despite *Star Trek*'s largely episodic nature, the coming-of-age formula provides much of the archetype's continuity which is revealed only when viewed synoptically. While it undergirds the character growth and development of all principal captains, it is most easily discernible in Captains James T. Kirk and Jean-Luc Picard. Kirk's overall career is repeatedly given space and airtime over the course of *ST:TOS* and then becomes the central theme for his character development in the motion pictures. More than once, we are reminded that he was unusually young for a Starfleet captain; something that he has in common with Horatio Nelson who assumed his first command as captain at the age of 23. Kirk's formative years are tackled in one of two ways. There are a number of references to events of the past such as him being a witness to and survivor of Governor Kodos's massacre as well as the attack of the vampiric cloud on the *Farragut*. One-time guest characters also serve as reminders of past tribulations like Finnegan, who bullied him at the academy, or Ben Finney, who saw his career curbed by Kirk's sense of duty. The series even commences with Kirk losing his closest friend, Gary Mitchell.[16] His coming-of-age arc continues in the movies with him being promoted, facing a midlife crisis, learning that he has a son, being demoted again, and ultimately losing his son at the hands of the Klingons.

The theme of family, or rather the lack/loss thereof, links Kirk and Picard in *Star Trek Generations* (David Carson, U.S. 1994). The latter's background is given a similar treatment over the seven seasons of *ST:TNG*. The road to developing his signature stern imperturbability and diplomatic finesse led him from being a brash young officer, who was stabbed in the heart in a bar brawl, to the disastrous loss of his first command. The *Stargazer* incident was followed by a rigorous court martial and his eventual acquittal. Friends and mentor figures such as Boothby, Starfleet Academy's groundskeeper, and Admiral Hanson contributed considerably to the maturation of Picard. Reconciling with his brother, Robert, in the wake of his assimilation by the Borg marked the beginning of a new phase in his life. Consequently, the trauma incurred by the death of Robert and his only son, René, first devastates Picard and then allows him to resign himself to the fact that he would be the last in a long line of Picards; one of whom, perhaps not surprisingly, served in the Royal Navy at the Battle of Trafalgar.[17]

While perhaps explored less elaborately, the Hornblower-esque coming-of-age formula also shapes the lives of Captains Benjamin Sisko, Kathryn Janeway, and Jonathan Archer. Sisko's arrival and decision to stay on *Deep Space 9* is facilitated by "divine" intervention which allows him to overcome the burden of his wife's death. Repeated visitations by the Prophets help him to cope with his trials and tribulations while at the same time they allow us to witness important moments of his life and people associated with them. Spanning three of the nine lifetimes of the Trill symbiont Dax, his friendship with the "old man" offers room for them to reminisce about past exploits.[18] Janeway is perhaps afforded the least character growth. Even so, the audience learns about her career through her close friendship with Lt. Tuvok (Tim Russ) which spans many years and different assignments. The frequent time travel adventures in *ST:VOY* offer us the occasional glimpse at mentor figures and advocates in her early career such as Admiral Patterson. Occasionally, Janeway's efforts to re-humanize Seven of Nine (Jeri Ryan) elicit personal anecdotes from her.[19] Friendships and flashbacks are also the main devices used to flesh out the character arc of Captain Archer. The origins of his long-time friendship with Charles "Trip" Tucker (Connor Trinneer) serve as an avenue to look back at the captain's rough and tumble rivalry with A.G. Robinson and his derring-do during the early years of the NX program. Though expedited by the cancellation of *ST:ENT*, we still witness him become a broker of interstellar peace and cooperation, leaving his own suspicions and personal grudges—harbored and held for Vulcans, Andorians, and Tellarites at one point or another—far behind.[20]

"Don't let them promote you": The Paradox of Success

Whether at sea or in space, being a captain, who bears sole responsibility for all his or her decisions, inevitably engenders a troubled psychological profile. Hence, a captain's desire to remain in a position of independent command points at a signature paradox of the archetype. Following the coming-of-age formula, the paradox stems from the meritocratic rise of the hero which turns into meritocratic anxiety once he has attained the rank of "post captain." Fueled by the fear about the anti-climax—i.e., the journey is the destination—and merged with an intrinsic lack of interest in politics, the meritocratic protagonist tries to keep the uneasy equilibrium between being a successful captain at sea and steering clear of political entanglements that tend come with success. Historically, attaining the rank of post captain was the goal of many young Royal Navy officers.[21] Once reached, they would enjoy a certain degree of "job security" and a guaranteed rise through the ranks based on their years of service. If they survived long enough, they could become admirals, receive a knighthood, and even a peerage. However, such a career path would inevitable bring them closer to home and thus involve them in the political machinations of the imperial center.

Forester said that "Hornblower was never a man to know complete happiness," because despite his "peerage and his flag ... he would not lose his old restlessness, his desire for action, his quickness of thought" (126). For example, that is why we find Hornblower trying everything in his power to steer clear of the political echelons once he had been made a knight of the Order of the Bath; this proves difficult for someone whose second wife is the fictional sister of the Duke of Wellington. Similarly, when he is placed in command of the West Indies station as a rear-admiral, i.e., a flag officer, he has a flag captain who is in charge of handling the admiral's ship. Hornblower "felt he could never grow used to his situation as Admiral, and having to stand by and be no more than an interested spectator while the ship he was in was being handled at decisive moments" (593). Needless to say, Forester's "man alone" cannot help but assume direct command and/or steer his flag captain on a course of his choosing on multiple occasions. Also, it is not surprising then that Roddenberry insisted on the starship captain staying "away from petty military politics" (24), in the guidelines for *ST:TOS*.

As representatives of a hierarchical, semi-military, naval service, all Starfleet captains are, of course, constantly employed in political negotiations; and they have to interact with a wide range of political entities. Their lack of intrinsic political ambitious and their meritocratic anxiety, however, comes to the fore in situations that lead to a promotion and/or transfer—even if it is only temporary—and thus away from their independent command. Like Kirk tells Picard: "Don't let them promote you. Don't let them transfer you. Don't let them do anything that takes you off the bridge of that ship, because while you're there, you can make a difference."[22] After all, Kirk should know. He was unsatisfied as an admiral working a desk job at Starfleet Command. He then became involved in a string of events which, while saving Earth in the process, still saw him being demoted. This produced a continuous subplot in the first four *Star*

Trek movies. In *Star Trek: The Motion Picture,* Admiral Kirk even goes so far as to take "over the center seat," and temporarily demotes the *Enterprise*'s new captain, Will Decker, to the rank of commander. In the sequel, Spock tells the admiral: "If I may be so bold, it was a mistake for you to accept promotion. Commanding a starship is your first best destiny."[23] Once again, Kirk assumes command which ultimately sends him on a course towards demotion in the fourth feature film. His disobedience to a direct order by a superior officer is then even used to validate the archetypal propensity of the Enlightenment mariner to go beyond orders. Issuing the verdict, the Federation president adds that "as a consequence of your new rank, you be given the duties for which you have repeatedly demonstrated unswerving ability. The command of a starship."[24] By demoting him, they actually do him a favor.

In a similar vein, Captain Sisko is asked twice to temporarily assume a higher posting.[25] Each time he expresses his reluctance while still accepting the assignment out of his sense of duty; and he repeatedly voices a yearning to return to his original command. His wish is always fulfilled once he successfully completed his tasks in the higher, more political/administrative position. For example, echoing Hornblower and Kirk, Sisko mournfully watches his science officer, Jadzia Dax (Terry Farrell), temporarily assuming command of the *Defiant.* She continues to perform a post-combat ritual which he had instituted. Sisko is made an admiral's adjutant and placed in charge of planning and coordinating squadrons of starships. The captain's reaction to his promotion is implied in the episode title—"Behind the Lines" (20 Oct 1997). Sisko articulates the emotional and psychological significance of a captain's independent command in an exchange with his admiral:

> ROSS: I know how you feel about your crew, but you and I are responsible for an entire tactical wing. Thousands of lives depend on the decisions we make tomorrow. You can't afford to be awake all night worrying about one ship.
>
> SISKO: Admiral, you can order me to my quarters, but there's no way I'm going to sleep. Not as long as the Defiant is out there.

It is the escapist freedom of an independent command, during which they often bend and/or break with their orders, that earns them recognition which then results in meritocratic anxiety. The captains also attribute the feeling of home to their ships which is irrevocably tied to the signature sense of family that their command style fosters among their crews. Captain Picard informs a visitor unfamiliar with the *Enterprise*: "Actually, I tend to think of this ship as home."[26]

Captain Janeway also advances in rank as evidenced in her guest appearance as admiral in *Star Trek Nemesis,* where she communicates a set of orders to Captain Picard. If the behavior of her future self (seen in the finale of *ST:VOY*), who put into motion a series of events which ensured her promotion to admiral, is any indication, then it is safe to assume that if there were any canonical continuation of Janeway's adventures, she would continue them as captain. Nurtured by their archetypal command culture, the allure of a captaincy, which is circumscribed by the self-contained habitats of their commands, is accentuated by a particular relationship pattern between the captains and their crew. All *Star Trek* captains lead their command in the vein of the romanticized Enlightenment mariner in that they lead by their own judicious example. They form an archetypal Nelsonian "band of brothers (and sisters)" with their subordinates, especially with their senior officers.

"The finest crew in Starfleet": A Perennial St. Crispin's Day

The romanticized Enlightenment mariner of the popular imagination is a "mild hero." He is perceived to be kinder and more just in the command of his subordinates than his contemporaries. Even though there is no longer any corporal punishment, nor any significant physical hardship on Starfleet ships, the set of behavioral patterns, which make Hornblower a stern yet beloved, paternalistic captain, is maintained in the archetypal Starfleet captain. Hornblower fosters a command style which rests on the interplay of trust, open communication, and delegation. Forester claimed that his command style is reminiscent of Nelson's in that "it would be the kind of leadership that owes much to tact and little to animal spirits" (89). He referred to the famed Nelson Touch, which is couched in St. Crispin's Day rhetoric. The admiral used the phrase "band of brothers" to refer to the captains and other senior officers under his command. Together, they formed a command culture which worked successfully based on clear communication, and mutual encouragement and support. It was a precursor for modern command paradigms, like Mission Command, in that all participants share the "commander's mind" (Vincent 99). Paradoxically, the paradigm emerged at a time when ship captains were neither required to discuss their strategies with their officers, nor were they obliged to elaborately explain their decisions to them.

Once Hornblower had achieved a certain maturity in command, the novels are replete with "band of brothers" rhetoric. He draws his officers into his confidence by allowing them to express their insights on a given situation. In the process, he gains vital information for his own decision-making process. Despite the fact that the final decision is ultimately his, he repeatedly falls back into the St. Crispin's Day paradigm not only to be able to make better decisions based on reciprocal communication, but also to ensure their successful implementation.[27] All of his officers always know exactly what their respective roles and tasks are, which leads them to identify positively with their missions. Consequently, it also increases the likelihood of their success. At the same time, however, Hornblower frantically tries to maintain a critical distance to his officers, wearing a mask of taciturnity and deliberate emotional detachment. For example, all of his subordinates know better than to interrupt him pacing up and down the "weather side of the quarter deck" (1937: 223). Many officers are stopped dead in their tracks by Hornblower's signature non-committal response "ha-h'm" (227). Even so, his men respect him to a point of worship and the captain cannot help but form a strong personal friendship with his long-term first lieutenant, William Bush. He also takes certain junior officers under his stringent albeit nurturing wings. "Forester's Hornblower would be far more lenient than most captains of the time he was presented in," as Sanford Sternlicht has observed, especially "when it came to flogging and other forms of corporal punishment" (22). By extrapolating Starfleet as a semi-military naval service, Roddenberry transferred the positively connoted "band of brothers" leadership style and made it another key characteristic of the archetypal starship captain.

Although still cast in the vein of the benign "man alone," the command style of Starfleet captains is often realized in a deceptively democratic discourse. Even so, once a captain has arrived at a decision, it is helpful, as Lt. Tuvok puts it, to remember the following guideline: "The captain is always right."[28] It echoes similar musings among Hornblower's men; e.g., "if Hornblower thought it right, it must be so, and there was no need to wonder about it" (1938a: 524). While Roddenberry focused more on the captain's narratological function and his psychological profile in his earliest draft for *ST:TOS*, he also included a few implicit pointers towards the "mild hero" and his judicious command style.[29] On top of that, he instilled into the starship captains the archetypal restlessness of the Enlightenment mariner which makes them, among other things, frontline leaders of men. A Starfleet captain has "a temptation to take the greatest risk onto himself" (5). While this is a universal characteristic of most heroes in general, the propensity to lead their men in the front rather than from the rear is an attribute that holds true for Hornblower, Nelson, and Cook. Whenever they landed on an "alien beach," Cook insisted to be among the first of his shore party to disembark from the boat. Already a commodore, Nelson famously led a boarding party at the Battle of St. Vincent (1797). Later, when he was already a rear-admiral, he repelled a gun-boat, fighting side-by-side with the common sailors who manned his barge. Hence, it is not surprising that Hornblower[30] and his descendants in outer space display similar daring. While this particular behavioral pattern may be the prerogative of Captain Kirk, as a naval swashbuckler in space, it is in fact an archetypal trait of all principal captains. After all, their tendency to go on away missions, while discreetly ignoring general regulations that state they must not do so without an escort, is a recurrent trope in *Star Trek*.

Roddenberry delineated the Nelsonian "band of brothers" command style in greater detail in the writers'/directors' guidelines for *ST:TOS*. Kirk is greatly admired by his subordinates in that the "crew respects him, some almost to the point of adoration" (10). In the vein of the Enlightenment mariner, he "will often solicit information and estimates," and his officers are "a trained team and are well able to anticipate information and action [sic] Kirk needs." Once again, this became the model that was reiterated in the series bible for *ST:TNG*—"the same 'band of brothers' feeling" (4)—and it was then presupposed as the character norm in the later series.[31]

The Captains and Their William Bush

A distinct outgrowth of Hornblower's leadership style, the special link between the captains and their second-in-command became a recurrent set of relationship patterns. Forester's novels chart not only the meritocratic career of his protagonist, but also the evolving friendship and deep bond between Hornblower and his long-term second-in-command—William Bush. His terse and "unexpected intimacy with Bush" (107), as Sternlicht has argued, is one of the few personal relationships that pierces the protagonist's idiosyncrasies which usually prevent him from forming elaborate emotional attachments. In fact, their bond is such that when Bush dies on a mission, following Hornblower's orders, the resulting emotional turmoil Hornblower experiences is disproportionately more intense than when he learned of the death of his first wife.[32] His relationship with Bush points to the high degree of male *philia* (trans. "brotherly love") which permeates the hyper-masculine world of sail in fiction. It even supersedes most gender normative relationships. The semi-fraternal/semi-paternal bond the two share results from Hornblower's judiciousness. And, it provided the archetypal relationship pattern between all principal *Star Trek* captains and their first officers.

In Roddenberry's first pitch for *ST:TOS*, we already find a character sketch titled the "First Lieutenant," whom he conceived as the "captain's right-hand man, the working level commander of the ship's functions" (8). Apart from his hierarchical position and the purview of his shipboard duties, Roddenberry also established a high level of male *philia* as the archetypal norm that circumscribes the captain's relationship with the first officer. Oscillating between fraternal and paternal articulations of their bond, *Star Trek*'s archetypal first officer can be read as a "William Bush in space." As a "man alone," it is not surprising to learn that, according to *ST:TOS* guidelines, "Captain Kirk has only a few opportunities for anything approaching friendship" (10). Spock, his first officer, is then one of two exceptions. Their bond amounts to "a strange friendship based upon logic, high mutual respect and Spock's strong Vulcan loyalty to a commander." Kirk's deeply felt fraternal bond with Spock provided the most revisited and most developed relationships throughout *ST:TOS*. In a literalization of metaphor, it even transcended death, furnishing the main plot line in *Star Trek III: The Search for Spock*. Their bond is, however, much more openly articulated, especially on a verbal level, than Hornblower's closely guarded feelings for Bush about which he rarely speaks. This is, of course, largely due to crucial differences in media. While they also closely guard their feelings, Starfleet captains have to articulate them in dialogs and other actions within the diegesis for the benefit of the audience. By comparison, readers of the Hornblower novels witness the protagonist's feelings unfold in extensive inner monologues. Hence, we essentially find a verbalization of the Hornblower-Bush relationship in *Star Trek*.

The bond between Kirk and Spock, which turned into one of the most beloved and thus iconic elements of *ST:TOS*, had a lasting impact on the relationships between the captains and their first officers in later shows. The discourse of male *philia*, however, shifted to a more paternal and, in some cases, nondescript tack. Consequently, Captain Picard has, according to Roddenberry, "an unspoken but deep father-son relationship with," his first officer William Riker, who in return regards his captain "with a mixture of awe and affection" (5). Even so, he also employed fraternal parameters to define Riker's point of view further in that "their relationship is that of a younger brother obedient to an elder brother whom he admires completely and hopes one day to successfully emulate" (25).

The relationships between the captains and their first officers in the post–Roddenberry series were increasingly accentuated by attempts on part of the writers to move beyond paternal/fraternal structures. Even so, the base tone of their bonds still carried the same connotations. More often than not, they were more powerful and much more important than real family ties. Captain Sisko was paired with a Bajoran woman, Kira Nerys (Nana Visitor), who, as first officer and liaison with the Bajoran government, oscillated between initial distrust for the benign colonialism the captain represents, and religious reverence for him as a divine "emissary." The paternal pattern still asserted itself in a leveling effect. Framed by religious devotion, they formed a kind of father-daughter relationship in the end which ultimately saw Kira "inherit" Sisko's command of the station.[33]

Even though he is the rebel leader she is initially tasked with apprehending, Chakotay (Robert Beltran) still "strikes an immediate and powerful bond with Janeway," as they find themselves hurled to the other side of the galaxy ("STAR TREK: Voyager Bible" 11). At first, showrunners haphazardly inserted romantic insinuations between them.[34] Ultimately, it was Janeway's increasing maternal tendencies which led her not only to betray the character premise for her gender role of professionalism, emotional distance, and moral principle, but also to mirror Kirk's *philia* for Spock. In the finale of *ST:VOY*, she breaks with all of her principles to bring Chakotay, her trusted friend and travel companion, back from the dead.

Similar to Sisko, Captain Archer was also coupled with an alien woman—the Vulcan, T'Pol (Jolene Blalock). Initially marked by indifference and distance, Archer gradually assumes the role of mentor and confidant as she grows more isolated from her people in the wake of a number of traumatic experiences.[35] As Archer grows more experienced at command, the series bible for *ST:ENT* states, "they will also develop a long-lasting friendship that is rather unique for its day—the bond between human and alien" (n.p.). Once again, this shows how the archetypal paternal/fraternal character constellation between the captain and their second-in-command is not only a product of a judicious command style, but also how it was perpetuated as a character norm after Roddenberry's death regardless of ethnicity or gender. *Star Trek*'s first officers also represent the most crucial node in the emotional bond the captains form with their surrogate families—their crews.

With Benevolence Towards All

Taken together, the Nelsonian command style and the benign sentiments of the Enlightenment mariner represent but one of two pillars of the archetype's judiciousness. Since the captain always finds himself in some form of geographic/temporal isolation, there is a need for him to expand his judiciousness beyond the domestically connoted hulls of his ship. Historical records show that the Golden Age of Sail did not necessarily experience a lack of naval men who were willing to fight against the Corsican tyrant hoping to earn riches and distinction in the process. Commanding officers who displayed foresight were, however, a rare commodity.[36] The naval heroes who served as inspiration for the romanticized Enlightenment mariner did not show any signs of being hampered by their isolation and disconnectedness. Instead, they were usually able to take the proverbial "bigger picture" into account and discern the significance of their assignment and their actions within the confines of the larger imperial project.

Ascribed to the Nelson(s) and Cook(s) of the Romantic imagination, Hornblower too displays an acute farsightedness. He is not just a "benevolent commander," as Sternlicht has noted, but he is also "a masterful tactician and a superb strategist ... and diplomat who could see the grand plans of early nineteenth-century Europe" (114). Yet another distinguishing character attribute, Hornblower's zeal to succeed at his independent command required a more enlightened and complex worldview. When he arrives at decisions, he tends to run multiple scenarios in his mind—which readers are privy to—to ensure the successful outcome of the immediate situation he is confronted with; he also tries to ascertain possible implications and repercussions his actions might have within a wider network of situations.[37] While most of his actions are covered by his initial orders, it is Hornblower's critical interpretation of them which ensures that the outcome transcends any narrow parameters of locality or personal motivations. Rather than restricting him, the trans-oceanic seascapes enable, and even ennoble the captain despite the isolation and oppressiveness that serve as possible sources for anxiety and uncertainty. An obvious extension of the "man alone" premise, the "writer would send his protagonist on independent duty far from home and diplomatic support; and further complicate matters" (105).

Based on the broad set of exploratory, defensive, and diplomatic orders that Starfleet captains act upon, it would have constituted a grave break in character if they had not obliged Hornblower in displaying similar farsightedness. Roddenberry's initial sketch of the starship captain only hints at the multiple layers of the character's judiciousness. In a memo to one of his associate producers, he stressed the captain's "humanistic nature and background" (qtd. Whitfield 238). Writers'/producers' guidelines expanded Captain Kirk's "highly mature perspective on command" to also include "alien life customs, however strange or repugnant they seem when measured against Earth standards" (10).[38] Even so, Captain Picard is arguably the epitome of a naval diplomat in space. He articulated it most succinctly at the wedding of Riker and Troi:

> A starship captain's life is filled with solemn duty. I have commanded men in battle. I have negotiated peace treaties between implacable enemies. I have represented the Federation in first contact with twenty-seven alien species.[39]

Even though his brief account is impressive, it is not that radically different from the diplomatic skill and shrewd political finesse the other captains display on their missions.

Captain Sisko faced situations that required the same level of judiciousness and farsighted judgment. As outlined in the series bible, "the political situation on the planet [Bajor] is terribly unstable," and it is Sisko's task "to try and 'tame' this ... atmosphere" (3–5). Right from the beginning he is placed in an intricate web of *realpolitk* which, unlike his fellow starship captains, he cannot easily escape by moving on to the next star system. Furthest from any diplomatic support, Captain Janeway, according to the showrunners, combines her "warmth, sensitivity, intellectual curiosity, and likability," with her "gift for doing the completely unexpected which has bailed her out on more than one scrape" (5). Even though he initially stumbles, causing more interstellar tension than any other captain, Jonathan Archer quickly finds his footing. He grows into the role of diplomatic mediator and his skill is sought by third parties on a number of occasions.[40] By nurturing and strengthening the "threads that bind"[41] the interstellar community together, he initiates the first steps towards a coalition of planets. Ultimately, Archer is instrumental in the formation of the United Federation of Planets. Following Forester's as well as Roddenberry's parameters for character construction and believability, Hornblower and his descendants in outer space would not be complete if they were flawless.

The Crucibles of the (Wo)Men Alone

So far, the Hornblower-esque Enlightenment mariner in space appears to be "something of a super sailor" (Sternlicht 113). The archetype is, however, tempered by two distinct character constraints. Incessant self-reflection, self-doubt, and the anxiety over failing in one's duty constitute the character's peculiar psychological struggle. It is exacerbated by a distinct lack of domestic happiness which is largely due to the archetype's passion for staying on independent commands. The domestic unhappiness is accentuated by the character's inability to resist the temptations of distant stations, and a generic oedipal desire for the ship. Invested with maternal qualities, a vessel is traditionally gendered since it envelops the lives within its hull. Thus, it protects the crew from the vagaries of harsh natural environments. Derived from the primal urge to possess a feminized entity in lieu of a human companion, a captain also ascribes sexual connotations to his ship.

Forester conceived of his stories primarily as psychological novels in that his attention to character always outweighed any emphasis on action-driven plots. Consequently, he delineated Hornblower's troubled psyche in countless pages of internal monologue. According to the author, the protagonist's

> struggle would go on as long as he was to live, for it was the struggle with himself. He was self-critical. Just as no man is supposed to be a hero to his own valet, so Hornblower could not be a hero to his own self. He would be too cynical about his own motives, too aware of his own weaknesses, ever to know content; ... struggle with himself and not subside into self-satisfaction or humility [1998: 87–8].

Hornblower barely shows his internal struggles to others. He keeps a close guard on his emotions at all times. Since he is, however, the narrative focalizer, readers are privileged albeit sometimes overburdened with having access to a steady stream of meticulously delineated self-criticism, self-loathing, and anxious self-chastisement. Ironically, the captain's predilection for self-reflection, and his often overlooked prudence, constitute his innate ability for command. His troubled psyche is both a crucial component and result of a captain who is successful while serving on an independent command. Forester put forth that his hero "had a great deal of ability, and his addiction to self-analysis called his attention to his own weaknesses so that he would make the effort to eliminate them, or at least render them ineffective" (118). In fact, the author condensed the repeatedly successful outcomes of Hornblower's struggles with himself into a stylistic play on the Shakespearean adage "discretion is the better part of valor."[42] In short, Hornblower's command ability necessitates a high degree of mental agony and a frantic desire to be prepared for any eventuality despite the hierarchical demand for an outward display of imperturbability.

In the pitch for *ST:TOS*, Roddenberry made it clear that even though the captain is "lean and capable both mentally and physically," he also "lives a continual battle with self-doubt" (5). In a note to one of his staff, he continued to map "the inner conflict between humanist and military commander," along the lines of "self-doubts, the moments of pettiness, the attention to the materiality of his career, etc." (qtd. Whitfield 238).[43] The captain's struggle within also exposes a precariously restrained temper. Occasionally, he lashes out at those surrounding him, only to immediately scold himself—just like Hornblower[44]—for losing his composure. The guidelines for writers state that Captain Kirk was to remain someone who is "constantly on trial with himself," thus setting the norm for all Starfleet captains who followed (10). Kirk's desire to live a life of independent command occasionally takes its toll regardless of his crew's devotion to and support of him. "Kirk feels these responsibilities strongly and is fully capable of letting the worry and frustration lead him into error" (*ibid.*). Similar to Hornblower, Kirk severely chastises himself whenever he does not live up to his self-imposed parameters of achievement and success. The same goes for situations where something does not go according to *his* plan.[45] Despite his maturity and experience, Captain Picard "has his share of idiosyncrasies," which undermine his shielded equanimity whenever "deep emotions are triggered" (1987: 23). Picard's doubts and his temper are exposed particularly well when he is turned into a cybernetic being. Violated and stripped of his free will, he is forced to inflict massive devastation on his own people. His assimilation by the Borg and subsequent rehabilitation, which remained incomplete, represent the few events in his life capable of triggering enormous psychological turmoil. We see him unable to draw the line between personal distress, the archetypal judiciousness towards his crew, and his ability to command as a "man alone."[46]

Captain Sisko is on the receiving end of the devastation that constitutes Picard's trauma—he lost his wife in the conflict with the Borg. Sisko is introduced being full of self-doubt. Upon receiving his mission orders from none other than Picard, he shares that he is thinking to going back to Earth and becoming a civilian.[47] By the end of the pilot episode, he has found renewed purpose and a degree of certainty, and he decides to stay on *Deep Space Nine*. From then on, Sisko adheres to the archetypal behavior of trying to maintain a calm, placid, and civil demeanor. He takes himself to task, however, when circumstances make him temporarily lose his temper, or when he fails in his duty. Echoing the coming-of-age formula in the series bible, Captain Sisko "as he's become more mature," he has "learned to stop and think twice before losing control" (7). When he becomes the only character who might successfully avert the Federation's downfall in an interstellar war, the surrealities of the conflict make him think that maybe "it's time for me to step down, let someone else make the tough calls."[48] Losing his closest advisor and friend in the war leads him to admit that "for the first time in my life I've failed in my duty as a Starfleet officer."[49] Yet, fueled by his self-doubt and self-criticism, the captain realizes (as does Hornblower on many occasions) that the only thing he can do is to proceed on, and finish the job he started.

Finding herself on the most distant station of all *Star Trek* captains, Captain Janeway's psychological turmoil stems from her relentless adherence to principles and her self-imposed facade of imperturbability. The gravity of her decision to strand her own crew on the other side of the galaxy in order to save a local alien people provides ample opportunities for her to revisit and question her choices.[50] Despite the fact that she could have hardly arrived at a different decision without defying the archetypal judiciousness of a Starfleet captain, her recurring doubts allow her to develop considerable zeal for her new mission—to get her *ersatz* family home. Whenever the survival of her crew does not require her utmost attention, doubts about her decision come to the surface. For example, when *Voyager* finds itself in the interstellar equivalent of doldrums (a sector of space completely devoid of stars and planetary systems) the captain grows despondent. She confides in her second-in-command: "I made an error in judgment, Chakotay. It was short-sighted and it was selfish, and now all of us are paying for my mistake.... If the crew asks for me tell them the Captain sends her regards."[51] On another occasion, when Janeway is presented with a possible way to make *Voyager*'s odyssey unhappen by changing the timeline, her doubts surface again. Once again, she turns to her first officer: "*Voyager* getting stranded. All these deaths, this entire future, it's my fault. I've got to do something to change it."[52] Ultimately, she is always plagued by residual doubts about her initial decision, the resulting zeal to bring her crew home, and a tinge of survivor's guilt. Triggered by her inability to protect some of her crew from harm, a future version of herself then decides to defy all the principles, which she tenaciously maintained for their entire sojourn, to expedite their journey. Janeway is likely the only captain whose initial character premise and promise—a believable professional feminine gender role—was betrayed on the part of the writers.

As humanity's first deep-space explorer, Jonathan Archer sets sail having the least troubled mind of all captains. At the beginning of his mission, he is fueled only by a self-imposed obligation to bring his father's legacy to fruition (i.e., the engine that powers his ship). The first steps he and his crew take to introduce humanity to the interstellar community are marked by a distinct naivety, a boyish sense of wonder, and a haphazardly concocted innocence. The captain's reflections betray a cumbersome reluctance to accept the fact that life among the stars might be less inviting than he had thought. Once he sees the unexpected and unintended effects of the decisions that he made and/or that were forced upon him, he painfully realizes that his intuitive approach of making up rules as they go along requires significant revision. Additionally, he faces psychological conundrums arising from moral and ethical issues. They translate into stories that speculate about the repercussions (serious and humorous) of viewing the vagaries of alien cultures through an unadulterated lens of humanity's first proto-imperialist venture in space.[53]

Becoming ever deeper embroiled in a trans-temporal conflict—the Temporal Cold War—the captain faces his first trial of self-doubt when he and his crew are wrongfully accused of destroying an alien colony. Falling short of assuming a defeatist attitude, Archer begins to slip into a despondent and melancholy mood. His second-in-command notices that the captain "seems to alternate between agitation, despondency and guilt."[54] Ultimately, he continues to adhere to the psychological profile of the "man alone" as he begins to feel Earth's weight on this shoulders in the wake of a devastating attack on Earth. A thinly disguised analogy of 9/11, and the wars in Afghanistan and Iraq, he is sent on a mission to apprehend the perpetrators. Archer succeeds in averting greater calamity but only after making a number of morally questionable decisions which ultimately lead him to develop post-traumatic stress disorder.[55] Archer begins to blame himself and the decisions he made during the first two years of his mission as being the reasons for why Earth was attacked. He finds comfort in the company of Captain Hernandez, the skipper of *Enterprise*'s sister ship.

> ARCHER: If we weren't out there stirring up trouble, seven million people might still be alive.
>
> HERNANDEZ: You weren't stirring up trouble. You were exploring.
>
> ARCHER: I'm not sure there's much of a difference....
>
> ARCHER: I lost something out there, and I don't know how to get it back.[56]

In fact, Archer did not lose anything. It is these battles with self-doubt that allow him to develop a more seasoned, Hornblower-esque command style.

While Hornblower's psychological struggles unfold in lengthy internal monologues, in *Star Trek* they are converted into a recognizable mix of narrative devices and character constellations. On the one hand, they are facilitated by a signature narrative device—the *captain's log*. Roddenberry pointed out to writers that "sometimes it [the captain's log] suggests the Captain's stream of consciousness, any fears or doubts he might have at the moment" (23). In the series bible for *ST:TNG*, he reiterated that the log allows the captain "to annotate their personal responses and feelings about a situation as it is occurring" (13). Like with Hornblower's inner monologues, it is only the television audience who is privy to the logs kept by the captains.[57] There are only a few exceptions in episodes and films where the logs are used as records and/or evidence in the respective story.[58] Log entries not only contain the respective captain's emotional and moral conundrums, but they also allow for additional insights into the psychological processes that shape the "man alone" paradigm.[59] The captain's log often echoes Hornblower's predilection for self-analysis. It is also an outlet where the captains may vent their preconceptions and prejudices which they are not supposed to display openly in their line of duty. Occasionally, the audience receives even deeper insights into the life of the captains by way of their personal logs. It is there they ponder the moral implications of the many decisions they have to make.[60] Due to their archetypal judiciousness, they always struggle with their inability to remain at a critical remove from their subordinates.

A recurring pair of confidants represents the second venue through which the captains express their worries. Occasionally, the captains ever so briefly let down their guard in the company of their closest advisors. Each principal *Star Trek* captain has two people they confide in; their second-in-command being one of them. The second fixture in this character constellation is either someone who the captain knows from a previous command, or someone with whom they formed a deep bond by way of shared personal trials. Following this recognizable pattern, Captain Kirk's fallibility, his preconceptions, and his anxieties come to the fore in his iconic friendship with Spock and Dr. McCoy.[61] Captain Picard's carefully crafted introspection and introversion can only be glimpsed at for any length of time in his conversations with Commander Riker and the ship's counselor, Deanna Troi (Marina Sirtis). At their wedding, the captain eloquently outlines the relationship he has enjoyed with them.

> Will Riker, you have been my trusted right arm for fifteen years. You have kept my course true and steady. Deanna Troi, you've been my guide and my conscience. You have helped me recognize the better parts of myself.[62]

In this case, the captain produces a summary statement about the level of trust and intimacy he has cultivated over years of serving with the counselor. She acts as a sounding board for Picard's psychological struggles. What is more, he is fortunate in that he occasionally receives sage advice from a non–Starfleet source—the civilian Guinan (Whoopi Goldberg). During their encounters the audience gains more insight into the captain's complex psyche.[63] Captain Sisko forms a strong bond with this second-in-command, Kira Nerys, once they have overcome their initial differences. His closest advisor, however, is his Trill science officer, Jadzia Dax. As outlined by the showrunners, "Dax and Ben Sisko have worked together before ... back then, Dax was still in the host body of an elderly man ... and was something of a mentor to Sisko" (12). Despite their initial ideological differences, Captain Janeway and her first officer, Chakotay, also follow the Hornblower-Bush paradigm. Even so, she tends to confide most of her doubts and her emotional conundrums in her tactical officer, Lt. Tuvok, whom she had known for approximately twenty years. Lastly, Captain Archer also forms a relationship of trust with his second-in-command. However, he embarks on the *Enterprise* with his life-long friend and confidant, Charles "Trip" Tucker (Connor Trinneer), as his chief engineer. A captain's lack of psychological equilibrium is but one of two crucibles in which their personality is continuously forged.

Hornblower's fallibility is not limited to his psychological struggles, but also includes his dealings with the opposite sex. His preferred naval lifestyle inevitably leads to a distinct lack of domestic happiness. Forester described his hero as "the sort of man with whom any woman might fall deeply in love, and yet whom a discerning or intuitive woman would recognize as one neither to hold nor to bind" (100). Hornblower's first marriage proved to be unsatisfactory and painful for him.[64] His second wife and his third child, Richard, bring him a certain degree of family life. Even so, their relationship is fraught with a few extramarital improprieties, especially his recurrent affair with a young French aristocratic widow. Even though Hornblower lives out his life at the side of his second wife, he "was never a man to know complete happiness, and he was the kind of cross-grained individual who would distrust it when it was waiting for him" (126).

Already in the first pitch for *ST:TOS*, Roddenberry made it clear that the starship captain "lives a continual battle with self-doubt and the loneliness of command" (5). In a memo to one of his associate producers, he emphasized that while women "might appeal to his [the captain's] sense of fun, his real mistress is the ship" (qtd. Whitfield 238).[65] Even though Kirk undoubtedly has a reputation as a ladies' man, it does nothing to alleviate his lack of domestic happiness. The only relationship that bore a certain degree of promise not only fails, but its aftermath also exacerbates his domestic unhappiness when his son, David, is killed. He is killed in a series of events triggered by Kirk who goes on a mission to bring his first officer back from the dead. In short, the captain regains his second-in-command as a consolatory constant at the cost of his son's life.[66] As Kirk grows older and more nostalgic, he questions the domestic life that he did not have only to underscore the fact that his "band of brothers" represents his surrogate, indeed, his true family.[67] Making it explicit that he is cast along the same Hornblower-esque lines, Roddenberry simply stated that Picard "has gone the way we saw Kirk going, content with a 'starship love'" (1987: 23). Most, if not all of his romantic interests are impeded either by his sense of duty, which is dressed in a mask of decorum and self-discipline, or a seemingly contrived sense of mature propriety; or, a combination of both.[68]

Sisko is likely the most tormented captain when it comes to the domestic sphere. Introduced as a family man, his wife, Jennifer (Felicia Bell), is killed in the first ten minutes of *ST:DS9*'s pilot episode, leaving him to care for his son alone. Hence, domestic unhappiness is a part of his everyday life. After a series of potential love affairs fail to progress beyond even the earliest of stages,[69] a more permanent romantic interest presents itself in freighter captain Kasidy Yates (Penny Johnson). However, even this relationship is fraught with disappointment. First, Sisko has to arrest her for smuggling and she serves time in prison.[70] Once she is back on the station, the promise of a content family life is cut short due to Sisko's predetermined role as a spiritual "emissary." He is whisked away onto a higher plane of existence, leaving his pregnant wife behind.[71] Finding herself on the most distant station, the archetypal lack of domestic happiness holds particularly true for Janeway. It is her singular zeal to keep traveling and return home which make it impossible for her to achieve any meaningful domestic happiness outside the "band of brothers" paradigm. Already engaged to a man when *Voyager* is hurled 70,000 light-years across the galaxy, she has little chance of ever seeing him again. After some time, contact with Earth is established and she learns that her fiancé abandoned hope and married someone else.[72] Once freed from her obligations, the captain hesitatingly pursues a handful of romantic encounters with transient aliens and holographic phantasms.[73] Ultimately, she resigns herself to protecting her surrogate family—her crew of interstellar voyagers.

Captain Archer does not add much substance or variation to the captains' archetypal lack of domestic happiness. Archer's most intimate and functional relationship is arguably with his pet beagle, Porthos. Even so, his life of restless adventures is not entirely devoid of romantic entanglements.[74] However, they all occur in passing since he is eager to make "history with every lightyear"[75] he travels. Archer briefly rekindles his relationship with a former colleague, Erika Hernandez. She is the captain of *Enterprise*'s sister ship. The irony of their romance is self-evident since Archer is taken with the one other starship captain who also serves on distant stations. She is physically as far removed from him as he is from her. At their first encounter, she reminds Archer: "I'm married to Starfleet. Just like you."[76] This serves to foreshadow that any serious prospect of making this relationship work is doubtful at best. Consequently, all captains are restless wanderers in their desire to remain in command of a ship on which they sail to the most distant destinations in outer space. As desirable as it may be for them, their geographic transience takes its toll since being a Hornblower-esque "fighting naturalist" in space precludes peace of mind and domestic happiness.

"Call me Horatio": Chroniclers of a Future Already Recorded

Who then are *Star Trek*'s intrepid starship captains? They are *not* space cowboys, riding off into the starry horizons of the "final frontier." Instead, they sail the ocean of outer space much like the idolized and idealized seafaring captains of the Romantic imagination—the Nelson(s) and Cook(s) of popular myth. Not since the Golden Age of Sail has a ship captain held so many different responsibilities, performed such a diverse range of functions, or acted so independently and out of touch with their superior officers like the captains in Starfleet. Just like the officers of the Royal Navy were the vectors of a supposedly enlightened imperial project, the Starfleet captains perform a similar role in the 22nd, 23rd and 24th centuries. Not only does Hornblower serve as an omnipresent (whether explicit or implied) reference point, he is also the central node in *Star Trek*'s transatlantic maritime endowment, amounting to a historicized telling of its narratives.

It is all in the name. When Roddenberry made his starship captain a "Hornblower in space," he inadvertently tapped into the onomastically encoded significance that Forester attributed to his hero's given name. He then adopted its narratological function as the basic narrative situation in *Star Trek.* According to Forester, the name "'Horatio' came first to mind, and oddly enough not because of Nelson but because of Hamlet" (90). The onomastic significance of the name could not be more obvious. Arguably Hamlet's only loyal friend, Horatio has to act upon the onomastic meaning of his name—*oratore.* Hamlet pleads with him not to drink the poison so that he can tell Hamlet's story. Consequently, by making the archetypal starship captain a "space-age Captain Horation [sic] Hornblower" (5), Roddenberry also transferred his narratological significance. He stated that the captain "will be the focus of many stories—in still others he may lead us into the introduction of the guest star" (*ibid.*). Even though all *Star Trek* series boast large ensemble casts, there is hardly ever any doubt as to who occupies the most narrative space (except for *ST:DSC*).[77] The character premise for the captains makes it unmistakably clear that the stories told in the *Star Trek* continuum will always be about the captain (whether implicitly or explicitly).[78] After all, the principal Starfleet captains are the keepers of the captain's log, serving as the historicizing chroniclers of a future history.

7. "Take her out"

Nautical Traditions and Re-imagined Nautical Life in Space

Upon entering a mysterious sector in space, Captain Picard likens it to the edge of the Earth during a time when people still believed that the world was flat. He then reminisces about naval traditions. Jokingly, he expresses his uneasiness because in the past "crews threatened to hang their captain from the yard arm" for continuing past what the crews would consider the point of no return—the edge of the Earth.[1] His first officer reassures him that none of the crew were contemplating such action. Starfleet officers are intimately familiar with a selective range of naval traditions. For example, debating the finer points of where and how to accommodate flag officers for a conference on *Deep Space Nine*, Lt. Cmdr. Worf (Michael Dorn) insists that it is "naval tradition."[2] Though somewhat oblivious to the ritualized significance of assigning quarters, security chief Odo (René Auberjonois) offers an irascible response: "So is keel-hauling." Naval traditions, like all traditions, achieve their status as cultural practices by being repeatedly performed, and thus legitimized by and within a community of people who share certain institutional and ideological affiliations. Traditions are re-enforced by a set of narratives which are also shared by this community. Consequently, it is not surprising that Captain Janeway calls her helmsman "an old salt"[3] when she learns about his affinity for sea stories. Naval traditions and maritime stories are an essential repository of meanings for script writers to tell stories in a future that Roddenberry had envisioned to be similar to the 18th century. In fact, the world of *Star Trek* propounds a covenant of old salts—a term used for seasoned sailors proficient in the art of telling sea yarns. Starfleet officers perform naval traditions, re-enact a specific range of naval practices, and repeatedly fall back on textual and/or haptic artifacts of the Age of Sail to draw a validating parallel of similitude between life at sea and life in space. The fact that one page of a Hornblower novel[4] is quoted visually in the form of a so-called "Easter Egg" in two episodes of *ST:DS9*[5] is portentous in that it is Jake Sisko (Cirroc Lofton) who turns to C.S. Forester's text for inspiration. While there is no specific commentary on the text, once discovered, these scenes emanate a meta-fictional hue. It is remarkable to find an aspiring writer reading a text, which had inspired a young Roddenberry to conceive his fictional future, in said future roughly thirty years after Roddenberry first codified his ideas.

In the series bible of *ST:TOS*, Roddenberry stated that "we do keep a flavor of Naval usage and terminology" (27). Striking a transatlantic chord by linking the Age of Sail with contemporary naval customs, he emphasized that "our own Navy today still retains remnants of tradition known to Nelson and Drake." His extrapolative trajectory is clear; if the U.S. Navy still observes traditions, which were followed by the heroes of a British maritime past, then Starfleet might have retained some of these traditions, too. He reiterated the importance of naval life, form, and customs in the series bible for *ST:TNG,* where Starfleet's "traditional" practices serve as "acknowledgement of the naval heritage of Starfleet" (40). Consequently, the post–Roddenberry series follow the norms of naval pomp and circumstance in order to maintain continuity, cohesion, and familiarity on the part of the audience. In some cases, they even expand on them. *Star Trek*'s re-imagined naval life in space derives from a romanticized life at sea.[6] The world of *Star Trek* offers a seaborne life transposed into space, which, in the process, has become sanitized and seemingly more civilized. Even so, it repeatedly asserts a nostalgic similitude between the customs that govern life in space and those that ruled life on wooden ships at sea.

Star Trek's fourth maritime dimension emerges as a pastiche-like veneer of naval customs, performative texts, and the naval performers who stage them. This naval veneer can be mapped along three lines. First, *Star Trek*'s naval heritage amounts to a historicized telling of its stories. A naval tradition and an archive, the captain's log is used to record events, chart spaces, and add explanatory commentaries. It is akin to the narrative logs written by naval officers, such as Captain Cook, whose privileged position as chroniclers allowed them to produce historical knowledge. Second, *Star Trek*'s covenant of old salts re-enacts[7] the past by going through the motions of celebrating seemingly archaic naval rituals. Most of these rituals are accompanied by a key auditory marker—the bosun's pipe. The echoes of the pipe often accentuate comments that invoke direct links to a bygone age of wind, sail, and wooden vessels. The "band of brothers" leadership style and its St. Crispin's Day rhetoric, both archetypally ascribed to the Starfleet captains, are then also perennially performed as part of this veneer of naval heritage. Third, *Star Trek*'s world is permeated by a romantic lament for the mythologized grandeur and simplicity of the past. The sophisticated technology of a starship is poetically reproached by way of maritime intertexts taken from a literary imaginarium connecting both sides of the Atlantic. *Star Trek* is populated by spacefaring sailors who lay claim to a naval heritage by way of reducing and compressing a range of naval customs into a veneer of naval performances.

"Captain's Log, Stardate": Histories of the Future

"Captain's Log, Stardate 1513.1,"[8] were the first words of *Star Trek* broadcast on television. The audience saw the *Enterprise* in orbit of a planet while the log was narrated in a voice-over. The log immediately localized the events, which would subsequently unfold, at a certain moment in history—a history of the future. The historic anchoring is achieved by the authoritative and privileged power generally attributed to logs of seafarers and explorers. Their logs are considered archives of historical knowledge not least because they presumably contain events and circumstances as they were witnessed and/or paraphrased by those who wrote them down. At the same time, however, these sources are problematic archives of knowledge in that they consist of highly selective, narrated sequences of events, places, circumstances and characters. The keeper of the log holds considerable discursive power and privilege in creating those sequences. Hence, they always have to scrutinized in terms of reliability. When the first episode of *ST:TOS* aired, it is difficult to imagine that anyone realized that the captain was performing the onomastically encoded role as the narrator bestowed upon him by Horatio Hornblower. Even though the etymological root from which the name derived (lat. *horatius*) is not entirely clear, there are pertinent pointers towards a person who keeps and/or tells the time. He is essentially a chronicler of time's progression, i.e., the sequence of time.[9] Such a person is invested with discursive power that allows them to order, and thus make sense of the passage of time. In narratological terms, it translates into Hornblower becoming the focalizer of the narratives. He is the privileged lens through which the readers see his world and the events unfolding around him. By the same token, Starfleet captains are charged with the role of narrators chronicling the future in their captain's log.

Within the first two sentences of the first *ST:TOS* episode,[10] the log established a naval tone. It might have reminded audiences of mariners, sailing the high seas, travelling to exotic places, meeting alien peoples, and making/writing history with every nautical mile they journeyed. The log immediately provided viewers with a temporal anchoring and a spatial locale. While both were far removed from the viewers' immediate context, they were validated by a date and visual cues which underscored the temporal trajectory. After all, there was a spaceship approaching a planet. Hence, the scene must be set in a distant future where they have a different format of time-keeping. Still, the log was presented as a record of events which have just happened and/or are happening as the captain is recording the log. Kirk subsequently identified the identity of the people who were going to beam down to the surface and he provided a bearing as to where the mission was headed. His narration guided viewers along and provided commentary which not only signaled emotional involvement, but also foreshadowed the possibility of conflict. The *Star Trek Encyclopedia* (1999) defines the captain's log as the "official record of mission progress kept by the commanding officer of a starship or a starbase" (Okuda 276). Though certainly accurate, the subtle intricacies already found in the very first captain's log point to slightly more complex processes. The captain's log is but one in an archive of accounts of the future which *have been*—the use of the present perfect is crucial—recorded by the keepers of the logbook. They record *virtually*[11] the history of a future which has not happened yet. They employ a historiographic narrative discourse reminiscent of many explorers' journals which were widely circulated during the Golden Age of Sail.

The journals of Captain Cook provide us with a paradigmatic example. His journals have enjoyed considerable scrutiny. Cook's logs and journals—a distinction that is not always easy to make—are, according to Dan O'Sullivan, "problematical texts due to their dual nature as historical sources or traces of the past on the one hand, and as themselves examples of history-making on the other" (60). Hence, it becomes feasible to problematize the captain's log vis-à-vis scholars' criticism of Cook's journals, and conflate them with Roddenberry's comments about the log's function. The log is a text type which enables us to expose the power of narrative discourse, ask questions about the reliability of narration, and delineate its historicizing function.

During the Age of Sail mariners kept more than one log-type of text on their ships. Logs were kept by different people for different purposes, and were intended for different audiences. Usually kept by the sailing master, every naval vessel had a ship's log. It contained sailing directions, bearings, information about the wind and the weather, and a range of events that bore specific importance for the ship's voyage. These logs, however, "do not as a rule express opinions, ascribe causes, or make comments of any sort" (O'Sullivan 52). A loose collection of information, they were tied together by only a rough chronology. Officers were also encouraged, and as far as voyages of discovery were concerned, they were required to keep an additional type of text. They "kept their own logs instead of, or in addition to, journals, and the distinction between the two is often blurred" (*ibid.*). The authors of these texts drew on the official ship's log and arranged the different elements it contained into an "enabling pattern" (53). In short, they arranged them in narrative form. The Admiralty ordered Cook to keep such a log. On his first voyage, he was somewhat overwhelmed by the demands and expectations placed on his written account. He was to produce meticulous observations along ethnographic, botanical, geological, hydrographic, and psychological lines. What is more, he was instructed to adhere to contemporary standards of authenticity, "validated by the language of Baconian empiricism" (33). The captain fell somewhat short of his objectives and his first journal was heavily revised and edited by John Hawksworth. On his second and third voyage, however, he kept his journals not only with a view to publish them, but also with the intention of addressing them to a wider range of readers. Ultimately, the corpus of texts he produced emerged as a series of "narrative logs" in which he assumed the discursive authority of a historian, writing history "on the fly."

Like a historian, James Cook recorded, transcribed, interpreted, processed, and arranged disparate units of information into an arguably coherent narrative. With "the help of bridging passages," the mariner also crafted "explanations, causal linkages, passages of speculation, references to other parts, and so forth" (54), to achieve coherence. He employed a range of discursive strategies which foreshadow similar practices in the logs recorded by the *Star Trek* captains. For example, the explorer relates a first contact situation with a group of indigenous people at Botany Bay in the following:

> 29 April 1770
>
> Saw as we cam in on both points of the bay [Botany Bay] Several of the natives and a few hutts, Men, women, and children on the south shore abreast of the Ship, to which place I went in hopes of speaking with them accompanied by Mr Banks Dr Solander and Tupia; as we approached the shore they all made off except two Men who seemd resolved to oppose our landing.... I thout that they beckon'd to us to come a shore; but in this we were mistaken, for as soon as we put the boat in they again came to oppose us upon which I fired a musket between the two which had no other effect than to make them retire back where bundles of thier darts lay [...] Emmidiatly after this we landed which we had no sooner done than they throw'd two darts at us, this obliged me to fire a third shott soon after which they both made off, [...] Mr Banks being of opinion that the darts were poisoned, made me cautious how I advanced into the woods. We found here a few Small hutts made of the bark of trees in one of which were four or five small children with whome we left some strings of beeds, etc. [qtd. O'Sullivan 20–1].

This passage points to the discursive strategies that govern a narrative log. Captain Cook establishes the scene by localizing the events in a specific place and at a specific time. He identifies the people and their respective roles as events unfold. In carefully stating his intentions for going ashore and in admitting to a misunderstanding, we see him try to construct an argument which would vindicate his actions in the eyes of the reader. In short, the captain justifies the steps he took which he perceives were actually forced upon him. He adds a dash of heroic self-portrayal by way of the belated dispersal of ignorance regarding the darts, which may or may not have been poisoned. Lastly, he relates the outcome of the incident in positive terms by emphasizing his benevolence towards the children. The journals were written from a position of hindsight because Cook never "saw the presence of a double point of view ... as a literary problem" (Edwards vii). The same temporal dissonance also affects the captain's log.

Detailing the function of the captain's log in the series bibles for *ST:TOS* and *ST:TNG*, Roddenberry made it clear that they serve as crucial narrative devices, employing the same discursive strategies found in an explorer's journal. Signaled by the stardate, Roddenberry also placed particular emphasis on the historicity of the log.[12] Mostly used as a voice-over, the log's narrative economics usually include temporal gaps between the events which already happened, those that are about to happen, and the recording itself. Hence, the log also serves as a bridge from one act to another. In the naval world of *Star Trek*, the bridging function of the log mirrors the many ellipses found in sea romances. For example, Hornblower often comments on the long periods of tedious waiting and/or monotonous routine which tend to fuel his archetypal restlessness.[13] Cook also abridged many days during his travels because he considered them uneventful. Consequently, when Captain Kirk engages an enemy vessel in a prolonged cat-and-mouse game of maneuvers and counter-maneuvers, his log reads: "With all engines and systems shut down, the Enterprise is also playing the silent waiting game in hope of regaining contact."[14] In a supplement, he adds: "Now motionless for nine hours, forty-seven minutes."

The captain's log is not just a tool of narrative expediency. In many episodes, the captain's narration provides a complete scaffolding for the diegesis, ranging from exposition and introduction to transitions and summary closure. *Star Trek*'s naval archive is replete with examples. Picard's log entries relating an incident on Moab IV, however, serves as paradigmatic examples.[15] Taken together, all log entries essentially provide a full synopsis of the episode. In the first log entry, the exposition is clear and concise. It delineates the crew's whereabouts as well as their mission objectives. Picard continues the log in additional entries all of which refer back to the main entry by way of marking them as "supplemental." While the episode's main conflict is carried by the dialogs, none of it finds its way into the captain's log. Picard continues his entries by describing their course of action and he provides more details about how they intend to avert disaster. The log concludes in a fourth entry which briefly recaps the immediate aftermath of their successful mission. Interestingly, Picard's report does not close the episode. It is recorded roughly five scenes before the conclusion. While we as the audience witness the action unfold, the process of selecting and arranging units of information, which comes to the fore in Picard's logs, highlights the power of discourse. It impacts the implied historical reliability and authenticity of the logs.

It goes without saying that "no diarist can begin to record literally everything that happened during his day" (O'Sullivan 54). This simple fact opens an avenue for us to problematize the intricacies of power, hierarchy, and authenticity that shape logs as archives of historical knowledge. For example, there were long stretches of time when Captain Cook did not write any entries, or when he simply copied entries from the journals of other crew members. On his third voyage, there is a two-week gap between his last journal entry and his death on Hawaii. While his supernumeraries left records about the incident, the controversies surrounding his death are in part due to the absence of the privileged "narrator" along with the conflicting information found in the texts that are available.[16] Similarly, there are other type of logs kept on Starfleet vessels like medical logs, science logs, the first officer's logs, combat logs, and personal logs. They are, however, used less frequently and hardly share any of the historiographic primacy ascribed to the captain's log. This particular imbalance of power can be better understood by revisiting the captain's log as a venue where the captain can articulate his doubts and anxieties. The captain's log serves as an analog to Hornblower's long inner monologues in order to transpose the latter's signature bouts with doubt into a format that works on television and film.

A captain's tendency to express their troubles and fears in their logs usually goes hand in hand with them trying to justify and rationalize whatever actions they took, or are about to take. These strategies are congruent with recent scholarship looking at historical/biographical texts, such as diaries, memoirs, journals, and logs, through a lens of life writing. Historians remapped Cook's journals along these lines and their findings point to two nodes that bear significance for the captain's log. First, there is a dualism in the intentions for writing a narrative log in the first place. Second, we must consider the position of authorial power assumed by and ascribed to the writer/narrator both in relation to those who belong to the same hierarchies, and to those in later generations (especially historians and editors). Cook fashioned his reports in such a way that they justified his actions and explained how he successfully fulfilled his orders. Additionally, he was conscious of "presenting not only his voyages but also a portrait of himself—as unchallenged commander, as successful explorer and navigator, as sympathetic humanist" (O'Sullivan 55). As the narrator, he was also in a more privileged position since he produced "an item of historical evidence, a treasured relic of the past" (*ibid.*). In other words, the commanding officer's log is always the official version of events; and, in the case of Cook's voyages, his journals often became the site of the "agreed-upon version of events" when views of other crew members diverged too much.

Like Cook's journals, or the records of any explorer for that matter, the captain's log is also affected by the fallacies of narratological reliability and historical authenticity. There is but one log that serves to illustrate this most clearly—the personal log recorded by Captain Sisko in the sixth season episode "In the Pale Moonlight" (15 Apr 1998). The story is told entirely in flashbacks structurally tied together by Sisko's narration as we see him recording his log. Facing staggering numbers of casualties in a war in which the Federation and the Klingon Empire could use an ally, Sisko single-handedly decides to bring the Romulans, who have maintained a pact of non-aggression with the enemy, into the conflict. His decision sets him on a path where he is forced to make choices that become increasingly questionable. The moral duplicities and the complexities of political intrigue draw on the fallacies of log-keeping on the level of narration. Even though the computer puts a date on the log, Sisko's inability to talk to anyone else, even his closest friend, foreshadows the fact that there will not be an official log/version of the events that follow. He makes it clear that his personal log is the only tangible piece of evidence/record available. Thus, he exposes the value and discursive power of the log. The captain then details all the steps he took and how his initial deception failed only to be mitigated by Garak (Andrew Robinson) who had played Sisko as a failsafe option.

In recording his personal log, Sisko exposes the fallacious claim to historical accuracy in the official version of the events. Even though it is not provided, the official version would include the mysterious disappearance of henchmen, a written order to package a restricted biogenic compound for classified purposes, and the destruction of a Romulan shuttle with a high-ranking official on board along with sufficient evidence to point to the enemy as the perpetrator. There is, however, no official version because these events are disparate elements in the official records, devoid of a narrative adhesive applied by a narrating agent. By first recording and then deleting his log, Sisko leaves the audience as both witnesses and accomplices. This particular log exposes most clearly the power of narrative discourse used to craft the very fabric of historicity that is maintained in the naval archive of logs in *Star Trek*'s fictional albeit historical future. Sisko's recording upholds as much as it subverts the processes of keeping a narrative log.

By adopting the naval tradition of log-keeping and by making it a privileged narrative device, *Star Trek* employs the power of a historiographic discourse to historicize, i.e., to record and validate its fictional future. As such, the captain's log is a key component in *Star Trek*'s veneer of naval heritage. Without the captain's log, which is the official/authoritative record of events encountered by the intrepid space-borne explorers, *Star Trek*'s fabric of historicity would be significantly weaker. As a discursive site, the logs conflate the processes of history-writing and storytelling. As naval artifacts, they oscillate between the imagined authenticity and the misremembered reliability that used to be attributed to the narrative logs written by explorers in the past. They also betray a nostalgic urge to record future history for the benefit of future explorers, and thus for posterity. This is particularly evident when writers and producers tried to fill the gaps in their fictional history books. The series bible for *ST:ENT* states that Captain Archer knows that his "Captain's Logs will be studied for years to come," and so "he keeps especially detailed reports" (n.p.). Similarly, when he receives the order for the *Enterprise* to be decommissioned, Kirk exploits the log's bridging function to pass on the history of his ship to another generation.[17] As *The Odyssey* comes to the reader courtesy of Odysseus, so *Star Trek*'s space odyssey comes to us courtesy of the "Horatio Hornblowers in space."

"In best maritime tradition": Performing a Perennial St. Crispin's Day

Echoes of naval nostalgia emanate from the moments and sites where Starfleet captains perform their archetypal judiciousness. Theirs is the Nelson Touch, which is couched in St. Crispin's Day rhetoric. Not only is Horatio Nelson invoked on a few occasions, his command style—as a nostalgic echo—is also the *modus operandi* for how Starfleet captains arrive at important decisions in a romanticized, naval fashion. When Captain Picard helps Data rehearsing a Shakespeare play (*Henry V*) on the holodeck, the significance with regards to the Nelson Touch could not be more obvious. They work through Act IV, Scene 1, the night before the Battle of Agincourt (1415). Data plays Henry, who, disguised as a commoner, mingles with his men, trying to ascertain their morale and hear their thoughts on his leadership. After a little while, Picard pauses the program and compliments Data on his performance, observing that there is no better way to learn about the human condition than by studying the Bard. However, Data is confused about the leadership lesson he was supposed to learn. He is puzzled by Henry's need to disguise himself while conversing with his men, rather than to simply lead by example of the power invested in him. The captain explains that Henry is an example of a leader who before a battle is willing to put himself in a position to experience, and share, first-hand the fears of his soldiers.[18] The concern for those under one's command provides the crucial link to the Nelson Touch. The admiral reportedly appropriated the phrase "band of brothers" from the play and used it to refer to his captains and other officers under his command. It then became synonymous with a command culture founded on clear communication, mutual encouragement, and trust.

Assuming the role of Henry V redux, Captain Picard performs one aspect of the Nelson Touch, explicitly invoking the admiral. Before joining battle with the Borg, Picard decides to hide the *Enterprise* in a nebula. While we hear the voice-over of him recording his log, we see him touring the ship on the lower decks. He talks to ordinary crewmen who give him their reports as he passes through the bowels of the ship. Ultimately, he arrives in Ten Forward, a lounge with large, forward-facing panorama windows, which at that point seems to be devoid of any patrons. Seeking respite, and believing that he is alone, Picard is startled by Guinan, the barkeeper, who asks about his apparent insomnia and inspection. Picard replies that it is "[s]omething of a tradition, Guinan. The Captain touring the ship before a battle." Guinan recalls that traditionally the inspection is one performed "[b]efore a hopeless battle." The captain responds, "Not necessarily. Nelson toured the HMS Victory before Trafalgar."[19] The ritualized performance of this naval tradition serves as a symbol for courage and hope regardless of the odds; and it is yet another articulation of the captain's genealogical ancestry. Unlike Henry at Agincourt, and Nelson at Trafalgar, Picard does not win the battle with the Borg at first—but, he wins the war. The captain repeats the ritual on the eve of another battle. Not only does he indirectly quote himself, but he also implicitly invokes Nelson again. While recording another log entry, we see him touring the ship, rallying and comforting the crew with this presence—"The crew has responded with the dedication I've come to expect of them. And like a thousand other commanders on a thousand other battlefields, I wait for the dawn."[20] The Nelson Touch, however, amounts to more than just touring the ship before battle. Even though Picard is the only captain to invoke Nelson directly, all principal captains practice the full range of the Nelson Touch.

The Nelson Touch circumscribes an entire command culture that allowed the historical admiral as well as his fictional descendants to make well-informed decisions, which in turn led to successful results. Nelson, Cook, and Hornblower belonged to a generation of naval officers who realized that if they involved their officers in the decision-making process, they could limit misunderstandings and miscommunication, and thus improve their chances for success. Such a "band of brothers" moment usually takes the form of an officers' meeting, or, in more contemporary terms, a mission briefing. Commanders of their class would invite every officer, who was going to play an essential part in a mission, to the ship's great cabin, where the captain would discuss the current situation and the impending action. Rather than simply informing his officers of his decision, and giving them his plans for how to execute them, he would propose a general course of action and invite his officers to present suggestions. The captain's goal was to draw on their expertise as specialists in a collective of specialists not only to collect more information, but also to test the ideas he harbors himself for flaws in logic. The captain would even allow for carefully-phrased criticism and/or objections. At no point was it a democratic process, however, because once the captain had listened to his officers' positions, and once he had reached his decision, the order was given—his was the final word. Such a process made subordinates identify with, and thus care more about the mission.

Once Forester's hero had achieved a certain level of maturity, the Hornblower stories are replete with examples of the Nelson Touch. For example, upon taking his squadron of ships on a mission into the Baltics, he encounters a French privateer which he intends to capture. He convenes a council of his officers to delineate his plan. Once outlined, he invites questions in order to instill "band of brothers" sentiments among his officers, who are still new to him at this point.

> "I think that is all perfectly plain, gentlemen?" said Hornblower, looking round his cabin at his assembled captains. There was a murmur of assent. Vickery of the Lotus and Cole of the Raven were looking grimly expectant. [...] It was Duncan who asked the next question. "If you please, sir, is Swedish Pomerania neutral?" "Whitehall would be glad to know the answer to that question, Mr Duncan," said Hornblower, with a grin. He wanted to appear stern and aloof, but it was not easy with these pleasant boys. They grinned back at him; it was with a curious pang that Hornblower realized that his subordinates were already fond of him. He thought, guiltily, that if only they knew all the truth about him they might not like him so much. "Any other questions, gentlemen? No? Then you can return to your ships and take your stations for the night" [1945: 210–1].

The scene also exposes Hornblower's struggle to remain emotionally distant from the men to whom he, of course, feels strongly connected. Similar scenes bring to the fore the different roles of advisors and doubters that are distributed among his officers. The structural sequence of such briefings remains the same. It usually begins with Hornblower providing a general outline of his plan. The Nelsonian hero then "tricks" his officers into being drawn into his confidence by allowing them to contribute to the decision-making process. If there is a point that Hornblower does not want to dwell on, he leaves hardly any room for arguments, let alone dissent. He allows room for suggestions and objections but if he deems them impractical, unnecessary, or otherwise, he provides cues to move on. Ultimately, he concludes the meeting, signaling that he has arrived at a decision.

A resonating echo of historicizing nostalgia, the Nelson Touch can be observed in almost any episode that includes a meeting of the senior officers under the auspices of the captain. These meetings are yet another way of how *Star Trek* draws a line of naval similitude with the Golden Age of Sail. The effect of similitude is further enhanced by the space where the meetings take place. In the past, officer meetings did not take place on the quarterdeck, which was considered too public, but rather in the enclosed sanctum of the captain's great cabin. The cabin was located at the stern of a ship and it was usually the single largest enclosed room available on a vessel. The rear of the cabin opened to a seascape vista through a series of windows. When Starfleet captains retreat to hold counsel with their officers, they do so in a room which is variably referred to as briefing room, conference and/or observation lounge. Most of them are directly adjacent to the bridge and feature large panorama windows which face out the stern of the ship. The rooms on the *Enterprise* (A, D, and E) and on *Voyager* serve as particularly good examples. *Deep Space Nine*'s wardroom also opens up to a starry vista. Consequently, the discursive particularities and the sequential structure of the Nelson Touch are re-enforced by a spatial similitude with wooden sailing vessels.

Performed in a discourse of gentlemanly civility, the range of meetings, which exemplify the perennial re-enactment of the Nelson Touch, is substantial. Starfleet captains convene senior staff meetings not only to discuss battle plans, but also to arrive at decisions on science projects, the investigation of natural phenomena, or rescue missions.[21] Even though this naval tradition is re-enacted with great regularity, the "band of brother" moments are still most powerfully articulated on the eve of battles. A case in point can be found in the staff meeting which Captain Picard calls in the observation lounge shortly before his second invocation of Nelson. Upon discovering the devastating weapons capability of their opponent, the captain draws on the support and advice of his fellow officers in order to devise a course of action that will thwart the enemy's plan. As the scene's tension gradually rises (accompanied by a riveting musical score), the "band of brothers" paradigm that governs the naval lives of all principal *Star Trek* crews becomes particularly evident. Once the captain has reached his decision to do everything in his power to stop the enemy, his officers' understanding is expressed in an unspoken display of loyalty, duty, and unerring trust. The curt acknowledgment by his first officer serves as a summarizing statement. The scene is also reminiscent of the strong emotional bonds Hornblower shares with his officers. The repetitive re-enactment of the

Nelson Touch is, however, but one of many rituals and traditions practiced on Starfleet ships which are endowed with naval significance.

"It is naval tradition": More Naval Rituals

Naval nostalgia serves as a continuous underpinning in *Star Trek*'s fourth maritime dimension. It also applies to a series of naval rituals which are re-enacted as "futurized" memories of a bygone age of wind and sail. Many of these rituals, such as weddings, space funerals vis-à-vis burials at sea, court-martials, command transfer and/or coming aboard ceremonies, are accompanied by the shrill signal of the bosun's pipe. We all remember that whenever someone was raised on the ship's intercom in *ST:TOS*, the call was prefigured by sounding the pipe over the speakers. The bosun's pipe became an iconic marker so much so that a leading British naval historian remarked upon it in a study of how the Royal Navy shaped the modern world. Brian Lavery has noted that "even in science fiction, the USS *Enterprise* kept up the naval custom of piping the captain on board, even when his molecules had been disassembled and reassembled for transport" (139). Even though the audience repeatedly sees crew members blowing the pipe, the signal remains a largely disembodied echo of naval heritage because the bosun, a warrant officer,[22] is not given any performative life in the hierarchies of Starfleet. While the bosun's pipe is still used to call the crew and/or to signal orders on Starfleet ships, it is used primarily to provide nostalgic resonance between the Golden Age of Sail and its re-imagined transposition in outer space.

Life on a sailing vessel was circumscribed by endless monotony and ritualized routine, which actually served to maintain a community governed by rigid hierarchies. Neither is this the naval life that readers find in sea novels, nor are those the aspects transposed into outer space in *Star Trek*'s maritime future. Seen through the eyes of Hornblower, naval life is monotony pierced by moments of intense strain, exhilarating action, and solemn duties. Many of these events, such as burials at sea, punishments, court-martials, and Sunday services, brought the ship's crew together as a community. Attendance was mostly mandatory and they were usually held in a public space, i.e., the open deck of the ship. Hence, repetitiously performed rituals re-enforced the crew's sense of belonging and identity as much as they maintained structures of hierarchy, power, and order. Roddenberry tapped into this rich repertoire of naval rituals, some of which are painstakingly described in the Hornblower novels.

Speaking as the best man at the wedding reception of Riker and Troi,

Captain Picard proposes the following toast: "And in best maritime tradition, I wish you both clear horizons. My good friends, make it so. The bride and groom."[23] It is not surprising then that we see Starfleet captains perform weddings. Certainly without precedent in the Hornblower stories, *Star Trek* occasionally taps into the popular misconception that ship captains inherently have the power to conduct weddings. It is believed that the ritual has its roots in the Age of Sails. In the absence of a minister, captains might have performed weddings since they were the only persons with a legal authority that was sufficiently high. Even so, sea captains normally need a license to join people in matrimony.[24] Nevertheless, this popular misconception is readily appropriated as one of the many naval echoes we find in *Star Trek.* On a few occasions, weddings also serve to invoke a direct link between life in space and life on wooden ships. Captain Kirk was the first to invoke such a link. Performing the wedding of two crew members, he states: "Since the days of the first wooden vessels, all shipmasters have had one happy privilege. That of uniting two people in the bonds of matrimony."[25] Similarly, Captain Picard conducts the wedding ceremony of Miles O'Brien and Keiko Ishikawa. The captain uses almost exactly the same formulation as Kirk, referencing "wooden sailing ships" when he proclaims his delight in having the honor of marrying the two.[26] Captain Sisko, who himself is also invested with religious sanctity, performs a number of weddings some of which are performed according to Bajoran beliefs.[27] Even though there is no reference to wooden vessels, Sisko's own wedding is still conducted in Starfleet's naval discourse by his superior officer Admiral Ross (Barry Jenner).[28] The ceremony is opened by Ensign Nog (Aron Eisenberg), who calls everyone to attention on the bosun's pipe. In the same vein, Captain Janeway joins B'Elanna Torres and Tom Paris in matrimony.[29] Even though misremembered as a tradition that was common during the Age of Sail, Starfleet captains use weddings to add more resonance to *Star Trek*'s veneer of naval heritage.

Opening his speech, Picard describes his role as best man as his "solemn duty"[30] vis-à-vis other duties that usually fall to the captain. A captain's most solemn duty, however, regards occasions wrought with grief and sadness. They also require another naval ritual to be performed—a burial in space. A burial at sea is as much a staple element in sea novels as the exchange of broad sides. The Hornblower novels are replete with examples which serve as paradigmatic models. Not only does Hornblower's inner monologue provide the reader with insights into the troubled feelings he has over every single death that occurs under his command, but in it he also comments on the rigid sequence of how the individual steps of the ceremony have to be performed. For example, after two battles with the *Natividad,* Hornblower has to perform the grim ritual a number of times.

> Without a word Hornblower strode forward down the starboard side gangway, taking his prayer book from his pocket. The fourteen dead were there, shrouded in their hammocks, two to a grating, a roundshot sewn into the foot of each hammock. Hornblower blew a long blast upon his silver whistle, and activity ceased on board while he read, compromising between haste and solemnity, the office for the burial of the dead at sea. "We therefore commit their bodies to the deep—" The cook and his mates tilted each grating in turn, and the bodies fell with sullen splashes overside while Hornblower read the concluding words of the service [1937: 317].

The symbolism of this naval tradition is largely maintained when transposed into outer space. Once again it is the echo of the bosun's pipe and certain discourse formulas, such as toasts and invocations, that are added to underscore the naval solemnity of the occasion. When Starfleet officers gather to give their last honors to one of their fallen shipmates, the ceremony usually takes place in a large, open, public space (similar to the open deck of a ship), so that as many crewmen as possible can attend. The service might take place in the mess hall, the wardroom, on the bridge, or more often than not in the ship's torpedo bay. Maintaining maritime symbolism, a sailor's hammock is replaced by a torpedo casket. Just like hammocks are placed on a grating, covered by the Union Jack, the torpedo caskets are placed on a platform, draped either with the flag of the Federation or that of Starfleet Command. The senior officers and various crew members gather and present an honor guard. This is followed by a brief eulogy delivered by whoever wants to share their thoughts about the deceased—usually this falls to the captain. The service concludes with the order to commit the casket to depths of space (usually accompanied by the bosun's pipe).

With the funeral service for Spock, *Star Trek II: The Wrath of Khan* set the in-universe precedent for the burial in space ritual. After having sacrificed his life to save the ship, Spock's body is placed in a torpedo casket which is lowered onto the torpedo ramp. The senior officers gather at its head while crewmen line the length of the ramp. Being reminiscent of Hornblower, who finds "his voice trembling and tears in his eyes as he read the service" (1937: 352), for a junior officer, Captain Kirk, who is quite visibly traumatized by the death of his closest friend, delivers an emotional eulogy. The burial in space ritual is repeated a number of times throughout *Star Trek*'s long history with few variations. In a second-season episode of *ST:TNG*, the crew holds a funeral service in the transporter room. With the casket perched upright on the transporter platform, Captain Picard asks those who are present if they would like to say a few words. Following a brief speech by Data, the captain concludes the service by proclaiming that the casket with the body inside will be committed "to the timeless depths of space."[31] Not only does the captain use the discursive formula customary for the ceremony, but space is also invested with oceanic depth, and thus it is once again likened to the sea. The hammock-turned-casket trope continues to surface in *ST:DS9*. For example, a casket containing the remains of a fellow captain is draped with a Federation flag and placed in the wardroom. The crew gives their comrade a memorial along the lines of an Irish wake. In another episode, Captain Sisko keeps vigil by the casket that holds the body of his closest friend.[32] With starship *Voyager* traversing dangerous space on the other side of the galaxy, the chances for fatalities rose; and so did the chances to see a full burial in space ceremony.[33] In an episode of *ST:ENT*, the remains of Commander Tucker's clone, who was grown the save the engineer's life in a thinly disguised comment on stem cell research, is also given a full ceremony.[34]

The transposition of the burial at sea ritual and the hammock-turned-casket trope are further accentuated by a specific discourse formula which is rooted in the traditions of the Royal Navy. *Star Trek* crews tend to follow the death of a close friend with a particular toast. Coming together with his senior staff after having returned from the mission that claimed Spock's life, Kirk raises his glass to the words: "Absent friends."[35] In the Royal Navy it was customary for the officers of the wardroom to follow the drinking of the Loyal Toast (the health of the sovereign) with yet another toast. There was a different toast for each day of the week. They usually drank "to absent friends" on Sundays. Captain Picard repeats the gesture following the loss of Data's life. He gathers his senior officers, opens two bottles of Chateau Picard, and solemnly toasts: "To absent friends. To family."[36] Once again, this goes to show how the Nelsonian command paradigm governs the captain's surrogate family. The fact that Starfleet's veneer of naval rituals is widely known can be seen whenever a member of an alien species appropriates Starfleet's naval heritage. Rewriting the toast for Klingon culture, which initially served as a stand-in for the Soviet Union, Dahar Master Kor (John Colicos) drinks "to absent comrades."[37] The imitation of naval symbolism and the re-enactment of discourse formulas are central to re-imagining life in space along maritime lines.

Throughout the *Star Trek* continuum we see a number of formal coming-aboard ceremonies along with a few command-transfer rituals which occasionally also involve the christening of a starship. Not only do these rituals maintain a familiar symbolism, but they also display naval similitude especially in terms of language. Drawing on the textual substance of the Hornblower novels for paradigmatic models, it is possible to map these rituals as yet another part of Starfleet's naval heritage. Following a distinct ritualized pattern, a ceremony is held whenever a foreign dignitary and/or a fellow naval officer of senior rank comes aboard. The same goes for captains when they board their own ships. Seen through Hornblower's eyes as he pulls alongside his ship, the following shows the ritual of welcoming the captain back on his ship:

> Hornblower could hear all the expected noises now, could see all the expected sights; the bustle and clatter as boatswain's mate and sideboys ran to the gangway, the measured tramp of the marines, the flickering of lanterns. The boat ran alongside and he sprang to the ladder. It was good to feel solid oak under his feet again. The pipes of the boatswain's mates twittered in chorus; the marines brought their muskets to the present, and Bush was at the gangway to receive him, with all the pomp and ceremony due to a Captain arriving on board [1937: 250].

Even though Hornblower is someone who does not particularly enjoy the rigors of protocol, he admits to himself that the pomp and circumstance have a certain appeal. The ceremony is essentially the same when Hornblower is on the receiving end. When representatives of foreign governments, or other naval officers come aboard, they are received with full honors regardless of whether they approach in a boat, or board by way of a gangway when the ship is docked. The ritual includes a presentation of his senior staff on the part of Hornblower[38]—an official courtesy which is replicated in *Star Trek*.

Starfleet officers, especially the captains, continue to go through the motions of this naval tradition. The boat and/or the gangway as well as the side of the ship are symbolically approximated either by a shuttle docking at a starship's airlock, or by visitors beaming aboard, materializing on a transporter platform. The captain and a small contingent of senior officers then personally receive visitors. Occasionally, someone will sound the bosun's pipe. Since this ritual is performed throughout the *Star Trek* continuum, there are a great number of examples. Even so, the most pertinent cases can be found in some of the feature films.[39]

The use of specific naval language is central to ceremonies that involve the captain assuming command of a starship and/or transferring command to someone else. In either case, the ceremony, which includes the reading of the commanding officer's orders, is held in attendance of the crew. The specific wording of the orders echoes the formulaic phrases "directed and required" and "requested and required," which, according to Hornblower, were "the cherished prerogative of his naval superiors" (1945: 237). A performative act, the public reading of these phrases initiates the transfer of command. Hornblower goes through such a ceremony when he hauls down his flag as Commander-In-Chief in the West Indies. The ceremony is meticulously executed on the quarterdeck of his flagship. Hornblower takes position with his senior staff on the starboard side while the marine band and the bosun's pipe accompany the arrival of the relieving officer and his staff. Hornblower steps forward and reads out the Admiralty's orders. He then gives his final order to haul down his flag which is followed by a 13-gun salute. The whole process is repeated in reverse as Rear-Admiral Henry Ransom reads his orders to assume command of the West Indies Station upon which his pendant is hoisted.[40]

A specific set of expressions marks the command-transfer ceremony as yet another naval ritual in *Star Trek*. We find one of the most powerful examples in a sixth-season episode of *ST:TNG* where Captain Picard is ordered to temporarily surrender command of the *Enterprise* so that he can go on a covert mission. He hands over command to Captain Edward Jellico (Ronny Cox). The senior officers and a contingent of crew members take position as the two captains conduct the ceremony in full dress uniform. Picard reads his orders: "You are hereby requested and required to relinquish command of your vessel to Captain Edward Jellico, Commanding Officer USS *Cairo* as of this date."[41] The same ritual is also performed when a captain takes command of a ship for the first time. We see Picard assume command of the *Enterprise* in a time travel/flashback scene in the series finale of *ST:TNG*. Arriving in a shuttlecraft, he is piped aboard and proceeds to read his orders to the assembled crew: "To Captain Jean-Luc Picard.... You are hereby requested and required to take command of the USS *Enterprise* as of this date."[42]

Yet another example, which also shows the intimate relationship of a captain with his ship, can be found when Captain Sisko receives a replacement for the *Defiant*. With the senior officers in attendance, the ceremony is conducted by Admiral Ross on the bridge of the new ship. He reads the captain's orders: "From Starfleet Headquarters, Office of the Admiralty, to Captain Benjamin L. Sisko. As of this date, you are requested and required to take command of USS *Sao Paulo*."[43] As everyone begins to file out to explore the new ship, the captain is left alone on the bridge so as to acquainted himself with her on his own terms.

The christening of a ship is a quintessential naval tradition which is used for effect in the opening credits of *Star Trek Generations*. Shot from different angles and at different distances, the camera follows a bottle of champagne tumbling through the blackness of zero gravity. The lengthy sequence is brought to an abrupt end when the bottle shatters upon hitting the white hull of the *Enterprise-B*. Even though there is no discursive act which accompanies the christening, this sequence foreshadows an instance where *Star Trek*'s naval heritage is literalized. The movie goes out of its way to establish an irrefutable link between *Star Trek*'s re-imagined naval life in space and the romanticized grandeur of wind and sail. Attending the christening and maiden voyage of the *Enterprise-B*, Captain Kirk is instrumental in saving the ship from being destroyed by a stellar phenomenon; and he is killed in the process. As the survivors enter the room from which the captain was blown into space, the camera begins to pan into the darkness of space. In a highly symbolic visual transition, the starry blackness of space dissolves into the deep blue of the sea, creating semiotic similitude.

In the following scene, the audience sees a sailing vessel set against a placid seascape. As the camera moves in closer, the name *Enterprise* becomes visible on the stern of the ship, written above the windows of the great cabin. Standing on the quarterdeck, we see two figures (Picard and Riker) dressed in historical naval uniforms. Even though they are reminiscent of Royal Navy uniforms, any specific affiliation to one particular naval service remains unstated. However, when the costumes were sold at Christie's *40 Years of Star Trek* auction, the lot description read: "British sailing ship uniforms ... worn in the *H.M.S. Enterprise* holodeck scene" (Christies.com, "Sale 1778 Lot 86"). Given the continued influence of Hornblower on *Star Trek*, it is safe to conclude that the crew re-enacts the lives of Royal Navy officers on the holodeck where they have gathered to perform the promotion ceremony for Worf. The ceremony takes the shape of a mock court-martial. The accused is led up on deck as if he were on his way to receive punishment at the grating. As indicated by Riker, it is an established tradition on the *Enterprise-D* to stage a promotion ceremony as a period re-enactment on the holodeck. Setting this tradition on a wooden sailing vessel opens an opportunity for the captain to articulate yet another naval echo that contributes to *Star Trek*'s forth maritime dimension. He acknowledges Starfleet's naval heritage by way of a romantic lament for the presumed simplicity of wind and sail.

Upon concluding Worf's ceremony, Picard withdraws to the port side, i.e., the weather side of the quarterdeck—incidentally, this is also Hornblower's favorite place to think[44]—where he begins to muse about a bygone age.

> PICARD: Will, just imagine what it was like. No engines. No computers. Just the wind and the sea and the stars to guide you.
>
> RIKER: Bad food, brutal discipline.... No women![45]

The captain acknowledges Starfleet's naval heritage in that he emphasizes its lure of escapism. His musings are validated when he receives a personal dispatch from Earth prompting him to say: "The best thing about a life at sea was that no one could reach you. This was freedom, Will." The message contains devastating news: his brother and nephew were killed in a fire. By poetically reproaching *Star Trek*'s hyper-technological future, Starfleet's re-imagined naval life in space folds in onto itself since the paradigmatic model of wind and sail is deemed more desirable when viewed through a lens of unadulterated, nostalgic heritage. The sequence closes with all officers being called to the bridge in response to an emergency. As they walk onto the bridge, the world of wind and sail, and the world of outer space coalesce visually with the senior staff still wearing their historic uniforms vis-à-vis the regular Starfleet uniforms of the crew.

"Well versed in the classics": Maritime Intertexts

By weaving specific maritime intertexts into a number of episodes and movies, *Star Trek*'s fourth maritime dimension also speaks to a romantic lament and a poetic reproach. These texts and the way they are rewritten provide an additional textual anchoring for *Star Trek*'s naval future in a broader transatlantic, Anglophone cultural continuum. Apart from Herman Melville's *Moby-Dick* (1851), the poem "Sea-Fever" (1902), written by British poet laureate John Masefield, is the most pertinent maritime intertext. By juxtaposing Masefield's poem with Gene Roddenberry's first publication, a poem titled "Sailor's Prayer" (1945), it becomes apparent how the former was likely appropriated and radically rewritten in the latter. Its original connotation and symbolism were discarded in order to install a romantic lament for the romanticized Golden Age of Sail by poetically reproaching *Star Trek*'s future of maritime similitude. Roddenberry's little-known poem appeared in the *New York Times*' literary supplement incidentally next to an uncredited text about transoceanic

Sea-Fever

1 I must down to the seas again, to the lonely sea
2 and the sky,
3 And all I ask is a tall ship and a star to steer her
4 by,
5 And the wheel's kick and the wind's song and the
6 white sail's shaking,
7 And a grey mist on the sea's face and a grey dawn
8 breaking.

9 I must down to the seas again, for the call of the
10 running tide
11 Is a wild call and a clear call that may not be
12 denied;
13 And all I ask is a windy day with the white clouds
14 flying,
15 And the flung spray and the blown spume, and the
16 sea-gulls crying.

17 I must down to the seas again to the vagrant gypsy
18 life,
19 To the gull's way and the whale's way where the
20 wind's like a whetted knife;
21 And all I ask is a merry yarn from a laughing
22 fellow-rover,
23 And quiet sleep and a sweet dream when the long
24 trick's over.

ILLUSTRATION 2. Poetic echoes from "Sea-Fever" are present throughout the *Star Trek* series and films.

rockets. By the time the poem was published, Roddenberry had already read the first Hornblower stories. Consequently, the poem demands closer attention since it provides an additional key for how Roddenberry saw the mythologized age of wind and sail, the romantic qualities he ascribed to it, and how they informed his view of a maritime future in space. Even though there is no direct textual link between the two poems, there are a number of notable parallels which provide an avenue for understanding how "Sea-Fever" was meaningfully woven into the intertextual fabric of *Star Trek*'s maritime future.

First published in his anthology *Salt-Water Ballads* (1902), June Dewyer contends that "Sea-Fever" "remains today one of the writer's best-known pieces" (5). The anthology was directly born out of the author's experiences as a teenager on a school ship. Even though he was inspired by the sea and intrigued by sailing vessels, he was not really a skilled sailor himself. Despite having successfully graduated in seamanship, his career as a British Tar in the Royal Navy was short. Still, he maintained his affinity for the sea together with his fascination for sailing ships. "He admired the sailors' storytelling abilities and tried hard to emulate them" (14), Deywer has argued, which is evident in his form and execution. His poems have little in common with other late Victorian poetry since his style is marked by a curt straightforwardness. Masefield saw himself as a speaker for the common sailor and his simple albeit disadvantaged lifestyle. Even though he could do little to alleviate sailors' hardship, he could speak to it by drawing on his own experiences. However, Masefield's admiration for the narrative power of old salts was tempered by his intent as well as the poem's content. The text was informed by the harshness which he was subjected to at the hands of some of those men. Consequently, the maritime characters in his *Salt-Water Ballads* are not the same Nelsonian heroes found in sea novels. He disregarded complex form in favor of "choral repetitions and the galloping anapests of the sea chantey" (18). "Sea-Fever" is thus imbued with a musical pattern which is further enhanced by auditory metaphors (lines 3, 5, 6, 8). He kept the rhyme simple and mostly restricted to couplets. The theme of the poem centers on the irresistible allure of the sea felt by the individual mariner. Yet, instead of being rooted in romanticized grandeur, sentimental heroism, and exotic escapism, the allure stems from irrationality, ambiguity, and a primal, almost fatalist urge. By equating the allure with a fever, the author "reinforces the impression that love of the sea is not an aesthetic experience; it is a visceral one" (23), in which the narrating old salt succumbs to pathologically real pyrexia. At first glance, there seems to be little that is compatible with the re-enforced and re-enacted naval nostalgia in *Star Trek*.

There is little known about Roddenberry's poem and what inspired him to write it. It was likely among the first pieces of creative output he generated while enrolled in a series of workshops for writers. The text incidentally echoes and amplifies many of Masefield's figurations. Roddenberry, however, replaced visceral irrationality with a romantic, boyish longing for a seaborne life of escapism and adventures. The title—"Sailor's Prayer"—already signals a significant change in that it places emphasis not only on the individual, but also on deference to a higher authority. Knowing Roddenberry's stance on religious beliefs, iconoclastic destiny is a more likely source for the mariner's evocative appeal than a resignation to divine intervention. Seeking only a "glimpse of the sea," at first, the text quickly gives way to the mariner's "thrill" of intimate contact with the physicality of the sea (lines 1–4). The drab loneliness of maritime life in Masefield seems to be left in the wake of Roddenberry's fascination with the sea. Not only does Roddenberry try to imitate the musical pattern of the sea chantey, but he also maintains (more successfully) the auditory metaphors found in Masefield. Even so, Roddenberry's romantic re-write comes to the fore in that Masefield's wailing cries and calls are substituted for more melodic sounds (like "sing," "tune," "music," and "beat"). The individual mariner hails the excitement and escapist adventures the sea offers. Rather than asking for a ship, he demands direct control of the wheel and thus the ship's destiny (line 6). Gone is the razor-sharp cutting of the wind as nothing less than a "northern gale" provides another voice in nature's choir. What remains resonant is both authors' clear appreciation for the narrative power and allure of old salts along with the promise of a "vagrant gypsy life" (lines 17–18). Indeed, once the life of Masefield's mariner is over, there is nothing but a "quiet sleep" waiting for him (line 23). Yet, a gypsy's presumed slyness emerges in the "cunning" soul of Roddenberry's sailor who refuses the eternal rest found on land. This is clearly reminiscent of the Nelsonian hero in that he is usually able to steal one more "trick"[46] from death so that he can continue his adventures. Hornblower and the *Star Trek* captains are cast in the same vein.

The way how "Sea-Fever" is woven into *Star Trek* amounts to it serving as a foil. It is used to imbue the future with the lament and longing that Roddenberry felt for the age of wind and sail. While the words are Masefield's, their rewritten meaning is Roddenberry's. Kirk commits the most salient appropriation of the poem when he tries to deal with the distinct possibility of being replaced by a machine. In a second-season episode of *ST:TOS*, the *Enterprise* becomes the testing ground for the revolutionary M5 computer system. Designed by Dr. Richard Daystrom, it can operate an entire starship without any crew. Not only would it be more efficient, but it would also reduce the risk of losing Starfleet personnel to the hazards of space. Kirk is dismayed and his ego is bruised when a fellow captain calls him "Captain Dunsel"[47]—a term used by midshipmen for parts that do not serve any purpose. Kirk confides in

McCoy about how helpless and how powerless he felt when the computer performed his job. He proposes a toast to himself as Captain Dunsel which McCoy counters with a toast to the real captain of the *Enterprise*. This prompts Kirk to quote the second line from "Sea-Fever" and he adds a comment to contextualize it.

> "All I ask is a tall ship, and a star to steer by." You could feel the wind at your back in those days. The sounds of the sea beneath you. And even if you take away the wind and the water, it's still the same. The ship is yours. You can feel her. And the stars are still there, Bones.

Kirk equates life on a starship directly with the naval life of wind and sail. Even though he emphasizes that the void of space has replaced the sea and the wind, it has already become clear that outer space is discursively likened to the ocean. Moreover, the "ocean of space" metaphor often becomes literalized.

The poem is also used to poetically reproach the move to take *Star Trek*'s naval paradigm away from its nostalgic wind-and-sail similitude and heritage, and move towards a stage that would be equivalent to the Age of Steam. The figure of the "poetic reproach" (240), has a nautical precedent in Herman Melville's *Billy Budd* (1924). In the chapter Melville dedicated to Nelson, he bemoans the loss of naval gallantry which he locates in the Golden Age of Sail. He addresses the reader as someone "who can hold the present at its worth without being inappreciative of the past" (*ibid.*), when he introduces Nelson's HMS *Victory* floating in Portsmouth harbor as an example. For him, the ship serves "not alone as the decaying monument of a fame incorruptible, but also as a *poetic reproach*, softened by its picturesqueness, to the Monitors and yet mightier hulls of the European ironclads" (*ibid.*, emphasis added). The poetic reproach is written in a discourse of nostalgia. During the heyday of the Age of Sail, a ship-of-the-line represented the epitome of technological progress and sophistication. At the same time, the new technology of steam power poured out of the workshops of burgeoning industrial nations. The protagonists of sea romances tend to view steam technology with suspicion because—like the M5 computer—it would make redundant a lot of manpower, and thus the art of seamanship. Hornblower voices his anxiety about this new technology upon being confronted with a small flotilla of steam tugs in the port of New Orleans.[48] Even though hyper-technological in its premise, Kirk re-enacts and reiterates the poetic reproach by maintaining *Star Trek*'s wind and sail paradigm for a little longer when he ultimately saves the human factor from the fallacies of the machine.

"Sea-Fever" is used as an intertext on three other occasions in the *Star Trek* continuum. Kirk quotes the second line of the poem again in *Star Trek V: The Final Frontier*, articulating even more of the boyish longing for adventure and escape found in Roddenberry's "Sailor's Prayer". At the beginning of the film, Kirk, Spock, and McCoy are on shore leave in Yosemite Valley. Their respite does not hold for long as the senior staff is recalled to the ship to respond to an emergency. Heading towards the Moon in a shuttle, the *Enterprise* comes into view. The ship hangs suspended, exposing its graceful lines in front of a full view of Earth's only satellite. The scene appears as a reflection on the shuttlecraft's window through which it is beheld by the three men. It prompts Kirk to quote Masefield which is followed by a brief argument over the poem's source. This scene shows once again how "Sea-Fever" was appropriated and rewritten to underscore *Star Trek*'s naval nostalgia. Kirk's "sailor's prayer" is answered when he is presented with the vehicle of his desires. He inscribes the ship with the empowering agency that lets him escape his landlocked retreat.

The repeated use of "Sea-Fever" inspired the writers of *ST:DS9* to continue the poem's intertextual presence, and to fold its appropriation in on itself by way of a parodical play on fans being familiar with it. Found on the ship's dedication plaque, the second line of the poem became the ship's motto for the *Defiant*. Despite being rather small when compared to the *Enterprise,* or even *Voyager,* the *Defiant* is a tall and proud ship since it is one of Starfleet's most powerful warships. It demands the same respect and adoration from its captain like all the other ships. The Ferengi, a gnome-like alien species who live in a hyper-capitalist society, delivered the parodical play on the poem. In one particular episode, Quark (Armin Shimerman), who owns the bar on the station, borrows a shuttle to fly his nephew to Earth (or so everyone thinks). Assured of the ship's space-worthiness, he admits to himself: "All I ask is a tall ship and a load of contraband to fill her with."[49] This goes to show that Masefield's poem has come a long way from being rewritten in order to emphasize *Star Trek*'s naval future vis-à-vis a romantic nostalgia for wind and sail. It is not, however, the only maritime intertext which was appropriated for this purpose.

Though quoted only once, the fact that Captain Picard sings the anthem of the Royal Navy, *Heart of Oak* (1759), bears considerable significance because it is used to hint at a Starfleet tradition. In fact, it is not the "real" captain who performs the song. In this particular episode, Picard is abducted by aliens who want to study his leadership style. They replace him with a *doppelgänger* who has all of the captain's memories. On one particular occasion, the captain visits Ten Forward which is full of patrons, including some of his senior officers. He approaches his chief engineer at the bar to commend him on increasing engine efficiency. Uncharacteristically for the captain, he seems to openly acknowledge and invite the attention of the patrons in the lounge. The captain then orders an ale for his officers and even buys a round for everyone present. Picard goes ahead and proposes a toast only to remember that when he was at Starfleet Academy they usually followed a toast with a song. While his senior officers are perplexed by his behavior, a group of regular crew members readily joins the captain and *Heart of Oak* reverberates in the room. It is the captain's insistence on tradition coupled with the crew being conversant with this old navy song which further corroborates Starfleet's covenant of old salts. Picard points to a naval heritage of wind and sail which is actively passed from one generation to another as part of their training.

The song's position in the myth of the British Golden Age of Sail is self-evident. Not only does it point out how Britons celebrated their seaborne identity during the Age of Sail, but it is also shows how Nelsonian heroes and their jolly tars have since become mythologized. The song resonates in a chorus of triumphalism which stems from Britain's realization that it was on the verge of ruling all trans-oceanic seascapes. The lyrics reiterate Britain's benign liberal ideas and the benevolence embodied by one of their principal agents—the men of the Royal Navy. Even though Starfleet's ships are no longer made of English Oak, they are populated by naval officers who continue to *remember* that jolly tars are a part of their collective genealogical ancestry.

Not only does Picard sing *Heart of Oak*, but he also continues the jolly-tars-in-space trope in another musical echo of naval heritage—*A British Tar*. Co-written by William Gilbert and Arthur Sullivan, the song is part of the comic opera *H.M.S. Pinafore* (1878). The opera is a satiric piece which investigates and pokes fun at Victorian social mores, its rigid class divisions, traditional gender roles, Nelsonian hero figures, and the presumed civility of naval discourse. It also enjoyed great success in the U.S.[50] The song served as a maritime intertext in the form of comic relief on the narration level and as a diversion in the diegesis of *Star Trek: Insurrection*. Captain Picard intervenes in a secret project designed to relocate a small group of aliens without their knowledge so that Starfleet can mine their planet's rings for a life-extending substance. Disguised as a non-invasive mission of observation, the project includes Data. When he learns the real reasons for their mission, he exposes the observers to the locals. Since Data is damaged in the process, his android programming enters a failsafe mode and he takes everyone hostage. When the Picard and Worf approach the planet in a shuttle, Data attacks them. Picard devises a diversion which would allow him and Worf to get closer to Data. The captain decides to sing *A British Tar* over the intercom so that Data might join in while Worf prepares to dock their shuttle. The android had been rehearsing the song before he left on his mission. Picard's plan works and the two go through nearly the entire musical routine, outlining the judicious character and righteous prowess of the British Tar which are rooted in his innate sense of honor and virtue.

In the opera, the song is distributed to the crew of the *Pinafore* by the First Lord of the Admiralty to "encourage independence of thought and action in the lower branches" (Silvers n.p.). It stresses the judiciousness of British sailors regardless of rank. Consequently, we see Data perform the role of the idealized tar which serves to foreshadow the impending vindication of his behavior. The song functions as a musical articulation of his innate sense of right and wrong, i.e., his failsafe programming. The reasons for why it was activated along with Starfleet's secret mission are revealed to Picard only after he has successfully apprehended Data. It goes to show that this maritime intertext, which might easily be mistaken as mere comic relief, also contributes to *Star Trek*'s continuous re-enactment of naval life in outer space.

The Melvillean Interlude

As a maritime intertext, Herman Melville's *Moby Dick* (1851) deserves particular attention. On the one hand, the *Star Trek* continuum repeatedly drew on the text's symbolism and the universal appeal of its characters to underscore its maritime future. On the other hand, the novel also provided an additional anchorage in *Star Trek*'s transatlantic maritime imaginarium. Framed by the sea yarns of James Fennimore Cooper and Edgar Allan Poe, and Jack London's *The Sea-Wolf* (1904), *Moby Dick* is arguably the most critically acclaimed sea novel in 19th century American literature. *Star Trek*'s appropriation of the tale amounts to a formulaic retelling of its quest and revenge plot which includes readily recognizable symbolism along with either misquoted or rewritten passages from the novel. It also serves to adorn *Star Trek*'s net of maritime intertexts with a claim to literary sophistication. Echoing Spock's conversation with Doctor McCoy, Starfleet's covenant of old salts is indeed "well versed in the classics,"[51] with Melville's masterpiece providing a transatlantic counterweight to Masefield's "Sea-Fever," Garrick's *Heart of Oak*, and Gilbert and Sullivan's *A British Tar*. Even so, *Star Trek*'s borrowings from *Moby Dick* amount only to a fraction of the palate offered by a text which "swallows as much of the world as it can, reaching out from cetology and the history of whaling to theology, philosophy, literature, art, and the farthest reaches of human history in meteoric flashes of analogy and metaphor" (Foulke 118). Even though the tale offers a plethora of meanings, *Star Trek* tapped into the text to systematically albeit reductively extract a particular set of character dynamics along with quotable material, and symbolic contours that added to its veneer of maritime intertextuality. *Moby Dick*'s intertextual presence has, of course, not gone entirely unnoticed. Barrett et al. have asserted that the tale is simply used as a "treatment of revenge" (23). While not entirely incorrect, they fall short of fully appreciating the systematicity and regularity with which the novel was woven into the maritime fabric of *Star Trek*. Only if we look at how the text was explicitly adapted and also rewritten on a total of five occasions[52] in the *Star Trek* continuum—and, only if we look at them in concert—can we see a particular pattern emerge.

Spliced into two guises of the monomaniacal captain, the Ahab character strain is articulated along two lines. First, there is *the forlorn Ahab* who pursues his quest until he meets his inevitable demise at the hands of the whale. Only characters who are not the principal *Star Trek* captains slip into the role of the 'original' Ahab. The similitude between the forlorn Ahab and the captain in the novel is further accentuated in that they share physical scars and/or metaphoric equivalents thereof; they look worse for wear.[53] However, there is also *the redemptive Ahab*. He echoes the captain in the novel when the latter revisits and briefly questions his own life in Chapter 132 (The Symphony).[54] The redemptive Ahab is actually prevailed upon to desist in his quest lest he lose everything he holds dear. Regardless of which permutation of Ahab manifests in *Star Trek*, they are used to comment on questions of rationalism. Whenever *Moby Dick* is woven into *Star Trek* stories, there is usually one or more characters who re-enact the role of Ahab's first mate, Starbuck. More specifically, the two permutations of Ahab are always the result of either a Starbuckian success or a Starbuckian failure in reasoning with the captain. In the novel, Starbuck represents the voice of reason, logic, and professional pragmatism. Despite being the only one entitled to question the captain's course of action, he ultimately fails to impart his reasoning to Ahab.[55] However, we see Starbuck succeed in some of *Star Trek*'s retellings of the tale. Regardless of whether they are forlorn or redeemable, *Star Trek*'s Ahabs serve only as a foil for elaborating on the characters' guilt that fuels their illogical need for revenge. All Ahabs feel guilty for having failed at something, or someone. Whether or not the captains come to terms with their guilt, ultimately depends on *Star Trek*'s Starbucks and how successful they are in employing a language of reason.

The white whale blew its intertextual presence for the first time in *ST:TOS*, "The Doomsday Machine" (20 Oct 1967). The *Enterprise* follows the distress call of her sister ship, the *Constellation*, only to discover that all the planets along their path have been destroyed by a monstrous space-borne leviathan—a planet killer. The *Constellation*'s captain, Commodore Matt Decker (William Windom) obviously dons the guise of the forlorn Ahab. His self-destructive need for revenge stems from an openly articulated feeling of guilt. It is revealed early in the episode when Kirk tells Decker about the destruction of the planet which the latter used as a safe haven for his crew.

Decker feels guilty for having abandoned them and for his inability to protect them from the planet killer. Even though Spock provides a reasonable, scientific explanation for the planet killer, reason cannot be imparted to Decker. Both Spock and later Kirk use a Starbuckian discourse of reason and logic but to no avail. Ultimately, it is his guilt as much as the planet killer that consume Decker.

Another intertextual appropriation of *Moby Dick* took its root in *ST:TOS*, "Space Seed" (16 Feb 1967), and then provided the plot for *Star Trek II: The Wrath of Khan*. In the film, some of the novel's symbolism gave way to a small corpus of quotable material which was rewritten to fit the maritime physicality of outer space. The antagonist Khan Noonian Singh (Ricardo Montalban), a genetically engineered *uebermensch*, assumes the role of the forlorn Ahab. He ascribes the role of the white leviathan to Kirk. Having been exiled by Kirk on what became an inhospitable planet, Khan blames the captain for the death of his wife and his superhuman followers. Khan's hatred and desire for revenge are once again but a foil for equipping the character with psychological depth rooted in guilt. He feels guilty because his "superior intellect,"[56] proved insufficient to save his loved ones. Kirk knows that Khan's quest for revenge belies a false sense of pride and excruciating guilt. "White Kirk" on his "white starship" taunts the forlorn Ahab by stabbing right into his sense of guilt upon having escaped yet another attempt on his life. Like Ahab, Khan meets his inevitable demise at the hands of the whale named Kirk in their third encounter.

Nearly the entire intertextual appropriation of *Moby Dick* is carried by Khan as the forlorn Ahab. It is already discernible in Khan's physique, which, apart from missing the wooden leg, is reminiscent of Ishmael's first impression of the captain.[57] When Kirk sees Khan for the first time in the movie, we see the latter as a tall, brawny man whose chest is half-exposed. He has long gray hair and a bronze skin complexion. Khan also bears a distinctive scar—instead of blemishing his face it marks his chest. Being a forlorn Ahab also means that Khan's Starbuck, a follower named Joachim (Judson Scott), fails to prevail upon him to cease his quest. Their exchanges give rise to a number of quotes from the novel which were rewritten so that they apply to *Star Trek*'s re-imagined maritime future in space. Not only does Khan paraphrase Ahab when the latter talks to Starbuck on the quarterdeck of the *Pequod*—"He tasks me; he heaps me" (136)—but, by rejecting Joachim's point, he also seals his fate much like Ahab sealed his upon rejecting Starbuck's last, frantic appeal—"Moby Dick seeks thee not. It is thou, thou, that madly seekest him!" (465). When Khan lies dying, his physical appearance echoes Ahab's descent into madness—"his torn body and gashed soul bled into another" (153)—and as he watches the *Enterprise* recede into the ocean of space, he quotes the captain again—"From hell's heart, I stab at thee; for hate's sake I spit my last breath at thee" (468). Such extensive borrowing was to be expected since *Moby Dick* is also quoted visually; a copy rests on Khan's bookshelf and it is safe to assume that he had enough time to study it during his exile.

Moby Dick was also used to craft the plot of a fifth-season episode of *ST:VOY*—"Bliss" (10 Feb 1999). It also features a forlorn Ahab. The crew encounters a massive space-dwelling entity which, unbeknownst to them, uses its telepathic abilities to create illusions based on its prey's desires to lure it within reach. The being feeds on starships. Seven of Nine (Jeri Ryan), the holographic doctor (Robert Picardo), and Naomi Wildman (Scarlett Pomers) are the only crew members who do not succumb to the creature's illusions because they do not share the crew's desire to return to Earth—*Voyager* is their home. Inside the creature's belly, they encounter a small alien ship which is manned by Qatai (Morgan Sheppard) who has been hunting the creature ever since it devoured his family. Together, they devise a plan to upset the being's digestive system so that it spits out their vessels. Having reached safety, Qatai tries to recruit the doctor for his quest to which the doctor responds: "An Ishmael to your Ahab? No thank you."[58] Qatai's monomaniacal need for revenge appears rather subdued. He is only a weak echo of Ahab when he is about to be drawn to the depths of the sea by the whale. Even so, Qatai definitely looks the part since he is a tall, burly figure with gray hair. His alien forehead is also crisscrossed with scars. Once again his obsessive quest briefly gives rise to a discussion of his real motivation—guilt. He feels guilty for having been too late to save his family and guilty for having survived. There is only a hint of Starbuckian reasoning in the Doctor's and Seven's scientific elaborations about the creature which are simply brushed aside by Qatai.

In the case of *ST:TOS*, "Obsession" (15 Dec 1967), Captain Kirk assumes the role of a redemptive Ahab, who, though reluctantly, listens to his Starbuckian advisors. In the episode, the crew encounters a vampiric cloud which feeds off the red blood cells of its victims. When Kirk was still a lieutenant on the *Farragut*, he encountered the same entity which killed two hundred crewmen, including his captain. Young Kirk manned the ship's weapons during the encounter and he happened to hesitate for a moment before he fired. He secretly blames himself for the casualties left in the wake of the attack. The captain's quest for revenge is once again but a foil for ascertaining the depth of his guilt so that he may come to terms with it. Kirk's obsessive pursuit of the cloud, during which he increasingly jeopardizes the ship and the crew, is ultimately redeemed in that he reluctantly begins to listen to voices of reason (Scotty, Spock, and McCoy). Starbuck's discourse of reason makes the captain finally realize that he could not have done anything to prevent the tragedy on the *Farragut*. In seeing reason, he succeeds in replacing his need for revenge with a more practical course of action—simply bait and kill the cloud once and for all.

In the same vein, Captain Picard also slips into the role of the redemptive Ahab when he confronts a nemesis from his past—the Borg Collective. Once assimilated by them,[59] Picard's violation at the hands of this cybernetic species comes to haunt him in *Star Trek: First Contact* when they travel back in time to change humanity's history. In the process, they take possession of the *Enterprise,* making Picard and his crew the last line of defense. As their situation becomes increasingly dire, the only chance for defeating the Borg seems to lie in self-destructing the ship. While his crew agrees on this course of action, the captain uncharacteristically rejects their suggestions. He is cornered and confronted by Lily Sloane (Alfre Woodard), a young woman from Earth's past, whom the captain has rescued from the Borg. Picard attempts to justify his irrational decisions which opens an avenue for Lily to glimpse at his rage and guilt. Shortly before breaking into a violent outburst, the captain states that this "is not about revenge."[60] Indeed, Ahab's quest for revenge serves yet again as a thinly disguised foil belying a deep sense of guilt. While he was a member of the Collective, the Borg misused him to defeat a large fleet of Starfleet ships. His guilt stems from him believing that he was too weak to resist the assimilation process. Like Kirk blames himself for the deaths on the *Farragut,* Picard blames himself for all the deaths he caused. Ultimately, it is Lily's Starbuckian discourse of reason which allows the captain to come to terms with his misguided revenge. Shocked by his violent outburst during which he smashes a few model ships, he retreats into contemplation and paraphrases Ishmael's description of Ahab's relationship with the whale—"And he piled upon the whale's white hump, a sum of all the rage and hate felt by his own race. If his chest had been a cannon, he would have shot his heart upon it."[61]

Star Trek's appropriation of *Moby Dick* also transferred the whiteness of the whale together with the creature's metaphysical ambiguities. Its whiteness is ascribed either to the skin tone of the symbolic whales that take on a humanoid form, or it is alluded to by way of cetacean contours and shapes in outer space. The planet killer, for example, was designed to be reminiscent of the white whale. Shaped like a cigar, the entity sports a small tail and a cavernous opening in the front. Its hull is colored in a silvery gray which is interspersed with brighter areas. It is strongly suggestive of Melville's white whale which was also not entirely white. Ishmael notes that "his body was so streaked, and spotted, and marbled with the same shrouded hue" (152).[62] The planet killer's visual pointers are underscored by the way the crew discusses its behavior, especially when they try to ascertain its nature and its intentions. The "space whale" echoes one of the central ambiguities in the novel which stems from a discussion about whether the whale's actions are rooted in *intent*—and, are thus perhaps indicative of a higher design and/or sentience—or, if they are simply a form of natural *instinct*. In the episode, Spock dispels any ambiguities since he concludes that the planet killer is an automated weapon used in a war millennia ago. The self-sustaining doomsday machine simply kept following its original programming (read: instincts) with none of the original programmers left alive to change it. Hence, this space whale is not a malicious devil.

The trope of the white whale is maintained on visual and metaphoric levels in "Obsession." Even though the creature appears to be amorphous most of the time, it takes on a cetacean appearance when shown on the ship's main viewer. As it heads towards the *Enterprise* to attack, its shape is reminiscent of a sperm whale charging a ship head on. The mystery of the whale's white hue is further accentuated by almost literalizing the metaphor of Moby Dick's ubiquity and presumed immortality.[63] After all, the cloud can easily expand to fill an entire room, contract to occupy the top of a rock, or disappear altogether. The creature's very existence, which is out of sync with normal space-time, also adds to its ambiguous state. The fact that the cloud finds its sustenance in human blood echoes Ishmael's thoughts on the leviathan. He invokes naturalists who opined the sperm whale "to be so incredibly ferocious as continually to be athirst for human blood" (150). The ambiguity the crew feels about the creature's intentions plays out in the course of the episode. Kirk remarks: "I can't help how I feel. There's an intelligence about it, Bones. A malevolence. It's evil. It must be destroyed."[64] Though initially doubtful about the cloud's sentience, Spock vaguely establishes the creature's intelligence, and thus its sentient intent. The argument provides sufficient reason for killing it, and Kirk-as-Ahab is redeemed.

"Bliss" also maintains a strong link to the white whale by way of the shape of the space-borne creature and the discussion about its intent. A scan reveals the creature's contours to be roughly cetacean. It has two large tail fins and a large body which extends to a sizable maw at its front. Further, the white whale's "ubiquity in time," and his "intelligent malignity," are echoed in an exchange between Qatai and the doctor (151–2). Ultimately, the doctor ascertains that the creature acts on instinct rather than malicious intent. Hence, Janeway refrains from rendering it harmless after having escaped from its clutches.

While Khan chases after "White Kirk" on his "white starship," the symbolic whiteness of the whale becomes the surface onto which Picard can project his guilt—the white/grayish faces of the Borg. The symbolic whiteness is inscribed onto those patches of skin which are not pierced by their harpoon-like cybernetic implants. The skin pigment loses its color in the assimilation process. A patchwork of gray lines, and white and gray blots is all that remains.

Since the Borg assimilate, i.e., consume, other races into their Collective, the discussion about the whale's intent and/or instinct also finds continuation. While a force to be reckoned with, the Borg are not supernatural. Their cybernetic evolution makes them posthuman, superhuman, and perhaps even post-nature. The leviathan that is Borg Collective is driven by the only spark of individuality allowed to remain at its governing center—the Borg Queen. Ultimately, her malicious intent indicts her to be slain by the redemptive Ahab.

This brief Melvillean interlude shows that Starfleet's covenant of old salts lays claim to an intertextual repertoire of maritime narratives which span the transatlantic Anglo-American imaginarium. While *Star Trek*'s British maritime intertexts are mostly used to establish a direct line of naval heritage with the Golden Age of Sail, the formulaic adaptation of Melville's novel is used to promote action-adventure-revenge plots, quotable material for both the forlorn and the redemptive Ahabs, and, most importantly, a foil for telling stories about guilt.

"Pointed in the right direction": Naval Paraphernalia

In a promotional video for the launch of *ST:ENT*, Captain Archer was introduced along a distinct leitmotif which adds to our understanding of *Star Trek*'s veneer of naval heritage. The voice-over tells the viewers: "For centuries, captains have guided their ships by the stars. But he'll be the first to guide one *to* the stars" (original emphasis). Like in the opening credits of the series, the captain is located in a genealogy which links the Age of Sail with 20th century aeronautical exploration and *Star Trek*'s re-imagined maritime future in space. It is Archer's mission to guide humanity to the stars. Guidance presupposes a sense of direction (literally and metaphorically) in the form a bearing and/or a heading. Navigational instruments, like the sextant, the compass, and the quadrant, together with other naval paraphernalia (especially model ships and pictures of sailing vessels), are repeatedly used to underscore Starfleet's naval heritage.

Drawing on essential precursors in the 17th century, the most significant inventions for ensuring accurate and reliable nautical navigation were made in the mid–18th century. Even though improvements to the "telescope," the "telescope-enhanced quadrant," "the filar micrometer," and the "technique of triangulation" were not dominated by the English in the 17th century—Dutch experts in optics and *l'Académie Royal des Sciences* were the important players—the British definitely led the way in the 18th century (Fernández-Armesto 249). For example, John Hadley's seaman's quadrant (1731), also known as the octant, served as a basis for Captain John Campbell, who invented the marine sextant (1757), which still serves as a prototype for modern models. John Harrison's marine chronometer H4 (1761/2) undoubtedly represents the pinnacle of nautical craftsmanship in the 18th century. He found an answer to "the Faustian yearning of the age" (251), i.e., the accurate determination of longitude which was a prerequisite for long-distance sailing endeavors like Cook's three voyages. These are but a few historical examples that writers drew on to craft Starfleet's naval heritage.

Not only do nautical artifacts serve as markers of naval heritage, but they also serve a distinct narratological function. They either simply appear as visual cues in the *mise-en-scène*, or they become the focus of a dialog whenever a direction is sought, questioned, tested and/or in the need of a course correction. For example, Starfleet's display of brass instruments, hardwood floors, and pieces of canvas manifests most conspicuously on the observation deck of the *Enterprise-A* in *Star Trek V: The Final Frontier*. The room is a tableau-like approximation of a quarterdeck adorned with the highest concentration of naval paraphernalia in the entire *Star Trek* continuum. The center piece is a wooden *steering wheel* located right in front of a large panorama window. Before they do what no one had ever successfully done before, i.e., crossing the great barrier into the center of the galaxy, we see Kirk briefly holding on to the wheel's base. In the next frame, we see a plaque, inserted in the base, which reads "to boldly go where no man has gone before." The iconic *Star Trek* credo echoes a journal entry by Captain Cook which he made upon having traveled further south than anyone had before him. Similar to Cook, the *Enterprise* crew penetrates further into the center of the galaxy than anyone had before them. The nautical flair of the observation deck is enhanced by the polished hardwood floor which shows a large *compass rose* in the middle of the room. There are also *brass fittings* and other nautical elements on the walls. *Brass oil lamps* provide sparse light. There is a *seaman's quadrant* on display just left of the steering wheel along with a *binnacle*. These additional accoutrements make it clear that the observation deck is a re-imagined quarterdeck because the binnacle is a "a box, found on the deck of the ship near the helm, that houses the compass" (King 109). There is also a *ring dial* towards the right side of the wheel. Lastly, the entrance to the observation lounge is framed by two more nautical instruments. There is what appears to be a *traverse board* which was a simple means for keeping track of a ship's speed and heading. And, we also find an *inclinometer* which indicates a vessel's angle of list. The observation deck is a visual archive resembling a traveling museum installation dedicated to Starfleet's naval heritage.

All scenes that take place on the observation deck deal with re-negotiations of the personal directions/bearings of the three lead characters. Once he learns that his Vulcan half-brother, Sybok (Laurence Lukinbill), returned from exile and leads a religious revolt, Spock retreats to the room for contemplation. Sybok brings Spock face-to-face with a central trauma in the latter's life—his father finding Spock's half-human characteristics repulsive. Wavering in his resolve and duty, Spock subsequently turns to Kirk and McCoy for help to stay on course. Similarly, the bearings of deep friendship and loyalty, which connect Kirk, Spock, and McCoy, are tested in the observation lounge when they face Sybok's "brainwashing" techniques. Even though their bond comes close to breaking, the triumvirate ultimately succeeds in staying on course. At the end of the film, Kirk re-affirms their "band of brothers" relationship and elevates it to the status of family in the observation lounge.

The negotiation of a character's bearing is central to other scenes in the *Star Trek* movies where we see especially Kirk's immediate surroundings draped with a veneer of naval paraphernalia. Kirk's apartment in *Star Trek II: The Wrath of Khan* is a case in point. In the opening shot of the scene, we see Kirk standing in front of a large window overlooking San Francisco Bay. Kirk has been on shore duty ever since he was promoted to the rank of admiral and placed in charge of Starfleet Academy. Not only are there *sailing ships* on his shelves, but there is also a *binnacle*, an *astrolabe*, various *brass lamps*, a *brass telescope* and a *brass ring dial*. The room is once again reminiscent of a museum installation dedicated to Starfleet's naval heritage. His promotion left him anxious and without a clear heading. This is the central issue in his conversation with McCoy who comes to visit him on his birthday. Bones tells him that he needs to obtain command of a starship again lest he himself become another museum piece for his collection. Kirk subsequently sets out on a mission to apprehend Khan, assumes command of the *Enterprise* again, while also losing his closest friend in the process. Hence, it is only fitting that the crew gathers in Kirk's maritime emporium to honor their fallen comrade in the sequel. Their gathering is interrupted by Spock's father, Sarek (Mark Lenard), who provides Kirk with information that sets him on a new course to bring his friend back from the dead.

In a similar vein, we see Kirk elaborate on his misgivings about the impending peace with the Klingons in *Star Trek VI: The Undiscovered Country*. He does so while recording his log in his quarters. Pacing up and down, trying to make sense of his course of action, we see a few maritime artifacts placed in the *mise-en-scène* to enhance the motif of direction. On a counter, there is a nondescript brass object in the form of an *anchor*. A *ship's bell* is mounted on the wall. And, when he asks himself how history can get past people like him, two engravings that show maritime scenes appear in the background. One depicts a lighthouse, seagulls, and a fishing boat heading into a bay. The other shows two tall ships-of-the-line sailing the ocean. The heading is clear—the captain has to change his bearing. He has to come to terms with his son's death at the hands of the Klingons so that a permanent interstellar peace can be ensured. The purposeful positioning of naval paraphernalia in the *mise-en-scène* is continued in the later series and films.

Even though its perpetual presence is easy to miss, Captain Picard's sextant is one of the most pertinent examples. Within a nautical context, the sextant is an instrument "for observing the angle of a celestial object above the horizon in determining longitude and latitude at sea" (King 395). Picard keeps one among his various possessions in his quarters. It is not surprising that the sextant tends to come into view in scenes where the captain makes important decisions, or when he deliberates on a course of action. For example, we see it behind the captain when he talks to the android B4, an earlier model of Data. Before Data sacrifices his life in the final battle in *Star Trek Nemesis,* he downloads all of his programming into B4. When Picard talks to B4 about Data's quest for becoming more human, some of Data's memories slowly begin to surface in B4. This gives the captain renewed hope after a personal trial which left a close friend dead and the *Enterprise* nearly destroyed. His sextant also cues and re-enforces Picard's decision to disobey orders and go rogue to save the Ba'ku from being forcible relocated in *Star Trek: Insurrection.* Having made his decision, he retreats to his quarters and removes his rank insignia. At that moment, the sextant appears in the background at the center of the frame. This actually points to a pattern which intermittently runs through all seven seasons of *ST:TNG.* In a first-season episode, the sextant is even foregrounded when Picard begins to suffer from severe headaches which prefigure a conflict with a specter from his previous command.[65] It also appears in the *mis-en-scène* of a third-season episode. We can see it in a scene where Picard's *doppelgänger* decides to take the platonic relationship which the captain maintains with Dr. Crusher into a new direction.[66] The discerning viewer will detect this nautical artifact on a number of other occasions.

The symbolic significance of nautical instruments and the act of using them to navigate in space are central elements in a third-season episode of *ST:DS9.*[67] Intent on proving the technological sophistication of ancient Bajorans, Sisko and his son build a lightship and set towards Cardassia Prime, a planet where ancient Bajorans supposedly landed centuries earlier. Barrett et al. have suggested that "Thor Hyerdahl's *Kon-Tiki* voyage, which showed that it was possible to sail from South America to Polynesia in a sail-powered-raft" (38), provided the model for the story. The episode goes a long way to literalize *Star Trek*'s veneer of nautical heritage in that it shows how Sisko and his son live in an enclosed, wood-paneled space. They sleep in hammocks and operate windlasses to set and/or to change solar sails. Navigating with ancient instruments, like an ornate Bajoran sextant, they also rely on an azimuth compass, which is a "compass for taking bearings of both heavenly and terrestrial bodies" (King 96). Ultimately, they make it to their destination but not because of any great navigational feat on their part. Even so, the episode maintains the narrative function of nautical instruments as visual cues signaling a character's personal course. After having deliberated for a while, Jake Sisko uses this father-son-adventure to tell the captain that he does not want to pursue a career in Starfleet. He decided to follow a different course in that he would like to build a career as a writer. And, Sisko approves of his son's course correction.

Nautical instruments also make obvious symbolic presents. For example, this happens in a fourth-season episode of *ST:VOY*. The crew encounters the Krenim, who have the power to make changes in the local space-time continuum. At the beginning of the episode, the senior officers gather to dedicate the new Astrometrics Lab designed to find a more efficient route back to Earth. The occasion prompts the first officer to draw a brief historical analogy between the lab and Starfleet's heritage of nautical/celestial navigation. Chakotay states: "Before there were maps and globes, let alone radar and subspace sensors, mariners navigated by the stars. We're returning to that tried and true method, but this time there's a difference."[68] The difference actually points back at the very nature and function of nautical instruments. Naval historian Simon Schaffer has asserted that these instruments were used to perform two interrelated functions:

> [T]he work of making reliable knowledge, in which instruments are understood as mediators between users and the world; and the work of making knowledge communities, in which instruments are understood as mediators between different users [87].

Instruments were a means to exchange, revise, and merge universally recognizable data. By extension, an 18th century sailing ship can then also be considered a nautical/scientific instrument in its own right.[69] The new Astrometrics Lab is conceived in the same vein. Mariners' need for greater accuracy—and, thus a means for ensuring that the ship does not get lost at sea, or run afoul of treacherous shores—was the central motivation for all those who sought to improve sea charts and instruments during the 17th, 18th and 19th century. Producing a reliable chronometer, John Harrison made the most crucial contribution. Naval historians have argued that having access to a precise time piece could have prevented many maritime disasters like the loss of Admiral Shovell's fleet off the coast of the Scilly Islands (1707), or Commodore Anson's ill-fated circumnavigation of the globe (1740–4).[70] The search for ever more accurate mapping and navigation techniques on the high seas was simply equated with a similar quest in outer space.

Voyager's sojourn through Krenim space is also fraught with disaster since they constantly come under attack for weeks on end. The ship is battered to a point where it is nearly uninhabitable and Captain Janeway gradually approaches a point where she loses her objectivity along with her personal bearings. Hence, the birthday gift she receives from her second-in-command, a marine chronometer, gains symbolic significance vis-à-vis the opening premise of the episode. Chakotay tells Janeway:

> It's a replica of the chronometer worn by Captain Cray of the British Navy. His ship was hit by a typhoon in the Pacific. Everyone back in England thought they were killed but eight months later Cray sailed his ship into London harbor. There wasn't much left of it, a few planks, half a sail, but he got his crew home.[71]

Even though Captain Cray appears to be a fictional character, Chakotay's reference serves once again to highlight Starfleet's naval heritage of wind and sail, and it maintains the leitmotif of direction. The symbolic meaning attributed to the chronometer could not be more obvious. James Cook brought a copy of Harrison's H4 chronometer with him on his second and third voyage, and he called it his "faithful guide" (qtd. Fernández-Armesto 301). Hornblower also believes the chronometer to be the marvel of his age and he points out the level of ignorance that older sailors show towards it.[72] Even though Janeway initially refuses to accept the present, she picks it up later and reminisces about what it was that Chakotay tried to tell her. As a symbolic gesture, she wears it as she heads into the final confrontation with the Krenim. Giving nautical instruments as symbolic presents is a tradition which was continued in *ST:ENT*. Captain Archer presents his first officer, T'Pol, with a nautical compass made of brass. He tells her: "It's your first official day of duty.... Should help keep you pointed in the right direction."[73] His gift follows in the wake of T'Pol's decision to resign her commission with the Vulcan High Command and join Starfleet instead.

Star Trek's veneer of nautical paraphernalia also includes a sizable array of model ships (as seen, for example, in Kirk's apartment on Earth). Models are also used to display the genealogy of ships that bear the same name which is made visible in the observation lounges on the *Enterprise* (*D* and *E*), and in Captain Archer's ready room. Pictures of ships and/or model ships visualize the naval heritage which links the sailing vessel HMS *Enterprize* (identified in the opening credits of *ST:ENT*), the U.S. aircraft carrier USS *Enterprise*, the Space Shuttle *Enterprise*, with the various Starfleet ships bearing the name. As is the case with the observation deck on the *Enterprise-A*, the ship's genealogy represents a visual archive like it would be found in a museum. We find model ships also outside the observation lounges. For instance, Captain Picard keeps a crystal model of a sailing yacht in his ready room. In a flashback scene, we see the "old salt" Lieutenant Paris playing with the model of a frigate when he as a child.[74]

Another obvious nod to the British Golden Age of Sail comes in the form of what is arguably one of the most famous sailing vessels of all time—HMS *Victory*. The *ST:TNG* episode in question opens with the *Enterprise* waiting to rendezvous with the starship *Victory*. Chief Engineer La Forge (LeVar Burton) calls his friend Data to show him the present which he intends to give to the captain of the starship *Victory*—a large model of Nelson's flagship.[75] In this scene, the naval heritage of Starfleet is once again couched in a romantic lament which has already emerged as a paradigmatic element of *Star Trek*'s fourth maritime dimension. The engineer remarks: "Wind and sail, that's the proper way to move a ship."[76] At the end of the episode, Captain Picard visits La Forge and demands a damage report on the sailing ship:

> LA FORGE: She cracked a spar when the Enterprise was shaken. Otherwise I think she weathered it quite nicely.
>
> PICARD: She's beautiful. A wonderful testimony to simpler times.... Well, soon she'll be ship-shape and Bristol-fashion.
>
> LA FORGE: Bristol fashion, sir?
>
> PICARD: It's an old navy phrase, meaning everything in perfect order.[77]

Not only does Picard reiterate the romantic lament and poetic reproach, but Starfleet's "old salts" in space display once again a sound command of sailor talk.

Roddenberry's initial call for "naval flavor" and his repeated statements about Starfleet boasting a transatlantic naval heritage that extends as far back as Nelson and Drake, manifest in a multi-layered veneer of naval practices, artifacts, and intertexts. They are used to craft similitude between naval life at sea and life in space. As "old salts," Starfleet officers are conversant with many archaic traditions and maritime stories which they repeatedly use to invoke a bygone age. By recording it in their logs, they also create historical knowledge of a fictional future. And, they adorn their re-imagined naval lives on the ocean of space with naval accoutrements that serve as heritage markers, romantic laments and/or as a source for metaphoric guidance. Nautical instruments were undoubtedly the products of observatory sciences, especially astronomy and practical engineering, which converged during the Age of Enlightenment. Consequently, as Schaffer reminds us, "the life of the sciences was implicated in rituals of colonial possession" (89). Similarly, by claiming that the future of *Star Trek* is roughly analogous to the Age of Sail during the 18th century on Earth, Roddenberry tapped into "epochs of imperial ambition," which "found astronomical stories useful in their political and ideological projects" (98). It was a time that marked the onset of modernity in the western world, which, in turn, would be shaped by two consecutive Anglophone hegemonies. It was a world of seaborne colonialism professing both the natural rights of man and a belief in scientific reason and progress. Continuing their histories, *Star Trek*'s benign colonial future—its fifth maritime dimension—draws on these hegemonies and their ideologies. *Star Trek*'s world offers us a continuous retelling of Anglocentric sagas of colonialism and imperialism.

8. "The benevolent empire of good intentions"
Star Trek's *Neo-Enlightenment*

Dedication plaques adorn the bridges of all Starfleet ships. Apart from their name, registry, and launch date, they all feature a brief quote which captures the spirit of the ship's mission and the core beliefs of Starfleet at large. The plaque of *Voyager* reads two lines from Alfred Tennyson's poem "Locksley Hall" (1842): "For I dipt into the future, far as human eye could see, Saw the Vision of the world, and all the wonder that would be" (qtd. Okuda 107). When it was published, the poem was poised at the height of *Pax Britannica*. Coinciding with the gradual advent of the Age of Steam in the 1840s/50s, the doctrine continued to shape Britain's perception of their providential role as the benign bringer/enforcer of world peace and progress until the early 20th century. Even so, the systematic roots of Britain's rise as a maritime superpower, which turned the Empire into a hegemonic force in the western world for most of the 19th and early 20th century, actually lay in the latter half of the 18th century. The utopian world envisioned by the poem's unidentified narrator delivers a triumphant view of the future. Couched in maritime motifs, it foreshadows a peaceful and prosperous milieu of Anglocentric modernity.

> Saw the *heavens fill with commerce, argosies of magic sails,*
> Pilots of the purple twilight dropping down with costly bales;
> Heard the heavens fill with shouting, and there rain'd a ghastly dew
> From the *nations' airy navies* grappling in the central blue;
> Far along the world-wide whisper of the south-wind rushing warm,
> With the *standards of the peoples* plunging thro' the thunder-storm;
> Till the war-drum throbb'd no longer, and the *battle-flags were furl'd*
> In the *Parliament of man*, the *Federation of the world.*
> There the *common sense* of most shall *hold a fretful realm in awe,*
> And the kindly earth shall slumber, lapt in *universal law.* ...

> Yet I doubt not thro' the ages on *increasing purpose runs,*
> And the *thoughts of men are widen'd* with the process of the suns [emphasis added].

For anyone who is even slightly familiar with *Star Trek*'s utopian future, these passages will radiate with prophetic qualities in the view of how Roddenberry imagined future space exploration. The poem's utopian musings found are indeed the most concise description of *Star Trek*'s maritime world in space.

"Locksley Hall" can easily be used as a shorthand for what is best described as *Star Trek*'s *maritime milieu*—its fifth maritime dimension. Largely confined to ideological constructs and the realm of ideas, it is the most abstract of the dimensions. This last layer of the *Rule Britannia* theme contributes to and also encapsulates all other maritime dimensions. Together, they coalesce into a holistic naval worldbuilding paradigm. Tennyson's text provides the ideological discourse which underlies what ultimately amounts to a naval Neo-Enlightenment in outer space. This future age espouses an Anglocentric teleology of reason, progress, and civilization which includes a dialectic relationship with the exotic/alien, colonial Other. Three constituent factors inform and shape *Star Trek*'s maritime milieu.

First, in describing the particulars of Starfleet's mission, Roddenberry informed writers and producers of *ST:TOS* that their mission is similar to that of Royal Navy ships in the past. The starship captain has "broad discretionary powers" (27), because outer space is analogous to Earth's oceans during the age of exploration. Consequently, the ship was to stay "far away and out of touch ... with the Admiralty" (24–7). Not only did his analogy yield the partially literalized metaphor of space as an ocean, but it also reconstituted *Star Trek*'s age of space exploration and colonization as an uncompressed maritime fabric of space and time. Such a conceptualization is largely out of step with our contemporary postmodern, postindustrial, and virtualized perceptions of space-time. *Star Trek*'s signature milieu of sailing starships draws dramatic substance, i.e., "dramatic decisions" (24), from how the vastness of the cosmos affects communication, the projection of force, and the execution of power, especially legal power. Apart from the conceptual isolation of the respective narrative habitats (the vessels and the space stations), this view of the future is largely channeled through the Starfleet captains. They embrace a modified Kantian ethics of reason which comes to the fore in a distinct practice of law—the law of equity. While it is in line with their broad discretionary powers and their Hornblower-esque archetype, it is wholly incompatible with contemporary 20th and 21st century legal procedures. The execution of legal power yet again underscores the similitude between life at sea in the past and future life in space. Within their maritime milieu, the captains' propensity for questioning and going beyond their orders manifests in the formulaic conflict between them and various representatives of the imperial/cosmopolitan center (who are staple characters in Napoleonic sea fiction). The captains' broad powers also point to a "politics of distance," which shaped the transatlantic history of Anglocentric modernity as much as it informs *Star Trek*'s space colonialism (qtd. Rothschild 90–1).

Second, when writers and producers conceived this particular milieu of the future, they imagined it to be "almost exactly analogous to the Earth of the eighteenth century" (Gerrold 11). Staying consistent with *Star Trek* chronology, the showrunners of *ST:ENT* (a prequel show) reiterated that the 22nd century was going to be a "new age of age of humanity's enlightenment" (Berman n.p.). Hence, the three centuries that form the core of *Star Trek*'s fictional history roughly correspond with the "long" Enlightenment between the late 17th and early 19th century on Earth. The heyday of the Age of Sail is the only correlative historical period which reflects Starfleet's mission in its entirety. Consequently, *Star Trek*'s maritime milieu poses as a Neo-Enlightenment informed by the romantic myths of discovery and their supposedly benign and disinterested form of exploration. This analogy, however, inevitably also replicated what Theodor Adorno and Max Horkheimer identified as the "dialectic of enlightenment" (qtd. Goulding 25). *Star Trek*'s future is also a new age of colonialism shaped by imperial forces that lead to interstellar conflict. It also replicates colonial encounters with the exotic/alien Other, and the process of their subsequent Othering. Such a pattern of colonial encounters applies almost universally to the western paradigm of Othering, and they are especially true for the Anglophone colonial experience at large. *Star Trek*'s Neo-Enlightenment thus embraces a largely scientific/rational belief in the telos of civilization's linear progress. It celebrates a normative, Anglocentric view of modernity which transcends American claims to national exceptionalism in favor of a transatlantic Anglophone saga.

Lastly, and perhaps most tellingly, *Star Trek*'s maritime milieu is also informed by what might easily be dismissed as an off-hand remark. Answering the question as to why Roddenberry gave the captain of *ST:TNG* a French name, he stated that it was "because the French have had a marvelous civilization and yet, everything we do is usually based on the English. I love the English" (qtd. Alexander 518). Following the *translatio studii et imperii* topos, his response provides yet another key to better understand the immediate context of *Star Trek*'s conception (as already explored), and the continued extrapolation and retelling of the benignly hegemonic, Anglocentric telos of modernity. Conceived at a crossroads that saw the transition of western leadership from a formal to an informal empire (and the "special relationship" linking them), the

United Federation of Planets (UFP) then emerges as a benevolent albeit disguised *empire of good intentions*. It can be understood as both a swan song for the myth of Britain's maritime supremacy and a celebration of its hegemonic continuation under the auspices of the United States. Roddenberry placed his creation in the 23rd and 24th century while looking back through a fictional maritime prism approximately two hundred years. He then extrapolated core values and beliefs which are arguably shared by all English-speaking peoples. They gravitate towards the centrality of the individual as a site of power and knowledge who is, however, restrained by a social contract/covenant which has been central to Anglophone histories since the *Magna Carta* (1215). The values shared by Anglophone peoples also bespeak a benign missionary zeal and a secular humanism.[1] Based on a polarized worldview (the west against the rest), the adventures of Hornblower offered a maritime milieu which remained—with a few modifications—compatible with America's role as the hegemonic heir to the British Empire until *Star Trek*'s waning days in the aftermath of 9/11. In other words, the *Rule Britannia* theme facilitates the fictional retelling of a continuous telos shared by two consecutive, Anglophone, cultural, political and economic hegemonies—from the British Empire, to the U.S., to the UFP. In a sense, the fifth maritime dimension then also encloses the frontier because it mirrors, extrapolates, and continues the hegemonic, Anglocentric telos of western modernity. After all, the frontier was but an outgrowth of this telos and manifested under the larger geo-political mantle of *Pax Britannica*.

"The only ship in the area": Power, Communication and the Decompression of Space and Time

Since outer space is a cosmic ocean, whose metaphoric qualities are partially literalized via aesthetic and physiognomic conceits, the often-invoked "starry ocean" also affects the manifestation and perception of distance and time. *Star Trek*'s maritime milieu has a telltale impact on the nature and modes of communication which, in turn, affect the execution of power. The space mariners' dependence on their vessels is conceptually rooted in the ships' spatial and thus also temporal isolation from other ships and the cosmic shores. Since *Star Trek* employs the "frigate trope" as its starship paradigm, the archetypal range of operations of this ship type also confers their naval "aloneness" onto the maritime milieu. The mournful lamentations of Coleridge's mariner are a powerful expression of the kind of isolation one could experience when confronted with the vastness of the ocean—"Alone, alone, all, all alone, Alone on a wide wide sea!" (qtd. Raban 152). As Thomas Richards has suggested, the "central experience of space exploration is the experience of solitude" (63). Solitude, however, does not automatically translate into outer space becoming a solitary frame of reference not least because in *Star Trek* (like during the Age of Exploration) space teems with different peoples, leading to many encounters. Yet, it is "the experience of solitude" (*ibid.*), that is still important since it makes *Star Trek*'s future a space where the actions of the individual are amplified. In short, actions seem to have a greater impact. This is facilitated by adopting an approximated sense of early modern space and time.

The understanding of space and time as being uncompressed is a constitute worldbuilding element in the Hornblower novels (as is the case in most other sea novels). These two dimensions are determined exclusively by the speed of the dominant mode of transportation at the time. During the late 18th and early 19th century (and, for quite some time after that) the sailing ship determined the speed of global travel. For example, the novels are replete with examples where Hornblower specifically remarks on the vastness of nautical distances and temporalities, providing meaningful correlatives for life in outer space. He makes plain the spatial and temporal bearings of his maritime world on the first few pages in *The Happy Return*.

> Here they were in the South Sea, with no other King's ship within two thousand miles of them.... Seven months at sea without once touching land.... He was certain about his latitude, and last night's lunar observations had seemed to confirm the chronometer's indication of the longitude.... Probably less than one hundred miles ahead, at most three hundred, lay the Pacific coast of Central America.... Anyway, two or three more days would see who was right [224–5].

The peculiarities of his spatial-temporal milieu are also often discernible in situations where the captain juxtaposes his current circumstances, especially moments where he has to make crucial a decision, with hypotheticals of what people back home might think about his actions.[2] Voyages of discovery are also suitable reference points not least because the South Sea and the explorations conducted thence led to the most pronounced experiences of "out-of-touchness" (Barrett 16).[3] The vast distances between their ship and their home together with the spaces that separated the various Pacific islands, and the time it took to traverse them, were always on the mind of explorers like James Cook. They appear mostly in the margins of his journals. For example, we can get a glimpse at them in the notes he made on location and the distances they travelled each day. While starships travel at speeds faster than that of light, the vast distances in outer space all but negate these awesome velocities so that the effect is *almost* the same. The long periods of waiting, the daily routine, and the travel time found on sailing ships are often fast-forwarded in sea fiction. Similarly, they are also abridged in *Star Trek* by way of an entry in the captain's log for instance.

Even though this paradigmatic model of early modern space and time was clearly encoded as a basic worldbuilding rule right from the beginning, it is also easy to miss because it is realized in the narrative margins of the respective episodes and films. Following *Star Trek* chronology, a new age of exploration begins with *ST:ENT*, where script writers were reminded that with "their star charts mostly empty ... it's taken humanity nearly a century to achieve warp 5. (At warp 2, only 18 inhabited planets were within a year's travel; at warp 5, the number increases to 10,000 planets!)" (n.p.). On the one hand, this note foreshadows the importance of technological progress in this space-borne age of Neo-Enlightenment. The 22nd century, however, is also reminiscent of the time immediately preceding the Golden Age of Sail. It was then that new advancements in shipbuilding (e.g., the jib sail), navigational sciences, and medicine ultimately made new latitudes, which had been out of reach, accessible to seafarers. In the latter half of the 18th century, they initiated a series of circumnavigations and a prolonged race for the Pacific. By insisting on keeping the ship and the captain out of reach, Roddenberry built maritime isolation into the fabric of his universe in order to facilitate drama which placed the individual in the spotlight. Throughout the production material of the later series, there are frequent reminders for writers not to treat "deep space as a local neighborhood," calling for "comprehension of the distances involved or the technologies required to support such travel" (1987: 11). The vastness of maritime space and time is particularly pronounced in *ST:VOY* in that naval "aloneness" became the very premise of a series about a starship that is lost on the other side of the cosmic ocean. At standard warp speeds, it would take them over seventy years to return home. Their distance from home and their isolation in the Delta Quadrant are leitmotifs especially in the early seasons of the show.[4] They gradually subside as the crew finds more shortcuts in later seasons.

Even though the actual traveling is often not shown, references to distances travelled and the time it took them to get from one place to another, are too numerous to be comprehensively charted. In space, distances are measured in light years. Depending on the ship's point of departure, the travel time of their cruises may range anywhere from a few hours at high warp to a few days, and even up to a couple of weeks. The rules of warp travel were not always consistent throughout the *Star Trek* continuum so much so that the audience experiences their own form of time dilation since the boundaries between time, speed, and distance are not only relative, but they are also blurry across the levels of narration. For example, before responding to a distress call in a distant sector of space, Captain Sisko asks how long it would take his crew to get there. Worf replies, "At maximum warp, six days." Not surprisingly, theirs is the only ship in the region.[5] Travel times increase dramatically as soon as a ship is restricted to lower warp speeds which may be due to any number of reasons, ranging from technical difficulties to bad space weather. Upon making contact with a Starfleet ship, which had been presumed lost, Jake Sisko and his friend, Nog, learn that the *Valiant* spent "seven months plodding along at warp three point two," in enemy waters.[6] On their trans-galactic sojourn, the *Voyager* crew encounters many phenomena which would add considerably to their journey lest they chart a better course. In the era of *ST:ENT*, outer space appears to be even bigger. Again asked to respond to a distress signal, Admiral Forrest tells Captain Archer the following: "We picked up an automated distress signal from a cargo freighter, the ECS Fortunate. The nearest Starfleet vessel is three weeks away at its maximum warp, but you could be there in a day and a half."[7]

The duration of starship missions, especially ships of deep space exploration, is also indicative of a world in which the effects of space/time-compression are largely reversed. There is, of course, the iconic five-year mission of the original *Enterprise*. Starfleet launched many long-term voyages of discovery, such as the eight-year mission of the *Olympia*, the Hansons' science mission to study the Borg which was expected to take more than three years, or Captain Sulu's three-year survey of gaseous planetary anomalies on the *Excelsior*.[8] There was also the much anticipated return of the *Lexington* from her mission which "ended up being more of a charting expedition," with "months between planetary systems."[9] These examples mirror the sense of space and time described by Hornblower and experienced by explorers such as Cook. Vast distances affect not only the crews' experience of isolation, but also interstellar communication.

Unless made possible by spatial proximity, communication is usually not instantaneous in outer space despite advanced technologies. Starships are effectively the primary conduits of communication and their captains are the primary agents in the ensuing interstellar dialog. In our contemporary frame of reference where global communication in real time is taken for granted, it requires conscious effort to think back to a time when global dissemination of information was determined exclusively by the speed of a sailing ship. Therefore, communication was also subject to the vagaries of maritime environments. Slow communication between the imperial center and its numerous satellites (stationary and floating), along with its inherent ironies, are a staple in Napoleonic sea fiction. The Hornblower novels offer many situations where the captain tries his best to carry out his orders without any recourse to direct consultation with his superiors. At one point, he usually receives the latest news and/or orders telling him that the essential context of his assignment has radically changed. For example, in *The Happy Return* he sets sail for the Pacific where he is to assist a renegade Spanish governor to begin a rebellion in order to destabilize the Spanish Crown. Spain was still allied with Napoleon at the time of his departure. Only after the captain had successfully captured a Spanish ship-of-the-line and handed it over to the revolutionaries, did he learn about Wellington's successful Peninsula campaign and the subsequent alliance with the former enemy. His new orders tell him to help suppress any insurrections in Spanish America. Having received the fateful news, Hornblower thinks to himself:

> In a world where news took months to travel, and where complete upheavals of international relationships were not merely possible but likely, he had learned now by bitter experience to keep in the closest contact with the shore [283].

Since such a maritime milieu undoubtedly creates an effect of estrangement, the postmodern reader of sea novels, who usually lacks essential contexts, is frequently reminded of these prosaic circumstances. The same goes for ships being the primary vehicles of communication, and the explicit, ritualized marking of their arrival as an *event*.[10] This model of early modern channels of communication was adapted and continued in approximated fashion as a part of *Star Trek*'s maritime milieu.

Once again it pays off to revisit the beginnings of *Star Trek* where this mode of communication, which included a crucial science fictional conceit, was established. Script writer David Gerrold intimated that a key word in the *Star Trek* world is "limit," i.e., the "implication here is that there are no other channels of interstellar communication. At least none as fast as the *Enterprise*" (6–9). Referring to the 18th century and Hornblower's frequent detached service, starships are "the only practical vehicle of interstellar dialogue"; their arrival "was always an event" (10). Even so, from the point of view of television production, such a rigid and impractical mode of communication had to be slightly modified by way of a science-fictional conceit—subspace communication. Once again, the keyword "limit" applies in that it is "a method of communication much faster than light, *but still not instantaneous*," since it is limited by spatial range and temporal distortion (9, original emphasis). The resulting model became the *modus operandi* for starships in the guidelines for writers and directors.[11]

Direct two-way communication is established as often as it is not throughout the entire *Star Trek* continuum. The ritual of receiving orders and/or news either by way of special envoy, simple text transmission, or even in a prerecorded video message, largely retains the qualities of receiving long-distance communiques that are reminiscent of a bygone age. Even though *Voyager* is undeniably out of range, they still manage to establish semi-regular communication with Starfleet Command by way of various technological conceits. Later in the series, the crew begins to receive a data package approximately once a month—a ritual reminiscent of receiving dispatches delivered by a packet ship.[12] Similarly, the arrival of another ship is specifically marked as an event of suddenness, anticipation, and suspense. Re-imagined in prosaic maritime fashion, starship rendezvous recall the sighting of a vessel on the oceanic horizon and the subsequent attempts to establish communication with it; such encounters are found in many, if not most, sea novels.[13] Interestingly, starships usually fail to call ahead more often than not which serves not only to create dramatic tension, but also to maintain maritime similitude with a bygone age. Instead, communication is established once a ship has arrived and direct dialog can be initiated either via ship-to-ship visual transmission, or by way of inviting visitors on board. The dramatic tension is then usually carried by the captain who is the main facilitator of interstellar dialog. The broad discretionary powers of Starfleet captains also add an archaic yet constituent legal dimension to the Hornblower-esque execution of these powers.

"There can be no justice as long as laws are absolute": Legal Power, Ethics and Naval Hierarchies

The powers held by a starship captain are essentially absolute and sovereign, and are thus, by definition, similar to those of sailing ship captains. Readers of Napoleonic sea fiction are constantly made aware of the awesome powers held by a commanding officer. Hornblower was keenly attuned to his powers after receiving his first command, he "was captain of his ship, with powers almost unlimited" (1962: 602). Referring to "the ordinary laws of England," i.e., the Common Law, he is only too aware of the fact that on "on a ship detached far from superior authority there was nothing a captain might not do" (1953: 118). The execution of these powers, their legal implications together with the ethics used to justify them, point to yet another analogy between *Star Trek* and the world of wind and sail. Made necessary by *Star Trek*'s early modern world of communication, writers also wrote an approximated pre–19th century legal tradition into its maritime milieu. Roddenberry made it repeatedly clear that "a Starship captain has unusually broad powers over both the lives and welfare of his crew, as well as over Earth people and activities encountered during these voyages" (1967: 10). As humanity's ambassador, a captain's range of power also extends beyond the ship. David Gerrold observed that "[j]ust as Captain Horatio Hornblower was the highest representative of English law in the far waters in which he sailed, so would Captain James T. Kirk of the *Enterprise* be the highest legal representative of Starfleet Command in the far reaches of the galaxy" (6). Consequently, we have to ask what kind of law do the captains then represent? More importantly perhaps, how do they translate it into practice, and how does it make *Star Trek*'s future correspond even more closely with the Golden Age of Sail?

The principal political and military hierarchies in *Star Trek*, i.e., the United Federation of Planets and Starfleet, are also legal bodies. However, this does not mean that writers and producers created a complete legal framework for the 23rd and 24th century; far from it. Even though legal disputes and conflicts are common in *Star Trek*, on ships as well as in interactions with alien peoples, they are mostly tackled case by case with implicit understanding that there is some sort of Federation-wide legal basis. Such an individualized case-based approach is not only paradigmatic of *Star Trek*'s maritime laws, but it also serves to underscore traditions which, according to legal scholars, "ring loud and long in Anglo-American legal history" (Charis and Chilton 22). In short, the legal baseline for *Star Trek* lies in a shared transatlantic heritage of English Common Law. What is more, it attests to a distinct relation between interstellar law and ship law which is decidedly out of step with 20th and 21st century American, and indeed, international legal procedures.

Interstellar relations are frequently fraught with legal disputes. They mostly concern territorial claims and settlements, interstellar peace treaties, trade agreements, war crimes, and extradition cases.[14] Going back to Hugo Grotius' *Mare Liberum* (1609), all of them incorporate "principles of international law," such as "treaty interpretations, state succession," and "law of the sea concepts" (Scharf and Robert 74). Hence, it would be easy to claim that interstellar relations simply reflect the state of American international relations which informed the production contexts of the respective episodes and films. Indeed, galactic legal disputes and accords allegorically point to (via the "frontier of politics" we could say) events in the international community that were of global significance. For example, the Khitomer Accords, ending the long Cold War between the Federation and the Klingon Empire, are a barely disguised reference to the series of steps it took to "un-thaw" American-Soviet relations, ranging from the Reykjavik Summit (1986) and the INF Treaty (1987), to the fall of the Berlin Wall (1989). Similar allegories can be read into the Treaty of Algeron which established the Neutral Zone between the Federation and the Romulan Empire (read: The Korean Armistice Agreement and the 38th parallel), or the formation of the Demilitarized Zone between the Federation and the Cardassian Union (read: the Gaza Strip and the West Bank, and/or the 38th parallel again), or the Treaty of Bajor which included obvious references to V-J Day (1945). There are, however, crucial differences between the interstellar law found in *Star Trek*, and 20th and 21st century legal customs. They become particularly apparent in the role afforded to the individual commanding officer, and they only make sense when viewed from a Hornblower-esque vantage point.

Neither is there customary interstellar law akin to contemporary international custom, indicating anything like a universally accepted legal standard, nor is there anything like an International Court of Justice in *Star Trek*'s maritime milieu. In other words, there is a weak, almost negligible presence of *jus cogens*.[15] Like the Royal Navy at the beginning of the 19th century, Starfleet takes it upon itself to interfere with and suppress piracy and especially slavery. Hornblower himself was also involved in the suppression of the slave trade during his tenure in the West Indies. These practices are still found in many parts of *Star Trek*'s maritime world. In the absence of a generally agreed upon practice of law, interstellar relations are instead governed almost exclusively by treaties and "a broader concept of foreign sovereign immunity than is currently applied" (Scharf and Robert 82).[16] Consequently, the practice of making and adhering to treaties in a universe of diverse peoples, long distances, and uncompressed time is significant since it mirrors international relations before globalization forced the development of international legal conventions.

In *Star Trek* we find a preference for early modern "sovereign discretion," rather than the contemporary practice of "obligations" (88). This comes to the fore in the execution and dispensation of the powers invested in a Starfleet captain.[17] Hence, questions could be raised as to whether captains make their decisions and thus dispense justice arbitrarily, i.e., beyond the boundaries of any law. In a sense they do because they are a seemingly benign permutation of a military despot. However, it makes sense if we take into account the peculiarities of *Star Trek*'s future representing a re-imagined Age of Sail in space. Chaires and Chilton have observed that what we see "on *Star Trek* is the operation of equity law" (21). This legal model conflicts with *absolute* approaches to the law, in which every case is treated identically, and even more so with the much hallowed legal paradigm of *due process*. After all, equity law

> rejected absolutes and was premised on the idea that justice can only occur when the particulars of the situation are considered. Thus, people in similar situation can and should be treated differently, and the fairness of the result is deemed more important than how [vis-à-vis due process] the decision was made [*ibid.*].

Equity law makes perfect sense in an environment which is similar to the floating world of sailing ships—a world governed by the moral fortitude and reason of characters who are the descendants of benevolent Nelsonian authority figures. Striving to find equitable solutions, it is their surroundings that force them to treat every situation as unique and independent from any they encountered previously.

From a contemporary American point of view, equity law might appear to be rather disturbing since central parts of U.S. national mythology are built on the legal tradition of inalienable rights. "There is much less concern about legal formalities" in *Star Trek*, Joseph and Carton have observed, and "lawyers or judges are almost never seen, formal procedure is minimized and informality is the rule" (30–1). In fact, there are often situations where starship captains gather *and* present evidence, usually for the defense; they then go ahead and judge the case that is before them which goes against every modern legal principle. However, what might be perceived as informal procedure, is in fact a distinct echo of an antiquated maritime practice in that it is a rather simple yet highly ritualized and efficient execution of power. While creatively circumventing the absolutism of the naval code (the infamous *Articles of War*), Hornblower always tries to find the most equitable solution. Characteristically, his decisions are accentuated by a liberal/sentimental ideology.[18] Legal experts decry this practice as "'a system of men and not of law,' which is the antithesis of our own [American] system" (38). And yet, in *Star Trek*, situational law and justice are portrayed as desirable as long as the people practicing it are inherently good and ethical. Moreover, from an antiquated and romanticized naval point of view, it contributes a constituent and narratologically sound element to *Star Trek*'s worldbuilding. Following the "Hornblower in space" model, the maritime milieu brings forth "ethical beings to do justice" (Chaires and Chilton 24). The ethical standards purported by *Star Trek* demand a reliance on and trust in reason.

Since *Star Trek*'s future was conceived as a Neo-Enlightenment, its central characters are guided by the *ethics of reason*. Ethical standards also indicative of *Star Trek*'s persistent belief in a rational teleology of linear progress that manifests in benign and seemingly disinterested forms of exploration, contact, and colonization. In her detailed study of the ethics found in *Star Trek*, Judith Barad has concluded that its "ethical tapestry" (353), rests on a modified Kantian ethics of reason, translating into an amalgam of equity, *prima facie* duties, and choice. Equity is undoubtedly the needle of a captain's moral and ethical compass. In extraordinary circumstances, "it provides a way for relaxing the rigor of the legal system from outside the system itself," and "it is a virtue for realizing what is actually just in a real situation ... a choice guided by reason" (123–4). Hornblower routinely exhibits such behavior with regards to the men under his command and even most of his enemies. For example, on one occasion his steward accidentally hits a superior officer. The incident places the captain in a morally difficult position. The unforgiving *Articles of War* do not allow for any mistakes, or extenuating circumstances. The penalty for striking a superior is death. The punishment would have been legally proscribed and legally just, yet morally objectionable and thus unjustifiable. Hence, the captain resorts to moral reasoning and finds a more equitable solution; in a sense, he cheats. By committing a mild form of negligence (while in port, he leaves open a window in the cabin in which the prisoner is held), he saves his servant's life without inviting harsh criticism from his superiors. His solution also allows him to save face in front of his crew.[19] Hornblower makes many similar choices which, if he had recourse to a higher authority, would never stand in the face of discipline, order, and duty. The extraordinariness of circumstance is built into a captain's situation, i.e., a maritime world of disconnectedness and discretionary powers. By definition, Starfleet captains are confronted with seemingly impossible situations, staggering odds, and difficult choices. They face a string of no-win scenarios. Yet, ever since Captain Kirk, *Star Trek* viewers know that despite their archetypal doubts, Starfleet captains (like Hornblower) "don't believe in no-win scenarios,"[20] as long as there is an opportunity (usually in a morally justifiable way) for reasoning one's way out of it.

Captain Picard provides us with a paradigmatic case for how Starfleet captains rely on arguments of equity and reason. In a first-season episode, he is confronted with making a grave decision. By committing a seemingly minor infraction, one of his crew members unknowingly breaks the law on a world where all infringements, as dictated by a powerful/divine alien entity, carry the death penalty. The native inhabitants demand that Picard honors their laws and allow the crew member to be executed. Their powerful alien protector steps in and threatens the entire crew of the *Enterprise* if the captain does not abide by their laws. Picard has to decide between submitting to their form of justice, or interfering with the customs of an alien people, which the Prime Directive forbids him to do. Having pondered all his options, Picard decides to interfere and he builds his defense in an argument of equity and moral reasoning, though he is not sure he can make himself understood: "[T]he question of justice has concerned me greatly of late. And I say to any creature who may be listening, there can be no justice so long as laws are absolute. Even life itself is an exercise in exceptions."[21] The alien "deity" relents and allows the crew to beam back to the ship. This is made possible in an anthropocentric universe that operates on moral reasoning as a widely-held common denominator. After all, despite having evolved to a "divine" multi-dimensional form of existence, the alien entity must, as Picard puts it, have once had similar values.

Circumscribing the captains' *modus operandi*, the ethics of reason and equity are woven into *Star Trek*'s maritime milieu. With a few exceptions, Starfleet captains routinely "use reason to decide what to do in a particular situation, as well as emphasize the role of context in determining what [they] should ultimately do" (Barad 355). Only captains Sisko and Janeway are intermittently shown in moments of "theistic existentialism" (307), which some[22] have interpreted as a radical break with, and even complete departure from *Star Trek*'s teleology of rational and benign progress. Even though postmodern discourses and postcolonial situations are introduced in *ST:DS9* and *ST:VOY*, they are simply there to critically interrogate the modern episteme without actually deconstructing it.[23] While these two captains branch out into irrational and spiritual spaces, the rational milieu of *Star Trek*'s future does not change. In fact, it reverts to a neo-conservative outlook in *ST:ENT*, and the captains always remain the central node.

The modified Kantian ethical tapestry is not woven solely with threads of equity. Instead, equity is interwoven with *prima facie* duty and choice, giving rise to a formulaic micro-pattern of conflict which is also found in Napoleonic sea fiction. The duties of Starfleet officers are such that they "may be overriden [sic] in the event of a more pressing moral demand" (354). Such a view on duty is compatible not only with the idea of equity, but also with the romanticized ideal of Nelsonian duty which, according to Laughton, says that "an officer is to obey orders, to submit his doubts to the Commander-in-Chief, and in a becoming manner to remonstrate against any order he conceives improper" (qtd. Czisnik 20). In a sense, *Star Trek*'s maritime milieu of disconnectedness and discretion then forces the freedom of choice onto the captains. Theirs is the choice to "disobey what others tell us to do, if we know the law to be inequitable ... or believe there's no moral context to justify that action" (Barad 355). Even on detached service, starships and their captains are still a part of the larger naval hierarchy of Starfleet. Orders are still issued from an imperial/cosmopolitan center. Hence, the moral, rational decision-making of the individual is positioned in such a way that it will inevitably clash with Starfleet's vertical power structure. The resulting encounters between the captains and representatives of the center resemble and closely follow the pattern of a signature trope in Napoleonic sea fiction. The Hornblower novels make an excellent example since they include many encounters where those who are either hierarchically and/or socially superior to the hero are portrayed as incompetent, decadent, effeminate, misguided, complacent, and/or lacking a sense of equity. The trope also ties into the manifestation of two of the signature characteristics of the "fighting naturalists" in space: (1) their propensity to critically question, go beyond, or even defy orders, and (2) their active resilience towards promotion to any rank higher than that of captain.

In Napoleonic sea fiction, this hierarchical conflict is generated by the tension between officers and officials, who obtain and/or hold positions due to interest and patronage, and the naval heroes who usually follow the meritocratic coming-of-age formula. Hornblower frequently articulates his criticism and even his disdain for his superiors. He aims his criticism usually at two distinct groups of people: (1) the admirals he serves under, and (2) various officials of the bureaucratic/political establishment who occasionally also present him with orders. Generally, these characters are all-orders-by-the-book-pencil-pusher-types who display little or no capacity for comprehending the complexities of the immediate situation. For example, when Hornblower is placed under the command of Admiral Leighton, he is frequently at odds with his superior who has very little experience in commanding men effectively. Moreover, the admiral is also dismissive of Hornblower's inclination to take the initiative and to suggest ideas of his own.[24] The captain and all his actions are, of course, vindicated whereas the admiral is proven wrong, and later even loses his life in an ill-conceived attack. Hornblower feels similarly about civilian government officials, like consular agents, ambassadors, and even the foreign secretary, who also happens to be his brother-in-law. They are all one-dimensional characters who consistently exhibit patronizing and bureaucratic posturing. In the captain's thoughts, these people convey "sublime ignorance and ... sublime contempt for matters nautical," and "lordly superiority over the uncouth sea-dog" (1945: 172). Characteristically, they issue orders which are "the usual combination of the barely-possible and the quite Quixotic" from a desk located thousands of miles from the real action (1937: 236).

The trope translated rather well into *Star Trek*'s maritime milieu where "[a]nyone at the rank of admiral is generally untrustworthy" (Richards 34). The list of Starfleet flag officers who fall into this particular category, along with the range of professional, moral, and ethical flaws they exhibit, is too extensive to be comprehensively delineated. For example, Vice Admiral Nechayev, who has a recurring role in *ST:TNG* and *ST:DS9*, is essentially a bully who shows little concern for the effects her orders might have on those further down the line, let alone civilians. At one point, she even tries to convince Picard to commit nothing less than genocide.[25] Admirals Haftel and Dougherty are willing to forego many of the Federation's principles and deprive individuals of their basic rights under the pretense of serving the greater good and/or progress.[26] Other admirals, such as Cartwright, Kennelly, Pressman, Satie, are shown to conspire in order to pursue anything ranging from maneuvering the Federation into a war and covering up illegal operations to witch-hunts for presumed spies.[27] Driven by paranoia, Admiral Leyton succeeds in radicalizing a segment of Starfleet and subsequently attempts a military coup on Earth. He is only narrowly thwarted by Captain Sisko.[28] Sisko also faces opposition in Admirals Coburn and Sitak who are the kind of officers who are by definition skeptical of initiatives taken by subordinates.[29] A few of Starfleet's flag officers (e.g., Jameson and Decker) develop psychotic and megalomaniac tendencies which are usually triggered by various traumas. They then try to assume more powers than they are legally entitled to.[30] Other admirals, like Commodore Stocker, lack any command experience and thus commit major blunders when placed in a tense situation.[31] The poor track record of Starfleet admirals corresponds with that of many Federation negotiators and special envoys, such as Robert Fox, Devinoni Ral, Ves Alkar, to name but a few.[32]

Even those flag officers who are the exception to the rule still follow a Hornblower-esque model in that they enjoy a close relationship with the respective starship captains. In most Napoleonic sea fiction, the burgeoning hero meets a paternalistic mentor figure and sponsor during the formative years of his career. Once the hero has matured, he leaves the tutelage of his mentor to make a name for himself. Over the years, they then either meet on various occasions, or the hero is periodically reminded of his tutor's support. As a young officer, Hornblower serves under Captain Sir Edward Pellew who takes a liking to the midshipman. He recognizes Hornblower's potential and begins to nurture his career as far as it is made possible by the strictures of the service. For example, Pellew's letters of recommendation contribute significantly to Hornblower receiving his own command. Years later, after having escaped from France and shortly before appearing before a court martial, the captain is reminded of Pellew's praise for him by another superior officer.[33] Similarly, while on a mission to quell a mutiny and subsequently orchestrate the return of Royalist forces to Le Havre, Hornblower sends a request for reinforcements which connects him directly with his old mentor.[34] Select admirals and the principal starship captains maintain similar relationships of paternalistic, mentor-like camaraderie, and friendship despite the vastness of *Star Trek*'s maritime milieu. They serve to counterbalance the cohort of archetypally untrustworthy flag offers.

Captain Archer and Admiral Maxwell Forrest undoubtedly enjoy the best-developed of these relationships. Not only did he advance Archer's career, but he also became an *ersatz* father figure whose support allowed the captain to bring Henry Archer's legacy (the engine that powers the *Enterprise*) to fruition. Captain Picard enjoyed an equally amicable rapport with Admiral J.P. Hanson. Shortly before the admiral loses his life in battle, he reminds Picard's senior officers of the captain's strength and determination. During the Dominion War, Sisko develops ties with his immediate superior officer, Admiral William Ross. Even so, as a young officer he was under the tutelage of another mentor figure, Curzon Dax, who also follows the pattern of the Hornblower-Pellew duo. While not an admiral, Curzon served as one of the most colorful ambassadors of the Federation. Captain Janeway found her supporter and sponsor in her old academy professor, Admiral Patterson. Not only does he call the captain "Katie," but upon handing over *Voyager* to her, he also comments that "she's quick and smart, like her captain."[35] It seems that only Captain Kirk did not have the good fortune of having been placed under the wings of a mentor at any point of his career.

Outer space simulates and stimulates a maritime milieu which adds a distinctively nautical context to the multi-faceted missions of Starfleet captains and their ships. Caused by the decompression of space and time, the milieu is shaped by disconnectedness and the broad discretionary powers of the captains. This, in turn, leads to them relying on moral reasoning and the laws of equity, creating mostly tension and conflict with those occupying the higher echelons of Starfleet. All of these are signature tropes, motifs, and characters found in the Hornblower novels. The mythologized world of sailing ships once again underscores that Starfleet, as a benign military organization, has more in common with the romanticized albeit bowdlerized naval hierarchies found in Napoleonic sea fiction. Challans has acknowledged that "Starfleet as benevolent as it appears" is still "a military dictatorship" in which the captain "stands as the bearer of Starfleet's conscience and an exemplar of moral autonomy," who "derives a moral understanding for action not from authority or sacred texts, but from justifiable principles arrived at through reason" (91–2). The mythologized Enlightenment mariners reign benevolently albeit supremely over the starry oceans in a world which is presented as a new age of reason and discovery. Consequently, it is also a new era of contact, conflict, and colonialism.

"We're on a mission of peaceful exploration": Voyages of Discovery, the Benign Power of the Enlightenment and the Colonial Other

Based on the initial claim that the future of *Star Trek* mirrors Earth history during the 18th century, it becomes clear that the resulting maritime milieu is informed by the dominant myths of benign and purely scientific voyages of discovery. James Cook and the ideologically charged "rhetoric of anti-conquest" (Gregg 14), commonly attributed to his voyages, served as useful points of reference for Roddenberry. A group of disinterested "fighting naturalists in space," Starfleet explorers thus inherited the reputation of leading similar voyages to the stars. Like Cook, they "exemplify the highest British values of peaceful exploration and enlightened intercultural contact" (*ibid.*). Since John O'Keeffe's pantomime *Omai* (1785) contributed significantly to the apotheosis of Cook, it also provides a shorthand for the character of the benign explorer. The final stanza of the play reads as follows:

> He *came* and he *saw*, not to *conquer*, but save;
> The *Ceasar* of Britain was he;
> Who scorn'd the ambition of making a slave
> While Briton's themselves are so free
> [qtd. Gregg 14, original emphasis].

The *Star Trek*'s future perpetuates an almost zealous belief in linear, humanistic progress which is used to "other" exotic aliens on the cosmic beaches of its starry ocean. Starfleet officers use their doctrine of reason to speak in a grammar of difference which simultaneously hierarchizes and racializes aliens. Regardless of their benign intentions, they also use it to map, assess, and categorize alien cultures and their resources for future colonization and assimilation. *Star Trek*'s maritime milieu of disinterested exploration is fueled by assumptions which derive from the highest ideas and ideals of the Enlightenment.

The central cornerstones of the Enlightenment are the following: (1) the belief in linear progress of civilization marked by (2) technological advancement, which, in turn, is achieved in the (3) application of scientific inquiry by (4) the individual as a site of reason, experience, knowledge, and power. Despite these benign and noble claims, the Enlightenment *Zeitgeist* also led to a separation between those who do not occupy the same level of civilization and those who do not espouse the same secular values, i.e., the exotic/savage/uncivilized Other. Hence, the teleology espoused by voyages of discovery exposes both the elements of their own myth-making and the subsequent racialization of the Other. The 18th century was a period of powerful European rivalries. As is the case in its 23rd and 24th century analog, "there is no such thing as exploration for exploration's sake" (Richards 13). The prime purpose of exploration is colonization which, in turn, leads to contact, conflict, and negotiation, and subsequently to hegemonic struggles for the dominance of empires.

In order to substantiate a transatlantic approach to *Star Trek*'s Neo-Enlightenment, it serves to draw on the latest scholarship on its historical antecedent. There is a growing need among historians to sidestep narrow claims of national cultures, periodization, and geographic localization. There is an impetus to apply trans-categorical paradigms, emphasizing agents, processes, and networks of similarity and connectedness. Isaac Kramnick has asserted that the Enlightenment was "an intellectual movement that knew no national boundaries" and its "intellectual ferment was transnational" (ix–x). Prior to Immanuel Kant's maxim *sapere aude*, the core of the Enlightenment *Zeitgeist* was often equated with the collected efforts of the French *philosophes*, such as Diderot, Montesquieu, Rouseau, Turgot, and Voltaire. It helps to remember that they dedicated the fruits of their labor, the *Encyclopédie* (1751–72), to three

Englishmen—Bacon, Locke, and Newton. Similarly, elaborating on the origins one of the most "hallowed" texts of the Enlightenment, Thomas Jefferson deferred to the "harmonizing sentiments of the day" (qtd. Hamowy 259). Thus, he laid the foundation for a prolonged scholarly debate over the Lockean versus the Hutchesonean influences on the *Declaration of Independence* (1776).[36] Consequently, Manning et al. have argued, the "Atlanticist perspective is also able to move beyond regional exceptionalist narratives (either contemporary or retrospectively imposed)" (3). Such a perspective affords us the critical understanding that many pillars of the Enlightenment were co-opted and retrospectively rearranged and/or geographically relocated for the projects of different national cultures. In the northern hemisphere, the Enlightenment was "by design ... primarily Protestant in denomination, and Anglophone in orientation" (Manning 9), and its proponents championed "a broad Anglocentric movement for civil liberties" (Giles 25).

The key concepts, beliefs, and paradigms of the Enlightenment, which continued to reverberate in *Star Trek*'s maritime milieu, also have to be set against the transatlantic redrawing of this historical period. The propensity to dare and think for themselves, using their reason, allowed practitioners of the Enlightenment to make the natural universe accessible; and hence, the advent of western techno-science arrived. Progress was equated with civilization, technology, and improvement, providing linear paradigms of universal progress which were used to systematize stages of social development in various models. Not only did this process place Anglophone cultures ahead of everyone else, but it also installed a teleology prescribing that all of humanity was destined to progress under their benevolent guidance. Enlightenment thinkers enshrined the individual at the center of the cosmos. The individual, however, remained constrained. While it was no longer by the power of a divinely ordained authority, the individual was restrained by "willful act[s] of contract" in government, commerce, and more (Kramnick xvi). The "ideal of equality of opportunity" ascribed to the newly freed individual "was both an effort to reduce inequality and to perpetuate it" in that it replaced the "secular and spiritual elite with a new meritocratic elite" (xviii). However, the idea and the ideal of the individual was still circumscribed by discourses of race, class, and gender. Last but not least, the most meaningful locale of the Enlightenment, its practices, and its practitioners was "at sea" (Gilje 165).

The maritime milieu which determined Anglophone mariners' existence was the single most important factor contributing to what appears to be a contradiction at first. Then again, the Enlightenment was riddled with contradictions since "it was easy enough for a philosophe both to call for a republican simplicity and to assume the superiority of gentlemen" (165). While mariners "supported equality" even without having access to the fruits of *philosophes*, they also "recognized and accepted that they lived and worked in a world dominated by hierarchy" (170). Framed by isolation and disconnectedness, their dependence on a vessel and on each other in an uncontrollable and unforgiving environment, makes such a peculiar dynamic meaningful.[37] It can easily observed in the many crises found in records of voyages of discovery and in sea fiction. The maritime milieu they found themselves in, like its outer space analog, "was simultaneously a geographical space over which ships, men and knowledge moved between communities on its margins *and* a subject of Enlightenment geographical science" (Withers 43, original emphasis). In short, the sea enabled as much as it circumscribed the Enlightenment.

While most of the ideas and ideals of the Enlightenment were articulated in transatlantic spaces, they were subsequently transported to the Pacific which became their principal proving ground. Mariners carried the Enlightenment *Zeitgeist* with them and then applied it to and inscribed it on the maritime networks they established. In other words, they were cartographic, hydrographic, and especially ethnographic navigators. The Pacific was the "final frontier" of the 18th century and early 19th century.[38] The resulting maritime milieu of contact and conflict is essentially the same in outer space. Despite steep competition, the Royal Navy dominated the exploration of the South Sea and James Cook's three voyages were enshrined at its zenith.[39] Hence, it only made sense for Roddenberry and his successors to use voyages of discovery as the paradigmatic model for *Star Trek*'s maritime milieu of "disinterested exploration."

The dialectic between purpose, directionality, and preconception, which fueled voyages of discovery, underscores why these seaborne ventures are the closest analogies for Starfleet's broad mission parameters. The orders given to James Cook by the Admiralty and the Royal Society are paradigmatic of Starfleet's mission of exploration. They attest to how imperial plans for expansion into the Pacific were draped in the mantle of scientific discovery. They share a teleology which puts on display the rhetoric of benign exploration and, at the same time, exposes ulterior colonial motives. The myth of Cook's disinterested form of exploration and its rhetoric of anti-conquest can in part be traced back to a "long historiographic tradition," which "prioritizes the scientific dimension of the voyages above strategic, political or even commercial considerations" (O'Sullivan 102). Historians compounded the myth by placing disproportionate emphasis on the strict and seemingly humane orders Cook issued to his men for how they were to conduct themselves with indigenous peoples. The first rule "to be observe'd by every person," was to "endeavour by every fair means to cultivate a friendship with the Natives and to treat them with all imaginable humanity" (qtd. Edwards 39–40). The myth was seemingly corroborated by favorable descriptions of Cook's actions found in the journals of his officers.[40] The rhetoric of showing civility, forbearance, and foresight in dealings with different native peoples was rooted in practical thinking and prudence rather than in good-natured humanism. While the dialectic of enlightenment afforded explorers a position of superiority, which they frequently used to intimidate and/or force their will on the indigenous Other, they could still be overpowered by sheer numbers.

The second set of orders given to Cook, which he was to open only after he had completed the expedition's task on Tahiti, paint an even clearer picture. Not only do they expose the actual colonial purpose of Cook's ethnographic navigation, but they also provide more building blocks for the myth of benign exploration.[41] The Lockean discourse used to delineate the particulars of when and how Cook could take possession of the lands he discovered also added to the myth. After all, the explorer was supposed to ask and/or negotiate with the native inhabitants for parcels of their land. If the land was cultivated (by western standards), it had to be purchased from the natives by way of a contract. If it was not for sale, the locals had to be "convinced" to accept colonial rule. Yet, if the land was not visibly cultivated, the *terra nullius* clause applied and it could be taken freely since it arguably belonged to no one.[42] It goes without saying that the underlying western paradigm of property and ownership, which was incompatible with most indigenous concepts of land-based religion and stewardship, tipped the balance in favor of the European intruders. There was hardly anything benign about it.

The myth was compounded further by the stance on the explorer's "fatal impact" popular among apologists, who argued that "it is a mistake to blame the discoverer for the subsequent misuse of the world he opened up" (Foulke 97). This points us to a clearly demarcated line between professions. The explorer/mariner is not the same person as the colonist/settler. Tellingly, this distinction is maintained in *Star Trek*. If *Star Trek*'s worldbuilding had followed the American frontier paradigm, the frontier would sooner or later be turned into a home. While planets are terraformed and settled by colonists, outer space is not the final frontier but rather an infinite ocean. Following the colonial/imperial experience of European powers, the Other remains exotic and is claimed for the mother country in the maritime milieu of the future. Like in sea novels, *Star Trek*'s mariners remain perpetually afloat, and their ships assume domestic qualities. In other words, Starfleet's space sailors make poor colonists.

Cook's maritime milieu of exploration and contact already laid bare the Enlightenment *Zeitgeist* and those who carried it to distant, alien places. The actual contact with the Other, which often resulted in conflict, was shaped by the interplay of the explorer's belief in progress, denoting civilization, and the subsequent inscribing of difference, i.e., being less civilized, onto the Other. The belief in progress was at the core of modernity. The basic idea was that "cultures attained 'civilization' by stages of moral awaking and material endeavor" (Bayly 7). Though a widely-held belief at the time, it was the writers of the Scottish Enlightenment in particular, who had the most powerful impact with their delineation of "the four stages of human progress" (Kramnick xiii). Comprising "the hunting, pasturage, agricultural, and commercial" stages, their model mapped "this evolutionary process as moving humanity from 'rude' simplicity to 'civilized' complexity" (*ibid.*). Essentially, they created a ladder of civilization. In this vein, "primitive societies had the capacity for self-improvement," which would be "greatly aided by contact with a superior nation" (Gregg 17). During the Age of Sail, and for quite some time afterwards, Britain laid the strongest claim to representing the epitome of western civilization—a claim backed primarily by its sea power.

The concept of linear progression from savageness to civilization was used to create hierarchies of difference. They are most pertinent in stories of contact between naval explorers and the diverse peoples they encountered. These stories are told in what Catherine Hall has called a "grammar of difference," which was "critical to empire building, for the British empire was legitimated on the grounds that Britons were suited to conquest and settlement, and would bring the benefits of their superior civilization to others" (136). Colonial difference is thus the product of "othering" the Other. In short, the Other was commonly defined by what they did not share with the representatives of civilization. The markers used to write in the "grammar of difference" were manifold and they always reflected the teleology of progress—architecture, the lack of written language, tools, weapons, the forms of dress, food, religious practices, social mores, and especially sexual behaviors. At its core, the process of "othering" was deeply racialized and gendered. While actually referring to Cook's competitor, Admiral Bougainville, Roddenberry found the wittiness which resulted from encounters with the colonial Other inspiring. He observed that "Bougainville was an enormously witty man and a great adventurer. He once stated that 'five Tahitian men could be clothed with one glove and a pair of scissors'" (qtd. Alexander 518).

Any of the journal entries in which Cook described his encounters with the diverse peoples of the Pacific can be used to illustrate the process of "othering." Cook's colonial gaze was suffused with pointers to the escapist lure of the South Sea. The way how he infantilized the natives points to the two different types of the savage—noble and ignoble. Set in the same time period, a similar colonial gaze was replicated in the Hornblower novels. Landing on the shores of Central America, the narrator sketches a setting of colonial encounter in an exotic town, including a telling description of its people.

> Little miry lanes, filthy and stinking, wound between the palmetto huts.... The Indian population were going about their usual avocations without regard for the man dying of thirst within fifty yards of them. They were all brown with a tinge of red, like Hernandez himself; the children ran naked, the women were dressed either in black or in dirty white; the few men to be seen wore only short white trousers to the knees and were naked from the waist up [1937: 243].

The benign, morally superior Enlightenment mariner offers the reader a racialized view down the ladder of civilization.

The archetypal setting of colonial encounters with the exotic Other was transposed wholesale into *Star Trek*'s future. Infused with a "cosmology of progress" (Wagner 141), and a "rational religion" (Kramnick xii), its maritime milieu mirrors the peaceful exploration its maritime antecedent. The built-in teleology of preconceptions, which fueled voyages of discovery, is used to denote the adventures of the starships along similar lines. While the *Enterprise*'s mission "to explore strange new worlds, to seek out new life and new civilizations" was limited to five years in *ST:TOS*, it became a "continuing mission" in *ST:TNG*. Not only is there a clear preconceived notion as to what and who they will encounter, but a basic purpose is also imparted to the audience. Though largely implied in the opening narrations, the rhetoric of anti-conquest can be found in Starfleet's mission statement. More importantly, it is used by the space-borne mariners themselves on innumerable occasions. It manifests in situations where we see them declare that they are "on a mission of peaceful exploration." Roddenberry outlined Starfleet's mission in a set of fictional orders to the captain of the *Enterprise* in the original pitch for *ST:TOS*.[43] The purpose of colonial interests that underlies voyages of disinterested discovery is thinly veiled in that the orders prioritize landings on planets which could support human life. Unlike Cook's instructions, Starfleet's orders do not contain any classified passages about taking possession of yet undiscovered lands. Instead, they are simply echoed in the actual practice of Starfleet on the cosmic beaches. On a number of occasions, we see Starfleet crews as vanguards of colonial interests. For example, in a third-season episode of *ST:TNG*, Captain Picard records in his log that the *Enterprise* is charting a system in tedious detail to prepare for colonizing the planet.[44] Similarly, the maritime milieu is highlighted in a later episode where "[a]fter weathering an unexpected magnascopic storm," the crew continues their quest to find more planets suitable for colonization.[45] The same telos applies to the many survey missions (cartographical, geological, biological, etc.) which the intrepid starship crews pursue at the beginning of innumerable episodes. Even though they often serve only as spring boards leading to encounters with the unexpected, their colonial intent is clear.[46]

The belief in linear, anthropocentric progress is another constituent element of *Star Trek*'s Neo-Enlightenment. Regardless of how far advanced and how alien they might be, all sentient life forms find themselves somewhere along the same, universal ladder of civilization. In *Star Trek* this belief assumes qualities of a cosmic imperative. Thus, all alien species are umbilically tied to humanity's cosmic voyage. This view of the cosmos can be inferred from Roddenberry's understanding of how sf is supposed to work, particularly with regards to extrapolating alien societies on a budget. He explained the "Parallel Worlds concept" in the sales pitch for *ST:TOS*, stating "that our stories deal with plant and animal life, plus people, quite similar to that on earth. Social evolution will also have interesting points of similarity with ours" (4). The belief in linear progress then served as the base tone for a rational/scientific worldview on the story level. Its telos is presented as if it automatically assumes the qualities of benign, disinterested modes of exploration. Even though it is articulated throughout the *Star Trek* continuum, we find one of the most paradigmatic examples in a third-season episode of *ST:TNG*.

"Who Watches the Watchers" (16 Oct 1989) produces both a commentary on and 24th century twist to a crucial albeit disputed segment of the myth of Cook—the details that led to his death at the hands of indigenous Hawaiians, who presumably viewed the explorer as their god Lono.[47] Not only is the episode a model of a colonial encounter story, but it also points to a caveat in *Star Trek*'s maritime milieu of exploration—Starfleet's directive of non-interference. The *Enterprise* is dispatched to an anthropological research post to help with repairs of its holographic duck blind. It allows the researchers to observe and study a Bronze Age people, the Mintakans. Their repairs fail and they are exposed to a Mintakan father and his daughter. The father is severely injured in the process and the ship's doctor insists on saving his life. While on the ship, she keeps him sedated lest they cause even more cultural contamination. Unfortunately, he awakens and sees Picard giving orders to his officers. In his frame of reference, "The Picard" corresponds with the ancient myth of the Overseer, who holds the power over life and death. He then goes on to share his fantastic resurrection story with his community. Having made great strides in rational thinking and logic, the community is now on the cusp of reverting to the "dark ages of superstition and fear." Picard decides to contain the situation by bringing the leader of the Mintakans onboard. She is the most level-headed and rational of her people. Echoing Plato's *Allegory of the Cave*, the captain intends to convince her that he is not a divine entity by explaining the telos of universal, linear progress to her. He does so in a lengthy allegorical argument which is paradigmatic of *Star Trek*'s humanist, anthropocentric discourse, stating that in important ways, humans and Mintakans are similar, having evolved from more primitive beings. Despite constant reminders about limiting their interference, the episode still affirms the myth of the benevolent, "disinterested" maritime explorer in the end. Picard visits the village one last time to tell the Mintakans why Starfleet studied them. He points them once again to the universal ladder of civilization. When asked why the Federation would want to study the Mintakan civilization, Picard replies: "To study you is to understand ourselves." Even though this is the case, the *Enterprise* plans to leave them alone, despite a Mintakan's insistence that they are willing to learn new ideas from the crew. Picard explains that staying would mean interfering: "You must progress in your own way." The Mintakan leader replies: "So we will. You have taught us there is nothing beyond our reach." The audience is put at ease with regards to the impact of the potential colonizer. Starfleet apparently does not stay to enlighten and assimilate the Other. Yet, we must not forget that Picard, as Nuria puts it, has already taught them. He benevolently dispensed knowledge about the inevitable progress they are going to make. Exemplifying encounters with the Other, the episode is paradigmatic of the maritime Neo-Enlightenment replicated and celebrated throughout the entire *Star Trek* continuum.

Though problematized and interrogated in *ST:DS9*, *Star Trek*'s humanist myth of progress is not discarded. Even when confronted with the antithesis of linearity in the most basic sense of existence, the universality of linear progress is reaffirmed and even imparted to the non-linear "Other." In the pilot episode, Commander Sisko discovers an artificially created wormhole near the station. The local Bajorans, however, view it as the Celestial Temple—an Olympian place where their divine prophets reside. During his first journey through the passage, Sisko initiates contact with aliens who inhabit a radically different plane of existence. They communicate with him by assuming the shape of people they find in his memories. Initially, they are hostile towards him, believing that he would disrupt their non-linear existence. They do not necessarily exist outside of time as we know it, but rather they perceive all of time simultaneously. At first, Sisko struggles to make himself understood and to make the nature of human existence meaningful to them. An avid baseball fan, Sisko uses the game as a metaphor to explain linear existence and its teleology to them.

> We are explorers. We explore our lives, day by day, and we explore the galaxy, trying to expand the boundaries of our knowledge. And that is why I am here. Not to conquer you either with weapons or with ideas, but to co-exist and learn.[48]

Even though he does not change the essence of their existence, he successfully makes them understand what it means to live a linear life. He literally imparts a different ontology to the aliens. Their encounter also reveals the intentions Sisko hides under the mantle of disinterested exploration. He seeks the right of passage through the wormhole even though the aliens tell him: "Our existence is disrupted whenever one of you enters the passage. Your linear nature is inherently destructive." Yet, after making linear existence meaningful to them, they consent to allow ships to travel through their realm. Despite occurring on a metaphysical level, the episode replicates the basic model of benign colonial encounters. What is more, *Star Trek*'s Neo-Enlightenment belief in the linearity of progress is even inscribed onto a non-linear form of existence.

The positivistic narrative of linear progress, technology, and history often replicates the four-stage model of civilization lionized by the Scottish Enlightenment. For example, it served as a visual backdrop in a sixth-season episode of *ST:VOY*[49] which is yet another showcase for the triumphalism attributed to the narrative of linear progress. *Voyager* takes a detour to investigate a most unusual planet which rotates around its axis more than fifty times a minute. Hence, a few seconds of ship time equal a few years on the surface. The ship is accidentally caught in the planet's gravity and is unable to leave. Their arrival coincides with a series of earthquakes on the surface as a bright new star appears in the night sky. At this point, the native population is shown to be at a late hunter-gatherer/early pastoral stage. It is also when the Ground Shaker star/deity enters their mythology. While working feverishly on a way to escape the planet's gravity, the crew relishes the fact that they can pursue ethnographic/anthropological observations at fast-forward speeds.

Over the course of the episode, the planet's progress is shown in four stages. They are visualized in scenes that show the same valley and how it changes over time. Means of communication become a leitmotif for the culture's progress which is driven by the need to establish contact with the Ground Shaker. At the hunter-gatherer stage, the indigenous population attempts to establish a rapport by way of religious invocation and the ritual offering of a valuable fruit. Even though the second stage appears to represent a medieval era, it is replete with pointers to an early Renaissance period. The local magistrate experiments with a hot air balloon to send a message to the Ground Shaker. Having progressed to a stage which is approximately analogous to the early 20th century, telescopes reveal that the Ground Shaker appears to be a ship in the sky. Consequently, astronomers attempt to make contact via radio. This is when the crew learns about the teleological impact their arrival had on the alien culture. Their observations are confirmed once the alien society has advanced to a point where they send a spacecraft to initiate direct contact. They learn that their ship had become the single most defining symbol in the alien culture's telos of progress; removing it might very well lead to a centripetal turnover of their culture. A representative of humanist culture, Seven of Nine suggests a more positivistic scenario for their continued progress. Ultimately, the aliens progress to a stage where they are able to come to the rescue of their civilization's inspiration and pull *Voyager* out of orbit. With the ship free to resume their journey, their fears about the culture slipping into stagnation, inevitably descending into a new dark age, might have been warranted. Predictably, however, the episode concludes by extolling how the sighting of *Voyager* has inadvertently albeit benevolently (and, we might add permanently) "improved" an entire civilization. In the final scene, we see an old alien man looking once again over the same valley. It now features the skyline of a high-tech future city. He then turns his wistful gaze towards the night sky. It is clear that thanks to *Voyager* his culture will eventually reach the stars. In fact, it is inevitable since it is written into *Star Trek*'s maritime milieu of linear progress.

The way in which the Enlightenment *Zeitgeist* was written into *Star Trek*'s maritime milieu also replicated the processes of "othering" which shaped the encounters between explorers and the colonial/exotic/alien Other during the Golden Age of Sail. On its voyages, Starfleet encounters a fair share of alien cultures that are visually "othered." Resorting to elements of stock stereotypes, they are reminiscent of indigenous peoples found along the maritime contours of Earth's oceans as well as in the North American West.[50] Despite the look of some alien species, *Star Trek*'s processes of 'othering' are primarily reduced to one defining marker which is, in part, the result of extrapolating a hyper-technological future version of a romanticized maritime past. The *level of technology* is the single most important benchmark used to define and categorize the Other. More than any other markers that are used to make aliens different (e.g., skin color, clothes, architecture, language, social, and religious mores, etc.), it is their level of technology which becomes the yardstick for comparison and categorization. All the differences perceived by the colonial gaze of the benevolent Starfleet explorer are the product of an institutionalized and hierarchically enforced framework built on the discourse of technology. Just as there were certain technologies that it took to build sailing ships (arguably the most complex machinery of their time), to construct western-style structures, and to record western knowledge, there are certain technologies necessary to travel to the stars, to build Starfleet ships and Federation-style buildings, etc. It goes without saying that the position of humanity, represented by the Federation and Starfleet, is marked as the most privileged and thus the most desirable. They provide the normative benchmark for the long cavalcade of alien cultures which we find either on the lower, similar, or higher rungs of the ladder of civilization. *Star Trek* writers used the fact of whether or not an alien race achieved space travel, more specifically warp technology, as the principal yardstick. Their basic assumption was that faster-than-light capability inevitably leads to contact with other alien cultures. Not only does this benchmark determine the rules of contact, interaction, and interference, but it also reveals *a three-tiered taxonomy* of the Other.

Not surprisingly, the large bulk of alien peoples is located somewhere (1) downward the spectrum of civilizations. We need, however, to distinguish between two sub-groups. Commonly referred to as pre-warp cultures, these "primitive" civilizations range from hunter-gatherer and agricultural communities to industrial and even postindustrial societies. There are also many aliens who are spacefaring cultures but who do not have the same level of technological and thus also "moral" sophistication like the Federation. They usually serve as simple story vehicles and thus we encounter them perhaps only once or twice. Then, there are those alien species who, over the years, have received elaborate histories and cultures of their own, and who occupy (2) roughly the same technological level as the Federation. They are the main contenders for the Federation's claim to a benevolent, imperial hegemony in their region of the galaxy. The group includes cultures such as the Klingons, the Romulans, the Cardassians, the Dominion, and, to a lesser degree, the Ferengi, the Breen, and the Gorn. Lastly, there is a much smaller circle of (3) more advanced aliens, such as the cybernetic Borg or Species 8472. There are also those who have evolved to a different plane of existence altogether like the Q Continuum, the Organians, the Metrons, the Nacene (Caretaker entity), the Traveler, and the individual known as Trelane.

The formulaic encounters between Starfleet explorers and the many aliens who are less advanced, reveal the most about how the myth of disinterested exploration was woven into *Star Trek*'s maritime milieu. The Prime Directive is the one law which overrules any other regulation. It "prohibits Starfleet personnel and spacecraft from interfering in the normal [read: normative] development of any society," especially those who are less advanced than Starfleet (Okuda 385). When Roddenberry outlined the directive in the series bible for *ST:TOS,* he noted that it "is a wise but often troublesome rule" (24). He introduced it because he acknowledged the detrimental impact that New World encounters and colonial projects had in Earth's past. Not surprisingly, he alluded to the Spanish *conquista* of South America and the ensuing genocide of the Aztecs and Mayans as representative examples.[51] Perpetuating *la leyenda negra,* Roddenberry's reference is quite telling since the "enlightened" brand of exploration conducted by Anglophone powers was always contrasted with the barbarism of early Spanish explorers. This is significant in two ways. First, it once again underscores how the historical period of the British Golden Age of Sail was singled out as the main inspiration for *Star Trek*'s future and how it was demarcated from earlier periods in the history of human exploration. Second, it also foreshadows how the frequent reference to the "normal development" of an alien culture (which occasionally became "natural development") in debates over the Prime Directive, can be understood from a normative Anglocentric perspective.

Needless to say, a mandate like the Prime Directive is wholly antithetical to Starfleet's mission of seeking out new life and new civilizations. If Starfleet were to adhere to what had better been rephrased as its "Prime Hypocrisy," then they would be doing very little exploring. It was also problematic from the point of view of writing and producing. David Gerrold remembered:

> [I]t was troublesome for the writers who had to work their stories around it. ... a bloody nuisance.... It keeps the *Enterprise* from being a cosmic meddler. And that's too much of a limitation on the format. It keeps [the captain] from being a moralist.... This is a very idealistic rule–but it keeps getting in the way of the story. Therefore, it has to be disregarded. Regularly [236–7].

As a dramatic device, the Prime Directive works only when Starfleet breaks it. This became the *modus operandi* for the entire *Star Trek* continuum. The directive is bent and broken more often than it is adhered to. A caveat in *Star Trek*'s maritime milieu, the Prime Directive brings to the fore more of the historio-mythical model that served as inspiration for Starfleet's form of disinterested exploration. It taps into additional layers of meaning used to perpetuate the myth of Captain Cook.

The Prime Directive echoes the sentiments expressed by explorers like Cook about the potential impact that contact with Europeans might have on the peoples of the South Sea. A number of passages in his journals, which were initially edited out for being too radical, were later quoted disproportionately often to add to the explorer's supposedly benevolent attitude towards indigenous people. Showing considerable foresight, Cook appeared to issue wistful warnings.[52] Even so, he still maintained the colonial gaze of someone who saw himself superior to those whom he "othered" by way of presuming an innate corruptibility of the natural man. On this second voyage, he commented on how their rapport with Europeans had detrimental effects on the Maori.

> [S]uch are the concequences of a commerce with Europeans and what is still more to our Shame civilized Christians, we debauch their Morals already too prone to vice and we interduce among them wants and perhaps diseases which they never before knew and which serves only to disturb that happy tranquility they and their and fore Fathers had injoy'd [qtd. Edwards 277].

He expressed similar concerns for Tahitian society and the indigenous population of New South Wales.[53] His sentiments, however, have to be set against the limits of his forbearance, his restraint, and his benevolence which are usually used to epitomize him as a disinterested explorer.

Cook was also very much aware of the power the dialectic of enlightenment afforded him. He made ample use of his powers whenever the self-imposed limits of his equanimity were crossed in encounters that jeopardized the success of his mission and/or the well-being of his crew. He resorted to force when he tried to quell the rampant thievery of native peoples, or when he was prevented from taking on fresh provisions. The kidnapping of indigenous elders was a common albeit flawed strategy to make natives compliant. Ultimately, it precipitated Cook's death on Hawaii. Occasionally, he also instructed his men to burn the huts and boats of native peoples. Since the latter were among the most prized possessions of many islanders, destroying them was a significant offense (as was the wanton violation of *tapus*). Cook's behavior points to the many,

> contradictions lying at the heart of his entire project. The realities inherent in a voyage of discovery were frequently incompatible with the ideals of ... humanism ... and the goals of the voyages, [were] exacerbated by underlying assumptions of superiority, and the need for Europeans to maintain "face" at all times [O'Sullivan 141–4].

Consequently, Picard's decision to "kidnap" the leader of the Mintakans in *ST:TNG*, "Who Watches the Watchers" is cast in a new albeit science-fictionally sanitized light. Starfleet's interactions have to be understood along similar lines. They benevolently "other" the alien in a framework of a technologically-encoded telos of progress which enfolds all other markers of cultural difference. They then bring the resulting power to bear on the alien Other. After all, stories of contact are inevitably also stories of conflict.

Whenever Starfleet encounters new alien cultures, the explorers always go out of their way in displaying benign interaction, restraint, and forbearance. This is especially true when they meet people who are clearly less advanced. They attempt to be observant of the peculiarities of alien customs (e.g., gestures, forms of address, bartering, etc.), pertaining to territory, resources, religious sites and/or artifacts. Moreover, they also inform the Other about their non-interference policy. However, whenever these self-imposed limits of "disinterest" are infringed upon, the space-borne explorers quickly reveal just how "interested" they really are, reaffirming once again their naval heritage of wind and sail. In a maritime milieu where progress and thus power is largely measured by technological superiority, should the need arise, Starfleet shows hardly any compunction of making use of it. A starship is invested with the same kind of power like an explorer's vessel. This dialectic is best revealed in situations where crew members go missing and/or are detained by aliens against their will.[54] Similarly, it comes to the fore in encounters where Starfleet property is stolen, or where aliens wantonly interfere with mission parameters.[55] While the actions taken by Starfleet are seemingly more benign in that they are not overtly destructive and/or violent, the imposition of power is equal in its transgressive severity to that of "disinterested" explorers during the Age of Sail.

Not only does Starfleet's audacious non-interference policy echo the seemingly benevolent practices attributed to Enlightenment mariners, but it is also integral for redrawing the contours of its space-borne Neo-Enlightenment along the lines of the mythologized British Golden Age of Sail. While a caveat in *Star Trek* storytelling, the Prime Directive seems to be unambiguous and straightforward. Yet, it acquires a hue of complexity when included in the transatlantic redrawing of *Star Trek*'s thematic make-up. It serves to add more texture to its maritime milieu in that it points to the underlying continuation of an Anglocentric hegemony. What is actually Starfleet's "interested" form of exploration becomes much clearer when equal, "imperial" Others try to interfere with the normal/natural development and progress of alien societies. Adding a more political layer to *Star Trek*'s fifth maritime dimension, the colonial gaze of the Federation supports a fictionalized continuation of Anglophone hegemonies. Hence, it only makes sense to ask as to *who* sets the standards for normal/natural development, and what do they tell us about the Anglocentric telos of western modernity woven into *Star Trek*'s maritime milieu. The four-stage model of social development provides us with a telling clue when we apply it to the narrative of linear human progress as visualized in the opening credits of *ST:ENT*. The credits are somewhat reminiscent of Senator Lyndon B. Johnson's sobering history lesson which he delivered in response to the launch of Sputnik in 1957.

> The Roman Empire controlled the world because it could build roads. Later—when men moved to the sea—the British Empire was dominant because it had ships. In the air age, we were powerful because we had airplanes. Now the communists have established a foothold in outer space [qtd. French 163].

He points to a shared, continuous heritage, singling out the two consecutive Anglophone hegemons (both of which imagined themselves as a New Rome) who shaped much of the modern western world in the last two centuries. While empires inevitably become decadent and ultimately decay, the future of human progress in outer space is shown to continue under some form of Anglocentric leadership. Not only does this foreshadow a continuum of Anglocentric hegemonies, but it also points to a specifically marked Anglocentrism woven into *Star Trek*'s maritime milieu of the future.

"The Best [and Worst] of Both Worlds": An Anglocentric Pax Galactica

Despite the many allegories on its surface, the world of *Star Trek* was never imagined as being just an All-American narrative. Instead, its world is such that it continued the telos of western modernity on a distinct Anglocentric trajectory. After all, it grew out of a moment of transatlantic convergence, transition, and continuation that linked Britain and the U.S. Volker Gentejohann has argued that hegemony can be best understood as "a process by which a dominant group imposes their world view on the whole of society or even on other cultures" (16). At the same time, however,

> hegemonic culture is never stable [because] to bring the greatest possible number of subjects under its sway, it either has to expand, adjusting its value system to accommodate for differences in its subjects or it must put restrictions on itself. ... It is therefore never a completed structure, but rather an ongoing, never-ending process [17].

From a more specific, Anglophone point of view, the narrative of cultural, political, and ideology hegemony has been told through the trope of *translatio studii et imperii*. Emphasizing that "virtues flee a decadent civilisation," Manning and Cogliano have asserted that the trope was used to "underwrite the transfer of power" along a built-in western trajectory (5). The range and power achieved by two consecutive Anglophone hegemonies has been severely undercut and debunked since the beginning of the 21st century. In the world of *Star Trek*, however, their influence found a historicized albeit fictional geography in outer space where it could theoretically continue indefinitely. Any form of centrism presupposes a center and/or a core marked by a "sharedness" which, in turn, allows for similarity and compatibility between culturally hegemonic and harmonious groups. Keeping the precise workings of *Star Trek*'s politics of distance vague, a series of basic values and experiences, which are shared by all Anglophone peoples, were written into its maritime milieu in their idealized form. Consequently, *Star Trek*'s maritime future cannot be seen as anything else than the extrapolation and continuation of transatlantic Anglophone hegemonies.

We can access the Anglocentrism in *Star Trek*'s maritime milieu by way of two symbolic entry points. The first helps us to constitute outer space in geographic terms, furnishing a symbolic spatial center. The process of visualizing geographies on a map not only creates knowledge, but it also betrays the discursive power used to generate it. In other words, "maps do not so much 'represent' the world as they act to 'constitute' it" (Withers 59). In *Star Trek*, the map of the Milky Way Galaxy is divided into four quadrants—Alpha, Beta, Gamma, and Delta. The center of the Federation, Earth, lies on the prime meridian which bisects the galaxy. While the format of the stardate has changed over the years, Earth always remained its central point of reference.[56] A telling Anglo-centrist entry point emerges when we juxtapose the galactic prime meridian with the maritime dimensions that shaped the history of determining the universal day and the measurement of time on Earth. The institutionalization of Greenwich Mean Time (GMT) was the product of hegemonic British maritime power. It was the result of a historical process which can be traced to Britain's rise to the leading position in observational sciences, especially hydrography and astronomy, in the late 18th century (e.g., the race for the exact measurement of longitude). Called at the behest of the United States, GMT was eventually validated, confirmed, and adopted on a global scale (much to the chagrin of the French) at the International Meridian Conference (1884).[57] GMT's successor, the Coordinated Universal Time (UTC), was in part also a maritime echo of Anglophone hegemonies in that it was coordinated between the U.S. Naval Observatory, the Royal Greenwich Observatory, and the UK National Physical Laboratory in the mid–20th century. While the Greenwich meridian is but an arbitrary line of longitude, it is also a latent expression of British maritime power. It then reverberates symbolically in *Star Trek*'s maritime milieu where Earth is located on the galactic prime meridian.

Star Trek's largely unexamined logocentrism, which some might dismiss as too general and/or irrelevant, offers a second symbolic entry point.[58] In the future, everyone speaks English. Most alien languages are usually also rendered in English. Naturally, this is rooted in the rather mundane dimensions of production. Featuring mostly speakers of American English, *Star Trek* is an artifact of American popular culture geared primarily towards American audiences. However, the ubiquity of the English language found in the interstellar community, and the lack of linguistic diversity, have gone largely unremarked. Roddenberry pointed to a "two-way scrambler" (1964: 11) which converts "all spoken language into English" (1967: 18). The formal introduction of the Universal Translator (a science-fictional conceit) in *ST:TNG* provided at least a plausible intradiegetic explanation. Even so, there remains a latent assumption of a linguistic common denominator—the so-called "Federation standard." A standard of English, it is spoken as a lingua franca throughout the Federation and even beyond its borders. The hegemonic significance of this linguistic standard becomes relevant if placed within *Star Trek*'s maritime milieu. English is carried to the shores of the cosmic ocean by *Star Trek*'s space-borne sailors. Starfleet replicates what Fernández-Armesto has identified as the most pertinent "residue" of British maritime power (7)—a residue which Jeremy Black has located at the center of "a symbiotic transfer of imperial hegemony from Britain to the USA," from "territorial control" to "economic advantage" (371).

Set against these two symbolic entry points, it serves to briefly revisit Roddenberry's off-hand remark that "everything we do is usually based on the English" (qtd. Alexander 518). Given the vagueness of his comment, we have to ask as to what exactly it was that they based on the English. It has become unequivocally clear that most of *Star Trek*'s worldbuilding paradigm was modeled on the myth of the British Golden Age of Sail. Yet, when we look beyond the thematic make-up of *Star Trek*, his remark also corroborates that he was very much aware of a shared transatlantic cultural bond which linked the hegemonic role played by Britain in the past with the geopolitical role assumed by the U.S. in the mid–20th century.

As a genre, sf is inherently historiographic and often also nostalgic. Many sf stories look through the lens of the past to imagine the future as a resuscitated and regenerated version of the past. Other sf narratives are set in an imagined/alternative past right from the beginning ("A long time ago in a galaxy far, far away..." for example). When he conceived *Star Trek*'s utopian world and its Anglocentric society of the future, Roddenberry branched out via the Hornblower novels to access a broader Anglophone experience. Chaires and Chilton have asked whether "Star Trek is [then] really only a philosophic extension to Locke's *Social Contract* or More's Utopia?" (8). While they did not answer the question, they still provided us with a useful trajectory. Simultaneously "no place" and "a good place," a utopia is imagined based on precarious foundations. While utopias show us better models of society, they are hazy on how these worlds/societies have been achieved. *Star Trek* repeatedly stands accused of leaving vague the path of how humanity has arrived in its re-imagined maritime future of space exploration. What we know is that sometime in the 21st century, Earth will experience a Third World War. Following the development of faster-than-light travel, our first contact with alien life will generate a centrifugal attitude towards space. The specifics, however, are left sketchy. Following the 21st century dark ages, humanity enters a Neo-Enlightenment in outer space. At this point it serves to remember that rather than being progressive, utopias are inherently more conservative, or at least reactionary and thus nostalgic.[59] In other words, the "future is seen in the terms of an outmoded form of social and political organization" in that it is viewed through a lens of "what has been lost rather than what can be gained" (Isaacs 189). Hence, what Roddenberry found when he looked to the past through the prism of sea fiction was the romanticized character of a maritime nation and its teleological role in western modernity. He found a set of beliefs, a heritage, and an ideology which were similar to and thus compatible with the American national experience as the rising Anglophone hegemon in the 20th century.

A constituent layer of meaning, the mythologized character of maritime nations is written all over *Star Trek*'s maritime milieu. Maritime cultures, as opposed to landlocked nations, tend to be portrayed as more progressive, liberal, and simply more open. In the national mythologies of predominant naval powers, especially in Britain, the national character became intimately tied to its naval agents. Historically, they coalesced in a national enterprise which touched many, if not most walks of life during the heyday of its maritime power.[60] The distorted reasons for why maritime nations were supposedly less repressive and less tyrannical have to do with the very nature of a navy. While the power of a large army could be brought to bear on the population at home, a large naval force could be used only indirectly to affect life on land. It is one of the most potent misconceptions in maritime mythologies which also became a dominant literary trope. For example, the Royal Army and its soldiers *tend* to be treated less sympathetically than the Royal Navy and its heroes, who were lionized as national idols. It goes without saying that this dynamic also became a staple in Napoleonic sea fiction. In a broader sense, "while powers that rule on land tend towards centralization and rigidity, those that rule the seas tend towards liberty and enterprise" (Barrett et al. 13). The character of maritime cultures seems to automatically imply a wider freedom of movement for individuals and thus more contact with the values of other cultures. Such a view is, of course, distorted, too. After all, there are problematic undercurrents which are traditionally sanitized in maritime mythologies. While "colonial exchanges broadened the horizons of European thinking," Manning et al. have observed, "assumptions about race and its implications for societal progress," actually hardened (8).

Despite pronounced allegorical treatment of certain American wars, such as World War II, Vietnam, and conflicts in the Middle East, we can detect the residue of other historical conflicts in *Star Trek* with the Napoleonic Wars providing the most obvious reference point. In the Hornblower novels, Roddenberry found a repressive aristocratic society that was romanticized and sanitized into the bringer and defender of liberty in the face of the Corsican tyrant. Throughout the novels, Forester takes great care not to portray Hornblower, the men under his command, and even the Royal Navy at large as the aggressors. Their goal is to free Europe from tyranny and to keep the peace for the benefit of everyone. The following excerpt from *The Commodore* (1945) is paradigmatic of the novels' ideological base tone:

> "The Navy," he said. "The guardian of the liberties of the world. The unswerving friend, the unremitting enemy. When the tyrant of Europe looks about him, seeking by fair means or foul to extend his dominion, it is the Navy that he finds in his path. It is the Navy which is slowly strangling that tyrant. It is the Navy which has baulked him at every turn, which is draining the life-blood from his boasted Empire and which will bring him down in ruin

> at the end. The tyrant may boast of unbroken victory on land, but he can only deplore unbroken defeat at sea" [270–1].

Epitomizing "disinterested" forms of ethnographic navigation, the Royal Navy was leading in scientific pursuits, too. While Roddenberry's ideas for *Star Trek* fermented during the late 1950s, and when he eventually committed them to paper in the early 1960s, he saw the role of the benevolent hegemon in the west falling to the U.S. as the ideological successor to the British Empire (as announced by President Kennedy). The U.S. would continue an Anglo-normative program for the western world, ensuring that it stayed under Anglophone leadership while facing yet another "tyrannical" force. The United Federation of Planets (UFP) and Starfleet would then continue to do the same (i.e., the best of both worlds) in a utopian world in outer space. Following Linda Hutcheon's arguments about the role of nostalgia in utopian thinking, these Anglo-normative bodies simultaneously served as a swan song for the maritime legacy of the British Empire and as a celebration of the U.S. taking up the baton in the 20th century. Even though utopian societies follow antiquated modes of government and administration, they are often draped with contemporary political discourse to obscure their conservative and/or reactionary leanings. While they espouse ideals that are widely shared by Anglophone peoples, a closer look at *Star Trek*'s political fabric reveals undemocratic structures. They were already foreshadowed by the practice of outmoded, mercantilist legal standards (see earlier in this chapter).

Adhering to the trope of *translatio studii et imperii*, the Federation and Starfleet are the product of the ideological extrapolation of hegemonic power held collectively by the Anglosphere. The trope was repeatedly used to indicate who represented the pinnacle of western civilization in the past. Manning and Cogliano have pointed out that "Norman kings invoked the *translatio imperii* trope to underwrite the transfer of power from the Classical civilizations to the French, and thence to England" (5). The trope then found pronounced and repeated articulation in the Anglocentric segment of western modernity. Peter Padfield has summarized the maritime dimensions of the *translatio* process as follows:

> So the liberating inspirations of the great trading cities of the United Provinces, transferred to England under William of Orange and spread under the shelter of British trading and naval supremacy to the North American colonies, were inscribed in the constitution of the infant United States of America [287].

These large-scale shifts of power and influence took place against the backdrop of the Enlightenment which was predominantly Protestant and Anglophone in the North Atlantic. Historically, however, the translated grandeur of Britain's hegemonic influence would not fully manifest for the U.S. until the mid–20th century. The American people first carried their Manifest Destiny across the North American continent which initially led to an isolationist mindset. Reframing this quintessentially American experience within a larger, global context, it was a phenomenon that was actually shielded by an often overlooked maritime dimension.

In 1823, President James Monroe unilaterally declared the Americas off limits for any further interference by European powers. With his foreign policy he intended not only to protect America's westward expansion, but also to aid the revolutionary fervor that was spreading throughout South America at the time. Labeled the Monroe Doctrine only later, the U.S. had little power to actually enforce it. Driven by its interests in trading with newly formed South American nations, Britain made overtures to the U.S. to conceive a joint declaration with the view of entering a more formal alliance in the wake of the War of 1812. The U.S., however, rejected the suggestion. Even so, upholding the Monroe Doctrine was, as Sue Parrill has pointed out, "a policy agreeable to Great Britain" and it was "successful mainly because it was supported by the British fleet" (83). The implicit concertedness between the two Anglophone powers points to the fetal stage of what Winston Churchill would later call the "special relationship." From a transatlantic perspective, Britain eventually incorporated the Monroe Doctrine into its own doctrine of *Pax Britannica*.[61]

Not surprisingly, the Hornblower novels incorporate the mutual interests of the two powers and use them as a geopolitical backdrop. While stationed in the West Indies, Hornblower has to enforce Britain's doctrine on the western side of the Atlantic. For example, he is tasked with enforcing the abolition of the slave trade without offending American interests. He is also concerned with keeping Spanish and French interference in the Caribbean and in South America at bay while supporting the revolutionary forces there. Set roughly between 1821 and 1823, *Hornblower in the West Indies* paints a tacitly amicable picture of the broader interests that are a part of Britain's hegemonic influence.

> Europe under the rule of absolute monarchy would turn a jaundiced eye upon the establishment of a whole new series of republics, no doubt. But it hardly mattered what Europe had to say, as long as the Royal Navy—even the depleted peacetime navy—controlled the seas, *and the two English-speaking governments continued in amity* [547, emphasis added].

The novel also served as an allegory for maintaining the special relationship in the face of the Soviet threat. After all, it was published less than a year before the U.S.–UK Mutual Defence Agreement (1958), which expanded cooperation on nuclear research and weapons.

The geopolitical context of the Monroe Doctrine also bears importance for *Star Trek*'s maritime milieu. After all, enforced by the Royal Navy, it amounted to a non-interference dictate which not only protected the rise of the U.S. as a global power in the long run, but ultimately also ensured that the western world would continue to be under the influence of an Anglophone hegemon. From a global point of view, it also guaranteed that Anglophone residues are now found along many maritime contours of the world. Hence, it is all but inevitable to draw a parallel between these historical processes (together with their hegemonic impact) and the Prime Directive. In an offhand comment, Chaires and Chilton have suggested that the directive appears to be "an odd variation of the 19th century Monroe Doctrine which reserved the western hemisphere to nations in it" (22). It makes sense to go even further and look at it as the Monroe Doctrine maintained perpetually. As such, it resonates with other geopolitical measures that ensured the continuation of an Anglophone hegemony in the west during the Cold War. Jay Goulding, for example, has suggested that it "is akin [to] the U.S.'s non-interference policy in the Third World or its *laissez-faire* philosophy for the national state" (36). More generally, it is also reminiscent of U.S. and NATO policies of containment which in turn echoed the earlier discourse of *cordon sanitaire*.[62]

While the Prime Directive is clothed in a discourse of anti-imperialism and decolonization with regards to alien cultures (spacefaring and non-spacefaring) who are on the lower rungs of civilization, it does *not* apply as soon as other imperial powers are involved. On the contrary, it is repeatedly used as an excuse to keep other powers from interfering with the normal/natural development of alien societies. Thomas Richards has observed that "the Directive completely disappears in a contest of equals" (14).[63] The Prime Directive is a mandate to ensure that as many members of the interstellar community as possible, especially 'primitive' civilizations, develop along the same normal/natural (read: normative) paradigm of linear process. As the only benevolent empire, the Federation provides the preferred model which is disseminated and enforced by its naval force—Starfleet. While the Federation may not look like an empire, it always acts like one without appearing to do so. For example, in what is arguably one of the most apt dialogs, two non–Federation citizens equate the imperial qualities of the Federation with root beer.

QUARK: What do you think?

GARAK: It's vile.

QUARK: I know. It's so bubbly and cloying and happy.

GARAK: Just like the Federation.

QUARK: But you know what's really frightening? If you drink enough of it, you begin to like it.

GARAK: It's insidious.

QUARK: Just like the Federation.[64]

However, the question has to be raised as to whether the way of the Federation is simply the American way. Putting aside the clamor of some critics who opted for surface simplicity, the fact that there is actually little known about the internal workings of Starfleet (and even less about Federation politics) points to a vague yet complex nostalgia governing the interstellar politics of the future. The Federation perpetuates the myth of broader Anglocentric ideals which in turn are undercut by romanticized hierarchies of power and the politics of distance.

At first it might seem a simple task to answer the question as to which contemporary political body the Federation resembles most closely. Apart from a few heavy-handed comments on American conflicts, the concepts of the contemporary nation state and transnational organizations, such as the UN or NATO, do not uniformly apply to *Star Trek*'s political entities once we look beyond their allegorical surfaces. *Star Trek*'s maritime milieu teems with empires and colonies. It actually replicates pre–20th century geopolitical structures. Even so, they could easily be draped with symbolic surfaces, if writers decided to do so, allowing them to become allegorical stand-ins for commenting on contemporary international events. Consequently, it seems impossible to equate the Federation and Starfleet with one single nation state, a political body, an alliance and/or a military hierarchy, respectively. Still, many critics attempted do just that. When viewed in concert, their observations reveal a certain discord which points back to the vagueness and nostalgia encoded in *Star Trek*'s political peculiarities. What is more, they serve to underscore the broad, historio-mythical Anglocentrism found in its future.[65] Delineating the Federation as "a voluntary confederation of worlds" (76), Richard has acknowledged the ill-defined contours of *Star Trek*'s politics.

Even on the surface, the Federation is compatible with a series of historical alliances. For example, it is reminiscent of the Confederation of the thirteen American colonies under the *Articles of Confederation* (1781–89).[66] Moreover, the Federation also echoes the sentiments on world governance found in Immanuel Kant's essay *Perpetual Peace* (1795) which reverberated in broad geopolitical formations after the Napoleonic Wars.[67] These included but were not limited to U.S.–British relations prior to and after the declaration of the Monroe Doctrine, the "growth of 'responsible government' ... and Dominion status" in the shade of *Pax Britannica*, and later, the genesis of both the Inter-Parliamentary Union (IPU) and the League of Nations (Black 191–2). While Chris Gregory has also equated the Federation with the U.S., he also pointed out that "Roddenberry's future-utopia *remains an ideal rather than a specific political construct*" (161, emphasis added). While he has not stated as to who this ideal might be and/or what it consists of, his remark opens up Roddenberry's deliberate vagueness about the political workings of his future.

Between Roddenberry's off-hand remark about basing much of *Star Trek* on the English, and the teleology that has come to the fore in its maritime milieu so far, it is clear that the ideals and ideas he found in the Hornblower novels and other naval stories were undoubtedly Anglocentric. Since they are accentuated with a considerable dose of nostalgia and romance, they were very compatible with the American national experience and Roddenberry's evolving career during the 1950s and early 1960s. In order to maintain the Hornblower-esque model of drama, he made it repeatedly clear that the ship has to "[s]tay away from petty military politics" (1967: 24).[68] This created a sort of reverence for Earth as an imperial metropolis, i.e., the center. Channeled through the politics of distance, it is the kind of reverence that is usually not warranted. We see the ambiguities and fallacies of the metropolitan center emerge on those infrequent visits that Starfleet's space mariners pay to Earth. Extrapolated from the Anglocentric telos of western modernity, the Federation represents a nostalgic ideal of the shared, transatlantic Anglophone experience. The base tone for this shared ideal are found in the North Atlantic Enlightenment. These are "the ideal of democracy," "the rights of the individuals," a rejection of "arbitrary demands of religion, favoring science and reason as the basis of belief," and "a detailed and sophisticated division of labour" (Barrett et al. 9). By approximating the maritime world of the 18th century Enlightenment, *Star Trek*'s maritime milieu embraces linear progress and a secular/rational humanism as its maxims. Resulting in a hierarchy of civilizations, it is the self-imposed duty of "those who are 'more enlightened' ... to 'alleviate' the ignorance of others" (Barad 76). In the future, Starfleet is the benign bringer of knowledge.

The Federation and Starfleet continue to put into practice the best and the worst of both Anglophone hegemons. Circumscribed by four trajectories, they tap into a broad Anglophone experience. They espouse (1) a Protestant missionary zeal, and (2) the belief in and recognition of the individual as a presumed site of power and knowledge who, however, is constrained by (3) a social contract/covenant which is further compromised by (4) the politics of distance. By ensuring the normal/natural development of the interstellar community, Starfleet employs an Anglocentric norm to "represent alien cultures as immature creatures in need of parental guidance" (Ono 170). In this vein, outer space becomes an extended Anglosphere where the human norm is decidedly Anglophone/Euro-American. In this process, the individual is idealized as the primary site of agency.

Starfleet crews, who are lionized as communities of highly individualized agents, are not particularly free though. While Roddenberry described the ranks and forms of address that govern their relationships as "courtesies" (qtd. Whitfield 185), they are still bound by rigid naval hierarchies. The philosophy of contractual formations permeates modern western thought. Individuals forego some of their natural freedoms in order to be governed by hierarchies which arguably protect their remaining rights more justly and effectively.[69] Contractual thinking is, however, a dominant marker of identity in the national mythologies of the two Anglophone hegemons. It links seemingly disparate "contracts" such as the *Charter of Liberties* (1100), the *Magna Carta* (1215), the *Mayflower Compact* (1620), the *Bill of Rights* (1689), the *Declaration of Independence* (1776), and the *United States Constitution* (1788). Consequently, contractual thinking emerges as a kind of meta-myth for the Anglophone experience. A necessity for financing a large naval force, naval historians usually point to the founding of the Bank of England (1694) as the direct result of Charles I's and II's financial trickery and disregard for Parliament. The subsequent contractual curtailment of the sovereign's powers speaks to the links between social contract theory and the maritime character of the nation.[70] Caught "between the social critique of the Enlightenment and the egalitarian currents intrinsic to Anglo-American maritime culture" (Gilje 170), it was sailors who "lived" the social contract on a daily basis. Consequently, contractual philosophy is carried to the stars by Starfleet's space-borne mariners. The Federation is conceived in a charter ratified by its four founding races (Humans, Vulcans, Andorians, and Tellarites) in 2161.[71] As idealized as these beliefs appear, they are compromised by yet another experience that shaped the collective psyche of all English-speaking peoples—the realities of controlling and governing vast territorial possessions in an era before space and time had become compressed.

In a political paradigm governed by distance in both space and time, there is an inevitable tension between the center and the periphery. Within an Anglophone frame of reference, this is more commonly referred to as the opposition between the *country* and the *court*. Gordon Wood has identified this conflict of power as an easily overlooked component which connects the two Anglophone hegemons. The "localist and grassroots opposition to far-removed central authorities was a recurring theme in English history as it would continue to be in American history" (59). The country/court opposition can also be detected in the tradition of sea fiction. It is particularly pertinent in stories set during the Napoleonic Wars. In the writings of Southey, Coleridge, and Austen, the archetype of the Nelsonian hero emerged as an empowering, masculine antidote to the effete ruling classes. Populating the home shores, they were vividly epitomized in the escapades of the Regency. Fraught by scandals, sexual and otherwise, and a descent into paralyzing decadence, these authors critiqued the "chivalry of the land" as the product of unrestrained empire (Fulford 162). Seen as the result of importing and consuming the Exotic, which was synonymous with the Orient, it had detrimental effects on the moral fiber and virtues of British manhood.[72] Often portrayed as the insidious intrusion of the exotic/colonial periphery upon the home shores, the fruits of empire made the metropolitan center incompetent, impotent, and prone to decay. Edward Gibbon's *The History of the Decline and Fall of the Roman Empire* (1776–89) served as a warning sign, which, incidentally, happens to be one of Hornblower's favorite books.[73] The Nelsonian naval officer then became the savior of the imperial fabric because his character (tempered by his experiences in a hostile, natural environment and his isolation from the home shores) remained untouched by the corruptive effects of the imported exotic. The country/court opposition was transposed into the maritime milieu of Napoleonic sea fiction (especially in the works of Frederick Marryat) which then provided the models for writers in the 20th century.

On those infrequent visits to the home shores, Hornblower's thoughts betray his deep apprehension and even disgust for the different nodes of the imperial center. It comes to the fore when he is invited to court to be presented to the Prince Regent, who makes the captain a knight of the realm. Scenes of opulence, pomp, nonsense, and foppish behavior frame the ceremony. The thoughts of the captain give the reader a distinct sense of disapproval and alienation.[74] Whenever Hornblower visits the metropolitan center, which usually includes the court, various political spheres, and even the Admiralty, they all show the signs of impending decay, corruption, and a lack of leadership hidden underneath a thin veneer of grandeur. The higher echelons are notoriously decadent, effeminate, bureaucratic, and, with a few exceptions, incapable to lead. The archetypal tension and conflict between the independent sea captain and his immediate superiors is thus a manifestation of the broader dichotomy between the *metropolitan center* and the *maritime periphery*.

Since *Star Trek*'s future approximates maritime politics of distance, similar structures, tensions, and conflicts between the idealized metropolitan center and the maritime periphery come to the fore. They expose the dark underbelly of the Federation's utopian ideal. Even though Roddenberry advocated for the ship to stay away from Earth, starting in the feature films, the audience occasionally sees the Federation's metropolitan center. Based on the little we see, it is clear that life on Earth may be less idyllic and flawless than we are led to believe. "While it is presented as a pleasant location," Barrett and Barrett have argued, "its function often serves to undermine rather than enforce, the *Star Trek* narrative" (201). Cloaked in a life of comfort and ease, the Federation and Starfleet repeatedly show explicit signs of corruption, incompetence, anxiety and/or decadence. Occasionally, we see the fruits of Starfleet's benevolent and disinterested form of exploration undermine the imperial center by way of an intrusion of the Exotic/Alien.

For example, in a first-season episode of *ST:TNG*, Captain Picard returns to Earth in order to expose and expel alien parasites that usurped the command echelons of Starfleet. Though presented in all its paradisiacal glory, Earth emerges as an environment that effeminates those who reside there, making them prone to fall prey to the Exotic.[75] On another occasion, the frailty of metropolitan politics and Starfleet's autocratic tendencies are exposed when "exotic" shapeshifting aliens infiltrate Earth. Sowing seeds of paranoia and fear at Starfleet Command, they intend to paralyze the Federation government, which has been lulled into a false sense of security and comfort. By essentially staging a coup, Starfleet plays into their hands and places Earth under temporary military protection. Tempered by his duty on the fringes of the Federation, it is up to Captain Sisko and his crew to fulfill their antidotal function.[76] Similarly, Captain Janeway narrowly thwarts another infiltration attempt by alien life forms who perceive their "exotic" existence in an extradimensional realm threatened by Starfleet's ventures.[77] Since the frailty of the metropolitan center together with its imperial anxiety are a part of a broader Anglophone experience, they also resonate well with invasion anxieties. Mythologically sustained by the trauma of 1066 and translated into a paradigmatic trope in sf by H. G. Wells, invasion fears are a condition commonly shared in the psyche of English-speaking peoples. They found pronounced articulation in the national imagination of the U.S. where they had been already present prior to the Red Scare of the late 1940s and 1950s. Hence, *Star Trek*'s maritime milieu allows for the telling of allegorical invasion stories (often believed as quintessentially American) which, in fact, are facilitated by an Anglophone experience of maritime empire-building and romanticized empire-maintenance.

Not only do visits to Earth expose the metropolitan center as effeminate and prone to subversion, but they also bring to the fore the nostalgic, reactionary, and thus undemocratic strictures that rule *Star Trek*'s maritime milieu. What "little we see," Murphy and Porter have suggested, "can be disturbing from a democratic point of view" (152). Indeed, there are hardly any active political processes at work in the immediate context of Starfleet's hierarchy. There is no participatory political culture (e.g., elections) which shape the course of the Federation. In short, there is "none of the political wranglings and constitutional debates found throughout series like Babylon 5," or in shows like the re-imagined *Battlestar Galactica* (153). Instead, the Federation offers a benign imperial hegemony which is equated with and maintained by a romanticized and sanitized naval force. In short, the maritime milieu in space is a process of empire. Regardless of how benevolent they profess to be, the imperial imperative builds on a hierarchy of subjects. Without even acknowledging the maritime endowment of *Star Trek*, Kent Ono has accurately asserted that its future offers "viewers the chance to reimagine the glories of past colonial power" and "to have faith in the authority and power of European and European American men so that the 'best of both worlds' ... is possible" (158–9). Yet, it also allows us to see the hierarchized and racialized specters projected forward in the process of *translatio studii et imperii,* continuing the Anglocentric telos of western modernity.

The excerpt of "Locksley Hall," quoted at the beginning of the chapter, delivers the blueprint for the vision of the world *Star Trek* offers. Poised at the heyday of Britain's maritime empire, which made its hegemonic impact felt along the oceanic contours of the world, it articulates Britain's benign self-image as the epitome of modern civilization as well as its inherent hubris. It paints in broad strokes the continuation of an Anglophone hegemony, and thus in a sense prefigured the type of nostalgia Roddenberry tapped into. Conceived at the transition from a formal (Britain) to an informal imperial hegemony (U.S.), the reactionary world of *Star Trek* mirrors and continues this process *ad infinitum*. Its maritime world in outer space grew out of the juncture of *Pax Britannica* and *Pax Americana*, and offered a perpetual Anglocentric *Pax Galactica*.

Conclusion
What You Leave Behind

In inceptum finis est. Before yachting and pleasure cruises became popular starting in the mid–19th century, a journey aboard a ship, especially a voyage of discovery, was defined by a clear goal; it was determined by the very nature of a seabound passage. Such voyages usually had clear mission parameters. Explorers had clear objectives for what they wanted to discover and what they were to accomplish. These were largely informed by presuppositions and assumptions as to what and who they would encounter. The process of making the unknown knowable, even before one actually dispels the qualities of the unknown, is a quintessential though often overlooked element of seabound voyages. Historical experience has taught us that these presuppositions, which usually amounted to wild speculations and unfounded expectations, did not correspond with what and/or who explorers ultimately discovered. For example, Columbus and Cook set out to discover and lay claim to something they ultimately did not find. Regardless of the thousands of nautical miles mariners traveled, no voyage was indefinite. Unless they ran afoul of treacherous shoals and were never seen or heard from again, their voyages were *also* guided by the presupposed return to their point of departure—their home port. We now also return to our point of departure after having successfully completed one circumnavigation of the entire *Star Trek* continuum following two thematic trajectories.

Most previous scholarship was hampered by the ongoing production of *Star Trek* together with its expansive nature. New circumstances—the cancellation of *ST:ENT* in 2005, the reboot of *Star Trek* in *Star Trek* (J.J. Abrams, U.S. 2009) and its two sequels,[1] *Star Trek*'s 50th anniversary in 2016, and the return to the Prime Universe on television with *Star Trek: Discovery* in 2017—allowed for a fresh and especially a synoptic look at the *continuities* which governed the

Star Trek continuum in a media-specific process of repetition and modulation for more than four decades. Guided by primary production material—a largely untapped resource—existing critical approaches to *Star Trek* served as a starting point for fully appreciating, understanding, contextualizing, and reconciling the multifaceted implications of Gene Roddenberry's shorthand definition for *Star Trek* as "Wagon Train to the stars" and "Hornblower in space." Sf uses and abuses histories/stories to create and maintain "imaginary frameworks," which are primarily rooted in the cognitive/scientific episteme. Hence, his rather straightforward reference opened an avenue for looking at how and why *Star Trek*'s science-fictional world partakes in the myth of the American West via the TV-Western *Wagon Train*, and the myth of the British Golden Age of Sail via the historical fiction of C.S. Forester's *Hornblower* novels.

Tending to these two acts of *vraisemblance* and relating the resulting thematic continuities that govern *Star Trek* to their multiple constituent contexts has allowed me to re-examine and problematize the roots of the continuum in a particular period of American history. The initial conception of *Star Trek* was framed by the prelude to and the aftermath of a moment in American history where, under the auspices of President Kennedy, the U.S. formally announced to the international community that it assumed the leadership as the defender of "the western world" from its previous self-proclaimed hegemonic leader—the British Empire. Drawing on the language of the contemporary Western, the president challenged the nation to get moving again by declaring the decade of the 1960s the "New Frontier." The actual world that *Star Trek* builds in outer space, however, is not reminiscent of any geographical or historical stages in America's westward expansion; neither do starships re-enact the overland trek of wagon trains which are led by interstellar wagon masters of the future. Enhanced by primary production material, I have made visible that which is hidden in plain sight and thus usually taken for granted. In short, *Star Trek*'s transatlantic double consciousness revealed a largely hidden British history/story embedded in its world. The theme of *Rule Britannia* governs the very ontology of *Star Trek*'s world in outer space—its worldbuilding paradigm. It is a historicized maritime future that is akin to the 18th century Age of Sail as it is commonly found in sea novels such as the *Hornblower* saga. Systematized and comprehensively charted, this second theme manifests in five interrelated maritime dimensions.

While its hyper-technological future builds on a rather singular technical discourse (so-called *Treknobabble*), it is undergirded by a distinct naval corpus drawing heavily on the nautical dictionary of the Age of Sail. It includes but is not limited to descriptive language for a ship's interiors and exteriors, structures of hierarchy and rank as well as sailing and battle orders. They are couched in a generic naval tone which echoes the presumed civility of gentlemanly discourse used by naval officers/heroes in sea novels. *Star Trek*'s corpus also borrows from the legacies of famous ships on both sides of the Atlantic, forming a core of Anglophone ship names; one of the most renowned ships in fiction, the *Enterprise*, traces its genealogy back to a vessel of the Royal Navy—HMS *Enterprize*. Placed in an oceanic paradigm which partially literalizes the "ocean of space" metaphor, starships are essentially disguised sailing vessels. Starfleet's broad mission parameters were likened to the multifaceted functions performed by Royal Navy ships in the past as representatives of maritime military might and maritime exploration. Instead of "space cowboys," it was the genealogical descendants of romanticized Enlightenment mariners who are in charge of this re-imagined maritime enterprise. Horatio Hornblower served as an archetypal character blueprint for *Star Trek*'s principal captains. Laying claim to an ancestry among maritime warriors and maritime explorers of the past, the captains emerged as "fighting naturalists" who continued to re-enact the famed Nelson Touch in outer space.

Guidelines for writers and directors also revealed that the space-borne sailors observe naval traditions and rituals which date back to the time of Nelson and Drake. As much as they serve to highlight the transatlantic cultural continuum between Britain and the U.S. by way of a shared set of naval traditions, they are also used to draw a validating parallel between life in space and a romanticized life at sea. Some traditions, like the captain's log, fulfill a crucial historiographic function. The historicized future archived therein is accentuated by a romantic lament for the presumed simplicity of a bygone age. Together with the presence of naval paraphernalia in the *mise-en-scène*, this is achieved by appropriating a specific range of naval intertexts, such as John Masefield's poem "Sea-Fever," and Herman Melville's *Moby Dick*. Being similar to the 18th century, the future of *Star Trek* resembles a maritime milieu in which space and time have become largely uncompressed again due to the vastness of interstellar space. Consequently, the future is governed by the laws, politics, and exigencies of distance. Shaped by a benign, imperial hegemony, it was extrapolated from the ideological succession of two Anglophone hegemons, the British Empire and the U.S., who were the self-declared leaders of western civilization in the last two hundred years. While occasionally draped with American surfaces, *Star Trek*'s maritime endowment points to a historio-mythical core which is of distinct British origin. Repeated references to the language, events, characters, spaces, and circumstances that constitute the myth of the British Golden Age of Sail served to celebrate the transatlantic cultural continuum the United States shares with Britain.

Ultimately, in revisiting the question of whose histories/stories *Star Trek* has been telling for more than forty years, we can then point to the reasons why its sf world became increasingly incompatible not only with American self-perception and the nation's geopolitical position at the onset of the 21st century, but also with the western *Weltbild* for humanity's future in general. Is it sufficient to claim that the *Star Trek* universe simply continued to tell "the American story" in outer space? No, not really. The assertion that *Star Trek* tells the human story at large, which a fair share of critics and fans often claim, is then equally imprecise. If anything, *Star Trek*'s transatlantic double consciousness has shown that its "imaginary framework" was extrapolated from two myths rooted in a rather specific segment of human history, i.e., an extended view of modernity seen through a privileged Anglocentric lens. More specifically, *Star Trek*'s world was based on and continued to re-imagine histories of an Anglocentric modernity represented by the succession of two Anglophone hegemons. The telos they shared, is articulated in the discourses of progressivism, positivism, liberalism, individualism, and secularism. Doubly encoded in its thematic make-up, the *Star Trek* continuum then provided a framework in which Anglo-dominated modernity, while occasionally interrogated, did not end. Instead, it was carried on by human space exploration in the 22nd, 23rd, and 24th century. *Star Trek*'s broad belief in scientific progress inevitably leads to technical advancements which, in turn, lead to social and intellectual progress. However, driven by a sense of mission and Protestant zeal, which permeate the Anglosphere, the telos is undermined by a patronizing and patriarchal benevolence. Realized in a hegemonically "enforced" peace, it continues to "other" those who are different.

From a geopolitical standpoint, the hegemonic vestiges of western modernity have increasingly been superseded and de-centered by the dynamics of geopolitics and transnational economics in the 21st century. Our contemporary western *Zeitgeist* is informed by trans-/supranational, multilateral, corporate, and virtual structures. The presumed certainties/truths offered by modernity have been replaced by postindustrial, postmodern, and growing post-national meanings of uncertainty, cynicism, irony and vagueness. They are indicative of a global turn from a *centrifugal* to a *centripetal Weltbild*. Since *Star Trek*'s world of perpetual Anglocentric modernity did not ostensibly change in its later incarnations, the dissonance with its immediate socio-cultural contexts continued to grow. *Star Trek*'s decline was exacerbated by significant changes in television programming, target demographics, and impending "franchise fatigue." The signs for the latter became discernible when *ST:TNG* concluded its seven-year run in 1994.[2] Juxtaposing *Star Trek*'s vision for a positivistic future where humanity travels to the stars with the predominant contemporary outlook for humanity's future in outer space allows us to understand this dissonance even better.

Star Trek's sf world became increasingly out of step with late 20th and early 21st century realities. We can employ the history of contemporary space exploration since the Moon Race vis-à-vis space-based sf television series and movies released in the past decade as useful points of reference. The way how they reflect the changing Anglophone/western mindset and attitude with regards to visions about humanity's future generates meaningful benchmarks. It does not take much to see how a centrifugal mind conceived *Star Trek* at a time in American history where the forward- and outward-looking optimism and progress (showcased among other things by the American space program) contributed much to the belief that *Pax Americana* had arrived. Paraphrasing President Kennedy, the eyes of Americans, and by extension the eyes of the western world, no longer seem to "look into space, to the moon and to the planets beyond" (1962). Funding for space ventures and public interest in a future where we journey out into space have steadily declined over the past five decades. This decline is reflected in popular culture artifacts, and sf television and film make obvious access points. It is, however, important to acknowledge a certain time lag. It marks the relationship between both the impulses that trigger large-scale changes in cultural communities, and the time it takes until they gain widespread traction, and even more until these changed attitudes affect mass media artifacts.

The first indications of the public's declining interest in space exploration, together with the initial steps towards a centripetal turn, emerged at the time of the last manned missions to the moon. For example, Apollo 16 and 17 received considerably less coverage than preceding missions. Even so, attitudes towards a possible future in space did not change overnight. NASA's space shuttle program continued to fuel the imagination of Americans and the western world in the 1970s and early 1980s. Unmanned missions, such as the two *Voyager* probes (launched in 1977) also contributed much to the public's sense of wonder and awe. After all, they delivered the first close-up views of our solar system. These new planetary shores still invited a sense of possibility. The *Challenger* disaster in 1986, on the other hand, was a major blow. Still, it was not until after the end of the Cold War that the "space shuttling" of astronauts and cargo between Earth and our "castles in the sky" met with the public's fatigue. It seems we began to attribute a sense of ordinariness to space missions. Continuous budget cuts and a persistent lack of commitment for a mission to Mars did not help either. Marking a clear point in the centripetal turn, it seems as if humanity's imagination had settled in low Earth orbit—first, on the Russian space station *Mir*, and now on the *International Space Station*.

The gradual decline of "real" space programs did not immediately affect the momentum of imagined space exploration and space adventures set in sf futures. On the contrary, the memory and legacy of human spaceflight, especially NASA's Apollo and shuttle programs, nurtured and sustained what became the second golden age of sf on television, which lasted roughly from the late 1980s to the early 2000s. While this period unarguably attested to the genre's diversity and range,[3] space-based sf series were the epicenter of the genre's prolific output. J.P. Telotte has observed that "the updated space opera mode of the *Star Trek* franchise" was paramount (24). The 1990s saw a proliferation of series either set in or oriented towards space. *Babylon 5* (U.S. 1993–8), the *Stargate* franchise (CAN/U.S. 1997–2011), which encompassed three series, and *Farscape* (AUS 1999–2003) are the best-known examples. This period also brought forth lesser known quality shows, such as *Space: Above and Beyond* (U.S. 1995–6), and *Earth 2* (U.S. 1994–5). Even though the premises and formats of these series differed greatly, they shared a base tone when it came to venturing into outer space. Regardless of the dangers, hardships, and conflicts that might lie in wait, a centrifugal momentum and a sense of curiosity permeated all of them. In short, imagined futures where humanity sets out into space still signaled that space exploration, space science, and a general spirit of inquiry were worthwhile, valuable, and meaningful. The fact that *ST:ENT* aired on September 26, 2001, however, reverberates with portentous symbolism.

The events of 9/11 and the trauma it incurred in the U.S., and in the western world at large, inarguably provided an additional push in the centripetal turn. Since 9/11, there seems to prevail a re-adjusted vision inward which has greatly affected attitudes about the future. Once again, space exploration and sf provide powerful reflections and refractions of these altered attitudes. Continuous budget cuts, the *Columbia* disaster in 2003, and the discontinuation of the space shuttle program in 2011 have severely curtailed NASA's space ventures. Other than our permanent residence in low Earth orbit, any current plans for revitalizing manned spaceflight remain vague and/or are fraught with a lack of vision and commitment. While the *Voyager* probes still fed the people's imagination in the 1970s and 1980s, recent robotic missions have failed to do so regardless of their astounding successes; the Mars rovers *Spirit* (2004), *Opportunity* (2004), *Curiosity* (2012), the *Cassini-Huygens* mission to Saturn and Titan (2004–5), and the *Rosetta* mission (2014), serve as cases in point. It seems as if the public's attention is only drawn towards space when tweeting astronauts become short-lived superstars on social media platforms. Even private space ventures, like Virgin Galactic, Space X, and Red Bull Stratos, do not really galvanize the public's imagination like the space programs, which were fueled by the vestiges of modernity, once did. The cognitive and imaginative receptors of the general public have grown numb with regards to nurturing science and historical literacy, and drawing inspiration from the exploration of space.

J.P. Telotte has summarized how the traumatic events which ushered in the new millennium have filtered into popular culture in general, and sf particular.

> [W]e confront an age in which history seems to have lost much of its relevance, the future is mysterious, and our humanity is often perceived as just a construct of various forces beyond our full understanding and control [26].

The re-imagined version of *Battlestar Galactica* (U.S. 2003–9) made it a point of tackling the trauma of 9/11, and the subsequent invasions of Afghanistan and Iraq, with allegorical and political finesse. Even so, humanity's exodus into space is not precipitated by intellectual curiosity, but rather necessity following a nuclear holocaust. *Star Trek*, on the other hand, failed to allegorically deal with the war on terror within the confines of its return to a new age of exploration in *ST:ENT*. A few space-based sf television series, like *Defying Gravity* (U.S./CAN 2009) and *Virtuality* (U.S. 2009), tried to recapture an outward drive into our solar system and beyond. Unfortunately, they were either canceled early, or did not make it past the pilot-stage. Recent space movies, including the *Star Trek* reboot, speak an even clearer and more questionable language with regards to humanity's future. When viewed collectively, they point out that whenever we as a species venture into space, it will inevitably lead either to exploitation and corruption, or simply end in disaster and death. The collective message about humanity's future conveyed in recent space-based sf films is perhaps best exemplified by astronaut Ryan Stone (Sandra Bullock) in *Gravity* (Alfonso Curaón, U.S. 2013). After surviving multiple disasters in orbit and making it safely back to Earth, we see her clutching the wet and nurturing soil near her landing zone. The image imparts a powerful image to the viewers, i.e., we should carefully reassess leaving humanity's cradle. The *Star Trek* reboot speaks a similar, and in many ways, a much more obvious language. While space as the "final frontier" provided a metaphoric geography of progress, change, opportunity, and hope in its original permutations, in *Star Trek* (J.J. Abrams, U.S. 2009) the "new" Doctor McCoy (Karl Urban) expresses his concerns about venturing into space. Tellingly, he defines space as "disease and danger wrapped in darkness and silence." In the same vein, the second installment of the reboot simply headed "into darkness." *Star Trek Beyond* (Justin Lin, U.S. 2016) does not venture beyond the danger and tragedy inherent in space exploration.

By comparison, the recent film/television landscape attests to the prolific output of fantasy proper. In the wake of the film adaptations of J.R.R. Tolkien's

The Lord of the Rings and *The Hobbit* as well as the *Harry Potter* novels, we have witnessed an increase in the number of fantasy television series. They range from revamped sword and sorcery formats to a number of vampire series, and adaptation of fairytales. Alien invasion stories and post-apocalyptic formats were the only type of stories (traditionally enveloped by the sf genre membrane) that made a somewhat predictable comeback since 9/11. The re-imagined series *V* (U.S. 2009–11), *Falling Skies* (2011–15), together with *The Andromeda Strain* (2008), *Revolution* (2012–14), and *Defiance* (2013–15), serve as cases in point. Consequently, by celebrating a perpetual Anglocentric modernity and centrifugal *Weltbild*, it is then not surprising that the *Star Trek* continuum became incompatible with a radically different, centripetal milieu.

Echoing the metaphor's progressivist and, indeed, humanist promise, the frontier allowed *Star Trek* to react to contextual changes—whether it was the new racial sensitivity in *ST:TNG*, the critical questioning of its own scientific eschatology in *ST:DS9*, or the belated acknowledgment of changing gender roles in *ST:VOY*. By employing the frontier as a metaphoric canvas onto which contemporary challenges, problems, and the "unfinished business" of race/ethnicity, gender, religion, politics and more, could be projected in allegorical form, *Star Trek* perpetuated the New Frontier promise for a liberal progressive future where these challenges can and will be resolved. By couching its morality plays in a maritime world modeled on the British Golden Age of Sail, *Star Trek* then *also* replicated and perpetuated the very structures, which, historically, caused inequities, discrimination, and subjugation. Hence, it is also no surprise that critics repeatedly pointed to the many failings of *Star Trek*. If we were to summarize the basic charge scholars usually bring against *Star Trek* on the whole and/or its individual parts, then it would be the following: while its sf world held great potential and promise, it did not do enough to follow through.

More importantly, however, it serves to acknowledge *Star Trek tried* to do more than many other sf television series and movies. Michèle Barrett et al. have reminded their readers that it makes sense "to put in context some of the more alarming judgements of practitioners in the often spiky academic debates about Star Trek" (9). More generally, astronomer and public educator Carl Sagan has commented on the overall value of a centrifugal mindset, space exploration, and intellectual curiosity like they are also found in *Star Trek*. "Projects that are future-oriented, that, despite their political difficulties, can be completed only in some distant decade are continuing reminders that there will be a future" (227).[4] Despite *Star Trek*'s ethno-/Anglocentrism, despite its positivism, and scientific eschatology, and despite its colonial and imperial power structures, its hopeful outlook for a future, i.e., an optimistic future in space where things would be better, was genuine. In the incompatibility of *Star Trek*'s world with our contemporary *Zeitgeist*, we can see a shortcoming with regards to a positivist and centrifugal outlook in the 21st century. In contrast, a centripetal mindset runs the danger of promoting ahistorical thinking, ignorance, suspicion and fear of the unknown over scientific knowledge, intellectual curiosity, and secularism. Yet, while it seemed the *Star Trek* idea had been moored indefinitely in port, a new ship embarked on a renewed voyage of discovery on the ocean of space in 2017. *Star Trek: Discovery* aimed at setting sail on a trajectory of renewed curiosity and hope. The polemic notwithstanding, Philip J. Fry's wistful remark is likely to reverberate in the years to come—"*The world needs Star Trek to give people hope for the future.*"[5]

Chapter Notes

Introduction

1. To date, there have been only two cursory forays into the myth of the British Golden Age of Sail. Both acknowledge C.S. Forester's *Hornblower* novels, but do not use them to chart the ways in which the myth is embedded in *Star Trek*'s worldbuilding. Michèle and Duncan Barrett used *Star Trek*'s "nautical metaphor" (10) only as a way into their critical investigation of the humanist values that fuel its persistent fascination with testing humanity. Jonathan Rayner noted many references to the myth in primary production material, but then came to the odd conclusion that "the model of eighteenth- and nineteenth-century European imperialist voyages seems inapplicable" (159).

2. The *Star Trek* continuum refers to the entirety of this science fiction universe: *Star Trek: The Original Series* (U.S. 1966–9, [*ST:TOS*]), *Star Trek: The Animated Series* (U.S. 1973–4, [*ST: TAS*]), *Star Trek: The Next Generation* (U.S. 1987–94, [*ST:TNG*]), *Star Trek: Deep Space Nine* (U.S. 1993–9, [*ST:DS9*]), *Star Trek: Voyager* (U.S. 1995–2001, [*ST:VOY*]), *Star Trek: Enterprise* (U.S. 2001–5, [*ST:ENT*]), and the first ten motion pictures.

3. The re-imagined version of *Battlestar Galactica* (U.S. 2003–9), the *Star Wars* universe (1977–), *Babylon 5* (U.S. 1993–8), both *Stargate SG-1* (Canada/U.S. 1997–2011) as well as *Stargate Atlantis* (Canada/U.S. 2004–9), and the short-lived series *Space: Above and Beyond* (U.S. 1995–6) serve as the most obvious reference points. They all celebrate the legacy of U.S. aircraft carriers during World War II and later conflicts.

4. Cf. George, 2013: 7–21; Selley, 1986: 89–104. As members of the pantheon of frontier heroes, Meriwether Lewis and William Clark bear the closest genealogical resemblance to Starfleet captains. However, there are no references to the two explorers and their Corps of Discovery in *Star Trek*.

5. The nature of the reboot is perhaps best understood as a form of parody (cf. Hutcheon, 1985: 1–20, 30–37, 50–54).

6. In the documents titled "STAR TREK IS..." (1964) and "THE STAR TREK GUIDE. THIRD REVISION" Roddenberry tapped into the two fields of maritime military might and maritime exploration, which form the core of the myth of the British Golden Age of Sail, to imbue *Star Trek* with a set of meanings that would ultimately become the *Rule Britannia* theme. An often-cited albeit largely unexamined passage describes the starship captain as "[a] space-age Captain Horation [sic] Hornblower" ("STAR TREK IS..." 5). On the same page, Roddenberry also established a link "with similar men in the past," like "Drake, Cook, Bougainville and Scott" (*ibid.*). Not only did he include "naval parlance" and a "slight naval flavor" in aesthetics and "general appearance," in delineating the starship's mission, he also appropriated a colonial, indeed imperialist rhetoric. Roddenberry and his team of writers established that their starship-driven future "*is almost exactly analogous to the Earth of the eighteenth century*" (qtd. Gerrold 11, original emphasis). Outlined as "a well-defined and long-range Exploration-Science-Security mission" ("STAR TREK IS..." 3), the endeavors of the starship and its crew was to be very similar to those of "English warships" ("THE STAR TREK GUIDE" 27). Over the years, Hornblower served as an omnipresent reference point behind the scenes of *Star Trek*'s production. Ronald D. Moore later remembered: "It was set up as a Navy command structure and Gene always

mentioned Horatio Hornblower [...] and I always thought of the Naval lineage as an important component of *Star Trek*" (2008).

Chapter 1

1. The contextual manual for *Star Trek*'s transatlantic double consciousness builds on a structuralist mix of theoretical and methodological tools drawn from sf genre criticism, television media criticism, comparative mythology, and cultural/historical contextualization. Sf literary critic Darko Suvin has argued that genres like sf are "socioaesthetic and not metaphysical entities" and that they "have an inner life and logic of their own, which do not exclude but on the contrary presuppose a dialectical permeability to themes, attitudes, and paradigms from other literary genres, science, philosophy, and everyday socioeconomic life" (16). The work of Mark Bould and Sherryl Vint, two leading sf film and television scholars, also informed my theoretical toolbox. They have argued that genres such as sf "are never, as frequently perceived, objects which already exist in the world and which are subsequently studied by genre critics, but fluid and tenuous constructions made by the interaction of various claims and practices by writers, producers, distributors, marketers, readers, fans, critics and other discursive agents" (48).

2. Already Darko Suvin has asserted that there is "a relationship of filiation" between these two protozoan impulses of sf, and that the "sea haunts this filiation" (22).

3. Histories of the future, and the discursive means to make them plausible, are inevitably tied to the grammatical realities and constraints of the English language. After all, any science-fictional framework demands cognition by way of knowing and understanding an unreal and fantastic world. In order to compensate, Peter Stockwell has argued, fictional futures make use of the "normative status of the past in narrative ... marking the fictional narrative as possessing verisimilitude" (36–43), and thus sustain cognition through a higher degree of grammatical plausibility.

4. When a TV writer/producer tells studio executives that he was "going to make a show about Captain Hornblower in outer space," David Gerrold recalls, they wanted to know: "*How* are you going to do it" (218, original emphasis). A screenwriter for *Star Trek* and its first chronicler, Gerrold also points to the significance that Hornblower had for *Star Trek*'s world-building. What he calls "a format" is essentially "a guide for whatever is to come later ... a flight plan for a series ... how he [a producer/writer] is going to tell his stories–what set of situations, characters, equipment, background, and physical laws of the universe will give him the broadest possible base for the stories he wants to tell" (*ibid.*).

5. I am in part indebted to the recently re-edited scholarly efforts of Matthew Kapell et al. in *Star Trek as Myth* (2010). The volume presented me with an initial stepping stone which was complemented by Chris Gregory's *Star Trek Parallel Narratives* (2000), and Jon Wagner et al. *Deep Space and Sacred Time: Star Trek in the American Mythos* (1998). Despite the wealth of their collective output, they outlined *Star Trek*'s mythological contours along the lines of only one national myth, i.e., the American story.

6. While "SF's analogical historicity may or may not be mythomorphic," Darko Suvin has argued, "it cannot be mythopoetic" (83).

7. The cosmology that dominates western thought has repeatedly changed over the centuries. Antiquity, the Middle Ages, and the Renaissance approximately circumscribe the major paradigms. Growing out of the Renaissance, the rise of modernity can be roughly traced back to the 18th century and the Age of Enlightenment. A teleology of progress then fueled the scientific and industrial revolutions. Over the course of the 19th century, this teleology fused with the popular (mis)understanding of Charles Darwin's evolutionary biology insofar as "natural change is guided by purpose and therefore works toward a goal, or at least toward movement in a preordained direction" (Wagner 145). It fostered a belief in linear and inevitable progress towards an ever more sophisticated and more positive stage of development, and "Western Europeans and Anglo-Americans had obviously come farther than others" (144).

8. Mapping the "symbiotic transfer of imperial hegemony from Britain to the USA" in the western world, Jeremy Black has distinguished between the formal character of the British Empire "as a result of territorial control, and its impact on government and education," and the informal qualities of the American Empire which "has largely been due to economic advantage outside the context of any such control" (371).

9. While the atheistic tendencies and presumptions found in *Star Trek*'s humanist worldview are critically examined in *ST:DS9*, they are never fully subverted. The benevolent and

hegemonic influence of the Federation and Starfleet are ultimately not in doubt either. Producer Michael Piller, Rick Berman's second-in-command, responded to initial criticism about the inclusion of religion by putting the writers' plans into perspective. He went on record in a DVD commentary: "We are not changing the rules of the *Star Trek* universe, we're simply exploring the rules of another alien race, and what they consider important, and we're seeing how we as humans in the 24th century might react to that, how we might learn from that" (2002).

10. Drawing on a film like *A Passage to India* (David Lean, UK 1984) and the TV serial *The Jewel in the Crown* (1984), Hutcheon has argued that the "intended anti-nostalgic exposé of the corruption and exploitation of empire in India may have been less the cause of their success than either a nostalgic liberal-utopian hope that two races might have been able to live as equals—despite history—or a nostalgic memory of the time when Britain was not a minor world power but, rather, ruler of an empire upon which the sun never set" (1998).

11. To attribute all the creative power of production in *auteur*-like fashion to one singular source is sheer folly in a multi-author/creator medium like television. It is particularly pertinent for *Star Trek* since the bulk of the continuum, i.e., the total number of hours of television and film, was actually produced after Gene Roddenberry's death in 1991. Even so, he had established certain "ground rules" before that; he also ensured that these rules were observed by other contributors as *Star Trek*'s world and thus its history grew not least because he nurtured and educated those, like Rick Berman and Michael Pillar, who would take the helm after his death. They, in turn, then mentored subsequent writers and producers, including Brannon Braga, Jeri Taylor, Ronald D. Moore and Ira Steven Behr. In other words, Roddenberry and his team working on early *Star Trek* regulated its world up to a point where its premise, promise, and mechanics could no longer be radically changed lest their successors endanger the degree of familiarity, narrative comfort, and recognition of the audience. By the time of Roddenberry's death, both the showrunners and the audience had already learned the fictional history of two television series and six motion pictures and had thus internalized the rules of *Star Trek*'s world by way of repetition and permutation. In the archive of production-related material writers and producers repeatedly refer to pre-existing and/or already established rules and formats, i.e., the *Star Trek* canon. The main premise of *Star Trek*'s world is treated as an *a priori* fact.

12. Simultaneously invoking Marshall McLuhan and Umberto Eco, Chris Gregory has put forth that in "the context of the resurgence of the oral mode of communication, television series (with their ever-developing and expanding storylines) have the capability of effectively 'mimicking' or reproducing the ancient mythological process" (8).

13. Vulcans base their entire culture on principles of logic and the subsequent rejection of emotion which arguably led to a profound sense of equality. After all, when viewed logically, the entire cosmos, i.e., all existence, is but infinite permutations of infinite manifestations of the same whole. IDIC is perhaps best understood as a brand of cultural relativism on a cosmic/universal scale. *Star Trek* fans also internalized IDIC as the central moral imperative, i.e., the message of *Star Trek*. Trekkies/Trekkers use it to form their community of practice, celebrating diversity and inclusion.

14. Geraghty has found "hints at there being a formula or blueprint to which *Star Trek* must stick lest it departs from Roddenberry's vision" (27). However, without the additional lens of primary production material—and, also because he pursued a different goal in his research—he has asserted that *Star Trek*'s foundational narratives can be subsumed under the American Puritan Jeremiad.

15. Attracted by re-runs of *ST:TOS* in syndication, a growing number of fans organized the first conventions in the 1970s. Conventions would become vibrant forums where like-minded aficionados of the show could exchange their ideas and engage in fan activities like costume contests, the trading of merchandise, and *filking*. There, they could also meet the series' creators/writers/producers and the cast members. Fans also began to write their own *Star Trek* stories, continuing the series in what would emerge as a new genre—fan fiction. First their stories were collected, edited, and published in so-called fanzines, and later they were disseminated on the internet.

Chapter 2

1. *Earth 2* (U.S. 1994–5) is a more convincing "Wagon Train to the stars." Driven by dissenting views, a group of colonists decides to leave an essentially uninhabitable Earth to establish a settlement on the nearest Earth-like

planet. Their transport, bearing the portentous call sign "VA-1587" (recalling the lost colony of Roanoke), crashes. They must embark on an overland trek in search of their original destination—New Pacifica. The colonists thus re-enact the quintessentially Puritan story of the errand into the wilderness.

2. In a sense *Wagon Train* told the American story of westward expansion in its entirety. On one day, they might encounter a band of hostile natives intent on raiding the train. Perhaps they even succeed in capturing some of the women and children who travel with the train. On another, they might run into a company of U.S. cavalry who seek vicious and undiscerning retribution from the natives. Estranged couples, who try to save their marriage out west, seek passage on the train as often as wives who try to escape from unhappy and/or abusive relationships. Children lose their parents to the vagaries of the wilderness and, as orphans, they are left to be cared for by the covenant of the train. They might also pick up survivors of another company of wagons who had been abandoned, cheated and/or lost. On other days, Civil War deserters, both Johnny Rebs and Billy Yanks, attempt to seek refuge with the train. There are of course cattle rustlers and horse thieves, con men trying to dupe the "simple" Western folk, quacks selling cure-it-all elixirs, Mexican revolutionaries importing their subversive fervor to the U.S., entrepreneurs intent on striking it rich out west, and idealistic albeit misguided school teachers on a mission to educate and civilize the savages.

3. The inter-genre contacts and exchanges between the Western and other modes of storytelling became increasingly more obvious in the mid–1960s. They were indicators for the rapid demise of the Western. Despite the growth of progressivist tendencies in the Western that reflected the growing social ills of the late 1950s, the genre was irrevocably tied to America's very own version of imperialism: the myth of American westward expansion. Thus, it was increasingly out of step with the times. "Many of the things that made the western so right for 1959," Gary Yoggy reminds us, "made it wrong for the sixties and painfully out of sync with the seventies" (179). The disastrous involvement of the U.S. in the jungles and in the rice fields of Vietnam provided the most potent impetus for the Western's swift decline in popularity. After all, it was there that America's imperialist jingoism met its gruesome self-image, sending ripples of disillusionment through the American national consciousness. As much as the frontier discourse informed President Kennedy's New Frontier manual for the opportunities and challenges of the new decade, it also provided much of the language initially used to justify the reasons for the U.S. becoming involved in Southeast Asia. While the decline of the Western did not "entail the disappearance of those underlying structures of myth and ideology," as Richard Slotkin has asserted, "those structures were abstracted from the elaborately historicized context of the Western and parceled out among genres that used their relationship to the Western to define both the disillusioning losses and the extravagant potential of the new era" (633). "[T]he matter of the Frontier was displaced into genres dealing with metropolitan crime, high-seas swashbuckling, and imperial or 'oriental adventure,'" and it fed into "a boom in fantasy and science fiction epics that were closely related in theme and visual style to the imperial epics of the 1930s" (634); "Like fairy tales," they "allegorize the condition and etiology of the present world" (636).

4. The myth of the American West as a continuous body, or archive of texts, artifacts, cultural practices, beliefs, and values evolved concurrently with the geographic and historical movement of this imagined space—the frontier—across North America. While the opening and conquest of the West is mostly placed within the confines of the 19th century, many of the roots that nurtured the myth can in fact be found much earlier. When the nation expanded into the Trans-Mississippi West, pre-19th century colonial folklore was adapted to new spaces. The archive of early colonial texts reflects the fear and wonder as well as the prejudice and respect with which Euro-Americans encountered the strange new world—new to the European experience—and its inhabitants. Much of it was permeated by a quintessential Eurocentric dichotomy that categorized indigenous people either as noble or ignoble savages. For example, captivity narratives were a particularly popular genre. These early story formats proved to be mobile and adaptable. Hence, they are found at most stages of U.S. westward expansion in one permutation or another. Howard McCurdy has outlined Frederick Jackson Turner's doctrinal addition to the myth as follows: "He traced many of the distinctive characteristics of American society to the influence of free land across an open frontier. Inquisitiveness, inventiveness, and individualism were American traits forged on the frontier, Turner argued. Once created, these traits persisted even after the actual conditions of frontier life

had disappeared. Turner traced the rise of American democracy and extended suffrage to social conditions on the frontier. Frontier life ... bred a love of liberty that found its expression in the political doctrine of self-rule, and migration to the frontier provided a powerful engine for the cross-fertilization of ideas and cultures that promoted America's sense of national identity" (144).

5. For example, like Robert Hine et al. argued, an iconic Western film such as John Ford's *Stagecoach* "is able to have it both ways," in that it "celebrates westering while it simultaneously debunks the civilization brought to the West by the East" (203).

6. TV Westerns were initially influenced by two medial precursors both in terms of narrative conventions and format. On the one hand, there were B-movie serials which had emerged in the 1940s and which would coexist in many reruns with TV Westerns until the mid-1960s. On the other hand, Western radio plays also provided an additional template.

7. Series such as *The Lone Ranger* were ideal vehicles to ensure that the tendrils of the "Red Threat" would not infiltrate the self-proclaimed stronghold of American values—the family. Thus, Westerns helped to inoculate the minds of the young generation against any subversive ideologies.

8. Movies like *Broken Arrow* (Delmer Daves, U.S. 1950) and *High Noon* (Fred Zinneman, U.S. 1952) are paradigmatic examples. They reflected the growing tensions of unresolved racial issues, and the excessive levels conformity that befell the U.S. as it feared Communist subversion, respectively.

9. Boiling its predominance down to numbers, Richard White has observed that in "1959 thirty prime-time television shows, including eight of the ten most watched, were Westerns" (613).

10. The show's impressive line-up also included three future *Star Trek* alumni: Leonard Nimoy, Richardo Montalban, and Louise Fletcher.

11. In addition to "engaging in social criticism that resembled current intellectual reservations," television and movie Westerns also included, according to John Lenihan, "themes and perspectives that were topical, if not altogether provocative" (122). He adds that "the postwar Western gives evidence of a disquieting mood and critical sensibility in the Truman-Eisenhower years that is often obscured by nostalgic and condescending hindsight" (125).

12. For the 20th anniversary of *ST:TOS*, its original pilot "The Cage," which had been rejected by studio executives, was restored and released on home video. The release featured a prolog and an afterword by Roddenberry in which he tells the viewers about the early days of producing *Star Trek*, his intentions and motivations, and the obstacles he and his team faced. About selling his idea to studios at the height of the Western craze, he had the following to say: "I wanted to sell my series. So, I promised the network that my *Star Trek* idea would be little more than a space western. A wagon train to the stars.... But as I began writing that pilot, I suddenly realized that here was a chance to do the kind of drama I'd always dreamed of doing.... Perhaps I could use this as an excuse to go to those far-off planets, with little polka-dotted people if necessary, and be able to talk about love, war, nature, god, sex; all those things that go to make up the excitement of the human condition. And maybe the TV censors would let it pass because it all seems so make-believe.... So, instead of a space western, I delivered a very different kind of story. [...] For the considerable money they put up, they certainly did not get a western space opera. In fact, nothing even faintly like it" (1986).

13. The lines Kennedy is most remembered for when it comes to the space race, he delivered at Rice University: "We choose to go to the moon. We choose to go to the moon in this decade and do the other things, not because they are easy, but because they are hard, because that goal will serve to organize and measure the best of our energies and skills, because that challenge is one that we are willing to accept, one we are unwilling to postpone, and one we intend to win, and the others, too."

14. The pertinent passage reads as follows: "[N]o nation which expects to be the leader of other nations can expect to stay behind in the race for space."

15. It stands to reason that Kennedy answered, at least implicitly, political economist Henry George when the latter bemoaned the closing of the frontier in *Progress and Poverty* (1879)—"But our advance has reached the Pacific... Further west we cannot go" (qtd. Hine 197)—in order to reopen it in the nation's imagination.

16. Kennedy invoked powerful seaborne images: "We set sail on this new sea because there is new knowledge to be gained ... we help decide whether this new ocean will be a sea of peace or a new terrifying theater of war.... And, therefore, as we set sail, we ask God's blessing on the most hazardous and dangerous and

greatest adventure on which man has ever embarked."

17. Devoting a book-length study to the tensions, overlaps, and continuities found in the early 1960s, W.J. Rorabaugh has opined that "[t]his ambiguous, in-between quality is this short era's most important characteristic" because "it truly did partake both of what had come before and of what would come after" (xxi).

18. The relevant segments of his speech read as follows: "For just as historians tell us that Richard I was not fit to fill the shoes of bold Henry II—and that Richard Cromwell was not fit to wear the mantle of his uncle—they might add in future years that Richard Nixon did not measure to the footsteps of Dwight D. Eisenhower.... As Winston Churchill said on taking office some twenty years ago: if we open a quarrel between the present and the past, we shall be in danger of losing the future.... A tired nation, said David Lloyd George, is a Tory nation—and the United States today cannot afford to be either tired or Tory."

19. After acknowledging the founding fathers, the president then announced that "the torch has been passed to a new generation of Americans." Domestically it had passed from the supposedly stagnant and complacent Eisenhower administration to the more vigorous, youthful, and heroic presidency of Kennedy. On an international scale, it had passed from Britain to the U.S. Kennedy symbolically took up the leadership role in the western world from the British Empire. He asserted that "[in] the long history of the world, only a few generations have been granted the role of defending freedom ... to those old allies whose cultural and spiritual origins we share, we pledge the loyalty of faithful friends ... I do not shrink from this responsibility—I welcome it."

20. In his critique of Kennedy's ideology, Richard Slotkin has pointed out the central hypocrisy of its presumed liberal progressivism. He has assessed the Kennedy administration as follows: "The 'liberal' strain in their thinking made them genuinely desirous of improving the living conditions of 'the poor' by engaging them in the dynamics of 'progress' and by extending the benefits of political democracy to those who had been prevented from enjoying them by tyranny, discrimination, and their own ignorance. But their way of defining progress incorporated the very structure of thought which justified the subjection of 'nonprogressive' races and peoples 'for their own good.' ... The paradox of the New Frontier ... aimed at achieving democratic goals through structures and methods that were elite-dominated and command oriented.... It obscures the elitist and anti-democratic implications of 'Camelot,' with respect to both the treatment of 'weaker' peoples and nations abroad and to the management and control of public opinion and Congressional consent at home" (496–504).

21. Kennedy's image as a hero essentially consisted of two parts: (1) a publicity narrative, and (2) a more personal historio-mythical core. While there were many authors who contributed to the image, such as his father Joe Kennedy, and his advisor and principle speechwriter Ted Sorensen, Jack was still the main source and the lead performer. Despite his disabling health issues and with the help of his father, Kennedy received a commission, served in the Pacific during World War II, and returned a naval war hero. Lieutenant Kennedy commanded a patrol torpedo boat (PT-109) in the Solomon Islands in 1943. On a routine night patrol, the vessel was rammed and sunk by a Japanese destroyer. Initially believed lost with all hands, the details of the crew's survival and subsequent rescue were then used to cast Jack in the role of a heroic leader who saved most of his men. Written by future Pulitzer Prize–winning author John Hersey, the story of the incident received national attention after it appeared under the title "Survival" in a 1944 issue of *The New Yorker*. To broaden the readership, Joe Kennedy's father lobbied hard for a reprint in *Reader's Digest*. The account served significant publicity purposes at every major step of his political career after the war—from him running for a seat in Congress in 1946, and for a Massachusetts Senate seat in 1952, to his presidential campaign in 1960. The war hero image spoke to scores of veterans who found it challenging to adapt to peace time. It also served to project a youthful and romantic image to the general public. "The image of Kennedy as a young man narrowly escaping death in war would prove," according to John Hellmann, "as resonant for readers of Kennedy-as-hero as his British heroes had for Kennedy himself" (36).

22. *The Lives of Bengal Lancer* (Henry Hathaway, U.S. 1935), *Mutiny on the Bounty* (Frank Lloyd, U.S. 1935), *That Hamilton Woman* (Alexander Korda, U.S. 1941), *The Charge of the Light Brigade* (Michael Curtiz, U.S. 1936), and *Captain Horatio Hornblower R.N.* (Raoul Walsh, U.S. 1951) serve as representative examples.

Chapter 3

1. When Britain first, at Heaven's command
Arose from out the azure main;
This was the charter of the land,
And guardian angels sang this strain:
'Rule, Britannia! rule the waves:
Britons never will be slaves.'

The nations, not so blest as thee,
Must, in their turns, to tyrants fall;
While thou shalt flourish great and free,
The dread and envy of them all.
[Chorus]

Still more majestic shalt thou rise,
More dreadful, from each foreign stroke;
As the loud blast that tears the skies,
Serves but to root thy native oak.
[Chorus]

Thee haughty tyrants ne'er shall tame:
All their attempts to bend thee down,
Will but arouse thy generous flame;
But work their woe, and thy renown.
[Chorus]

To thee belongs the rural reign;
Thy cities shall with commerce shine:
All thine shall be the subject main,
And every shore it circles thine.
[Chorus]

The Muses, still with freedom found,
Shall to thy happy coast repair;
Blest Isle! With matchless beauty crown'd,
And manly hearts to guard the fair.
[Chorus] (qtd. Gregg 87–8).

2. *ST:DS9*, "Sacrifice of Angels" (3 Nov 1997).

3. *ST:VOY*, "Scorpion" (21 May 1997).

4. The rapidly expanding pantheon of celebrated naval commanders ranged from Edward Vernon and George Anson, who were among the architects of Britain's maritime triumphalism following the Seven Years' War, to Edward Hawke and Richard Howe, who had prefigured Nelson's patterns of audacity and ingenuity during the *annus mirabilis* of 1759.

5. Sue Parrill delineated maritime historical fiction as "novels written in English during the nineteenth, twentieth, and twenty-first centuries which treat the Royal Navy during the time of the French Revolutionary and Napoleonic Wars" (1).

6. Forester's strength lay in meticulously outlining his stories. Following a linear trajectory, he admitted that he could write only by starting at the beginning. Predictably, he never learned to revise or to rewrite. While diligent and prolific right from the beginning, "overwriting" thousands of words a day for weeks in a row, he produced little successful output at first. His early texts were fraught with an unrefined style and a disjointed structure. Labeling Forester as "never arty," Sanford Sternlicht has observed that his approach to "literature was from the beginning pragmatic, perhaps even bourgeois, reflecting his very strong middle-class background" (26).

7. Forester published no less than twenty-four books before he began working on the Hornblower stories. He also continued to accumulate writing credits for films such as *Eagle Squadron* (Arthur Lubin, U.S. 1942), *Forever and a Day* (Multiple Directors, U.S. 1943), and *The Pride and the Passion* (Stanley Kramer, U.S. 1957). The latter starred Cary Grant, Frank Sinatra and Sophia Loren.

8. Unlike the contemporary meaning of the word, a *cruise* was a technical naval term that describes the broad assignments and long, independent missions of vessels labeled *cruisers*, like frigates.

9. Sue Parrill (2009) and Sanford Sternlicht (1999) provide more extensive summaries of the individual novels. Readers are introduced to an unlikely hero in *Mr. Midshipman Hornblower* (1950), which tells of Horatio's entry into the Royal Navy in an anthology of episodic stories. He joins the service at the behest of his father at an age which is considered too advanced for entering officer training. *Lieutenant Hornblower* (1952) is narrated from the point of view of Lt. William Bush, who serves as Horatio's senior officer in HMS *Renown*. Bush would become Hornblower's long-term friend and second-in-command. The novel is essentially a story about a somewhat precariously justified mutiny. Finding himself demoted to Lieutenant, reduced to half-pay and out of work since the Peace of Amiens (1802), *Hornblower and the Hotspur* (1962) almost seamlessly ties into the previous narrative. As commander of the *Hotspur*, he is sent on a reconnaissance mission along the French coast where he is to assess the enemy's readiness for another conflict. *Hornblower During the Crisis* (1966) remains unfinished. It was the novel Forester had been working on when he died. He intended the story to have his hero indirectly contribute to the events that led to the most famous naval battle in the history of wind and sail—Trafalgar. *Hornblower and the Atropos* (1953) serves as transition between the adventures of young Hornblower and him attaining greater independence in command. He embarks on a series of adventures in the Mediterranean which see him salvage a large treasure from a sunken British ship with the help of Malay pearl divers while being threatened by Turkish guns.

10. Not only was *The Happy Return* (1937) the first Hornblower novel, but it was also the first installment in what would become the initial Hornblower trilogy. The reader joins him as post-captain of the frigate *Lydia*. He was sent to the Pacific coast of Nicaragua to aid a local Spanish renegade, Don Julian Alvarado, in inciting a rebellion in order to destabilize the Spanish crown which at that point was still allied with Napoleon. Upon arrival he learns that the renegade, who calls himself El Supremo, is monomaniacally obsessed with his own godhood. El Supremo served as a thinly disguised stand-in for Adolf Hitler and General Franco. Following his exploits in the Pacific, the captain is given command of a larger vessel in *Ship of the Line* (1938). He is, however, placed in a squadron under the command of Admiral Leighton who is Hornblower's social and military superior; even so, he is neither a particularly adept seaman, nor a great leader of men. The admiral has the squadron go on ill-conceived missions all of which end in narrowly avoided disaster. The last of these missions finds Hornblower out of reach of his squadron, facing four French ships. While bravely holding his ground, damaging three of the four enemies beyond repair, Hornblower's vessel is incapacitated and with most of his crew dead, he is forced to surrender. *Flying Colors* (1938) picks up the story line from there. Hornblower and the remaining survivors are imprisoned in Rosas. Together they affect an escape behind enemy lines and ultimately return to Britain. Hornblower returns to a hero's welcome and receives knighthood. While seemingly enjoying all that he has achieved, Hornblower is itching to set sail again at the beginning *The Commodore* (1945). Promoted to commodore, Hornblower is given his own small squadron to go on a mission to the Baltics. His mission entails fending off French privateers and navigating the pitfalls of complex diplomatic maneuvers between all political players who have a stake in the Baltics which is further hampered by a Babylonian cacophony of languages. Forester made the conscious decision to set the story in the Baltics in order not to offend his vast American readership by having his protagonist fight the nascent U.S. Navy during the War of 1812. *Lord Hornblower* (1946) served as a transition piece set against the backdrop of the imminent conclusion of World War II. Another step in the evolution of Hornblower's career, Forester wrote much of the novel while working on U.S. Navy and Royal Navy vessels in the Pacific where he found himself "preoccupied with the fall of empires" (1998: 112–3). Hornblower is given command of a small ship and full discretionary powers to deal with a potentially embarrassing mutiny on a British ship just off the coast of Normandy. Not only does Horatio contrive a way to pardon all mutineers except the ringleader, whom he shoots in cold blood, but he also succeeds in overpowering a French vessel. It allows him to open a backdoor into the French heartland via the city of Le Havre which is ready to break with Napoleon's cause. Written while in harbor in Tokyo Bay on V-J Day, Forester considered the last page of the novel "the best ten minutes' work I had ever done ... a complexity of action and emotion ... in the most economical and fitting wording" (115).

11. Hornblower's later career as a more seasoned vice-admiral in command of the West Indies squadron is chronicled in an anthology of stories which constitutes *Hornblower in the West Indies* (1958). While set during peace time, he is kept busy with patrolling the Caribbean, enforcing the hegemonic rule of *Pax Britannica*, and engaging with the intricate *Realpolitik* of the West Indies. Hornblower also apprehends slavers who are in violation of the Slave Trade Act of 1807. Even so, Forester is particularly careful to show Hornblower as respectful towards American interests. He even goes so far as to stress the shared Anglo-American stake in ensuring the spread of Anglocentric modernity throughout the western hemisphere. The Hornblower's saga is concluded in the short story *The Last Encounter* (1967) which was published posthumously. Horatio helps Prince Louis Napoleon to catch the Dover packet in time so that the latter can be proclaimed the first president of France.

12. Sanford Sternlicht has noted that the "growing popularity of the novels caused the British Admiralty and the United States Navy Department to compete with each other to get the popular sea writer aboard their ships" (35). In the darkest hours before and during the war, Forester brought forth this heroic figure, "one fictional Englishman, a man of intelligence, courage, compassion, integrity, and great resourcefulness" (160). And, he "rose to do battle, successfully, with a seemingly multi-headed monster, and *all English-speaking people took heart*" (*ibid.*, original emphasis).

13. Upon returning early from the war in 1943, he began to fly for PanAm and he also enrolled in writer's classes at various colleges, working towards a career as a writer. "Sailor's Prayer" was published in the literary supplement of *The New York Times* on 17 June 1945, appearing next

to an "uncredited piece, 'Transoceanic Rockets,' describing the future of the rocket for interplanetary travel" (Alexander 80). The poem encapsulates Roddenberry's distinct affinity for the Golden Age of Sail. Apart from the romantic overtones, which bespeak a yearning for the mythologized glory and the fictional unpretentiousness of that age, Roddenberry also exhibits an adept use of nautical jargon, and a boyish longing for a supposedly simpler time.

14. In one of the last interviews he gave, Roddenberry reiterated: "I have always said Captain Horatio Hornblower was a great hero of mine–and in some ways, he still is. Yes, he is" (qtd. Fern 89). *Star Trek* veteran producer, director, and scriptwriter, Nicholas Meyer, recalled that "indeed, Gene Roddenberry had certainly been a Hornblower fan" (102).

15. Sue Parrill has observed that while "nineteenth-century novelists either justified or ignored he practice of flogging, the heroic captains in twentieth- and twenty-first-century novels rarely authorize floggings, following the dictum that flogging ruins a good man and makes a bad man worse. Modern readers could not admire a captain who flogged his men" (14).

16. For example, Hornblower thinks to himself in *A Ship of the Line*: "He had managed to evade having a chaplain on board—Hornblower hated parsons.... Religion was the only power which could ever pit itself against the bonds of discipline" (1938a: 445–6).

17. Sharon Monteith has defined 1960s counterculture as follows: "The 'counterculture' contained the tension between democratic ideals and undemocratic practices, a disillusion with a national or 'official' culture as signified by government, the military and 'the establishment'—in all its forms from stifling parents to party politics" (6).

18. Following the intermittent breaks in its isolationist stance in the first two decades of the 20th century, the U.S. moved rapidly from interventionism to the preservation of a hegemonic balance of power in the wake of World War II. The U.S. quickly learned how to become a benign meddler on the global stage as evidenced by their support of the Jewish State, the Berlin Airlift, and the Marshall Plan. The "special relationship" between Britain and the U.S. was occasionally tense in the process towards "world governance" under the auspices of the United Nations and NATO, and the subsequent efforts to decolonize the "old sovereignties" (Foertsch 22). Even so, their bond has remained the transatlantic backbone of the western hemisphere ever since.

19. In the words of the preeminent Korean War poet William Childress, it was a conflict in which soldiers "dumbly follow / leaders whose careers / hung on victory" (qtd. Halliwell 6).

20. In addition to *Captain Horatio Hornblower R.N.*, *Midshipman Easy* (Carol Reed UK 1934), adapted from Marryat's 1836 novel, *Clive of India* (Richard Boleslawski U.S. 1935), *The Lives of a Bengal Lancer* (Henry Hathaway U.S. 1935), *Mutiny on the Bounty* (Frank Lloyd U.S. 1935), *That Hamilton Woman* (Alexander Korda U.S. 1941) and *The Charge of the Light Brigade* (Michael Curtiz U.S. 1936) exemplify the "Anglophilia" (Glancy 67) that permeated Hollywood at the time.

Chapter 4

1. *ST:VOY*, "Thirty Days" (9 Dec 1998).

2. See, for example, *Mr Midshipman Hornblower* (24) and *Lieutenant Hornblower* (229).

3. "Make it so" was also the ritualized response by the captain to the officer of the watch reporting noon to him; it was up to the captain to make noon. "By tradition, the day officially began at noon, when the date and day of the week were changed on the log-board ... and eight strokes were struck on the ship's bell, followed by the Boatswain's 'pipe to dinner'" (King 17). The phrase thus exemplifies the vast powers held by the captain.

4. See *Hornblower in the West Indies* (589).

5. As Jonathan Raban has observed, even "the most landlubberly speaker of colloquial English is prone to talk unconsciously in terms that come out of the sea" (7).

6. *ST:TNG*, "The Last Outpost" (19 Oct 1987).

7. *ST:DS9*, "Soldiers of the Empire" (29 Apr 1997).

8. *Star Trek III: The Search for Spock* (Leonard Nimoy U.S. 1984).

9. Starfleet's use of naval jargon has to be understood as a particular permutation of a continuous process of linguistic borrowings which becomes evident when set against the backdrop of discursive characteristics in space-based stories at large. Such stories readily appropriate jargons which usually correspond with the predominant paradigms of transportation and military engagement found in the historio-cultural context they emerge from. In many sf universes this translates into either a nautical or a more *aero*nautical form of usage. A clear-cut distinction between both sets of jargon often proves difficult for obvious reasons.

"Nautical terminology haunts space travel fiction generally," as Bedford reminds us, in that pointing back to "the previous great age of exploration seems natural, with a silky inevitability" (qtd. Westfahl, 2009: 11–2). Equally important is the fact that the "basic vocabulary of the sea voyage has been transplanted wholesale to flight" (Foulke xiii), and thus has been modified and expanded to apply to aeronautical spaces.

10. Roddenberry made it a point to highlight the fact that the contemporary U.S. Navy—and by extension then also Starfleet—shares nautical discourses with the Royal Navy of wind and sail. Starfleet was to maintain "a flavor of Naval usage and terminology.... After all, our own Navy today still retains remnants of tradition known to Nelson and Drake" ("The Star Trek Guide" 27).

11. *ST:TOS*, "The Man Trap" (8 Sep 1966).

12. For examples see, *ST:TOS*, "Court Martial" (2 Feb 1967), and *Star Trek II: The Wrath of Khan* (Nicholas Meyer, U.S. 1982).

13. For examples see, *ST:TOS*, "The Ultimate Computer" (8 Mar 1968), *ST:TOS*, "The Alternative Factor" (30 Mar 1967), and *ST:ENT*, "First Flight" (14 May 2003).

14. Correspondingly, there are two types of surgeons in Napoleonic sea fiction; one is rather inept and perpetually drunk, while the other "is well-educated, perhaps even a physician, competent in the practice of medicine, and perhaps a natural scientist" (Parrill 100). Stephen Maturin in Patrick O'Brian's Aubrey/Maturin series is a paradigmatic example for the latter.

15. This is the author's conclusion following a number of debates at international conferences such as the 2012 *Film & History* Conference in Milwaukee, the 2012 *Transatlantic Studies Association*'s Annual Conference in Cork, and the 2016 Annual Conference of the *Science Fiction Research Association* in Liverpool.

16. Traditionally, Royal Marines "were to go ashore during landings, to do sentry duty at the captain's cabin.... During a ship-action, they would fire muskets and swivel guns from the tops or from the bulwarks, help with the big guns ... and participate in boardings" (Parrill 15).

17. In *A Ship of the Line*, "Hornblower turned aside to begin his inspection. He walked up and down the quadruple ranks of the marines, but although he ran his eye mechanically over the men he took notice of nothing.... Marines could be drilled and disciplined into machines in a way sailors could not be; he could take the marines for granted and he was not interested in them. Even now, after ten days, he hardly knew the faces and names of six out of the ninety marines on board" (444).

18. *ST:TOS*, "Elaan of Troyius" (20 Dec 1968).

19. Hornblower's engagement with the *Natividad* in *The Happy Return* provides a good example: "On the starboard tack, sir, same course as us. Her masts are in one line. Now she's altering course, sir. She's wearing round. She must have seen us, sir. Now she's on the port tack, sir, heading up to wind'ard of us, close hauled, sir." ... "Man the braces, there!" he shouted, and then to the man at the wheel: "Port your helm. And mark ye, fellow, keep her as near the wind as she'll lie. Mr Bush, beat to quarters, if you please, and clear for action." ... "Stand by, Mr Rayner. Fire as your guns bear," he called. ... "Put your helm a-weather. Catch her! Hold her so!" ... "Stand by to go about," rasped Hornblower (305–7).

20. *ST:DS9*, "Rules of Engagement" (8 Apr 1996).

21. In the guidelines for writers of *ST:TOS*, Roddenberry made the case for "omitting features which are heavily authoritarian" (27). The language of Starfleet was to sound "semi-military and seminavigational [sic]" (qtd. Whitfield 173).

22. For example, at one point in *Hornblower in the West Indies*, our hero reminds himself and the readers that "so far he had never forgotten to make use of polite forms of request when giving orders" (240).

23. *ST:ENT*, "First Flight" (14 May 2003).

24. The term "con" goes back to "sailing directions [given] to the steersman" as much as to the action of directing "the steering from some commanding position on shipboard" (King 155).

25. *ST:TAS*, "Albatross" (28 Sept 1974), *ST:DS9*, "The Passenger" (21 Feb 1993).

26. *ST:TNG*, "Lower Decks" (7 Feb 1994), *ST:VOY*, "Good Shepherd" (15 Mar 2000).

27. *ST:ENT*, "Affliction" (18 Feb 2005).

28. The historical vessels *Santa Maria, Bounty, Victory, Constitution, Bismarck, Titanic* and *Missouri* come to mind. In fiction, the *Enterprise* is on par with the *Argo, Pequod*, the *Flying Dutchman, Nautilus*, the *Millennium Falcon, Nostromo*, and the *Normandy*.

29. From a purely symbolic point of view, the prefix maintains familiarity and recognition on part of the main target audience, while it also discursively encodes difference to that what people associate with it. It helps to hark

back to the conception of *Star Trek* to contextualize the unmasking of the deceiving symbolic qualities inherent in the prefix USS. The earliest pitch for the show listed the simple prefix "S.S." which stood for "starship" ("STAR TREK Is..." 3). This changed once the producers had decided on the name of the ship. The guidelines for writers of *ST:TOS* included a self-test which highlighted popular mistakes that scriptwriters usually made with regards to the format and terminology. The relevant segment reads, "the U.S.S. (United States Spaceship)," which is immediately rectified by the statement that the "Enterprise is more correctly an international vessel, the United Spaceship Enterprise" (1). Early during the production, Roddenberry had to defend many of his decisions which included the designation for the ship. People asked "[w]hy couldn't it be a good, safe patriotic *United States* spaceship? [since] this 'one world' concept would be unpopular" (qtd. Whitfield 97, original emphasis). Roddenberry held his ground since he believed that only a unified humanity under a United Earth government could successfully venture into space.

30. Roddenberry and his co-producers, Bob Justman and D.C. Fontana, decided that the name was unsuitable. In a series of memos, they discussed a number of variations opting to "include the names of some famous fighting ships of the past, plus a couple of international variations we might consider, Star Fleet [sic] being composed of a united service" (qtd. Whitfield 144). Names that circulated right from the beginning were *Enterprise, Lexington, Endeavour, El Dorado, Hood, Hornet, Constellation, Ari, Krieger*, etc. The final list of names for Starfleet vessels that was established read: "*Enterprise, Exeter, Excalibur, Lexington, Yorktown, Potemkin, Republic, Hood, Constitution, Kongo, Constellation, Farragut, Valiant*, and *Intrepid*" (145).

31. After all, the *Enterprise* (CV-6) was the only aircraft carrier which had not been sunk by the Japanese. After it had been decommissioned, the name was transferred to the first nuclear-powered carrier, the *Enterprise* (CV-65).

32. *ST:ENT*, "United" (4 Feb 2005).

33. Senior producer Ron Moore has stated that this was an homage to C.S. Forester's Hornblower stories and the influence they had on Roddenberry.

34. For example, the sailing brig USS *Enterprise* served with distinction during the conflict with the Barbary States whose raiders harassed American shipping, provoking a full-scale naval retaliation.

35. Lincoln Geraghty has opined that the selection and particular arrangement of these historical moments "locate *Enterprise*, and therefore *Star Trek*, within a very specific American narrative: the history of spaceflight and exploration.... Celebrating American achievements on the sea, in the air, and in space eliminated all vestiges of humanity's international achievements and replaced them with images of America's attempts at exploring space" (2008: 17–8).

36. Variously spelled with an "s" or a "z," it is likely that the ship was based on a sixth-rate frigate launched in 1774. It served in the American Revolutionary War as well as the Napoleonic Wars.

37. Further substantiated by *The Sail & Steam Navy List* (2004), David Davies has defined "a class being [sic] ships built to a particular design. Classes might vary slightly in dimensions and details of design" (24).

38. In 2012, the space shuttle was transferred from the Smithsonian in Washington, D.C., to the Intrepid Sea, Air and Space Museum in New York. Leonard Nimoy was invited as a guest speaker at the welcoming ceremony. As he reminisced about the fan-letter campaign, he repeatedly refers to the space shuttle as "this wonderful ship," rather than as an orbiter, which is the term most commonly used for the shuttle in the aeronautical community (youtube.com, "Nimoy salutes Enterprise"). This goes to show that the nautical discourses which shaped *Star Trek*'s future were used to overwrite aeronautical realities.

Chapter 5

1. According to Roddenberry, the ship's base color was to be "a metallic battleship gray" ("WRITER/DIRECTOR'S GUIDE STAR TREK: The Next Generation" 18). Following modern naval conventions, the ships also display their registration, i.e., pennant numbers, and their name on their hulls. However, the pennant of the aircraft carrier *Enterprise* (CVN-65) is not easily recalled when decoding the starship's registration of NCC-1701. While the meaning of the prefix was never verified on screen, it is safe to assume that it too carries a residue of naval meaning since production notes variously defined it as Naval Construction Contract, Naval Construction Code Number, and Naval Contact Code. Unlike modern navy vessels, however, Starfleet ships actually display their names along with their registries.

2. Cf. Rayner, 2007: 152–6.

3. Anthony Price has defined frigates as "the Navy's true all-purpose cruisers sweeping the seas clean of enemy merchant shipping and raiding cruisers (frigates themselves), while making short work of weaker enemy privateers ... with that protective role went actual convoy escort, together with blockading duties and the combined operations which came to go with that work" (26–7).

4. According to Roddenberry, their missions included but were not limited to "regulating trade, fighting bush wars, putting down slave traders, lending aid to scientific expeditions, conducting exploration on a broad scale, engaging in diplomatic exchanges and affairs, and even becoming involved in such minor matters as searching for lost explorers" (qtd. Whitfield 179).

5. "Since space knows no north or south, and no 'up' or 'down,' directions are given in two planes rather than one.... The 'space horizon' is a plane bisecting the galaxy at its widest point, and 'zero' horizon is the line from Earth to the center of the galaxy. The vertical plane, 'up' and 'down,' is at right angles to the galaxy 'horizon.' ... It is therefore very much like having two compass circles through the galaxy, one through the thick 'horizontal' plane and the other circle through the thin 'vertical plane'" (Whitfield 173).

6. We can take the description of any peaceful meeting of ships found in the Hornblower novels as a baseline example for comparison. The following passage is taken from *The Happy Return*: "The *Lydia*, close hauled, was heading for Panama one day's sail ahead when the guardacosta lugger which had encountered them before hove up over the horizon to windward. At sight of the *Lydia* she altered course and came running own wind towards her, while Hornblower kept steadily on his course.... The lugger hove-to a couple of cables' lengths away, and a few minutes later the same smart officer in the brilliant uniform came clambering on to the *Lydia*'s deck" (353).

7. Any of Forester's elaborate descriptions of Hornblower's many ship-to-ship engagements may serve as a paradigmatic model for comparison. For example, in *A Ship of the Line*, the captain faces a French enemy vessel: "Bow to bow the *Sutherland* was approaching the eighty-gun ship, unwavering; if both captains held their courses steadily there would be a collision which might sink both ships ... the *Sutherland* was lying as near to the wind as she could, with her sails on the point of flapping.... At half a mile smoke suddenly eddied round the Frenchman's bows, and a shot came humming overhead. She was firing her bow chasers.... The bowsprits were only a hundred yards apart now, and Hornblower set his teeth so as not to give the instinctive order to up helm.... The two ships were overlapping now, not thirty yards apart, and the Frenchman's guns were beginning to bear.... The *Sutherland* began to wear round slowly, beginning her turn to cross the Frenchman's stern before the two ships were alongside.... The *Sutherland* shook and jarred with the impact of the shot; ... Then with a series of heavy crashes, one following another as the *Sutherland* crossed her enemy's stern and each section of guns bore in turn, she fired her broadside into her, heeling slightly at each discharge, with every shot tearing its destructive course from end to end of the ship.... The Frenchman came on undeviating, not disdaining a broadside to broadside duel, but not attempting to manoeuvre, especially against an enemy who had proved himself alert, at a time when manoeuvring meant delay in gaining the shelter of Rosas. The ships inclined together, growing nearer and nearer.... A word from Hornblower swung the *Sutherland* round till she lay parallel to her opponent, and as she steadied on her new course" (563–5).

8. During the Age of Sail, "most battles took place at relatively close range. They often didn't begin until the ships were as close as 1,000 yards" (King 8).

9. *ST:DS9*, "Sacrifice of Angels" (3 Nov 1997).

10. *Star Trek Nemesis* (Stuart Baird, U.S. 2002), *Star Trek: First Contact* (Jonathan Frakes, U.S. 1996), *ST:TNG*, "The Best of Both Worlds, Part II" (24 Sep 1990).

11. Cf. Gregory, 2000: 69–78; Wagner, 1998: 187–9; Westfahl, 2009: 190.

12. Sanford Sternlicht has summarized Hornblower's situation in the Indies as follows: "There is much to do.... Hornblower learns of a French plot to rescue Napoleon from St. Helena and return him to the throne of France, with the probable outcome that the world would be torn by war once more.... Hornblower captures a speedy Spanish slaver by cleverly having a drogue attached to the faster's ship's rudder. Then Hornblower is kidnapped by pirates in Jamaica, and after his release he destroys their lair ... Hornblower then is witness to the victory of General Simón Bolívar at the turning point of the war for Venezuelan liberation.... His sympathies are with the rebels, who are aided by British mercenaries" (101).

13. "It never failed to raise a wry smile on his face when he looked about him at 'His Majesty's ships and vessels in the West Indies' under his command. In wartime he would have had a powerful fleet; now he had three small frigates and a motley collection of brigs and schooners. But they would serve his purpose; in his scheme the frigates became three-deckers and the brigs seventy-fours and the schooners frigates" (1958: 677).

14. "Starfleet has stationed three mid-sized Runabout Class patrol ships at DS9 which allow our characters to travel to the numerous star systems in the sector.... These ships are twenty meters long.... They can transport up to forty people but that's a crowd.... These ships are the symbol of the Federation presence in this sector" ("Star Trek DS9 Bible" 6).

15. Cf. Forester, 1937: 362; 1938b: 96; 1958: 629, 658, 682.

16. Jonathan Raban has outlined that while "the sea itself was beginning to be invaded by industrial machinery," the romance of sailing ships, as it is still readily entertained in popular culture memory, ossified into the common belief that "the sea still belongs to sail" since "[t]he ship moves in nature, propelled by the natural force of wind" (17).

17. Already during the 1960 presidential campaign he stated that "[i]f the Soviets control space they can control earth, as in the past centuries the nation that controlled the seas dominated the continents" (qtd. McCurdy 75). He conceived of space not only as being analogous to the sea, but he also implicitly referred to Britain's seaborne empire. Even in the president's famous moon speech, he proclaimed that "[w]e set sail on this new sea because there is new knowledge to be gained ... we help decide whether this new ocean will be a sea of peace or a new terrifying theater of war" (1962).

18. *ST:TOS*, "The Ultimate Computer" (8 Mar 1968).

19. *Star Trek Nemesis* (Stuart Baird, U.S. 2002).

20. *ST:ENT*, "Broken Bow" (26 Sep 2001).

21. *ST:VOY*, "Threshold" (29 Jan 1996).

22. As noted earlier with regards to the effects of near misses in combat, Roddenberry stated that whenever ships encounter rough weather in space "we found that we had to make the ship rock in such situations. We had to have our people knocked out of their chairs.... Otherwise an earthbound audience simply cannot relate emotionally to the jeopardy going on" (qtd. Whitfield 102).

23. The following excerpt from *A Ship of the Line* serves as a representative example for a basic comparison: "The black sky was suddenly split by dazzling lightning, followed almost instantaneously by a tremendous crash of thunder, and the squall came racing down upon them; they could see its hard, metallic line on the surface of the grey sea. Almost taken aback, the *Sutherland* shuddered and plunged.... *Sutherland* lurched and plunged, her storm canvas slatting like a discharge of guns, before she paid off again. The hail had given place to torrential rain now, driven along almost horizontally by the howling wind, and the sudden change in the wind called up a short, lumpy sea over which the *Sutherland* bucked and plunged in ungainly fashion" (515–7).

24. *ST:TOS*, "Where No Man Has Gone Before" (22 Sept 1966), *ST:TOS*, "Mirror Mirror" (6 Oct 1967), *ST:TOS*, "Court Martial" (2 Feb 1967).

25. *ST:TNG*, "Time Squared" (4 Apr 1989).

26. *ST:DS9*, "Invasive Procedures" (17 Oct 1993).

27. *ST:VOY*, "Night" (14 Oct 1998).

28. Once again we can turn to the Hornblower texts, in this case *Mr Midshipman Hornblower*, to extract a relevant example for comparison: "In the faint growing light he had seen shreds of denser mist blowing past them—a clear indication that they could not hope for continuous fog. At that moment they ran out of a fog bank into a clear patch of water.... Less than a cable's length away a three-decked ship of the line was standing along parallel to them on their starboard side. Ahead and on the port side could be seen the outlines, still shadowy, of other battleships.... Another shred of fog drifted past them, and then they were deep in a fresh fog bank.... The horizon ahead expanded rapidly, from a few yards to a hundred, from a hundred yards to half a mile. The sea was covered with ships.... "Wear ship again, Mr Hunter," said Hornblower. "Back into the fog." That was the one chance of safety" (163–5).

29. *ST:TNG*, "Best of Both Worlds" (17 Jun 1990), *ST:DS9*, "Defiant" (21 Nov 1994), *ST:DS9*, "Rocks and Shoals" (6 Oct 1997), *ST:VOY*, "Year of Hell" (5 Nov 1997).

30. *ST:TNG*, "Chain of Command, Part II" (21 Dec 1992), *ST:TNG*, "Preemptive Strike" (16 May 1994), *ST:DS9*, "In Purgatory's Shadow" (10 Feb 1997), *ST:ENT*, "Kir'Shara" (3 Dec 2004).

31. *ST:TNG*, "Galaxy's Child" (11 Mar 1991), *ST:TNG*, "Tin Man" (23 Apr 1990), *ST:TOS*, "The Doomsday Machine" (20 Oct 1967), *ST:VOY*, "Bliss" (10 Feb 1999).

32. *ST:DSC*, "Magic to Make the Sanest Man Go Mad" (29 Oct 2017).

33. *ST:DS9*, "Q-Less' (7 Feb 1993), *ST:DS9*, "Chimera" (17 Feb 1999), *ST:VOY*, "Elogium" (18 Sep 1995), *ST:TNG*, "Encounter at Farpoint" (28 Sep 1987), *ST:TOS*, "The Immunity Syndrome" (19 Jan 1968).

34. Journal entries of explorers and descriptions of the sighting of land in Napoleonic sea fiction serve as meaningful reference points. Upon approaching the Society Islands on his first voyage, James Cook made the following entry on the day they sighted land for the first time: "Tuesday, 4th. A Steady fresh Trade and clear weather. At ½ past 10 a.m. saw land bearing south, distance 3 or 4 Leagues. Haul'd up for it, and soon found it to be an Island of about 2 Leagues in Circuit and of an Oval form, with a Lagoon in the Middle, for which I named it Lagoon Island. The Border of land Circumscribing this Lagoon is in many places very low and narrow, particularly on the south side, where it is mostly a Beach or Reef of rocks; it is the same on the North side in 3 places, and these disjoins the firm land and make it appear like so many Islands covered with wood.... This Island lies in the Latitude of 18 degrees 47 minutes and Longitude 139 degrees 28 minutes West from the Meridian of Greenwich" (qtd. Edwards 36–7).

Similarly, when Captain Hornblower finally sights the Pacific coast of Spanish America after having sailed for weeks without making landfall, the reader is given the following description: ""Land ho!" he heard. "Deck there! Land two points on the larboard bow, sir." That was the lookout in the foretop hailing the deck.... Everyone would be wildly excited at the sight of land, the first for three months, on this voyage to an unknown destination. He was excited himself. There was not merely the imminent thrill of discovering whether he had made a good landfall; there was also the thought that perhaps within twenty-four hours he would be in the thick of the dangerous and difficult mission upon which my lords of the Admiralty had dispatched him.... "Looks like a burning mountain, sir. Two burning mountains. Volcanoes, sir." ... There were volcanoes all along this coast; the presence of two of the larboard bow was no sure indication of the ship's position. And yet—and yet—the entrance of the Gulf of Fonseca would undoubtedly be marked by two volcanoes to larboard" (1937: 230–1).

35. *ST:TNG*, "Clues" (11 Feb 1991).

36. Once again we can draw on Cook and Hornblower for conceptual models that showcase the significance and the function of the bay as a quintessential maritime space. Trying to find an anchorage, Cook wrote: "Sunday, 15th. P.M. stood over for the Southermost Land or South point of the Bay, having a light breeze at North-East, our soundings from 12 to 8 fathoms.... On each side of the Cape are Tolerable high white steep Cliffs ... Tuesday, 17th. P.M. for the most part looks like our high Downs in England, and to all appearance well inhabited, for we saw several Villages as we run along shore, not only in the Vallies, but on the Tops and sides of the Hills, and Smokes in other places" (qtd. Edwards 76–7).

Upon making landfall in *The Happy Return*, Hornblower meticulously surveys the coastline: "It was a strange landscape which the telescope revealed to him.... Besides these cones there was a long mountain range of which the peaks appeared to be spurs, but the range itself seemed to be made up of a chain of old volcanoes, truncated and weathered down by the passage of centuries; ... lower he could see what looked like green cataracts which must be vegetation stretching up along gullies in the mountain sides.... On each side of the breakers was a stretch of clear water on the horizon, and beyond that again, on each side, was a medium-sized volcano. A wide bay, an island in the middle of the entrance, and two flanking volcanoes.... "Get the courses in," said Hornblower. "Keep that lead going in the chains, there." ... The channel was shoaling fast. They would have to anchor soon in this case" (232–9).

37. *ST:TNG*, "The Chase" (26 Apr 1993).

38. *Star Trek Generations* (David Carson, U.S. 1994).

39. *ST:VOY*, "Timeless" (18 Nov 1998).

40. Cook-scholar, Glyn Williams, has offered: "What may be unique to the Pacific is the status of 'the beach.' In one sense this was a well-defined physical entity, a boundary separating land and water; in another it was a more ambivalent area, a zone of confrontation and conflict, but also a space where intercourse, commercial and sexual, took place" (2004: 242).

41. According to Roddenberry, planetary landings are one of *Star Trek*'s "keys" and they are "made for a wide variety of reasons—scheduled ports of call, resupplying the cruiser, aid to Earth colonies, scrutiny of an Earth commercial activity, collection of rare animal or plant specimens, a courtesy call on alien life contacted by earlier explorers, a survey of mineral deposits, or any combination of scientific, political, security, or supply needs" (qtd. Whitfield 24).

42. *Captain Horatio Hornblower R.N.* (Raoul Walsh, U.S. 1951).

Chapter 6

1. *ST:TOS*, "Spectre of the Gun" (25 Oct 1968).
2. *ST:TNG*, "Time's Arrow" (15 June 1992), *ST:TNG*, "Time's Arrow, Part II" (21 Sep 1992), *ST:TNG*, "A Fistful of Datas" (9 Nov 1992), *ST:ENT*, "North Star" (12 Nov 2003).
3. Cf. George, 2013: 7–21; Selley, 1986: 89–104.
4. *Master and Commander: The Far Side of the World* (Peter Weir, U.S. 2003).
5. Trans. He who has earned the palm, let him bear it.
6. Cf. Vincent, 2005: 94–9; White, 2005: 53–7.
7. In film and television, Nelson is portrayed, for example, in *That Hamilton Woman* (Alexander Korda, U.S. 1941), *The Nelson Affair* (James Cellan Jones, U.S. 1973), and the four-part series *I Remember Nelson* (UK 1982). Cook's voyages were turned into the miniseries *Captain James Cook* (AUS 1987), and his exploits were the subject of numerous documentary films.
8. Among the many decisions Nelson had to make, there are three which are often referred to vis-à-vis his archetypal propensity to question and to go beyond his orders. While stationed in the West Indies, he decided to disobey the instructions of Admiral Hughes. He went against his original mission to enforce the Navigation Acts, preventing illegal trade with the U.S. Arguing for a higher cause, he presented his reasons to his superior and placed the situation into a larger context. When his ideas were rejected, Nelson asserted his own judgment and chose what he thought to be the best course of action. A few years later, he freely interpreted "vague" battle orders during an engagement off the Cape of St. Vincent. Nelson took the initiative and made a name for himself. He left his squadron's line-of-battle formation, headed straight at two enemy ships, which were more powerful than his, engaged them, and successfully captured both (much to the dismay of his commanding officer, Sir John Jervis). Lastly, Vice-Admiral Nelson famously turned a blind eye to the signal of his superior who ordered him to discontinue action at the Battle of Copenhagen (1801). Once again, he saw an opportunity to achieve his mission. He successfully pressured the Danes and then singlehandedly opened negotiations with them.
9. *ST:TNG*, "Redemption II" (23 Sep 1991).
10. While refitting in Batavia during his first voyage, Cook noted: "I had consulted with the Carpenter and all the officers concerning the leake [sic], and they were all unanimously of the opinion that it was not safe to proceed to Europe without first seeing her bottom" (qtd. O'Sullivan 23).
11. Forester, 1998: 90.
12. *Lieutenant Hornblower* (1952).
13. Forester delineated this archetypal character trait of his hero as follows: "The man who has to make unaided decisions. The man alone; he may have technical help, he may even have friends, but as regards the crisis he is facing he can only act on his own judgment, and in case of failure he has only himself to blame. This Man Alone—the captain of a ship" (1998: 82).
14. The starship captain is a commanding officer who with "the Starship out of communication with Earth and Starfleet bases for long periods of time, [has] unusually broad powers over both the lives and welfare of his crew, as well as over Earth people and activities encountered during these voyages. He also has broad power as an Earth Ambassador to alien societies in his galaxy sector or on new worlds he may discover" (10).
15. In fact, the "Hornblower in space" label applies to seven captains which is in part due to *Star Trek*'s peculiar beginnings. In the first pitch for *ST:TOS*, Roddenberry gave the captain the name Robert M. April. He did not receive any screen time except for a brief guest appearance (voiced by James Doohan) in an episode of *ST:TAS*. In his short appearance, Captain April articulates at least two attributes of the archetypal starship captain—taking the initiative of command and the bond that a captain has with his ship (*ST:TAS*, "The Counter-Clock Incident" [12 Oct 1974]). The first actor to assume the role of "Hornblower in space" was Jeffrey Hunter, who portrayed Captain Christopher Pike in the original pilot for *ST:TOS*—"The Cage." Even though it is but one episode, it provides sufficient substance to recognize Hornblower-esque contours, such as Pike's troubled psyche.
16. *ST:TOS*, "The Conscience of the King" (8 Dec 1966), *ST:TOS*, "Obsession" (15 Dec 1967), *ST:TOS*, "Shore Leave" (29 Dec 1966), *ST:TOS*, "Court Martial" (2 Feb 1967), *ST:TOS*, "Where No Man Has Gone Before" (22 Sep 1966), *Star Trek: The Motion Picture* (Robert

Wise, U.S. 1979), *Star Trek II: The Wrath of Khan* (Nicholas Meyer, U.S. 1982), *Star Trek III: The Search for Spock* (Leonard Nimoy, U.S. 1984).

17. *ST:TNG*, "Tapestry" (15 Feb 1993), *ST:TNG*, "The Battle" (16 Nov 1987), *ST:TNG*, "Measure of a Man" (13 Feb 1989), *ST:TNG*, "First Duty" (30 Mar 1992), *ST:TNG*, "Best of Both Worlds" (18 Jun 1990), *ST:TNG*, "Family" (1 Oct 1990).

18. *ST:DS9*, "Emissary" (3 Jan 1993), *ST:DS9*, "Image in the Sand" (30 Sep 1998), *ST:DS9*, "Penumbra" (7 Apr 1999), *ST:DS9*, "Dax" (14 Feb 1993), *ST:DS9*, "Invasive Procedures" (17 Oct 1993), *ST:DS9*, "Facets" (12 Jun 1995).

19. *ST:VOY*, "Prime Factors" (20 Mar 1995), *ST:VOY*, "Flashback" (11 Sep 1996), *ST:VOY*, "Revulsion" (1 Oct 1997), *ST:VOY*, "Relativity" (12 May 1999), *ST:VOY*, "The Raven" (8 Oct 1997), *ST:VOY*, "Natural Law" (2 May 2001).

20. *ST:ENT*, "Desert Crossing" (8 May 2002), *ST:ENT*, "First Flight" (14 May 2003), *ST:ENT*, "Fallen Hero" (8 May 2002), *ST:ENT*, "Cease Fire" (12 Feb 2003), *ST:ENT*, "Kir'Shara" (3 Dec 2004), *ST:ENT*, "Babel One" (28 Jan 2005).

21. Richard Woodman has argued that "more than professional security [that] came with this almost mystical elevation ... if free of the close control of an admiral or senior captain, the post-captain was on his own, at liberty to conduct his ship according to the spirit and letter of his orders by means of his own initiative and interpretation" (16–7).

22. *Star Trek Generations* (David Carson, U.S. 1994).

23. *Star Trek II: The Wrath of Khan* (Nicholas Meyer, U.S. 1982).

24. *Star Trek IV: The Voyage Home* (Leonard Nimoy, U.S. 1986).

25. *ST:DS9*, "Homefront" (1 Jan 1996), *ST:DS9*, "Paradise Lost" (8 Jan 1996), *ST:DS9*, "Behind the Lines" (20 Oct 1997).

26. *Star Trek: First Contact* (Jonathan Frakes, U.S. 1996).

27. Cf. Forester, 1945: 210–1; 1946: 429–30; 1958: 574–5.

28. *ST:VOY*, "Year of Hell, Part II" (12 Nov 1997).

29. Not only does the captain have "an almost compulsive compassion for the plight of others, alien as well as human," but he also "must continually fight the temptation to risk many to save one" ("STAR TREK Is..." 4).

30. For example, during the siege of Riga, Commodore Hornblower personally leads a counterattack on land (1945: 347–8). He also spearheads a boarding party charged with subduing British mutineers and recapturing their ship off the coast of Le Havre (1946: 411–20).

31. Captain Sisko assumes command of *Deep Space Nine* with his "gentle, strong and soft-spoken demeanor" ("Star Trek DS9 Bible" 7). "[I]ntelligent, thoughtful, perspicacious, sensitive to the feeling of others," Captain Janeway "is respected and loved by the members of her crew" ("STAR TREK: Voyager Bible" 5). Captain Archer also takes "comfort in his crew, which has proved to be one of the most loyal in the galaxy" (startrek.com, "Archer").

32. Cf. Forester, 1938b: 136; 1946: 458–9, 461, 466–7.

33. *ST:DS9*, "Starship Down" (6 Nov 1995), *ST:DS9*, "What You Leave Behind" (2 Jun 1999).

34. *ST:VOY*, "Resolutions" (13 May 1996).

35. *ST:ENT*, "The Seventh" (6 Nov 2002), *ST:ENT*, "Azati Prime" (3 Mar 2004), *ST:ENT*, "These Are the Voyages..." (13 May 2005).

36. Anthony Price has observed: "Meritorious officers were two-a-penny, insanely brave ones the norm.... More and more there would be a premium on judgement in complex situations, tact in handling foreigners (allied or neutral) and superiors, and even real diplomatic skills requiring an understanding of higher policy" (157–8).

37. For example, Hornblower acts with notable caution when he faces shifting geopolitical circumstances while on a secret mission to destabilize Britain's enemies in South America in *The Happy Return*. The same is true in *A Ship of the Line* where he decides to go on an independent cruise to interfere with Napoleon's supply lines rather than (as his orders "implied") to wait idly for his superior to arrive. In *The Commodore*, his diplomatic interference and cunning during the siege of Riga prompted Prussian troops to rethink and then abandon their alliance with Napoleon. Lastly, *Lord Hornblower* is a testament to the hero's farsightedness in that he takes the initiative to support a royalist rebellion in Le Havre even though his mission was to apprehend British mutineers.

38. After all, Kirk "also has broad power as an Earth Ambassador to alien societies in his galaxy sector or on new world he may discover" ("THE STAR TREK GUIDE 10").

39. *Star Trek Nemesis* (Stuart Baird, U.S. 2002).

40. *ST:ENT*, "Cease Fire" (12 Feb 2003), *ST:ENT*, "Babel One" (28 Jan 2005).

41. *ST:ENT*, "Terra Prime" (13 May 2005).

42. A product of Forester's literary finesse,

the omniscient narrator reminds the reader on more than one occasion that the "lucky man ... is usually the man who knows how much to leave to chance" (1938b: 153).

43. This aspect of the archetype found pronounced articulation in Captain Pike. In "The Cage" we see him struggling with, and almost succumbing to, the tremendous strain caused by his responsibilities. Pike is deeply troubled by the loss of three crewmen, including his yeoman, for which he blames himself, regretting the decisions he made. Confiding in his doctor, he even goes so far as to say that "I'm tired of deciding ... to the point of considering resigning." Still, it is his qualities as a *decider* that save the day.

44. Cf. Forester, 1937: 230; 1938a: 441; 1938b: 40; 1946: 376.

45. Roddenberry added that Kirk "is also capable of fatigue and inclined to push himself beyond human limits then condemn himself because he is not superhuman" (10).

46. *ST:TNG*, "The Best of Both Worlds, Part II" (24 Sep 1990), *ST:TNG*, "Family" (1 Oct 1990), *Star Trek: First Contact* (Jonathan Frakes, U.S. 1996).

47. *ST:DS9*, "Emissary" (3 Jan 1993).

48. *ST:DS9*, "Far Beyond the Stars" (11 Feb 1998).

49. *ST:DS9*, "Sacrifice of Angels" (3 Nov 1997).

50. According to the series bible, the captain's "thoughts [of doubt] held at bay during the day, tend to surface in the middle of the night when it's hard to sleep" (6).

51. *ST:VOY*, "Night" (14 Oct 1998).

52. *ST:VOY*, "Shattered" (17 Jan 2001).

53. *ST:ENT*, "The Andorian Incident" (31 Oct 2001), *ST:ENT*, "Shadows of P'Jem" (6 Feb 2002), *ST:ENT*, "Detained" (24 Apr 2002), *ST:ENT*, "A Night in Sickbay" (16 Oct 2002), *ST:ENT*, "Stigma" (5 Feb 2003).

54. *ST:ENT*, "Shockwave" (22 May 2002).

55. *ST:ENT*, "Anomaly" (17 Sep 2003), *ST:ENT*, "Damage" (21 Apr 2004).

56. *ST:ENT*, "Home" (22 Oct 2004).

57. The logs serve to "verbalize the arguments the captain must consider," as Judith Barad and Ed Robertson have argued, since "we cannot get into the captain's head to hear what he is thinking" (60).

58. *Star Trek VI: The Undiscovered Country* (Nicholas Meyer, U.S. 1991), *ST:DS9*, "Whispers" (6 Feb 1994), *ST:VOY*, "Bliss" (10 Feb 1999), *ST:ENT*, "Chosen Realm" (14 Jan 2004).

59. *ST:TOS*, "Court Martial" (2 Feb 1967), *ST:TOS*, "Obsession" (15 Dec 1967).

60. *ST:DS9*, "Playing God" (27 Feb 1994), *ST:VOY*, "The Cloud" (13 Feb 1995).

61. In his guidelines for writers and directors, Roddenberry outlined that Spock and Bones "can approach [him] on the most intimate personal levels relating to the Captain's physical, mental and emotional well-being" (12).

62. *Star Trek Nemesis* (Stuart Baird, U.S. 2002).

63. *ST:TNG*, "The Measure of A Man" (13 Feb 1989), *ST:TNG*, "The Best of Both Worlds" (18 Jun 1990), *ST:TNG*, "I Borg" (11 May 1992), *Star Trek Generations* (David Carson, U.S. 1994).

64. He could never really love his first wife, Maria, since he found everything about her too plain and too mundane. Made clear in many of his introverted fits, her very character disagreed with him. Her death in childbirth and the loss of his first two children to the pox added even more psychological baggage to a mind which was already emotionally conflicted and compromised.

65. It is already evident with Captain Pike who longs for a life that is more serene than his gallivanting about the stars. Even so, the quirkiness of his character makes him suspicious of anything which resembles his escapist dreams. He might have been briefly intrigued by the illusion of female beauty and the illusive promise of domestic harmony in the face of his psychological fatigue. The captain, however, rejects all of it, knowing what his doctor meant when he met the captain's claim that there are other kinds of life available for him with certain reservations.

66. *Star Trek II: The Wrath of Khan* (Nicholas Meyer, U.S. 1982), *Star Trek III: The Search for Spock* (Leonard Nimoy, U.S. 1984).

67. *Star Trek V: The Final Frontier* (William Shatner, U.S. 1989), *Star Trek Generations* (David Carson, U.S. 1994).

68. *ST:TNG*, "Captain's Holiday" (2 Apr 1990), *ST:TNG*, "The Perfect Mate" (27 Apr 1992), *ST:TNG*, "Lessons" (5 Apr 1993), *Star Trek: Insurrection* (Jonathan Frakes, U.S. 1998).

69. *ST:DS9*, "Second Sight" (21 Nov 1993), *ST:DS9*, "Through the Looking Glass" (17 Apr 1995), *ST:DS9*, "Shattered Mirror" (22 Apr 1996).

70. *ST:DS9*, "Family Business" (15 May 1995), *ST:DS9*, "For the Cause" (6 May 1996), *ST:DS9*, "Rapture" (30 Dec 1996).

71. *ST:DS9*, "Penumbra" (7 Apr 1999), *ST:DS9*, "'Til Death Do Us Part" (14 Apr 1999), *ST:DS9*, "What You Leave Behind" (2 Jun 1999).

72. *ST:VOY*, "Hunters" (11 Feb 1998).

73. *ST:VOY*, "Counterpoint" (16 Dec 1998), *ST:VOY*, "Fair Haven" (12 Jan 2000), *ST:VOY*, "Workforce" (21 Feb 2001), *ST:VOY*, "Workforce, Part II" (28 Feb 2001).

74. *ST:ENT*, "Civilization' (14 Nov 2001), *ST:ENT*, "Two Days and Two Nights" (15 May 2002), *ST:ENT*, "Rajiin" (1 Oct 2003), *ST:ENT*, "Storm Front" (8 Oct 2004), *ST:ENT*, "Storm Front, Part II" (15 Oct 2004).

75. *ST:ENT*, "Fight or Flight" (3 Oct 2001).

76. *ST:ENT*, "Home" (22 Oct 2004).

77. *ST:DSC* significantly departed from this format. Not only does the show start out with two captains—Captains Georgiou (Michelle Yeoh) and Lorca (Jason Isaacs)—but the main narrative focalizer is the first officer of the titular ship, Commander Burnham (Sonequa Martin-Green).

78. *ST:DSC* diverges from the focus on the captain in that the show's main focalizer, Michael Burnham (Sonequa Martin-Green), starts out as a first officer who is subsequently stripped of her rank.

Chapter 7

1. *ST:TNG*, "Where Silence Has Lease" (28 Nov 1988).

2. *ST:DS9*, "Rapture" (30 Dec 1996).

3. *ST:VOY*, "Thirty Days" (9 Dec 1998).

4. The page in question was taken from the first chapter of *The Commodore* (1945). Forester describes how Hornblower is officially welcomed to his estate by the mayor of the town.

5. *ST:DS9*, "The Visitor" (9 Oct 1995), *ST:DS9*, "The Muse" (29 Apr 1996).

6. Even though the authors of sea novels are often credited with being historically accurate—which is particularly true for the two preeminent authors of the genre in the 20th century, Forester and O'Brian—they still tone down the harsh realities of life at sea for both the officer elite and the common sailor. In their works, Dean King has noted, readers "escape into a world where etiquette and order seem to rule ... and where even war has its civilities" (xiii).

7. Re-enactment can best be understood as "retrospective travel," according to Vanessa Agnew, in that it is "a body-based discourse in which the past is reanimated through physical and psychological experience" (329–30).

8. *ST:TOS*, "The Man Trap" (8 Sep 1966).

9. *Perseus.tufts.edu*, "Horatius."

10. "Captain's Log, Stardate 1513.1. Our position, orbiting planet M-113. Onboard the Enterprise, Mr Spock, temporarily in command. On the planet, the ruins of an ancient and long dead civilization. Ship's surgeon McCoy and myself are now beaming down to the planet's surface. Our mission, routine medical examination of archaeologist Robert Crater, and his wife, Nancy. Routine, but for the fact that Nancy Crater is that one woman in Dr. McCoy's past."

11. That is, if virtual is understood as being such "in essence or effect, although not formally or actually" (Oed.com, "Virtual").

12. Even though the format of the stardate has changed considerably in terms of consistency over the years, it was invented as a narrative ploy to avoid having to deal with the difficulties of employing standard dates in the future. According to Roddenberry, the stardate is "computed against the speed of the vessel, the space warp, and its position within our galaxy" (qtd. Whitfield 175).

13. Cf. Forester, 1937: 373–5; 1938a: 452; 1958: 684–5.

14. *ST:TOS*, "Balance of Terror" (15 Dec 1966).

15. *ST:TNG*, "The Masterpiece Society" (10 Feb 1992).

16. O'Sullivan, 2008: 221–5.

17. "Captain's Log, U.S.S. Enterprise, Stardate 9529.1. This is the final cruise of the Starship Enterprise under my command. This ship and her history will shortly become the care of another crew. To them and their posterity will we commit our future. They will continue the voyages we have begun and journey to all the undiscovered countries, boldly going where no man, where no one, has gone before" (*Star Trek VI: The Undiscovered Country*).

18. *ST:TNG*, "The Defector" (1 Jan 1990).

19. *ST:TNG*, "Best of Both Worlds" (17 Jun 1990).

20. *Star Trek Nemesis* (Stuart Baird, U.S. 2002).

21. *ST:TOS*, "Balance of Terror" (15 Dec 1966), *ST:DS9*, "Destiny" (13 Feb 1995), *ST:VOY*, "Eye of the Needle" (20 Feb 1995).

22. The bosun was a warrant officer who "was in charge of all deck activities" on a sailing vessel (King 113).

23. *Star Trek Nemesis* (Stuart Baird, U.S. 2002).

24. *Tvtropes.org*, "Married at Sea."

25. *ST:TOS*, "Balance of Terror" (15 Dec 1966).

26. *ST:TNG*, "Data's Day" (7 Jan 1991).

27. *ST:DS9*, "Call to Arms" (16 Jun 1997), *ST:DS9*, "The Ship" (7 Oct 1996).
28. *ST:DS9*, "'Til Death Do Us Part" (14 Apr 1999).
29. *ST:VOY*, "Course: Oblivion" (3 Mar 1999), *ST:VOY*, "Drive" (18 Oct 2000).
30. *Star Trek Nemesis* (Stuart Baird, U.S. 2002).
31. *ST:TNG*, "The Schizoid Man" (23 Jan 1989).
32. *ST:DS9*, "The Sound of Her Voice" (10 Jun 1998), *ST:DS9*, "Tears of the Prophets" (17 Jun 1998).
33. *ST:VOY*, "Alliances" (22 Jan 1996), *ST:VOY*, "Coda" (29 Jan 1997), *ST:VOY*, "One Small Step" (17 Nov 1999).
34. *ST:ENT*, "Similitude" (19 Nov 2003).
35. *Star Trek III: The Search for Spock* (Leonard Nimoy, U.S. 1984).
36. *Star Trek Nemesis* (Stuart Baird, U.S. 2002).
37. *ST:DS9*, "Once More Unto the Breach" (11 Nov 1998).
38. *A Ship of the Line* furnishes a concise description of such a situation when the captain of an East Indiaman and one of his passengers visit Hornblower's ship after the latter had successfully repelled an attack by coastal pirates. "The boat ran alongside, and Hornblower walked forward to receive his own guests—Captain Osborn of the *Lord Mornington*, in his formal frock coat, and someone else, tall and bony, resplendent in civilian full dress with ribbon and star. 'Good afternoon, Captain,' said Osborn. 'I wish to present you to Lord Eastlake, Governor-designate of Bombay.' … Once more that was a handsome gesture; Hornblower called them up and presented them one by one; horny-handed Bush, and Gerard handsome and elegant, Captain Morris of the marines and his two gawky subalterns, the other lieutenants and the master, down to the junior midshipman, all of them delighted and embarrassed at this encounter with a lord" (448–9).
39. *Star Trek II: The Wrath of Khan* (Nicholas Meyer, U.S. 1982), *Star Trek VI: The Undiscovered Country* (Nicholas Meyer, U.S. 1991).
40. Cf. Forester, 1958: 719–20.
41. *ST:TNG*, "Chain of Command, Part I" (14 Dec 1992).
42. *ST:TNG*, "All Good Things…" (23 May 1994).
43. *ST:DS9*, "The Dogs of War" (26 May 1999).
44. Cf. Forester, 1937: 223–4.
45. *Star Trek Generations* (David Carson, U.S. 1994).
46. It serves to remember that the term "trick" also carries a pertinent nautical meaning. King defines trick as a "period of time during which a helmsman stands duty at the wheel" (447).
47. *ST:TOS*, "The Ultimate Computer" (8 Mar 1968).
48. Cf. Forester, 1958: 546–7.
49. *ST:DS9*, "Little Green Men" (15 Nov 1995).
50. Cf. Jones, 2004: 8.
51. *Star Trek V: The Final Frontier* (William Shatner, U.S. 1989).
52. In chronological order: *ST:TOS*, "The Doomsday Machine" (20 Oct 1967), *ST:TOS*, "Obsession" (15 Dec 1967), *Star Trek II: The Wrath of Khan* (Nicholas Meyer, U.S. 1982), *Star Trek: First Contact* (Jonathan Frakes, U.S. 1996), *ST:VOY*, "Bliss" (10 Feb 1999).
53. Cf. Melville, 1993 [1851]: 102.
54. *Ibid.* 443–4.
55. *Ibid.* 95–7.
56. *Star Trek II: The Wrath of Khan* (Nicholas Meyer, U.S. 1982).
57. Ishmael notes: "He looked like a man cut away from the stake … made of solid bronze…. Threading its way out from among his grey hairs, and continuing right down one side of his tawny scorched face and neck, till it disappeared in his clothing, you saw a slender rod-like mark, lividly whitish" (102).
58. *ST:VOY*, "Bliss" (10 Feb 1999).
59. *ST:TNG*, "The Best of Both Worlds" (18 Jun 1990), *ST:TNG*, "The Best of Both Worlds, Part II" (24 Sep 1990), *ST:TNG*, "Family" (1 Oct 1990).
60. *Star Trek: First Contact* (Jonathan Frakes, U.S. 1996).
61. *Ibid.*
62. Melville dedicated an entire chapter (Chapter 42) to the whiteness of the while in which he elaborates on the whale's distinctive hue vis-à-vis a cultural history of the symbolism of whiteness.
63. Ishmael relates "the unearthly conceit" that Moby Dick was "not only ubiquitous, but immortal (for immortality is but ubiquity in time)" (151).
64. *ST:TOS*, "Obsession" (15 Dec 1967).
65. *ST:TNG*, "The Battle" (16 Nov 1987).
66. *ST:TNG*, "Allegiance" (26 Mar 1990).
67. *ST:DS9*, "Explorers" (8 May 1995).
68. *ST:VOY*, "Year of Hell" (5 Nov 1997).
69. Cf. Sorrenson, 1996: 221–36.
70. Cf. Lavery, 2009: 84–5, 105, 118.
71. *ST:VOY*, "Year of Hell" (5 Nov 1997).
72. "Hornblower's mind began to run back

through his recent calculations of the ship's position. He was certain about his latitude, and last night's lunar observations had seemed to confirm the chronometer's indication of the longitude—even though it seemed incredible that chronometers could be relied upon at all after a seven months' voyage.... Crystal the master had shaken his head in doubt at Hornblower's positiveness, but Crystal was an old fool, and of no use as a navigator" (1937: 225).

73. *ST:ENT*, "Borderland" (20 Oct 2004).

74. *ST:VOY*, "Thirty Days" (9 Dec 1998).

75. The model of the HMS *Victory* belonged to Gene Roddenberry himself. He used to keep it in his office.

76. *ST:TNG*, "Elementary, Dear Data" (5 Dec 1988).

77. *Ibid.*

Chapter 8

1. Cf. Perkins, 1968: 82–6.

2. For example, after engaging an enemy vessel during a severe storm, Hornblower has to temporarily cease his pursuit lest his ship take more damage: "He could imagine what would be said in service circles when he sent in his report to the Admiralty. His statement that the weather was too bad to renew the action, after having received such a severe handling, would be received with pitying smiles and knowing wags of the head.... Cowardice, moral or even perhaps physical, would be the unspoken comment on every side—*at ten thousand miles distance no one could judge of the strength of a storm*" (1937: 321, emphasis added).

3. Cf. Withers, 2008: 37–9; O'Sullivan, 2008: 206–11.

4. *ST:VOY*, "Eye of the Needle" (20 Feb 1995), *ST:VOY*, "Resolutions" (13 May 1996), *ST:VOY*, "False Profits" (2 Oct 1996).

5. *ST:DS9*, "The Sound of Her Voice" (10 Jun 1998).

6. *ST:DS9*, "Valiant" (8 May 1998).

7. *ST:ENT*, "Fortunate Son" (21 Nov 2001).

8. *ST:DS9*, "The Sound of Her Voice" (10 Jun 1998), *ST:VOY*, "The Raven" (8 Oct 1997), *ST:VOY*, "Flashback" (11 Sep 1996).

9. *ST:DS9*, "Explorers" (8 May 1995).

10. In *Hornblower and the Atropos*, we find this paradigmatic situation: "It was at least a month—it might well be two—since any letters had reached the Fleet from England. Not a newspaper, not a word.... There was so much to do that it was not until evening that Hornblower had leisure to open the two private letters that were awaiting him. The second one was only six weeks old, having made a quick passage out from England and not having waited long for *Atropos* to come in to Palermo" (1953: 105, 210).

11. In the guidelines for *ST:TOS*, Roddenberry stated that "[w]hen necessary, we can establish our distance from a Starfleet Base is such that it takes hours or even many days for subspace radio messages to be exchanged" (24). This directive was continued in the later series where we are reminded that "[s]ubspace radio waves allow us near-instantaneous contact with a starbase when we are within a few dozen light years. Beyond that, subspace messages take several hours or days" (1987: 40). Since *ST:ENT* is chronologically set before *ST:TOS*, the peculiarities of communication are reiterated once again and they are given even more importance in individual episodes. "Long range, subspace communications are only possible while the ship is at warp. As a result, our ability to contact Starfleet Command will be extremely limited" (Berman, et al. 2001: n.p.).

12. Cf. King, 2000: 325; *ST:VOY*, "Pathfinder" (1 Dec 1999), *ST:VOY*, "Life Line" (10 May 2000).

13. For paradigmatic examples see Forester, 1937: 279–80; 1945: 233–7.

14. *ST:TOS*, "Errand of Mercy" (23 Mar 1967), *ST:TNG*, "The Price" (13 Nov 1989), *ST:TNG*, "The Ensigns of Command" (2 Oct 1989), *ST:DS9*, "Rapture" (30 Dec 1996), *ST:ENT*, "United" (4 Feb 2005).

15. Scharf and Robert, 2003: 99.

16. Acknowledging the function/mission of a Starfleet ship, Scharf and Robert have elaborated: "Its function is really more akin to that naval vessels in the early age of mercantilism.... Perhaps not coincidentally, it was in response to the needs of international relations during the mercantile period that modern international law evolved. It is therefore appropriate that the universe of *Star Trek* would develop an analogous system of interstellar law" (75–6).

17. *ST:TNG*, "The Defector" (1 Jan 1990), *ST:TNG*, "A Matter of Perspective" (12 Feb 1990), *ST:TNG*, "The Masterpiece Society" (10 Feb 1992), *ST:VOY*, "Death Wish" (19 Feb 1996), *ST:VOY*, "Counterpoint" (16 Dec 1998).

18. Cf. Parrill, 2009: 14; King, 2000: 89–92.

19. Cf. Forester, 1962: 606–11.

20. *Star Trek II: The Wrath of Khan* (Nicholas Meyer, U.S. 1982).

21. *ST:TNG*, "Justice" (9 Nov 1987).

22. Cf. Barrett et al., 2001: 133, 137, 156; Wagner, 1998: 186–7.

23. *ST:DS9*, "Rapture" (30 Dec 1996), *ST:DS9*, "Image in the Sand" (30 Sep 1998), *ST:DS9*, "Shadows and Symbols" (7 Oct 1998), *ST:VOY*, "Sacred Ground" (30 Oct 1996), *ST:VOY*, "Coda" (29 Jan 1997), *ST:VOY*, "Endgame" (23 May 2001).

24. "Clearly Leighton was not the sort of admiral to welcome suggestions from his inferiors.... 'I am extremely annoyed, Captain Hornblower, that you should have acted in such a fashion. I have already admonished Captain Bolton for allowing you to go, and now that I find you were within ten miles of here two nights ago I find it difficult to express my displeasure.... Please understand, Captain Hornblower, that I am very annoyed indeed, and I shall have to report my annoyance to the admiral commanding in the Mediterranean, for him to take any action he thinks necessary.' ... Hornblower began to describe the action against the Italian divisions. He could see by Leighton's expression that he attached little importance to the moral effect achieved, and that his imagination was not powerful enough to allow him to gauge the effect on the Italians of an ignominious retreat before an invulnerable enemy" (1938a: 513–4).

25. *ST:TNG*, "Descent" (21 Jun 1993), *ST:TNG*, "Journey's End" (28 Mar 1994), *ST:DS9*, "The Maquis, Part II" (1 May 1994).

26. *Star Trek: Insurrection* (Jonathan Frakes, U.S. 1998), *ST:TNG*, "The Offspring" (12 Mar 1990).

27. *Star Trek VI: The Undiscovered Country* (Nicholas Meyer, U.S. 1991), *ST:TNG*, "Ensign Ro" (7 Oct 1991), *ST:TNG*, "The Pegasus" (10 Jan 1994), *ST:TNG*, "The Drumhead" (29 Apr 1991).

28. *ST:DS9*, "Homefront" (1 Jan 1996), *ST:DS9*, "Paradise Lost" (8 Jan 1996).

29. *ST:DS9*, "Favor the Bold" (27 Oct 1997).

30. *ST:TOS*, "The Doomsday Machine" (20 Oct 1967), *ST:TNG*, "Too Short a Season" (8 Feb 1988).

31. *ST:TOS*, "The Deadly Years" (8 Dec 1967).

32. *ST:TOS*, "A Taste of Armageddon" (23 Feb 1967), *ST:TNG*, "The Price" (13 Nov 1989), *ST:TNG*, "Man of the People" (5 Oct 1992).

33. "'I remember you plainly,' said Calendar. 'I remember hearing what Pellew had to say about you.' Whatever Pellew said about him would be favourable—he had owed his promotion to Pellew's enthusiastic recommendation—and it was pleasant of Calendar to remind him of it at this crisis of his career" (1938b: 131).

34. "Pellew would send them [reinforcements], he knew. It was fifteen years since they had last met; nearly twenty years since Pellew had promoted him to a lieutenancy in the *Indefatigable*. Now Pellew was an admiral and a commander-in-chief, and he was commodore, but Pellew would be the loyal friend and the helpful colleague he had always been" (1946: 426–7).

35. *ST:VOY*, "Relativity" (12 May 1999).

36. Cf. Kramnick, 2000: 88–93; Zuckert, 2000: 691–695; Lewis, 2000: 655–659.

37. Cf. Foulke, 2000: 8–15.

38. Charles Withers has observed that "[i]slands in the 'Southern Seas' were the source of new flora and fauna ... home of peoples whose existence and social structures raised profound questions to do with humanity's origins and differences and whose classification an depiction helped to usher in new 'modern' methods of understanding in art and in science" (43).

39. Cf. Foulke, 2000: 97–101.

40. Cf. O'Sullivan, 2008: 13.

41. Nzetc.victoria.ac.nz, "Cook's Secret Orders."

42. Cf. O'Sullivan, 2008: 191–2.

43. "Nature and duration of command: Galaxy exploration and Class M investigation: 5 years ... You will conduct ... exploration of intelligence and social systems ... Scientific investigation to add to the earth's body of knowledge of life forms and social systems ... you will confine your landings and contacts to planets approximating Earth-Mars" (9).

44. *ST:TNG*, "Tin Man" (23 Apr 1990).

45. *ST:TNG*, "Emergence" (9 May 1994).

46. *ST:TNG*, "Violations" (3 Feb 1992), *ST:DS9*, "Paradise" (13 Feb 1994), *ST:DS9*, "The Ship" (7 Oct 1996), *ST:ENT*, "Strange New World" (10 Oct 2001), *ST:ENT*, "The Catwalk" (18 Dec 2002).

47. Cf. Obeyesekere, 1997; Sahlins, 1995.

48. *ST:DS9*, "Emissary" (3 Jan 1993).

49. *ST:VOY*, "Blink of an Eye" (19 Jan 2000).

50. *ST:TOS*, "The Apple" (13 Oct 1967), *ST:TOS*, "A Private Little War" (2 Feb 1968), *ST:TOS*, "The Paradise Syndrome" (4 Oct 1968), *ST:TNG*, "Code of Honor" (12 Oct 1987), *ST:VOY*, "Caretaker" (16 Jan 1995), *ST:VOY*, "Basics, Part II" (4 Sep 1996), *ST:VOY*, "Natural Law" (2 May 2001), *ST:ENT*, "A Night in Sickbay" (16 Oct 2002).

51. Cf. Whitfield, 1991: 177.

52. Cf. O'Sullivan, 2008: 44, 137–46.

53. Cf. Edwards, 2003: 65, 173–4.

54. *ST:TOS*, "A Taste of Armageddon" (23 Feb 1967), *ST:TNG*, "The High Ground" (29 Jan 1990), *ST:TNG*, "The Most Toys" (7 May 1990), *ST:TNG*, "First Contact" (18 Feb 1991), *ST:VOY*, "Innocence" (8 Apr 1996), *ST:VOY*, "Natural Law" (2 May 2001), *ST:ENT*, "Detained" (24 Apr 2002), *ST:ENT*, "Precious Cargo" (11 Dec 2002).

55. *ST:TNG*, "The Vengeance Factor" (20 Nov 1989), *ST:TNG*, "Rascals" (2 Nov 1992), *ST:DS9*, "Armageddon Game" (30 Jan 1994), *ST:VOY*, "Concerning Flight" (26 Nov 1997), *ST:VOY*, "Critical Care" (1 Nov 2000), *ST: VOY*, "The Void" (14 Feb 2001), *ST:ENT*, "Civilization" (14 Nov 2001), *ST:ENT*, "Anomaly" (17 Sep 2003).

56. Cf. Okuda, 1999: 467; Roddenberry, 1967: 25; 1987: 13; Whitfield, 1991: 175.

57. Cf. Fernández-Armesto, 2006: 292–4; Howse, 1980.

58. Cf. Wagner, 1998: 155–6; Jones, 2010: 129–32; Gentejohann, 2000: 76.

59. Hutcheon, 1998.

60. Cf. Lavery, 2009: 11–3; 82.

61. Cf. Murphy, 2005: 9–14, 125–6, 153–4; Black, 2004: 171–2, 180, 194, 219; Burk, 2012: 1–23.

62. Cf. Foertsch, 2008: 25–6; Gaddis, 2005: 3–52.

63. Exposing the double standard of the Prime Directive, a playful albeit apt Foucauldian "internet meme" reads as follows: "Superficially, it constitutes the limit that the Federation sets for itself, but in practice, it is the justification for constant intervention in the colonial ambitions of other Post-Warp civilizations. Far from being opposed to the Federations [sic] own extension of power, it appears to be the correlate of a colonial technology of Government" (Stickyembraces.tumblr.com, "Foucault and the Prime Directive").

64. *ST:DS9*, "The Way of the Warrior" (2 Oct 1995).

65. Barrett and Barrett have defined the Federation and Starfleet as "a global 'anti-Bonapartist' alliance" (43). Chaires and Chilton have debated whether "the UFP is more akin to the strong internal federalism of the contemporary U.S., Germany and Canada than the weak federalism of today's United Nations," only to tentatively conclude that "the only viable model ... is the United Nations" (20–1). While they observed that "the Federation maintains a standing 'military arm,' Starfleet" (*ibid.*), as an indicator for a strong federalist structure, it is crucial to point out that the Federation does *not* have *a standing army*. While some allegories made Scharf and Robert draw a parallel to the "North Atlantic Treaty Organization" (77–8), others, such as Goulding, firmly concluded that it is "a metaphor for the United States" (16). Joseph has also described the Federation as "a much looser federal system than our own [U.S.]" (40). Gentejohann has emphasized the "all-pervasive parallels between the Federation and the USA" (152), and Ono has simply stated, "Federation (read: U.S.)" (159).

66. Preeminent Revolutionary War scholar Gordon Wood has defined it as "something very different from a real national government," in that it was more like "a firm league of friendship" (72).

67. Cf. Kramnick, 1995: 552–9.

68. In the series bible for *ST:TOS*, Roddenberry preempted any questions about Earth as the metropolitan center of the Federation. He asserted that "we'll never take a story back there and therefore don't expect to get into subjects which would create great problems, technical and otherwise" (29). Moreover, *Star Trek* stories "will not let us get into details of Earth's politics ... indicating (without troublesome specifics) that mankind has found some unity on Earth, perhaps at long last even peace" (*ibid.*).

69. Cf. Friend, 2004.

70. Cf. Lavery, 2009: 11, 37–41, 80–1.

71. Roddenberry also pointed to the social contract as an Anglocentric norm, echoing its commercial roots and economic pragmatism. "The history of this Earth is replete with examples of ... groups joining together in a "union," "congress," or "federation." As man reaches out into the stars and makes contact, it is entirely probable that some sort of cooperative union will result—if not from a need for mutual self-defense, then certainly to enjoy the benefits of interplanetary trade and commerce" (qtd. Whitfield 40).

72. Cf. Fulford, 1999: 168–70; Gregg, 2005: 20–4.

73. Cf. Forester, 1937: 301, 373; 1938a: 445; 1945: 186.

74. Cf. Forester, 1938b: 150–3.

75. *ST:TNG*, "Conspiracy" (9 May 1988).

76. *ST:DS9*, "Homefront" (1 Jan 1996), *ST:DS9*, "Paradise Lost" (8 Jan 1996).

77. *ST:VOY*, "In the Flesh" (4 Nov 1998).

Conclusion

1. With the *Star Trek* reboot, a new creative team marketed a re-imagined version of the

original *Star Trek* world by way of creating a parallel universe. In this new "imaginary framework," the rules and parameters of the original world no longer applied, freeing the reboot from most constraints that the historiographic archive of more than three hundred years of fictional history would have placed on it.

2. Cf. Hark, 2008: 41–59.

3. For example, time travel shows, sf-themed sitcoms, teenage drama/alien story crossovers, and *The X-Files* (U.S. 1993–2002) as a category in its own right, etc.

4. Sagan continued: "Exploratory spaceflight puts scientific ideas, scientific thinking, and scientific vocabulary in the public eye. It elevates the general level of intellectual inquiry. The idea that we've now understood something never grasped by anyone who ever lived before—that exhilaration, especially intense for scientists involved, but perceptible to nearly everyone—propagates through the society, bounces off walls, and comes back at us. It encourages us to address problems in other fields that have also never been solved before. It increases the general sense of optimism in the society. It gives currency to critical thinking of the sort urgently needed if we are to solve hitherto intractable social issues.... [T]his is also, we may note, the first time that a species has become able to journey to the planets and the stars.... Sailors on a becalmed sea, we sense the stirring of a breeze" (227–312).

5. *Futurama*, "Where No Fan Has Gone Before" (21 Apr 2002).

Works Cited

Monographs

Abbott, Carl. *Frontiers Past and Future: Science Fiction and the American West*. Lawrence: University of Kansas Press, 2006.

Aldiss, Brian, and David Wingrove. *Trillion Year Spree: The History of Science Fiction*. New York: Atheneum, 1986.

Alexander, David. *Star Trek Creator: The Authorized Biography of Gene Roddenberry*. New York: Penguin, 1994.

Ambrose, Stephen. *Undaunted Courage: Meriwether Lewis, Thomas Jefferson, and the Opening of the American West*. New York: Simon & Schuster, 1997.

Barad, Judith, and Ed Robertson. *The Ethics of Star Trek*. New York: HarperCollins, 2001.

Barrett, Michèle, and Duncan Barrett. *Star Trek: The Human Frontier*. Cambridge: Polity, 2001.

Bayly, Christopher. *Imperial Meridian: The British Empire and the World 1780–1830*. Essex: Pearson, 1989.

Benedict, Anderson. *Imagined Communities: Reflections on the Origin and Spread of Nationalism*. Revised edition. London: Verso, 1994.

Bernardi, Daniel L. *Star Trek and History: Race-ing Toward a White Future*. New Brunswick: Rutgers University Press, 1998.

Black, Jeremy. *The British Seaborne Empire*. New Haven: Yale University Press, 2004.

Booker, Keith M. 2004. *Science Fiction Television*. Westport: Praeger, 2004.

Chapman, James, and Nicholas J. Cull. *Projecting Empire: Imperialism and Popular Cinema*. New York: I.B. Tauris, 2009.

Chomsky, Noam. *Rethinking Camelot: JFK, the Vietnam War, and U.S. Political Culture*. Boston: South End Press, 1993.

Cornea, Christine. *Science Fiction Cinema: Between Fantasy and Reality*. Edinburgh: Edinburgh University Press, 2007.

Csicsery-Ronay, Istvan. *The Seven Beauties of Science Fiction*. Middletown: Wesleyan University Press, 2008.

Culler, Jonathan D. *Structuralist Poetics: Structuralism, Linguistics and the Study of Literature*. London: Routledge, 1975.

Czisnik, Marianne. *Horatio Nelson: A Controversial Hero*. London: Hodder, 2005.

Dallek, Robert. *John F. Kennedy*. Oxford: Oxford University Press, 2011.

Danaher, Geoff, et al. *Understanding Foucault*. London: SAGE, 2007.

Darby, William. *John Ford's Westerns: A Thematic Analysis, with a Filmography*. Jefferson, NC: McFarland, 2006.

Davies, David. *A Brief History of Fighting Ships*. London: Constable & Robinson, 2002.

Dillard, J.M. *Star Trek: Where No One Has Gone Before: A History in Pictures*. New York: Simon & Schuster, 1996.

Dweyer, June. *John Masefield*. New York: Ungar, 1987.

Engel, Joel. *Gene Roddenberry: The Man and the Myth*. London: Virgin, 1995.

Fern, Yvonne. *Gene Roddenberry: The Last Conversation*. New York: Pocket Books, 1996.

Fernández-Armesto, Felipe. *Pathfinders: A Global History of Exploration*. New York: W.W. Norton, 2006.

Foertsch, Jacqueline. *American Culture in the 1940s*. Edinburgh: Edinburgh University Press, 2008.

Foulke, Robert. *The Sea Voyage Narrative*. New York: Routledge, 2002.

Freedman, Carl. *Critical Theory and Science Fiction*. Middletown: Wesleyan University Press, 2000.

Fremont-Barnes, Gregory. *The Royal Navy, 1793–1815*. Oxford: Osprey, 2007.
French, Francis, and Colin Burgess. *Into That Silent Sea: Trailblazers of the Space Era, 1961–1965*. Lincoln: University of Nebraska Press, 2009.
Gaddis, John Lewis. *Strategies of Containment: A Critical Appraisal of American National Security Policy during the Cold War*. Oxford: Oxford University Press, 2005.
Gentejohann, Volker. *Narratives of the Final Frontier: A Postcolonial Reading of the Original Star Trek Series*. Frankfurt: Peter Lang, 2000.
Geraghty, Lincoln. *American Science Fiction Film and Television*. Oxford: Berg, 2009.
______. *Living with Star Trek: American Culture and the Star Trek Universe*. New York: I.B. Tauris, 2007.
Gerrold, David. *The World of Star Trek*. New York: Ballantine, 1973.
Giglio, James N. *The Presidency of John F. Kennedy*, second edition. Lawrence: University of Kansas Press, 2006.
Glancy, H. Mark. *When Hollywood Loved Britain: The Hollywood "British" Film 1939–45*. Manchester: Manchester University Press, 1999.
Goulding, Jay. *Empire, Aliens, and Conquest: A Critique of American Ideology in Star Trek and Other Science Fiction Adventures*. Toronto: Sisyphus, 1985.
Greenwald, Jeff. *Future Perfect: How Star Trek Conquered the World*. New York: Viking, 1998.
Gregory, Chris. *Star Trek Parallel Narratives*. London: Macmillan, 2000.
Grossman, James R., et al. *The Frontier in American Culture: An Exhibition at the Newberry Library*. Berkeley: University of California Press, 1994.
Halliwell, Martin. *American Culture in the 1950s*. Edinburgh: Edinburgh University Press, 2007.
Hanfling, Barrie. *Westerns and the Trail of Tradition: A Year-by-Year History, 1929–1962*. Jefferson, NC: McFarland, 2001.
Hanley, Richard. *The Metaphysics of Star Trek*. New York: Basic Books, 1997.
Hark, Ina Rae. *Star Trek*. London: BFI, 2008.
Hawes, William. *Filmed Television Drama, 1952–1958*. Jefferson, NC: McFarland, 2002.
Hearn, Chester G. *The Illustrated Directory of the United States Navy*. St. Paul: MBI Publishing, 2003.
Hellmann, John. *The Kennedy Obsession: The American Myth of JKF*. New York: Columbia University Press, 1997.
Hine, Robert, and John Mack Faragher. *Frontiers: A Short History of the American West*. New Haven: Yale University Press, 2007.
Howse, Derek. *Greenwich Time and the Discovery of Longitude*. Oxford: Oxford University Press, 1980.
Hutcheon, Linda. *A Poetics of Postmodernism: History, Theory, Fiction*. New York: Routledge, 1992.
______. *A Theory of Adaptation*. New York: Routledge, 2006.
______. *A Theory of Parody: The Teachings of 20th Century Art Forms*. London: Methuen, 1985.
Jenkins, Henry. *Science Fiction Audiences: Watching Star Trek and Doctor Who*. New York: Routledge, 1995.
______. *Textual Poachers: Television Fans and Participatory Culture*. New York: Routledge, 1992.
Johnson, Sarah L. *Historical Fiction: A Guide to the Genre*. Westport: Libraries Unlimited, 2005.
Johnson-Smith, Jan. *American Science Fiction TV—Star Trek, Stargate and Beyond*. New York: I.B. Tauris, 2005.
Jones, John B. *Our Musicals, Ourselves: A Social History of the American Musical Theatre*. Lebanon: University Press of New England, 2004.
King, Dean. *A Sea of Words: A Lexicon and Companion to the Complete Seafaring Tales of Patrick O'Brian*, revised edition. New York: Holt, 2000.
King, Geoff. *Science Fiction Cinema from Outerspace to Cyberspace*. London: Wallflower, 2000.
Kraemer, Ross, et al. *Religions of Star Trek*. Boulder: Westview, 2003.
Krause, Lawrence M. *The Physics of Star Trek*. New York: Basic Books, 1995.
Latham, Michael E. *Modernization as Ideology: American Social Science and "Nation Building" in the Kennedy Era*. Chapel Hill: University of North Carolina Press, 2000.
Lavery, Brian. *Empire of the Seas—How the Navy Forged the Modern World*. London: Conway, 2009.
______. *Nelson's Navy: The Ships, Men and Organization 1793–1815*. London: Conway, 1989.
Levy, Bill. *John Ford: A Bio-Bibliography*. Westport: Greenwood Press, 1998.
Lyon, David, and Rif Winfield. *The Sail & Steam Navy List*. London: Chatham Publishing, 2004.
Malmgren, Carl D. *Worlds Apart: Narratology*

of Science Fiction. Bloomington: Indiana University Press, 1991.

Marill, Alvin H. *Television Westerns: Six Decades of Sagebrush, Sheriffs, Scalawags, and Sidewinders*. Lanham: Scarecrow Press, 2011.

Masefield, John. *Salt-Water Ballads*. London: Grant Richards, 1902.

McCurdy, Howard E. *Space and the American Imagination*. Washington, D.C.: Smithsonian Institute, 1997.

McMurtry, Larry. *Sacagawea's Nickname: Essays on the American West*. New York: New York Review Books, 2001.

Melville, Herman. *Moby-Dick; or, The Whale*. Ware: Wordsworth Editions, 1993.

Meyer, Nicholas. *The View from the Bridge: Memories of Star Trek and a Life in Hollywood*. New York: Plume, 2010.

Miller, Nathan. *Broadsides: The Age of Fighting Sail, 1775–1815*. New York: Wiley & Sons, 2001.

Mogen, David. *Wilderness Visions: The Western Theme in Science Fiction Literature*. San Bernardino: The Borgo Press, 1993.

Monteith, Sharon. *American Culture in the 1960s*. Edinburgh: Edinburgh University Press, 2008.

Murphy, Gretchen. *Hemispheric Imaginings: The Monroe Doctrine and Narratives of U.S. Empire*. Durham: Duke University Press, 2005.

Murray, Janet. *Hamlet on the Holodeck: The Future of Narrative in Cyberspace*. New York: The Free Press, 1997.

Nye, David E. *America as Second Creation: Technology and Narratives of New Beginnings*. Cambridge: MIT Press, 2004.

Obeyesekere, Gananath. *The Apotheosis of Captain Cook: European Mythmaking in the Pacific*. Princeton: Princeton University Press, 1997.

Okuda, Michael, and Denise Okuda. *The Star Trek Encyclopedia: A Reference Guide to the Future*, expanded edition. New York: Simon & Schuster, 1999.

O'Sullivan, Dan. *In the Search of Captain Cook: Exploring the Man Through His Own Words*. New York: I.B. Tauris, 2008.

Padfield, Peter. *Maritime Supremacy and the Opening of the Western Mind: Naval Campaigns That Shaped the Modern World, 1588–1782*. London: John Murray, 1999.

Paino, Troy D. *Social History of the United States: The 1960s*. Santa Barbara: ABC–Clio, 2009.

Parkinson, C. Northcote. *Portsmouth Point: The Navy in Fiction 1793–1815*. Liverpool: Liverpool University Press, 2005.

______. *The True Story of Horatio Hornblower*. Phoenix Mill: Sutton Publishing, 2003.

Parrill, Sue. *Nelson's Navy in Fiction and Film*. Jefferson, NC: McFarland, 2009.

Penley, Constance. *NASA/TREK: Popular Science and Sex in America*. London: Verso, 1997.

Perkins, Bradford. *The Great Rapprochement: England and the United States, 1895–1914*. New York: Atheneum, 1968.

Perrett, Bryan. *The Real Hornblower*. London: Arms and Armour, 1998.

Perrin, W.G. *The Naval Miscellany*, Vol. 3. London: Navy Records Society, 1928.

Perry, Barbara A. *Jacqueline Kennedy: First Lady of the New Frontier*. Lawrence: University Press of Kansas, 2004.

Poe, Stephen Edward. *A Vision of the Future—Star Trek: Voyager*. New York: Pocket Books, 1998.

Pounds, Michael C. *Race in Space: The Representation of Ethnicity in Star Trek and Star Trek: The Next Generation*. Lanham: Scarecrow Press, 1999.

Price, Anthony. *The Eyes of the Fleet: A Popular History of Frigates and Frigate Captains 1793–1815*. London: HarperCollins, 1992.

Reeves-Stevens, Judith, and Garfield Reeves-Stevens. *Star Trek Phase II: The Lost Series*. New York: Pocket Books, 1997.

Richards, Thomas. *The Meaning of Star Trek*. New York: Doubleday, 1997.

Rieder, John. *Colonialism and the Emergence of Science Fiction*. Middletown: Wesleyan University Press, 2008.

Roberts, Adam. *Science Fiction: The New Critical Idiom*. New York: Routledge, 2006.

Rorabaugh, W.J. *Kennedy and the Promise of the Sixties*. Cambridge: Cambridge University Press, 2002.

Ryall, Tom. *Britain and the American Cinema*. London: SAGE, 2001.

Sackett, Susan. *Inside Trek: My Secret Life with Star Trek Creator Gene Roddenberry*. Tulsa: Hawk Publishing, 2002.

Sagan, Carl. *Pale Blue Dot: A Vision of the Human Future in Space*. New York: Random House, 1994.

Sahlins, Marshall. *How "Natives" Think About Captain Cook, for Example*. Chicago: University of Chicago Press, 1995.

Slotkin, Richard. *Gunfighter Nation: The Myth of the Frontier in 20th Century America*. New York: Harper Perennial, 1995.

Sobchack, Vivian. *Screening Space: The American Science Fiction Film*. New Brunswick: Rutgers University Press, 1997.

Solow, Herbert F., and Robert H. Justman. *Inside Star Trek: The Real Story*. New York: Simon & Schuster, 1996.
Southgate, Beverley. *History Meets Fiction*. Harlow: Longman, 2009.
Stempel, Tom. *Storytellers to the Nation: A History of American Television Writing*. Syracuse: Syracuse University Press, 1996.
Sternlicht, Sanford. *C.S. Forester and the Hornblower Saga*, revised edition. Syracuse: Syracuse University Press, 1999.
Stockwell, Peter. *The Poetics of Science Fiction*. Harlow: Longman, 2000.
Suvin, Darko. *Metamorphoses of Science Fiction: On the Poetics and History of a Literary Genre*. New Haven: Yale University Press, 1980.
______. *Positions and Presuppositions in Science Fiction*. Basingstoke: Macmillan, 1988.
Swann, Paul. *The Hollywood Feature Film in Postwar Britain*. London: Croom Helm, 1987.
Taves, Brian. *The Romance of Adventure: The Genre of Historical Adventure Movies*. Jackson: University Press of Mississippi, 1993.
Tracy, Nicholas. *Nelson's Battles: The Art of Victory in the Age of Sail*. Barnsley: Chatham Publishing, 1996.
Veil, Martha. *Exploring the Pacific*. New York: Facts on File, 2005.
Wagner, Jon G., and Jan Lundeen. *Deep Space and Sacred Time: Star Trek in the American Mythos*. Westport: Praeger, 1998.
Westfahl, Gary. *Islands in the Sky: The Space Station Theme in Science Fiction Literature*. San Bernardino: The Borgo Press, 2009.
White, Richard. *"It's your misfortune and none of my own": A New History of the American West*. Norman: University of Oklahoma Press, 1991.
Whitfield, Stephen, and Gene Roddenberry. *The Making of Star Trek*. London: Titan, 1991.
Williams, Glyndwr. *The Death of Captain Cook: A Hero Made and Unmade*. Cambridge: Harvard University Press, 2008.
Wood, Gordon S. *The American Revolution: A History*. New York: Random House, 2003.
Woodman, Richard. *The Sea Warriors, Fighting Captains and Frigate Warfare in the Age of Nelson*. London: Constable & Robinson, 2002.

Edited Volumes

Altherr, Thomas L. "Let 'er Rip: Popular Culture Images of the American West in Wild West Shows, Rodeos, and Rendezvous." *Wanted Dead or Alive: The American West in Popular Culture*. Ed. Richard Aquila. Champaign: University of Illinois Press, 1996. 73–104.
Aquila, Richard, ed. *Wanted Dead or Alive: The American West in Popular Culture*. Champaign: University of Illinois Press, 1996.
Asa, Robert. "Classic Star Trek and the Death of God: A Case Study of 'Who Mourns for Adonais?'" *Star Trek and Sacred Ground: Explorations of Star Trek, Religion, and American Culture*. Eds. Jennifer E. Porter and D. McLaren. Albany: State University of New York Press, 1999. 33–60.
Attebery, Brian. "Science Fictional Parabolas: Jazz, Geometry, and Generation Starships." *Parabolas of Science Fiction*. Eds. Brian Attebery and Veronica Hollinger. Middletown: Wesleyan University Press, 2013. 3–23.
Attebery, Brian, and Veronica Hollinger, eds. *Parabolas of Science Fiction*. Middletown: Wesleyan University Press, 2013.
Baker, Neal. "Creole Identity Politics, Race, and Star Trek: Voyager." *Into Darkness Peering: Race and Color in the Fantastic*. Ed. Elizabeth A. Leonard. Westport: Greenwood Press, 1997: 119–29.
Barr, Marleen S. "'All Good Things…': The End of Star Trek: The Next Generation, The End of Camelot—The End of the Tale About Woman as Handmaid to Patriarchy as Superman." *Enterprise Zones: Critical Positions on Star Trek*. Eds. Taylor Harrison et al. Boulder: Westview Press, 1996. 231–44.
Barr, Marleen S., ed. *Future Females, The Next Generation: New Voices and Velocities in Feminist Science Fiction Criticism*. Lanham: Rowman and Littlefield, 2000.
Bloodworth, William. "Writers of the Purple Sage: Novelists and the American West." *Wanted Dead or Alive: The American West in Popular Culture*. Ed. Richard Aquila. Champaign: University of Illinois Press, 1996. 43–68.
Booker, M. Keith. "The Politics of Star Trek." *The Essential Science Fiction Television Reader*. Ed. Jay P. Telotte. Lexington: University Press of Kentucky, 2008. 195–208.
Bould, Mark, and Andrew M. Butler, eds. *The Routledge Companion to Science Fiction*. Oxon: Routledge, 2009.
Bould, Mark, and Sherryl Vint. "There Is No Such Thing as Science Fiction." *Reading Science Fiction*. Eds. James Gunn and Marleen Barr. New York: Palgrave, 2009. 43–51.
Browne, Ray B., and Pat Browne, eds. *The Guide to United States Popular Culture*. Madison: University of Wisconsin Press, 2001.

Cannadine, David, ed. *Empire, the Sea and Global History: Britain's Maritime World.* Basingstoke: Palgrave Macmillan, 2007.
Cartmell, Deborah, ed. *Adaptations: From Text to Screen, Screen to Text.* London: Routledge, 1999.
Chaires, Robert, and Bradley Chilton. "Law, Justice and Star Trek." *Star Trek Visions of Law and Justice.* Eds. Robert Chaires and Bradley Chilton. Dallas: Adios Press, 2003. 13–25.
Chaires, Robert, and Bradley Chilton, eds. *Star Trek Visions of Law and Justice.* Dallas: Adios Press, 2003.
Challans, Tim. "The Enterprise of Military Ethics: Jean-Luc Picard as Starfleet's Conscience." *Star Trek and Philosophy: The Wrath of Kant.* Eds. Jason T. Eberl and Kevin S. Decker. Chicago: Open Court, 2008. 91–104.
Conway, Stephen. "Empire, Europe and British Naval Power." *Empire, the Sea and Global History: Britain's Maritime World.* Ed. David Cannadine. Basingstoke: Palgrave Macmillan, 2007. 22–40.
Dixon, Wheeler Winston. "Tomorrowland TV: The Space Opera and Early Science Fiction Television." *The Essential Science Fiction Television Reader.* Ed. Jay P. Telotte. Lexington: University Press of Kentucky, 2008. 93–110.
Drayton, Richard. "Maritime Networks and the Making of Knowledge." *Empire, the Sea and Global History: Britain's Maritime World.* Ed. David Cannadine. Basingstoke: Palgrave Macmillan, 2007. 72–82.
DuPree, M.G. "Alien Babes and Alternate Universes: The Women of Star Trek." *Star Trek and History.* Ed. Nancy R. Reagin. New York: Wiley & Sons, 2013. 280–94.
Eberl, Jason T., and Kevin S. Decker, eds. *Star Trek and Philosophy: The Wrath of Kant.* Chicago: Open Court, 2008.
Edwards, Philip. Ed. *James Cook, The Journals.* London: Penguin Books, 2003.
Fernández-Armesto. "Britain, the Sea, the Empire, the World." *Empire, the Sea and Global History: Britain's Maritime World.* Ed. David Cannadine. Basingstoke: Palgrave Macmillan, 2007. 6–21.
Forester, C.S. "The Commodore." [1945]. *Admiral Hornblower.* London: Penguin Books, 1996. 158–364.
______. "Flying Colors." [1938b]. *Admiral Hornblower.* London: Penguin Books, 1996. 9–155.
______. "The Happy Return." [1937]. *Captain Hornblower R.N.* London: Penguin Books, 1987. 221–386.
______. "Hornblower and the Atropos." [1953]. *Captain Hornblower R.N.* London: Penguin Books, 1987. 7–219.
______. "Hornblower and the Hotspur." [1962]. *The Young Hornblower Omnibus.* London: Penguin Books, 1998. 387–633.
______. "Hornblower in the West Indies." [1958]. *Admiral Hornblower.* London: Penguin Books, 1996. 545–758.
______. "Lieutenant Hornblower." [1952]. *The Young Hornblower Omnibus.* London: Penguin Books, 1998. 189–383.
______. "Lord Hornblower." [1946]. *Admiral Hornblower.* London: Penguin Books, 1996. 367–541.
______. "Mr Midshipman Hornblower." [1950]. *The Young Hornblower Omnibus.* London: Penguin Books, 1998. 9–186.
______. "A Ship of the Line." [1938a]. *Captain Hornblower R.N.* London: Penguin Books, 1987. 387–572.
George, Alice L. "Riding Posse on the Final Frontier: James T. Kirk, Hero of the Old West." *Star Trek and History.* Ed. Nancy R. Reagin. New York: Wiley & Sons, 2013. 7–21.
Geraghty, Lincoln. Ed. *The Influence of* Star Trek *on Television, Film and Culture.* Jefferson, NC: McFarland, 2008.
Giles, Paul. "Enlightenment Historiography and Cultural Civil Wars." *The Atlantic Enlightenment.* Eds. Susan Manning and Francis D. Cogliano. Farnham: Ashgate, 2008. 19–36.
Gilje, Paul A. "The Enlightenment at Sea in the Atlantic World." *The Atlantic Enlightenment.* Eds. Susan Manning and Francis D. Cogliano. Farnham: Ashgate, 2008. 165–78.
Green, Jack P., and J.R. Pole, eds. *A Companion to the American Revolution.* Malden: Blackwell, 2000.
Gregg, Stephen H., ed. *Empire and Identity: An Eighteenth Century Sourcebook.* Basingstoke: Palgrave Macmillan, 2005.
Hall, Catherine. 2007. "Gender and Empire." *Empire, the Sea and Global History: Britain's Maritime World.* Ed. David Cannadine. Basingstoke: Palgrave Macmillan, 2007. 134–152.
Hamowy, Ronald. "The Declaration of Independence." *A Companion to the American Revolution.* Eds. Jack P. Green and J.R. Pole. Malden: Blackwell Publishers, 2000. 258–61.
Harrison, Taylor, and Sarah Projansky, eds. *Enterprise Zones: Critical Positions on Star Trek.* Boulder: Westview Press, 1996.
Helford, Elyce R. "'A Part of Myself No Man Should Ever See': Reading Captain Kirk's Multiple Masculinities." *Enterprise Zones:*

Critical Positions on Star Trek. Eds. Taylor Harrison et al. Boulder: Westview Press, 1996. 10–32.

Isaacs, Bruce. "A Vision of a Time and Place: Spiritual Humanism and the Utopian Impulse." Star Trek *as Myth: Essays on Symbol and Archetype at the Final Frontier*. Ed. Matthew W. Kapell. Jefferson, NC: McFarland, 2010. 182–96.

James, Edward, and Farah Mendlesohn, eds. *The Cambridge Companion to Science Fiction*. Cambridge: Cambridge University Press, 2003.

Jancovich, Mark, and Derek Johnston. "Film and Television, the 1950s." *The Routledge Companion to Science Fiction*. Eds. Mark Bould and Andrew M. Butler. Oxon: Routledge, 2009. 71–79.

Jones, Gwyneth. "The Icons of Science Fiction." *The Cambridge Companion to Science Fiction*. Eds. Edward James and Farah Mendlesohn. Cambridge: Cambridge University Press, 2003. 163–73.

Jones, Richard R. "Course in Federation Linguistics." Star Trek *as Myth: Essays on Symbol and Archetype at the Final Frontier*. Ed. Matthew W. Kapell. Jefferson, NC: McFarland, 2010. 129–43.

Jones, Stephanie. "The Isolation of the Spirit: Captain Horatio Hornblower, RN." *Fictional Leaders: Heroes, Villains and Absent Friends*. Eds. Jonathan Gosling and Peter Villiers. Basingstoke: Palgrave Macmillan, 2012. 37–49.

Joseph, Paul, and Sharon Carton. "The Law of the Federation: Images of Law, Lawyers, and the Legal System in Star Trek: The Next Generation." *Star Trek Visions of Law and Justice*. Eds. Robert Chaires and Bradley Chilton. Dallas: Adios Press, 2003. 26–72.

Kant, Immanuel. "Perpetual Peace." [1795]. *The Portable Enlightenment Reader*. Ed. Isaac Kramnick. London: Penguin Books, 1995. 552–9.

Kapell, Matthew W. "Introduction: The Significance of the Star Trek Mythos." Star Trek *as Myth: Essays on Symbol and Archetype at the Final Frontier*. Ed. Matthew W. Kapell. Jefferson, NC: McFarland, 2010. 1–16.

______, ed. Star Trek *as Myth: Essays on Symbol and Archetype at the Final Frontier*. Jefferson, NC: McFarland, 2010.

Kincaid, Paul. "Through Time and Space: A Brief History of Science Fiction." *Teaching Science Fiction*. Eds. Andrew Sawyer and Peter Wright. Basingstoke: Palgrave Macmillan, 2011. 21–37.

Kramnick, Isaac. "Ideological Background." *A Companion to the American Revolution*. Eds. Jack P. Green and J. R. Pole. Malden: Blackwell Publishers, 2000. 88–93.

Kramnick, Isaac, ed. *The Portable Enlightenment Reader*. London: Penguin Books, 1995.

Lawrence, John S. "Star Trek as American Monomyth." Star Trek *as Myth: Essays on Symbol and Archetype at the Final Frontier*. Ed. Matthew W. Kapell. Jefferson, NC: McFarland, 2010. 93–111.

Lenihan, John H. "Westbound: Feature Films and the American West." *Wanted Dead or Alive: The American West in Popular Culture*. Ed. Richard Aquila. Champaign: University of Illinois Press, 1996. 109–34.

Leone, Matthew C. "Visions of Corrections in Star Trek: Something Old, Nothing New." *Star Trek Visions of Law and Justice*. Eds. Robert Chaires and Bradley Chilton. Dallas: Adios Press, 2003. 160–73.

Manning, Susan, and Francis D. Cogliano, eds. *The Atlantic Enlightenment*. Farnham: Ashgate, 2008.

Marshall, P.J. "Empire and British Identity: The Maritime Dimension." *Empire, the Sea and Global History, Britain's Maritime World*. Ed. David Cannadine. Basingstoke: Palgrave Macmillan, 2007. 41–59.

Mendlesohn, Farah. "Fiction, 1926–1949." *The Routledge Companion to Science Fiction*. Eds. Mark Bould and Andrew M. Butler. Oxon: Routledge, 2009. 52–61.

Newman, Neville. "C.S. Forester." *British Novelists Between the Wars, Dictionary of Literary Biography*. Ed. George M. Johnson. Detroit: Gale, 1998. 95–106.

Ono, Kent. "Domesticating Terrorism: A Neocolonial Economy of *Différance*." *Enterprise Zones: Critical Positions on Star Trek*. Eds. Taylor Harrison et al. Boulder: Westview Press, 1996. 157–85.

Pickering, Michael, ed. *Research Methods for Cultural Studies*. Edinburgh: Edinburgh University Press, 2008.

Pilkington, Ace G. "*Star Trek*: American Dream, Myth and Reality." Star Trek *as Myth: Essays on Symbol and Archetype at the Final Frontier*. Ed. Matthew W. Kapell. Jefferson, NC: McFarland, 2010. 54–66.

Porter, J., and D. McLaren, eds. *Star Trek and Sacred Ground: Explorations of Star Trek, Religion, and American Culture*. Albany: State University of New York Press, 1999.

Raban, Jonathan, ed. *The Oxford Book of the Sea*. Oxford: Oxford University Press, 1992.

Rayner, Jonathan. "'Damn the photon torpedoes!' Star Trek and the Transfiguration of

Naval History." *The Naval War Film: Genre, History, National Cinema*. Ed. Jonathan Rayner. Manchester: Manchester University Press, 2007. 153–72.

Reagin, Nancy R., ed. *Star Trek and History*. New York: Wiley & Sons, 2013.

Roberts, Robin. "Science, Race, and Gender in Star Trek: Voyager." *Fantasy Girls: Gender in the New Universe of Science Fiction and Fantasy Television*. Ed. Elyce R. Helford. Lanham: Rowman and Littlefield, 2000. 203–22.

______. "The Woman Scientist in Star Trek: Voyager." *Future Females, The Next Generation: New Voices and Velocities in Feminist Science Fiction Criticism*. Ed. Marleen S. Barr. Lanham: Rowman and Littlefield, 2000. 277–90.

Rollins, Peter C., and John E. O'Connor. eds. *Hollywood's West: The American Frontier in Film, Television, and History*. Lexington: University Press of Kentucky, 2005.

Rotschild, Emma. 2008. "David Hume and the Seagods of the Atlantic." *The Atlantic Enlightenment*. Eds. Susan Manning and Francis D. Cogliano. Farnham: Ashgate, 2008. 81–96.

Saunders, Stephen, ed. *Jane's Fighting Ships: Yearbook 2003–2004*. London: Jane's Information Group, 2003.

Sawyer, Andrew, and Peter Wright, eds. *Teaching Science Fiction*. Basingstoke: Palgrave Macmillan, 2011.

Schaffer, Simon. "Instruments, Surveys and Maritime Empire." *Empire, the Sea and Global History, Britain's Maritime World*. Ed. David Cannadine. Basingstoke: Palgrave Macmillan, 2007. 83–104.

Scharf, Michael, and Lawrence Robert. "The Interstellar Relation of the Federation: International Law and 'Star Trek: The Next Generation.'" *Star Trek Visions of Law and Justice*. Eds. Robert Chaires and Bradley Chilton. Dallas: Adios Press, 2003. 73–113.

Stilwell, Alexander, ed. *The Trafalgar Companion*. Oxford: Osprey Publishing, 2005.

Taylor, Philip M., ed. *Britain and the Cinema in the Second World War*. Basingstoke: Palgrave Macmillan, 1988.

Telotte, Jay P., ed. *The Essential Science Fiction Television Reader*. Lexington: University Press of Kentucky, 2008.

______. "Introduction: The Trajectory of Science Fiction Television." *The Essential Science Fiction Television Reader*. Ed. Jay P. Telotte. Lexington: University Press of Kentucky, 2008. 1–36.

Vincent, Edgar. "Nelson the Commander." *The Trafalgar Companion*. Ed. Alexander Stilwell. Oxford: Osprey Publishing, 2005. 83–101.

______. "Nelson the Man." *The Trafalgar Companion*. Ed. Alexander Stilwell. Oxford: Osprey Publishing, 2005. 61–81.

Westfahl, Gary, ed. *Space and Beyond: The Frontier Theme in Science Fiction*. Westport: Greenwood Press, 2000.

______. "Space Opera." *The Cambridge Companion to Science Fiction*. Eds. Edward James and Farah Mendlesohn. Cambridge: Cambridge University Press, 2003. 197–208.

______. "The True Frontier: Confronting and Avoiding the Realities of Space in American Science Fiction Films." *Space and Beyond: The Frontier Theme in Science Fiction*. Ed. Gary Westfahl. Westport: Greenwood Press, 2000. 55–66.

White, Colin, ed. *Nelson: The New Letters*. Woodbridge: The Boydell Press, 2005.

White, Ray. "The Good Guys Wore White Hats: The B Western in American Culture." *Wanted Dead or Alive: The American West in Popular Culture*. Ed. Richard Aquila. Champaign: University of Illinois Press, 1996. 135–59.

Williams, Glyndwr, ed. "'As befits our age, there are no more heroes': Reassessing Captain Cook." *Captain Cook: Explorations and Reassessments*. Ed. Glyndwr Williams. Suffolk: The Boydell Press, 2004. 230–45.

______. *Captain Cook: Explorations and Reassessments*. Suffolk: The Boydell Press, 2004.

Williamson, Jack. "Space vs. Time." *Space and Beyond: The Frontier Theme in Science Fiction*. Ed. Gary Westfahl. Westport: Greenwood Press, 2000. 9–11.

Withers, Charles. "Where Was the Atlantic Enlightenment?—Questions of Geography." *The Atlantic Enlightenment*. Eds. Susan Manning and Francis D. Cogliano. Farnham: Ashgate, 2008. 37–60.

Wolfe, Gary K. "Theorizing Science Fiction: The Question of Terminology." *Teaching Science Fiction*. Eds. Andrew Sawyer and Peter Wright. Basingstoke: Palgrave Macmillan, 2011. 38–54.

Wright, Peter. "Film and Television, 1960–1980." *The Routledge Companion to Science Fiction*. Eds. Mark Bould and Andrew M. Butler. Oxon: Routledge, 2009. 80–101.

Yaszek, Lisa. "Shadows on the Cathode Ray Tube: Adapting Print Science Fiction for Television." *The Essential Science Fiction Television Reader*. Ed. Jay P. Telotte. Lexington: University Press of Kentucky, 2008. 55–67.

Yoggy, Gary A. "Prime-Time Bonanza! The Western on Television." *Wanted Dead or*

Alive: The American West in Popular Culture. Ed. Richard Aquila. Champaign: University of Illinois Press, 1996. 160–85.

Journal Articles

Agnew, Vanessa. "Introduction: What Is Reenactment?" *Criticism* 46/3 (2004): 327–9.

Alexander, David. "Gene Roddenberry: Writer, Producer, Philosopher, Humanist." *The Humanist* 51/2 (1991): 5–30.

Alryyes, Ala. "War at a Distance: Court-Martial Narratives in the Eighteenth Century." *Eighteenth-Century Studies* 41/4 (2008): 525–42.

Baker, Djoymi. "'Every Old Trick Is New Again': Myth in Quotations and the *Star Trek* Franchise." *Popular Culture Review* 12/1 (2001): 67–77.

Bennett, Todd. "The Celluloid War: State and Studio in Anglo-American Propaganda Film-Making, 1939–1941." *The International History Review* 24/1 (2002): 64–102.

Bowring, M. C. "Resistance Is Not Futile: Liberating Captain Janeway from the Masculine-Feminine Dualism of Leadership." *Gender, Work and Organization* 11/4 (2004): 381–405.

Brackbill, Hervey. "Midshipman Jargon." *American Speech: A Quarterly of Linguistic Usage* 3/6 (1928): 451–5.

Buhler, Stephen. "'Who Calls Me Villain?' Blank Verse and the Black Hat." *Extrapolation* 36/1 (1995): 18–27.

Cohen, Robin. "Fuzzy Frontiers of Identity: The British Case." *Social Identities* 1/1 (1995): 35–62.

Consalvo, Mia. "Borg Babes, Drones, and the Collective: Reading Gender and the Body in Star Trek." *Women's Studies in Communication* 27/2 (2004): 177–203.

Cook, Alexander. "Sailing on the Ship: Re-Enactment and the Quest for Popular History." *History Workshop Journal* 57 (2004): 247–55.

Decherney, Peter. "Race in Space." *Cineaste: America's Leading Magazine on the Art and Politics of the Cinema* 26/3 (2001): 38–9.

Duncan, Jody. "Star Trek: Insurrection, Lost in the Briar Patch." *Cinefex* 77 (1999): 68–95.

Dutta, Mary. "'Very bad poetry, Captain': Shakespeare in Star Trek." *Extrapolation* 36/1 (1995): 38–45.

Felner, Julie. "Where No Woman Has Trekked Before." *Ms. Arlington* 5/6 (1995): 80–1.

Forester, John. "Father's Tales." *American Scholar* 66 (1997): 533–45.

Fulford, Tim. "Romanticizing the Empire: The Naval Heroes of Southey, Coleridge, Austen, and Marryat." *Modern Language Quarterly: A Journal of Literary History* 60/2 (1999): 161–96.

Golumbia, David. "Black and White World: Race, Ideology, and Utopia in Triton and Star Trek." *Cultural Critique* 32 (1995): 75–95.

Greven, David. "The Twilight of Identity: Enterprise, Neo-Conservatism and the Death of Star Trek." *Jump Cut: A Review of Contemporary Media* 50 (2008): n.p.

Hardy, Sarah, and Kukla, Rebecca. "A Paramount Narrative: Exploring Space on the Starship Enterprise." *Journal of Aesthetics and Art Criticism* 57/2 (1999): 177–91.

Harris, Jocelyn. "Domestic Virtues and National Importance: Lord Nelson, Captain Wentworth, and the English Napoleonic War Hero." *Eighteenth-Century Fiction* 19/1–2 (2006): 181–205.

Houlahan, Mark. "Cosmic Hamlets? Contesting Shakespeare in Federation Space." *Extrapolation* 36/1 (1995): 28–37.

Hurd, Denise Alessandria. "The Monster Inside: 19th Century Racial Constructs in the 24th Century Mythos of Star Trek." *Journal of Popular Culture* 31/1 (1997): 23–35.

Joyrich, Lynne. "Feminist Enterprise? Star Trek: The Next Generation and the Occupation of Femininity." *Cinema Journal* 35/2 (1996): 61–84.

Knellwolf, C. "The Exotic Frontier of the Imperial Imagination." *Eighteenth-Century Life* 26/3 (2002): 10.

Kreitzer, Larry. "The Cultural Veneer of Star Trek." *Journal of Popular Culture* 30/2 (1996): 1–28.

Lagon, Mark P. "'We Owe It to Them to Interfere': Star Trek and U.S. Statecraft in the 1960s and the 1990s." *Extrapolation* 34/3 (1993): 251–64.

Lamb, Jonathan. "Cook and the Question of Naval History." *Eighteenth-Century Life* 30/2 (2006): 98–115.

Lloyd, Francis V. "Masefield's Sea Fever." *Explicator* 3/36 (1945): n.p.

Paxman, David. "'Distance Getting Close': Gesture, Language, and Space in the Pacific." *Eighteenth-Century Life* 26/3 (2002): 78–97.

Pendergast, John. "A Nation of Hamlets: Shakespeare and Cultural Politics." *Extrapolation* 36/1 (1995): 10–17.

Rieder, John. "On Defining SF, or Not: Genre Theory, SF, and History." *Science Fiction Studies* 37/2 (2010): 191–209.

Roddenberry, Gene. "Sailor's Prayer." *The New York Times*, 17 June 1945, E8.

Sorrenson, Richard. "The Ship as a Scientific Instrument in the Eighteenth Century." *Osiris* 11 (1996): 221–36.

Stubbs, Jonathan. "'Blocked' Currency, Runaway Production in Britain and Captain Horatio Hornblower (1951)." *Historical Journal of Film, Radio and Television* 28/3 (2008): 335–51.

Westfahl, Gary. "A Civilized Frontier." *Science Fiction Studies* 29/2 (2002): 272–76.

Manuscripts

Berman, Rick, and Michel Piller. "Star Trek DS9 Bible." Unpublished manuscript, 1992.

Berman, Rick, et al. "STAR TREK ENTERPRISE Bible." Unpublished manuscript, 2001.

______. "STAR TREK: Voyager Bible." Unpublished manuscript, 1995.

Roddenberry, Gene. "THE STAR TREK GUIDE. THIRD REVISION." Unpublished manuscript, 1967.

______. "STAR TREK IS...." Unpublished manuscript, 1964.

Roddenberry, Gene. "WRITER/DIRECTOR'S GUIDE STAR TREK: The Next Generation." Unpublished manuscript, 1987.

Websites

"British Sailing Uniforms." Christies.com. 2006. http://www.christies.com/Lotfinder/lot_details.aspx?sid=&intObjectID=4779650&AllObjectIDs=&SRObjectID=&AllSaleIDs=&SRSaleID=&RefineQueryURL=. Accessed 7 Sep 2017.

Burk, Kathleen. "How Did the Anglo-American Relationship Become 'Essential'?" Britishscholar.org. 2012. http://britishscholar.org/wp-content/uploads/2012/09/KB-Anglo-American-Relations2.pdf. Accessed 6 Aug 2017.

D'Allesandro, K.C. "Wagon Train." Museumtv.tv. n.d. http://www.museum.tv/eotv/wagontrain.htm. Accessed 14 Jun 2017.

"Database: Archer, Jonathan." Startrek.com. n.d. http://www.startrek.com/database_article/jonathan-archer. Accessed 20 Feb 2017.

"Database: Tucker, Charles 'Trip.'" Startrek.com. n.d. http://www.startrek.com/database_article/charles-trip-tucker. Accessed 16 Mar 2017.

"Enterprise Boldly Goes on Deployment Once More." Navynews.co.uk. 2011. https://navynews.co.uk/archive/news/item/2661. Accessed 3 Aug 2017.

"Enterprise Launch Promo 9: First Captain." Youtube.com. 2001. http://www.youtube.com/watch?v=l4XE09M3ytI. Accessed 3 Sep 2017.

"FAQ: Articles for the Government of the United States Navy." History.navy.mil. 2001. http://www.history.navy.mil/faqs/faq59-7.htm. Accessed 21 Jan 2017.

Fisher, Craig. "Royal Navy & Marine Customs and Traditions." Hmsrichmond.org. n.d. http://www.hmsrichmond.org/avast/customs.htm. Accessed 24 Aug 2017.

"Foucault and the Prime Directive." Stickyembraces.tumblr.com. n.d. http://stickyembraces.tumblr.com/post/26346995036. Accessed 20 Jul 2017.

Friend, Celeste. "Social Contract Theory." Utm.edu. 2004. http://www.iep.utm.edu/soc-cont/. Accessed 22 Jul 2017.

Gunn, James. "Teaching Science Fiction." Sfcenter.ku.edu. n.d. http://www.sfcenter.ku.edu/teaching.htm. Accessed 22 Feb 2017.

Hawke, Edward, et al. "Cook's Secret Orders." Victoria.ac.nz. 1768. http://nzetc.victoria.ac.nz/tm/scholarly/tei-MacHist-t1-body-d3-d7.html. Accessed 13 Jul 2017.

Holpuch, Amanda, and Ruth Spencer. "Your TV Pitches Reviewed: Writers and Producers Dish out the Tough Love." Theguardian.com. 2013. http://www.theguardian.com/tv-and-radio/interactive/2013/sep/25/reader-tv-pitch-review#Mainee. Accessed 15 Nov 2017.

"Horatius." Perseus.tufts.edu. n.d. http://www.perseus.tufts.edu/hopper/text?doc=Perseus%3Atext%3A1999.04.0059%3Aentry%3DHoratius1. Accessed 12 Aug 2017.

Hutcheon, Linda. "Irony, Nostalgia, and the Postmodern." Utoronto.ca. 1998. http://www.library.utoronto.ca/utel/criticism/hutchinp.html. Accessed 20 Jul 2017.

Kennedy, John F. "Address at Rice University on the Nation's Space Effort." Jfklibrary.org. 1962. http://www.jfklibrary.org/Asset-Viewer/MkATdOcdU06X5uNHbmqm1Q.aspx. Accessed 10 Jan 2017.

______. "Address of Senator John F. Kennedy Accepting the Democratic Party Nomination of the Presidency of the United States." Jfklibrary.org. 1960. http://www.jfklibrary.org/Asset-Viewer/AS08q5oYz0SFUZg9uOi4iw.aspx. Accessed 10 Jan 2017.

______. "Address to Joint Session of Congress, May 25, 1961." Jfklibrary.org. 1961. http://

www.jfklibrary.org/Asset-Viewer/xzw1gaee TES6khED14P1Iw.aspx. Accessed 10 Jan 2017.

______. "Inaugural Address." Jfklibrary.org. 1961. http://www.jfklibrary.org/Asset-Viewer/BqXIEM9F4024ntFl7SVAjA.aspx. Accessed 10 Jan 2017.

"Leonard Nimoy Salutes Space Shuttle Enterprise." Youtube.com. 2012. http://www.youtube.com/watch?v=Tu_NfWVYb78. Accessed 30 Apr 2017.

"Married at Sea." Tvtropes.org. n.d. http://tvtropes.org/pmwiki/pmwiki.php/Main/MarriedAtSea. Accessed 31 Aug 2017.

Moore, Ronald D. "AOL Chat: Answers." Memory-alpha.org. 1997. http://en.memory-alpha.org/wiki/Memory_Alpha:AOL_chats/Ronald_D._Moore/ron017.txt. Accessed 13 Aug 2017.

______. "Exclusive Interview: Ron Moore—Fighting the Star Trek Clichés." Trekmovie.com. http://trekmovie.com/2008/06/21/exclusive-interview-ron-moore-fighting-the-trek-cliches/. Accessed 13 Aug 2017.

"Navy Traditions and Customs, Lieutenant Commander." History.navy.mil. n.d. http://www.history.navy.mil/trivia/triv4–5g.htm. Accessed 21 Jan 2017.

"NCC." Memory-alpha.com. n.d. http://en.memory-alpha.org/wiki/NCC. Accessed 22 Feb 2017.

O'Keeffe, John. "A Short Account of the New Pantomime called Omai, or, A Trip Round the World." Archive.org. 1785. http://archive.org/stream/shortaccountofne00shie#page/n5/mode/2up. Accessed 9 Jul 2017.

"Old salt." Oed.com. 2012. http://www.oed.com/viewdictionaryentry/Entry/130955#eid33427513. Accessed 7 Sep 2017.

"Redshirt." Memory-alpha.com. n.d. http://en.memory-alpha.org/wiki/Redshirt. Accessed 12 Feb 2017.

Schwartz, Debora. "Translatio Studii et Imperii." Calpoly.edu. 2002. http://cla.calpoly.edu/~dschwart/engl513/courtly/translat.htm. Accessed 20 Jul 2017.

Silvers, Samuel. "Gilbert and Sullivan Archive: H.M.S. Pinafore." Boisestate.edu. 2012. http://math.boisestate.edu/GaS/pinafore/html/index.html. Accessed 27 Aug 2017.

"Starfleet Ranks." Memory-alpha.com. n.d. http://en.memory-alpha.org/wiki/Starfleet_ranks. Accessed 11 Feb 2017.

Straczynski, J. Michael. "Well, Now That the Official Announcement…." Jmsnews.com. 1991. http://www.jmsnews.com/msg.aspx?id=1–21388&topic=Writing. Accessed 15 Nov 2017.

Tennyson, Alfred. "Locksley Hall." Utoronto.ca. 1842. http://rpo.library.utoronto.ca/poems/locksley-hall. Accessed 1 Jul 2017.

"Virtual, adj. (and n.)." Oed.com. 2012. http://www.oed.com/view/Entry/223829?redirectedFrom=virtual&. Accessed 23 Aug 2017.

Wharton, W.J., ed. "Captain Cook's Journal During His First Voyage Round the World." Gutenberg.org. 1893. http://www.gutenberg.org/files/8106/8106-h/8106-h.htm. Accessed 13 Jul 2017.

"What If—Why Educators Should Teach Science Fiction." Youtube.com. 2011. http://www.youtube.com/watch?v=gOHM9qeNcRE. Accessed 22 Feb 2017.

Index